HEGELIAN LITERARY PERSPECTIVES

ESSAYS ON

HEGEL'S INFLUENCE AND REPUTATION

THE *AESTHETICS*

COMEDY, SOCIAL DRAMA, VERSE DRAMA

SHAKESPEARE, A. C. BRADLEY, T. S. ELIOT

THEATER OF THE ABSURD

LUIGI PIRANDELLO, EDWARD ALBEE

SOPHOCLES, DANTE, ARTHUR MILLER

ANNE PAOLUCCI

HENRY PAOLUCCI

PREFACE BY
ANNE PAOLUCCI

Library of Congress Cataloging in Processing Data

Paolucci, Anne
    Hegelian literary perspectives / Anne Paolucci and
Henry Paolucci; preface by Anne Paolucci.
    p. cm.
Includes bibliographical references.
    ISBN 0-918680-99-9 — ISBN 0-918680-80-8 (pbk.)
    1. Literature, Modern—History and criticism. 2. Hegel,
Georg Wilhelm Friedrich, 1770-1831 —Contribution in
philosophy of literature. I. Paolucci, Henry. II. Title.
PN701 .P36 2002
809—dc21

                            2002018372

Published for
THE BAGEHOT COUNCIL
by
GRIFFON HOUSE PUBLICATIONS
P. O. BOX 468
SMYRNA DE 19977

Contents

PREFACE

The eminent Italian critic-philosopher, Benedetto Croce, the most influential Hegelian of the twentieth century, took pains to explain and to illustrate in his own writings that the study of a subject was the study of the *history* of that subject. The Greeks, we know, were the first to realize this and to act on that understanding. The pre-Socratics led the way in exploring philosophic inquiry, and, in so doing, laid the groundwork for that burst of intellectual activity we associate with Socrates, Plato, and Aristotle. The Greeks were also the first to record scrupulously and systematically the phenomena of the heavens, the first to catalog the rich diversity of plants and animals that share our planet, the first to approach history itself as an organic evolution rather than a chronicle of events.

Hegel, the modern Aristotle, approaches the world of intellectual inquiry in the same spirit as the Greeks. Like his early predecessors, his interests were wide-reaching; he studied subjects with the same systematic method of inquiry that set the Greeks apart from all who came before them. Most important, like the Greeks, he saw the particulars of a subject as part of a larger whole, part of a continuity that was both logical and historical.

He set the modern example for others who followed: in Italy, the Italian literary critic and historian, Francesco De Sanctis; the philosopher, scholar and educational reformer, Giovanni Gentile; and, of course, Croce. In the United States, the New Critics absorbed some measure of Hegelian thought through the writings of Croce. In England, Hegel's influence was equally profound and pervasive, especially among the Oxford Idealists— F. H. Bradley and his brother A. C. Bradley (perhaps the most interesting and challenging critic ever to write on Shakespeare); and Bernard Bosanquet, whose translation of the first 100 or so pages of *The Philosophy of Fine Art* is by far the most readable and accurate introduction to Hegel. In "Hegel's Theory of Tragedy" *(Oxford Lectures on Poetry),* but also in many other places, A. C. Bradley acknowledges his debt to Hegel and brings Hegelian ideas to bear on his discussion. The most striking applications are to be found in his essays on "Macbeth" *(Shakespearean Tragedy)* and "The Rejection of Falstaff" *(Oxford Lectures on Poetry).*

Hegel's influence goes far beyond philosophy and literary studies. He gave new direction to anthropological studies; he has been credited for much that is found in the teachings of Christian Science; his influence on the thought of Karl Marx is common knowledge.

Even the great poet and critic of the twentieth century, T. S. Eliot — notoriously silent on the influences that shaped his poetry and his style as a critic — wrote in *The Criterion* (XIV, April 1935, 433) that he regretted not having read more Hegel when he was younger. In fact, late in life, he turned again to the dissertation started at Harvard many years earlier and completed at Oxford, on F. H. Bradley's philosophical Idealism. Hegel's impact on Eliot remains a rich source for literary exploration. That Hegel had, directly or indirectly, exerted a deep and lasting influence on him is clear enough to anyone who has read his provocative pages in "Hamlet," for instance, or his essay on "The Three Voices of Poetry," where the discussion of the literary genres (he does not hesitate to tell us, in this instance) is drawn from the German expressionist critic and acknowledged Hegelian, Gottfried Benn.

My own long and profitable study of Hegel, particularly of *The Philosophy of Fine Art,* is reflected in the several essays here included under my name; but my insights and applications of Hegel's aesthetic theory would not have been possible without the guidance of Professor Henry Paolucci, who generously shared with me (as he did with so many other colleagues and scholars) his extraordinary knowledge of the Hegelian texts and his compelling appreciation of them. He made Hegel accessible to anyone willing to listen. Those who accepted the challenge were rewarded with an exciting intellectual experience and encouraged to explore the Hegelian world for the rich possibilities it offers in so many different fields of study.

Anne Paolucci
February 15, 2002

PUBLISHER'S NOTE

A number of the essays included in this volume were originally published in scholarly-academic journals or as chapters in
books. Many of them have been out of print for some time or
have become rarities, in many cases difficult to find. Given their
unusual nature — literary analyses from an Hegelian point of
view — we felt an obligation to collect a sampling of the more
important ones and make them available in a single volume.
Scholars in the various subjects represented in this collection
will find these essays provocative reading.

No effort has been made to delete recurring references to
certain basic arguments and key passages from Hegel. They serve
to emphasize different aspects of those arguments, thus helping
readers (especially those unfamiliar with Hegel) to grasp the es-
sentials, at least, of Hegel's thought. Approached from different
directions and in a variety of contexts, those arguments are clarified and sustained in the large literary mosaic of which they are
an integral part.

References and notes provided in the original text have
been retained. Where no such references or notes were included
in the original text, there has been no presumption to search
them out.

The name of the author of each essay appears in the table
of contents.

PART ONE
(9-50)

HEGEL'S INFLUENCE AND REPUTATION;

THE *AESTHETICS*

The two essays of "Part One," by Henry Paolucci, appear for the first time in this volume. A number of other writings by Professor Paolucci, in which Hegelian ideas and themes are explored, are now available again and include:

"Hegel and the Celestial Mechanics of Newton and Einstein," in *Henry Paolucci: Selected Writings on Literature and the Arts; Science and Astronomy; Law, Government, and Political Philosophy*. The Bagehot Council/Griffon House Publications, Wilmington Delaware, 1999, pp. 152-189.

"Truth in the Philosophical Sciences of Society, Politics, and History," *Henry Paolucci: Selected Writings . . .* pp. 190-226. First published in *Beyond Epistemology*, ed. Frederick G. Weiss. Martinus Nijhoff, The Hague, 1974. See also: *The Political Thought of G. W. Hegel*. The Bagehot Council/Griffon House Publications, Wilmington Delaware, 1978.

"The Poetics of Aristotle and Hegel," (originally in *Hegel in Comparative Literature* [*Review of National Literatures*, Vol. I, No. 2, Fall 1970], Council on National Literatures, New York, 1970, pp. 165-213.) Reissued in *Henry Paolucci: Selected Writings . . .* pp.165-213. (The *RNL* volume also contains articles by Albert Hofstadter, Daisy Fornacca Kouzel, Robert I. Perkins, Richard C. Clark, Frank D. Grande, and a selection from T. M. Knox's "Introduction to Aesthetics.")

"Hegel and the Idea of Artistic Beauty or the Ideal," in *Henry Paolucci: Selected Writings . . .* pp. 45-93. First published in *Hegel on the Arts*, abridged (from Hegel's *Philosophy of Fine Art*) and translated by Henry Paolucci. Frederick Ungar Publishing Co., 1979. Reissued by The Bagehot Council/Griffon House Publications, Smyrna, Delaware, 2001. See especially, "Introduction," pp, vii-xxi.

CHAPTER 1

DIALECTICAL INVERSIONS: HEGEL'S INFLUENCE AND REPUTATION

Hegel, like Aristotle, has been more often refuted than read; and, unhappily, more often praised than read, also.

One reason perhaps is that, like Aristotle, Hegel isn't easy reading. His pages offer much intellectual excitement: at some point, one shuts the book; goes for a walk perhaps, brooding about what he has read; and then suddenly there comes a flash of intuition, and a sense of having seen, in the thrill of a momentary, trembling glance, how everything in the universe, from the very least to the greatest, somehow "fits" together. Bertrand Russell started his intellectual career on the strength of such a flash of insight that came to him out of the pages of Hegel. In an autobiographical essay, written late in his career, he gives this account of the experience: "I remember the precise moment, one day in 1894, as I was walking along Trinity Lane, when I saw (or thought I saw) that the ontological argument is valid." Spurred on by his teacher at Cambridge, the Hegelian-idealist J. E. McTaggart, Russell went off to study philosophy in Germany and there, as he tells it, he had a similar but richer flash of insight:

> I remember a spring morning when I walked in the Tiergarten, and planned to write a series of books on the philosophy of the sciences, growing gradually more concrete as I passed from mathematics to biology; I thought I would also write a series of books on social and political questions, growing gradually more abstract. At last I would achieve a Hegelian synthesis in an encyclopedic work dealing equally with theory and practice. The scheme was inspired by Hegel, and yet something survived the change in my philosophy. The moment had a certain importance.

Bertrand Russell's Hegelian "moment" lasted from 1894 through 1898. "During 1898," he wrote, "various things caused me to abandon . . . Hegel"; but he also abandoned other more abiding favorites, like Kant and Leibnitz, in order to pioneer for himself in mathematical philosophy.

John Dewey, Russell's American counterpart, records a similar experience in a comparable autobiographical essay — although Dewey, as he himself explains, never really rejected Hegel. It was at The Johns Hopkins University that Dewey first came under a powerful Hegelian influence when he studied with the outstanding American Hegelian of the time, George Sylvester Morris. Of Morris, Dewey wrote: "I should be happy to believe that the influence of the spirit of his teaching has been an enduring influence." In fact, Dewey goes on to say, Morris's teaching "was far from being the only source of my own 'Hegelianism'." He had already felt the force of the English Hegelians, reacting to the philosophies of "atomic individualism and sensationalistic empiricism" — for it was the time, as he says, of the *Essays in Philosophical Criticism,* cooperatively produced by a younger group under the leadership of the late Lord Haldane. That movement was at the time "the vital and constructive one in philosophy," and its influence "fell in with and reinforced that of Professor Morris." But there were also "subjective" reasons, Dewey acknowledges, "for the appeal that Hegel's thought made to many." Focusing on this subjective side of it, Dewey says with candor that what he then read in Hegel

> supplied a demand for unification that was doubtless an intense emotional craving, and yet was a hunger that only an intellectual subject-matter could satisfy. It is more than difficult, it is impossible, to recover that early mood. But the sense of divisions and separations that were, I suppose, borne in upon me as a consequence of a heritage of New England culture, divisions by way of isolation of self from the world, of soul from body, of nature from God, brought a painful oppression — rather, they were an inward laceration. My earlier philosophic study had been an intellectual gymnastic. Hegel's synthesis of subject and object, matter and spirit, the divine and the human, was, however, no mere intellectual formula; it operated as an immense release, a liberation. Hegel's treatment of human culture, of institutions and the arts, involved the same dissolution of hard-and-fast dividing walls, and had a special attraction for me.

Dewey says that fifteen years passed before he gradually began to "drift away," imperceptibly at first, from Hegel. But there was to be left upon his thinking, he acknowledges, a "permanent deposit" of Hegelianism. This was not an influence of method, or form, he explains, but of content. For "in the content of his ideas," Dewey goes on to say, "there is often an extraordinary depth," as there is in his analyses "an extraordinary acuteness. Were it possible for me to be a devotee of any system, I still should believe that there is greater richness and greater variety of insight in Hegel than in any other single systematic philosopher."

Dewey became a pragmatist, prepared, as he felt, to face a confused and disorderly reality piece by piece. But he always acknowledged that his experience with Hegel — an experience that healed him of his original internal laceration, both intellectually and spiritually — is what armed him to live a philosophic life of permanent pragmatic doubt. Had he felt himself up to it, he might have attempted, at a later date, to systematize his thought. But he never felt up to it, concluding, rather, that it would take more power of integration than he had to surpass Hegel's effort, however unsatisfactory he deemed the result of that effort to be. Perhaps Hegel might one day have a worthy successor. "Meantime," he concluded, "a chief task of those who call themselves philosophers is to help get rid of the useless lumber that blocks our highways of thought, and strive to make straight and open the paths that lead to the future. Forty years spent in wandering in a wilderness like that of the present is not a sad fate — unless one attempts to make himself believe that the wilderness is after all itself the promised land."

Dewey and Russell, typical thinkers of our time, started with Hegel and, for diverse reasons, either rejected him or drifted away. George Santayana, an American thinker of comparable stature, had a reverse experience later in life, and it made him regret that he had not had it earlier. At Harvard University, where he taught for decades, Santayana had written his doctoral dissertation on the German philosopher R. H. Lotze, who had been presented to him as a thinker whose achievement had surpassed Hegel's and, in effect, eclipsed it. Santayana himself had said disparaging things about Hegel without having read him. But many years later, in 1945, after he had published scores of books covering every conceivable subject, Santayana looked back on his Lotze days with regret, observing:

> I wish now that my thesis might have been on Hegel; it would have meant harder work, it would have been more inadequate; yet it would have prepared me better for professional controversies and for understanding the mind of my time. Lotze was stillborn, and I have forgotten everything that I then had to read in him and to ponder: I liked Hegel's *Phaenomenologie*; it set me planning my *Life of Reason;* and now I like even his *Logik*, not the dialectical sophistry in it, but the historical and critical lights that appear by the way. I could have written, even then, a critical thesis, say on *Logic, Sophistry and Truth in Hegel's Philosophy*. This would have knit my

own doctrine together at the beginning of my career, as I have scarcely had the chance of doing at the end. My warhorse would not have been so much blinded and hidden under his trappings.

Lotze had been popular in Santayana's days as a student, even as a number of neo-Kantian and neo-Liebnitzian German philosophers are popular today; and it may be that some budding American philosopher will later regret having given years to their study, as Santayana regretted having studied Lotze, when Hegel is at hand, almost completely translated, at last.

Neither Russell nor Santayana ever pretended, of course, to have been thoroughly schooled in Hegel. Where the major Hegelian influence on modern thought has run is aptly summed up by Morris Raphael Cohen: "His ideas dominate our evolutionary social sciences as well as most diverse schools of philosophy and theology. We can see this in the dialectic materialism of the orthodox Marxism which is disturbing the world, as well as in the Oxford idealism of our Anglo-American thought, which offers solace and support to the established order of spiritual values. Popular as well as radical philosophic thought seems to be ruled by his dogma that the abstract is unreal. Above all, Hegel still fashions our concepts of the history of social institutions, art, religion, and philosophy. Indeed, as to the history of philosophy, his method of approach seems to be in almost exclusive possession of the field, though few recognize it as Hegelian in origin." The Marxist-socialist philosopher and educator Sidney Hook notes more specifically that, as a significant measure of Hegel's influence,

> one need but remember the names Zeller, K. Fischer and Erdmann in the history of philosophy; Gans, Lasalle, Köhler in law; T. H. Vischer and Rosencranz in aesthetics; Riegl and his disciples in the history of art; in political economy, Marx, on the one hand, and in certain respects the historical school from Kniess to Sombart and Weber, on the other; in religion, F. C. Bauer and the Tübingen school, D. F. Stone and Bruno Baur in the middle of the century and Troeltsch and Dilthey towards the end. The influence of Hegel on Lamprecht, Spengler, Friedell and other popular historians of culture is obvious. No less profound is the influence of his organic logic, mediated by Marx, upon all who subscribe to the materialistic interpretation of history.

Carl Friedrich, professor of government at Harvard, brings the account of Hegel's influence somewhat more up to date:

> It is indeed startling to reflect upon the fact that Hegel has been credited with and discredited, by his evident connection with Communism and Fascism, with the moderate socialism of T. H. Green,

or the conservative constitutionalism of a Hocking. The cultural anthropologists of contemporary America are as much indebted to him as are the philosophers of history in the style of Toynbee. Northrop has suggested that the Hegelian heritage is the peculiar and distinguishing feature of the East (in the sense of the countries East of the Rhine); but surely the impact of the neo-Hegelians in England [Bernard Bosanquet, F. H. Bradley] and the Hegelians in Italy, notably Benedetto Croce, makes such a construction more than doubtful. Hegel's influence on existentialism, on Kierkegaard and Jaspers, on Heidegger and Sartre, is tremendous. His influence on Dewey is well known; it is less generally appreciated that as the first philosopher stressing process, he must be seen as the precursor not only of Dewey, but also of Bergson and Whitehead. His viewpoint antedated and reinforced the impact of Darwin and Darwinism. As an "anti-reductionist," he sought to build defenses against subjectivism and materialism which link him with modern philosophers. All of historicism's world-wide sweep traces the impact of the Hegelian concern with history as the concretization of what he epitomized as the world spirit. We may be critically inclined toward this Hegelian heritage, as the writer certain is, but we cannot gainsay its universal significance. No one interested in the clash of ideas that is rending the world today can afford to neglect the work of Hegel.

In spite of his objections to Hegel, Friedrich leaves no doubt as to the tremendous impact of Hegel on those who followed:

The influence of the Hegelian philosophy . . . has been so all-engulfing that a tracing of it would fall little short of an intellectual history of the years since his death . . . . Marxism and Fascism, especially in its Italian form, no less than existentialism and pragmatism, are clearly unthinkable without Hegel. But apart from these philosophical and political impacts of the broadest and most comprehensive sort, Hegel's influence has flown through many smaller channels to shape the thought of a large part of the social sciences not only in Germany, but throughout Europe and especially in the United States . . . . It is manifestly impossible to do more than give a few hints. For example, Max Weber's crucial categories of "understanding" and of "ideal types," derived from the methodological work of Rickert and Windelband, are Hegelian, especially in their teleological implications. Similarly, the work of Toynbee is rooted in Hegel's philosophy of history, and indeed closer to Hegel than some of the intervening work in the field. [T]he work of the cultural anthropologists, such as Ruth Benedict, is derived from Hegel's philosophy . . . . The list could be much further extended. In consent and in dissent, and often in absorbing while rejecting, the modern social sciences carry a heavy and in many ways fateful Hegelian heritage. When Benedetto Croce made his famous as-

sessment of *What is Alive and What is Dead in Hegel's Philosophy*
there had as yet been no Communist revolution, no Fascism, no
existentialism. His was the estimate of a nineteenth-century liberal
which showed how difficult it is to evaluate a thinker's
vitality . . . . The cosmic purposes of a universal meaning, read in
the mind of man — such was the bold challenge of Hegel. Marx
mocked at it: "The ideal is nothing else than the material world
reflected by the human mind, and translated into the forms of
thought." Marx's materialist dialectic confronts us today in the
power of the Soviet Union. Hegel is no answer. Yet much of the
Western response is at best Hegelian.

Candidly acknowledging a personal "prejudice" against
Hegel, whose philosophy "has always seemed to me fundamentally wrong," Professor Friedrich — like so many others — felt
moved at a certain point to attempt a re-evaluation of that philosophy precisely because he had been "increasingly impressed
with the vast scope" of its influence.

That influence went far beyond Germany and central Europe, as Otto Pöggler has pointed out. In his essay "Hegel Edit-
ing and Hegel Research," Pöggler distinguishes, for purposes of
generalization, "three geographical regions of philosophizing,
three great spheres . . . which, to be sure, overlap and interpen-
etrate," where Hegel's influence has been strongly, if not always
directly and positively, felt. They are: continental Europe; the
Marxist East, extending through China; and the Anglo-American West, with the Scandinavian countries included, while those
of South America and Japan, too, receive rather more strongly
the European current of influence. Stressing how the reception
and response varies in each "region," Pöggler draws this rapid
but highly apt sketch:

> To English analytical philosophy Hegel's thought is a pseudo-phi-
> losophy, which produced more unclarity than it eliminated, and
> which rendered itself politically suspect by its ambiguous relation-
> ship to the "open society" which today is felt worthy of support.
> Nevertheless, whoever inquires about the original philosophical
> meaning of American pragmatism and returns to the thought of
> Pierce, sees there a parallel to the starting point of Hegel (which
> Pierce himself stressed). When, on the other hand, the socialist
> countries today seek a "more humanitarian" socialism, the rela-
> tion between Hegel and Marx becomes problematic in a new way:
> there is a positive turn toward the young Marx and, through him,
> toward Hegel. Further, in some eastern European countries, Hegel
> is the thinker who represents the philosophical tradition itself (in-
> sofar as it anticipated dialectical materialism). In continental Eu-
> rope during the last two decades Hegel has been something like a

Klassiker vom Dienst, that is, he has been that thinker treated most often in university seminars and lectures, his thought serving as that popular medium in which the various philosophical tendencies could be understood. But continental Europe's interest in Hegel has not meant "Hegelianism"; if Hegel's thought is taken as somehow the "completion of metaphysics," this is only in the sense that in him and with him "metaphysical" thinking in general is to be dismissed . . . . But again and again, every philosophizing that tries to be more than methodology and theory of science finds itself referring to Hegel, whether positively, by studying with Hegel the problems of *philosophia perennis,* or by taking his thought as a hermeneutic of the western world; or negatively, as in Marxism, where the relation to Hegel has become a matter of life and death since the political condemnation of the Hegelianizing tendencies of Lukacs and Bloch.

Implicit in the geographical or regional distinctions Professor Pöggler has traced to define the main currents of Hegelian influence is recognition of the fact that Hegel's wealth of thought is now and can become increasingly in the future a common legacy for all three — the Marxist east and the Anglo-American west, as well as Europe. Before Hegel's time, European culture had passed through a period of rationalist universalism that denied any value to ethnic or national diversity, insisting that all traditional cultural and conventional differences were obstructions to human progress, in the cultural and scientific as well as in the political spheres. It had been, in other words, as Jacques Barzun aptly observes in his *Romanticism and the Modern Ego,* a false or abstract universalism that really amounted to a narrow-minded imperialist ambition to project or impose upon the entire world what was really a characteristically French penchant for abstract reason in opposition to historical diversity. Against that "rationalist mistake that the French Revolution had attempted to carry out," there arose an "historical-minded and cultural nationalism, which cherishes diverse nationalities" whose "peoples" are deemed to be as "a unique product of history . . . worth preserving in its integrity."

Hegel, it had seemed to his immediate disciples as well as to later critics like Barzun, had managed better than any thinker before him to give cultural, ethnic, and religious diversity its due. Edmond Scherer (1815-1889), who, in Irving Babbit's judgment, ranks as one of the "masters of modern French criticism," wrote a highly influential article on Hegel in 1861 in which he thus summed up this important side of the Hegelian influence:

Hegel has taught us the respect and intelligence of the facts.

Through him we know that what is has a right to be . . . . We no
longer make the world over in our image; on the contrary, we
allow ourselves to be modified and fashioned by it . . . ; the place
of every truth constitutes its sequence! How it lives again before
our eyes! The affiliations of the peoples, the advance of civiliza-
tions, the character of different times, the genius of languages, the
sense of mythologies, the inspiration of the national poetries, the
essence of religions, are so many revelations due to [the Hegelian
impact on] our aesthetic. It prefers to contemplate and study rather
than judge . . . . It has given up the barren method which consists
in opposing one form of beauty to another, in preferring, in ex-
cluding. It bears with everything. It is as vast as the world, tolerant
as nature.

What Scherer has here praised is the result of Hegel's dialectical approach to the otherwise overwhelming materials of
cultural history in its aesthetic, religious, and philosophic phases.

There is a pattern, it would appear, in the response of
intelligent students to a first enthusiastic acquaintance with Hegel.
Benedetto Croce, who with Giovanni Gentile, ranks as Italy's
most influential thinker of the twentieth century, has explained
the phenomenon in dialectical terms. In an autobiographical
essay about his intellectual development he notes why it is virtually impossible to come under Hegel's influence, as he and Gentile, as well as Russell and Dewey and Marx and Lenin did, and
not break wholly away — at least for a time. As he explains in
"Concerning My Philosophic Labors" (1945), in personal love
and friendship we deem it a supreme if rarely realized good to
maintain permanent and constant ties; but it cannot be so, and
should not be so — we must realize — in our intellectual relations
with our teachers, no matter how great they may be and no matter
how much we in fact owe them intellectually. The reason is that,
if they are genuine teachers, conveying *living* thought with their
instruction, they must have the effect of "helping our own thought
to be genuinely free by stimulating it to become productive independently, in its own turn; and in that way, whether they be
conscious of it or not, they make us different from what they
are, and even opposites or adversaries."

Of course if, after having established ourselves independently on our own — which is to say, after having turned Hegel
upside down to prove that our soul's not dead — we let it go at
that, ceasing to be critical in our so-called independence, the
result is certain to be eventual *fossilization* in opposition: thought
in rigor mortis, most dead when it vaunts its independence. It is
a danger to which many of Croce's Italian disciples, like so many

of the uncritical Marxists of our day, have only too readily suc-
cumbed. The greatness of Lenin, it has been argued, for instance,
consists in the fact that, while Marx and Engels professed to
have turned Hegel upside down to establish their originality,
their great Russian disciple had the boldness, when the necessity presented itself, to do the same to them. Marx and Engels
had reversed Hegel by insisting that the state with its artistic,
religious, and philosophic culture, was a mere superstructure,
raised after the fact, upon the material economic base of civil
society. But Lenin, imbued as his champions are apt to say with
the living spirit of Hegelian dialectical thought, reversed that
Marxian reversal, thus setting Hegel right-side up again, so that
as supreme architect of the Russian Revolution, he could build a
revolutionary state first and then proceed to raise on its solidly
political foundations a state-capitalist, thoroughly state-dominated
system of economic productivity. Lenin, as Y. S. Brenner explains half-apologetically, "accepted Marx's idea that 'with the
change in economic foundations, the entire immense superstructure is more or less rapidly transformed,' but he did to it what
Marx had once done to Hegel's dialectic — he turned it upside
down." Marx, Brenner notes with precision, "had always looked
upon the state as part of the social superstructure, as a dependent variable of growth: Lenin turned it into an independent
agent." (In *Theories of Economic Development and Growth,* Praeger,
New York, 1966, p. 225.)

Of course, as we all know, Lenin professed always that he
was the most Marxian of the Marxists — precisely because he
was willing to think the dialectic through for the actual Russian
situation. But such Marxist reversals of reversals of Hegel by no
means exhaust the ways of returning to Hegel after one has experienced his power and rejected it in order to take independent possession of it for oneself.

One of the usual reasons for "breaking" with Hegel is to
charge, as Croce did in his *What is Living and What is Dead in
Hegel,* that Hegel has stubbornly applied his dialectical method
in the spheres of human experience where it really can't apply
and where its stubborn application therefore serves only to dis-
tort the reality of the matter. Croce argued that this was especially true in the spheres of history, art, religion, and philosophy — which is to say, on the highest reaches of cultural activity.
Having made that charge, Croce proceeded to establish himself
as an independent "contributor" to critical philosophic thought
in those very fields, starting with fine art. Indeed, in his own

Aesthetics, which served to establish him as the twentieth century authority in the field — the *Encyclopedia Britanica* asked him, in consequence, to provide its long article on the subject — Croce concluded his account of Hegel's contribution to the field with a contemptuous *tour de force,* even though it is obvious that the best insights of the entire volume derive from Hegel, usually from expositions of positions Hegel criticizes in order to salvage. Hegel, Croce there acknowledges, was a "fervid lover of the arts," and indeed a philosopher "endowed with a warm aesthetic spirit." But he was driven, we are told, by his stubborn adherence to the dialectic, to subordinate art to religion, and the two of them in turn to philosophy, so that, in the end, his philosophy shows itself to be essentially "hostile to art." As it progresses dialectically, wrote Croce in what has become his most influential critical judgment, Hegel's philosophy of art "passes in review the successive forms of art, shows the progressive steps of internal consumption and lays the whole in its grave, leaving philosophy to write its epitaph."

It was Croce's colleague, Giovanni Gentile, who called for a return to Hegel after noting the sterility that had gradually overtaken the critical activity of those who attached themselves to Croce without having shared Croce's long and continuing absorption in the life of Hegelian dialectical thought, which generates and justifies the kind of productive criticism that is the chief merit of Croce's own labors.

Often rejection of Hegel after early acceptance is justified on grounds of content rather than method. Experts in fields where the Hegelian dialectic has been profitably applied have sometimes concluded that Hegel's "results" or conclusions have been superceded because empirical study has brought to light enormous quantities of relevant materials that Hegel and his contemporaries did not know and could not possibly have known. The orientalist Kurt F. Leidecher, who finds much to disagree with in Hegel, notes in an essay entitled "Hegel and the Orientals" (1971) evidences of how little Hegel really knew about China and India, in order to pose the questions: "In view of this, should we still read Hegel's evaluation of the Oriental world or consign it to oblivion?" Much of Hegel's "links with Buddhism" and much that he accepts as historical reality about China and India is far from the truth, writes Professor Leidecker. And yet, taking the Hegelian system as a whole, with its method of thought — so essentially oriental in itself, according to Leidecker — nothing could be more valuable for the *organization* of oriental studies today. "The dialectic," he concludes, "is the greatest and permanent achievement of Hegel and within its context he can be and was the trailblazer for the synthesis between Orient and Occident."

But what Hegel can do for the synthesis of East and West he can also do, and indeed has already done, according to William F. Albright — the most eminent archeologist of our time — for the synthesis of pre-historic and dawn-of-history studies, on the one hand, and traditional historiography, on the other. Albright too sees the dialectic as the crucial tool, "the dominant concept of Hegel's philosophical thought." In his classic work, *From the Stone Age to Christianity: Monotheism and the Historical Process,* Albright characterizes the trailblazing achievement of Hegel in this sphere:

> Hegel impressed his contemporaries and successors both with the originality and sweep of his philosophical conceptions and the wealth of illustration from world-history which he gave to support them . . . . [B]oth philosophers and historians must remain for ever in his debt. For the first time he brought together the data of history in a rational synthesis, exhibiting the progress of humanity from its Asiatic cradle to modern Western Europe and clearly recognizing the fact of cultural evolution.

Through the dialectic, Albright tells us, the remotest past is linked in a most meaningful way with our living sense of the origins of the present — another sphere in which Hegel has proved to be a trailblazer:

> This triad means that every concept or experience involves the existence of its opposite, which follows and reacts against its activity. The inevitable conflict is reconciled by the synthesis, which comprehends and elevates [the opposites] . . . . Owing to Hegel's dominant interest in fields related to man, such as political science, aesthetics, and religion, he was able without difficulty to classify practically all phenomena on which he touched in triads, a plan which gives his philosophy a strangely artificial appearance, at the same time that it imposes itself by its simplicity and harmony.

One should note here that Albright's religious focus is backward: he uses Hegel's dialectical method and his profound insights about art and philosophy as well as religion to organize our knowledge of the origins of Christianity in a Greco-Roman, Mesopotamian-Egyptian and Judaic past. Still, his conclusion accords with that of Pöggler, Friedrich, and others in its unequivocal assessment of Hegel's influence as a continuing phenomenon, expanding and dividing itself to inundate all of Europe, spilling outward in main currents flooding through the Marxist East to the limits of China and across the European and Anglo-American West to the shores of the Pacific. And everywhere, it seems, there has been a repetition of the sort of experience Professor Friedrich and others have had. Leading thinkers, scholars, revolutionary masters of statecraft have initially felt the force of Hegel's thought in such a way as to prompt them to take a stand against him; but then, realistically sensing the omnipresence of the Hegelian influence, they have almost invariably undertaken, or inspired others to undertake, a re-assessment that has served to contribute and broaden the range of that influence.

But Albright also records the danger implicit in that pervasive influence. Hegel, he points out,

> continued to influence thinker after thinker, who in turn built up schools from which new branches sprang — until the wine of Hegelianism is sometimes extraordinarily watered. Marx and Engels converted Hegel's dialectical idealism into dialectical materialism and a whole army of lesser fry has tried to apply Marxianism to historical research, with the most fantastic results, since biblical and ancient Oriental facts are forcibly adapted to the Marxist pattern.

Virtually the same materials served a very forward-looking Moses Hess, founder of modern philosophic Zionism, to look far ahead to an eventual founding of a Jewish state, on notions derived directly from Hegel, of the relations between Judaism and Christianity, on the one hand, and Judaism and the nation-state system, on the other.

As Emil L. Fackenheim has observed in "Hegel and Judaism: A Flaw in the Hegelian Mediation" (1973), there are passages in Hegel which, "if understood in Hegelian terms, can mean only that there is a future for the Jewish people in the modern world . . . a view lending more than poetic truth to the fact that the first Western Zionist philosophy — that of Moses Hess — was largely Hegelian." Fackenheim reviews what he considers to be the flaw in Hegel's treatment of Judaism while noting, at the same time, the elements in it that "helped produce Moses Hess's Zionism." Then he asks, as Professor Leidecker had asked about Hegel's judgments on the Orient generally, whether Hegel's approach to the subject does "justice" to the Jewish experience in its essential truth, and he concludes: "Surprisingly, our answer . . . must be emphatically affirmative: Hegel not only *might* have developed an adequate *Grundidee* as his thought emphatically exposed itself to the Jewish religious self-understanding;

his philosophy is, perhaps, of all philosophies the *only one* capable of doing so."

The response of thoughtful readers to Hegel — of which we have presented only a select sampling to illustrate divergences and similarities — suggests that what one is apt to feel most powerfully, in studying his works, is the comprehensive *potential* of his method. One must use the word *potential* to indicate that the effect is not one of narrowing or restrictive comprehensiveness, but outward, expansive pressure toward ever-receding horizons.

For Hegel, as for great dramatists, there was a dramatic necessity to let personality in history as in art and statecraft have its due, without prejudgment. It is a spirit of tolerance which has offended the pseudo-tolerant who wished not to give certain realities — like the state of Prussia, or the Christian religion, or bourgeois society — their due. But whatever makes history has, according to Hegel, its reasons which are to be understood by a comprehensive philosophy, most of all in the spheres where human willfulness is most directly objectified, namely politics, political history, and the art, religion, and philosophy of peoples that make history or have made it in the past. Compared with these spheres where the human will informs the materials of study, the sphere of natural phenomena is relatively simple. Yet the method of finding rationality in the objective things, whether natural or willful, ought to be the same; and it is Hegel who, as he explains in the Preface to his *Philosophy of Right,* insists on identity of method. The Marxist revolutionaries have shown the utility of the method for organizing practical revolutionary activity, and also, when such activity succeeds, for organizing genuinely productive statecraft. We have suggested how useful the method has appeared to be for practicing philosophers seeking to organize their thought, for orientalists, archeologists, theologians, historians, etc. The most striking results are attained with it in fields where the facts under study involve a multiplicity that threatens to overwhelm our intellects. That is especially true in the sphere of art.

Writing in 1955, the eminent critic Rene Wellek observed that, in the sphere of aesthetics, as in so many others, "Hegel, we now recognize, is one of the most influential figures in the history of mankind," particularly "if we think of the long line of Hegelians in Germany, of his influence on Taine and De Sanctis, on Belinsky, Peter, Croce, and any number of others." In England it was the philosopher Bernard Bosanquet who first gave Hegel's *Philosophy of Fine Art* its due by translating Hegel's "Introduction" to it in 1886 and by appending a large portion of that "Introduction" — the section on the "Division of the Sub-ject" — to his now classic *History of Aesthetic,* which was published in 1892. Bosanquet observed that Hegel, building on the insights of Johann Winckelmann, had sought to demonstrate that purely natural beauty is essentially defective in itself; that our conscious perception of it is essentially artistic, re-creative rather than pas-sive, and that the ideal beauty is what the artist produces when with his mind absorbed in the non-sensuous expression of a "liv-ing" idea he "frees" the idea so that it can "proceed as it were to repeat consciously the process by which it was unconsciously embodied in nature and construct for itself a more adequate representation equally actual for sense in the second nature of art." The Ideal, as Hegel develops the concept out of Winkelmann, is, in other words, the subjective idea "so trans-lated into the terms or tendencies of the imagination as to be capable of direct or indirect presentation to sense."

We are so used to this Hegelian notion, which is at the basis of the modern rejection of "imitation" of nature as the fundamental principle of fine art, that we are apt not to realize how revolutionary its introduction was in the history of aesthet-ics. In Bosanquet's words:

> Hegel's treatment of the Ideal is the greatest single step that has ever been made in aesthetic. Winckelmann had portrayed the ideal as in its perfection one and abstract. Kant, while recognizing it as an embodiment of life, had on this very ground excluded it from aesthetic, because relative to the will. It was Hegel who while main-taining its aesthetic nobility in the sense of Winckelmann, and cred-iting it with the full aesthetic purity demanded but denied to it by Kant, at the same time accepted the extension and differentiations of it so as to constitute the principle and matter of art in all its phases and limits.

For the benefit of students who hesitate to read Hegel because they have heard that his "method" makes reading difficult, Bosanquet has noted that the lectures on the *Philosophy of Fine Art* make "no parade of the dialectic method which constitutes the essential difficulty of his other philosophical works." The dialectic is "at work" in Hegel's exposition, and it serves to give the whole an organic unity not to be found in other works of comparable scope; but Bosanquet's conviction is, as he says, "that in the aesthetic we possess a specimen of the reasonable connec-tion which the dialectic was intended to emphasize, without the constant parade of unfamiliar terms which have been thought to be mere lurking-places of fallacy."

In their widely influential *Introduction to the Methods and Materials of Literary Criticism: The Bases in Aesthetics and Poetics*, first published in 1898, the American scholars S. M. Gayley and F. N. Scott said of the *Philosophy of Fine Art*: "It is at once the most elaborate and the most profound of all attempts to philosophize about the history of art. Nor is it all pure speculation. Its conclusions are based upon observations both wide and minute, and the keenness of Hegel's criticisms upon particular types and specimens of art is acknowledged by all who have read them." In this, Gayley and Scott confirm Bosanquet's observation that "here, as often happens, the wealth of Hegel's knowledge and industry has disconcerted his critics and even his followers."

Professor Carl Friedrich reminds us that "Hegel's approach to art was rooted in vital personal experience. He spent a great deal of time in art galleries; during his Berlin professorship he made three long trips, to the Low Countries and Brussels in 1822, to Austria and Vienna, in 1824, and to France and Paris in 1827, and perhaps their main purpose was to see the great works of art and architecture." Friedrich notes further that, while in Vienna, Hegel "was enchanted with Italian opera, and his letters to his wife expressed not only general joy, but detailed appreciation. When Mendelsohn produced in Berlin, for the first time after generations, Bach's 'Passion according to St. Matthew,' Hegel was greatly impressed. His taste in music, contrary to Schopenhauer's, was altogether of a high order."

We know what high praise Schopenhauer has received from composers and music-worshippers because he acclaims music as the highest of the arts. Yet it is a fact that Schopenhauer's taste in music fell far short of his enthusiasm for it, whereas Hegel, who gives each of the arts its due, while defining characteristic differences in terms of content as well as form, in all parts of the world, and through the entire course of history, withstands even today the closest sort of scrutiny at the hands of genuine arbiters of taste. What is astounding, when one has read through all the lectures on fine art, is precisely the wealth of appreciative analyses and judgments, about architecture, sculpture, painting, and poetry, as well as music. For specialists in any one field, there are bound to be quite evident shortcomings; yet, as Professor Friedrich concludes, in spite of such shortcomings, "Hegel's *Aesthetik* was a trailblazer . . . . Hegel was the first of the great modern philosophers to outline a philosophy of the beautiful in art; what is more, he was the first to work out an over-all developmen-

tal pattern. And while many . . . of his specific suggestions have
now been rejected, the attentive reader soon discovers a substantial sediment of ideas originally suggested by Hegel in contemporary works on the history and philosophy of art and culture."

It was in the sphere of aesthetics that Croce first and most
conspicuously "broke" with Hegel. In his own *Aesthetics,* he argues against Hegel that his dialectical analysis of the concrete
work of art into three dialectically related phases was invalid.
Hegel had distinguished in the concrete work of art a content,
which ought to be inherently artistic, and a form, which ought
also, of course, to be inherently artistic. An artist can turn to an
inherently artistic content or subject matter (Inhalt, Sache), like,
for instance, the story of Macbeth as reported in Holinshed's
Chronicles, or that of Antony and Cleopatra, as reported in
Plutarch. Everyone who reads Holinshed or Plutarch can sense
for himself the artistic promise of those stories. But the artist
can then reform the stories in his mind, think them through in a
new form, eliminating elements in the original and adding new
elements, as Shakespeare so obviously did. And then comes the
artistic realization of the content consistently with the new form
in the concrete work of art which, in Shakespeare's case, are
literally the very plays themselves as we can read them or see
them performed. Croce insisted, to the contrary, that the formal
side of this Hegelian triad is really already the entire work of art,
that "intuition" and external "expression" are really one and in-
divisible, and that what the artist does after he has expressed his
intuition to himself internally — what he does to externalize it —
is really a matter of communication, not art.

The English theoretician of art, E. F. Carritt, had accepted
this Crocian criticism of Hegel — a criticism that in essence rejects the Hegelian dialectical analysis *in toto* – and had made that
criticism the basis of his doctrine in his own highly influential
Theory of Beauty (1923). But years later, he too experienced what
the neo-Marxists and the new-Crocians or Gentilians in Italy were
to experience: the need to oppose dialectically their own opposition to Hegel by returning to the vitality of the Hegelian dialectic itself, which justifies our critical attitudes, provided we
persist in them long enough to become self-critical. In his *Introduction to Aesthetics,* written years later, Carritt acknowledges that,
in spite "of a deep-seated philosophic reluctance [to do so] in
the past, under the influence of Croce," he now felt constrained
to abandon his criticism of Hegel's distinction of content (Inhalt,

Sache) and form (Vorstellung) in the concrete, actual work of art, and more particularly, Hegel's insistence that the distinguishable content as well as the form in a truly great work must be inherently artistic and appreciable as such in itself, Carritt saw that, among other things, Hegel's distinctions made it possible to understand how a great literary work can inspire sculptors, painters, and musicians to re-express it content in other mediums, and also why it has been obviously possible for the greatness of Homer and Virgil and Dante to be "known" by millions who have not been able to read the originals and have often indeed had to rely on prose versions. One is even able to recall to mind, without the distinguishable notes and instruments, the substantive greatness of music, as perhaps a deaf Beethoven could also conceive such greatness without hearing it in any physical sense.

What has a good translation in common with the original if not the artistic content? And if the "form" of the translation can be distinguished from the content it shares with the original, Carritt acknowledges against Croce, we must accept the reality of an artistic form in the original that is also distinguishable from the content. In the concrete work of art the beauties of separable form and content, "each capable of existence outside that fusion," writes Carritt, would indeed be fused and produce one beauty "probably much greater than the sum of the two," though that is apt to be truer of an original work of poetry, for instance, than of a translation, however successful.

There can be no doubt that Hegel's influence has been and continues to be pervasive. Critics like Croce, who repudiated Hegel in order to assert their independence as thinkers, have acknowledged — each in his own way — their profound debt to the German philosopher, assessing their own efforts as part of an inescapable dialectic that makes the very rejection of Hegel part of the continuing spiraling to new levels of understanding.

CHAPTER 2

INTRODUCTION TO HEGEL'S
AESTHETICS

Hegel is the philosopher who gives us an Aesthetics, including a theory of literature, that makes it possible for the first time to integrate the achievements of classical (Greco-Roman) art and romantic (medieval, Christian-European) art with critical insights worthy of an Aristotle, yet on a far more comprehensive scale.

Aristotle and Hegel

As far as theory of literature goes, Hegel's poetics is as comprehensive as Aristotle's is fragmentary. Aristotle says nothing about architecture (the symbolic art *par excellence* of non-Greek, non-Western peoples of the ancient world); he barely hints at an aesthetics of sculpture, painting, and music (though he has powerful things to say about the cathartic effects of music in the last book of the *Politics*); and in the *Poetics*, of the three voices of poetry only one, the dramatic, is treated at length, and even of that voice, only one manner, that of tragic drama, is treated with completeness. Hegel's theory of literature, by contrast, is the culmination of an aesthetics that is elaborated through three large volumes . . . and treats equally of epic, lyric, and dramatic poetry, supplying what is missing in Aristotle's treatise with respect to Greek literature, at the same time that he reinterprets the Aristotelian insights in the light of the literary experiences of other peoples.

Aristotle's method in his *Poetics* was comparative; but whereas his comparative study is limited to a single literature, Hegel's is comparative in the modern sense, ranging beyond ancient Classical poetry to comprehend also the Symbolic poetry of the Far and Near East and the Romantic poetry of medieval Christendom and the modern Western nations.

Italian Humanism, the German Reformation, and the "Moderns"

In this context we should recall the Renaissance humanistic rejection of what we now refer to as the medieval "aesthetic consciousness." The experience that produced the iconoclastic controversy — that insisted on the possibility of representative art for God's sake, despite the neo-platonic, Hebraic, Islamic, and Eastern imperial rejection of such art; the experience that produced the great Gothic cathedrals, the medieval hymns, the Christian chivalric epics, and so much else, and, finally, Dante and, some say, even Shakespeare — that experience was too much for Italian humanism to cope with.

Italian humanism turned instead to the neglected legacy of Greece and Rome and found, within that legacy, a criticism, a theory of literature competent to explain it. But that criticism manifestly could not deal with the aesthetic experience of medieval Christendom in the centuries of the formation of the modern European peoples. So we find Italian humanists who regarded everything "modern" as Germanic or/and Barbarian, insisting that the entire previous millennium, the preceding 1,000 years, had been a mistake. Let's stop writing "medieval," they said, and return to the ancient style, where there are standards of criticism and a theory of literature ready-made for us. Such is the basic significance, the thrust, of the Italian humanistic renaissance, from 1321, the year of Dante's death, to the sack of Rome in 1525.

The Italian rejection of the "Christian thousand years" of the formation of the modern European nations was reinforced by the German Reformation. Luther and Calvin, for example, also reject those thousand years — but for apparently opposite reasons. The Renaissance humanists wanted secular literature the way it was written and appreciated before the centuries of German barbarism; the Protestant reformers wanted Christian literature (the Bible, the writings of the Fathers of the Church) that was written before the centuries of Germanized medieval Christianity.

Clearly there is a tension here.

If we "moderns" refuse to be medieval in substance and nevertheless cannot really become ancient, no matter how hard we strain ourselves to write in Ciceronian and Virgilian Latin and even learn to read Greek, what are we?

Spingarn notes that as it passed out of Italy in the sixteenth century, renaissance humanism — originally Platonic or *Idealistic* in emphasis — soon became Aristotelian or *Naturalistic,* and eventually became thoroughly *Rationalistic,* which is to say, *antihistorical* in emphasis. In the famous Battle of the Books — the quarrel between the ancients and the moderns — the so-called

moderns totally reject the middle-age's experience even as the
so-called ancients do. But, in addition, they assert their own value,
as moderns, against the ancients as well.

This is an important point. History has given us the Greek
experience, followed by the Roman apprenticeship and absorption and universalizing of that Greek experience. Into the Roman world had come all the other values of the Near Eastern
and North African peoples, and most powerfully, the values of
the Jews, with their Bible and their Messianic expectations. In
the form of Christianity, those values come to dominate the
Roman world spiritually and culturally. Then, in a daze of longing for a life beyond this world of tears, the Roman world ceases
to be Roman. It becomes Oriental in the East, and in that form,
"survives" until the middle of the fifteenth century; and Germanic in the West, where it becomes the cradle for the nourish-
ment of the emerging European nations.

*The Rationalist Rejection of History and the Romantic Rejection of
that Rejection*

It is a continuous history. Italian humanism is the first phase
of a process of rejecting that history. Hegel, and Marx under his
influence, will explain that, always, history moves forward by a
process of dialectical rejections. We have to say "No" to the last
most powerful experience we have lived through if we are going
to have a critical (as contrasted with a naive) comprehension of
what it was all about. The Romans rejected their Greek heritage,
briefly, before they absorbed it. The Germanic peoples rejected
the Greco-Roman culture of the ancient world, but not the Judeo-
Christian culture. Indeed, they answered the Christian monastic
call to abandon the world and entered the Church — naively,
though by no means unconsciously.

The Italian humanist renaissance and the Protestant Reformation both rejected that naiveté. They threw out the baby
with the dirty bath water, however. They pretended for a long
time to be content to go back, to Cicero and Virgil, Plato and
Aristotle, the Bible and St. Augustine. But time moves forward.
Without a past they were willing to call their own, the moderns
did indeed look like spiders as contrasted with bees. The humanists gathered sweetness and light only from ancient flowers.
For them all the achievements of medieval aesthetic, religious
and philosophic consciousness were weeds. The moderns applied the same attitude to the ancients as well as the medieval
achievements; and the moderns won out.

Rationalism emptied criticism and literary theory of its entire historical content. The entire past is rejected, antiquity together with the middle ages. The spiders spin out their own web of historically rootless culture. The culmination is, in France, the enlightenment of the Goddess Reason on the High Altar of Notre Dame. Root out the past; excavate all that made up the Ancient Regime; and, in the resultant hole, build an Age, a Reign of Reason.

It became instead a Reign of Terror. The Germans, who used to do everything in their heads first, showed the annihilating power of historically rootless reason in the great Kantian critiques of pure and practical reason, and of judgment — Reason overthrows not only the past, but itself, when it uproots itself from history. The result is skeptical idealism that rejects not only the evidence of things unseen (Faith), but also the evidence of things seen (Natural Science) and the evidence of things thought (Philosophy).

That ends an era. It is called the Neo-classical period, the Age of Rationalism. It ends in a thorough reversal of itself, in an age which is properly called the Age of Historicism, of the reawakening of the historical sense. In the midst of their orgy of anti-historical rationalism, the rationalists themselves were suddenly sobered up out of their rationalist revel. It was as if the voice of Silenus had suddenly been heard at a Dionysian revel.

The rationalists recognized abruptly that their rationalism itself was a child of history. History is triumphant in the very claim of rationalism to be liberating itself from history. That is, of course, a profounder sense of history than the ordinary one. It is the Romantic sense of history.

France's reason, the French rationalists and the rationalists in other lands suddenly say, is an expression of the historically deeply rooted French national spirit, even as Germany's idealist skepticism is characteristically German. All over Europe, there suddenly leaps into consciousness an awareness of what it means to be English, French, German, Italian, Spanish, etc. And with it, awareness that it had all happened — this formation of national identities — during those doubly- and triply-rejected middle ages.

By acknowledging their distinctive identities, as against the Rationalist claims of the essential oneness of all mankind, the critics and literary theoreticians of the Romantic age — and the *Aesthetics* of Hegel is the culmination of all this — became simultaneously appreciative of the Aesthetic Consciousness of the middle ages and of the ancient Hebrews, Persians, Arabs, Turks, Hindus, and Chinese, as well as the classical Greeks and Romans.

On how rationalism tends to be culturally imperialistic, imposing its rationalist standards everywhere, to the point of destroying cultural identity, Jacques Barzun has described especially well in his *Romanticism and the Modern Ego:*

> The romantics' nationalism is cultural nationalism. They spoke less of the nations than of "peoples," whom they considered the creators and repositories of distinct cultures. The romantics could hardly have overlooked this and remained good historians, or even good critics. But they went further and maintained that each human group, being a unique product of history, was worth preserving in its integrity. They compared Europe to a bouquet, each flower in its appointed soil . . . . To them the idea of imposing any nation's ways, speech, or art upon another was repellent. For this was precisely the rationalist mistake that the French Revolution had attempted to carry out and that they were combating.

This respect of the national identities of the European peoples made the European word suddenly receptive to non-European cultures. It was no longer the case of using fake Chinese or Persian, or Ethiopic visitors (Rasselas of Dr. Johnson, the Orientals of Goldsmith, Voltaire, Montesquieu, etc.) to show the absurdity of differences. It was now a case of deciphering the hieroglyphs of Egypt, recovering ancient Persian inscriptions, learning Chinese, Indian, etc. etc.

We should remember that most non-Western literatures really had no contact with one another until, by reaching out to them, Westerns scholars joined them together in the Western mind. This is important and should be acknowledged by those literatures, once the flush of self-assertion has subsided. It's the old Socratic precept writ large: *know thyself.* Not only as individuals but also as entire peoples and nations. Know your limitations, your true history, your true goals, your true accomplishments — whatever they are, howsoever rich or meager, provincial or cosmopolitan, particular or universal.

The relative isolation of the Far Eastern and Middle Eastern literatures from one another is well put by Arthur E. Kunst in "Literatures of Asia" *(Comparative Literature: Methods and Perspectives,* ed. Stallknecht and Frenz):

> A superficial acquaintance with the literatures of India and China shows that they have relatively little decisively in common; few literary prejudgments could be more absurd than the assumption of Europeans that an "Oriental" mode of literature exists. Before

modern times, South Asian and East Asian literature have no more relation to each other than they do to Middle Eastern or to European literature.

Hegel's Comprehensive Aesthetic and Theory of Literature

This is the moment of the stupendously successful Hegelian effort to provide a comprehensive Aesthetic, including a theory of literature — perhaps the only one in the history of the subject — that "saves" for the Western experience the humanist respect for the classical tradition of imitation; the rationalist-modern eagerness to spin everything out of the self, rationally at first; and the aesthetic consciousness of the Middle Ages which gives moderns the Romantic impulse to transcend classical art, to include God-centered art in its Symbolic as well as Romantic forms.

In focusing on this comprehensive analysis of the sphere of fine art, we must not isolate it from the organic whole of which it is a part. For Hegel, the *Aesthetics* derives its vitality from the integrated life of the whole. If we cut it off from the rest of the system, we do it fatal violence.

Hegel, we should keep in mind, is not speaking figuratively when he characterizes his system of philosophy as *organic* – as a body of *living* thought. On the contrary, for him thought is literally what Aristotle long ago said it was: one of the three characteristic forms of life. We tend to think of plants and animals as the only forms of life. A third and, as Aristotle said, manifestly higher, *completer* form of life is *thought*. Thought has its vegetative and animal-sensory aspects: it nourishes itself, grows, moves, reproduces, receives impressions. And when freed by rational habituation from having to give attention to those aspects, when it concentrates upon itself and becomes *thought thinking thought (noesis noeseos noesis),* it is life in its highest form, capable of the time-arresting experience of art, religion, and philosophy — for which the vegetative-nutritional and animal-sensory forms of life are but a crude anticipation.

Through his Science of Logic and Philosophy of Nature, and even more directly through the sciences of the Philosophy of Subjective and Objective Mind, Hegel prepares us to grasp as our own experience the comprehensive vitality of the life of thought. He discusses at length the Aristotelian judgment in the *Metaphysics* which is that the "actuality of thought is life," and that "God is that actuality in self-dependence, life most good and eternal. We say therefore that God is a living being, eternal, most good, so that life and duration as continuous and eternal

belong to God; for this *is* God . . . . It is of itself that divine thought
thinks . . . and its thinking is a thinking on thinking." In his *Ethics,* Aristotle had concluded that the purpose or end of human
existence is precisely to rise in thoughtful activity so as to experience for a time the life of thought thinking thought, which is
God's actuality. According to Hegel, the thoughtful activity that
raises man to such heights is that which unites the objective experience of God-inspired art and the subjective experience of
religious worship in the thoughtful whole of God-centered philosophical thought.

Is such a level of life an illusion, beyond human capacity?
Aristotle had raised the question, and Hegel cites the Aristotelian answer with full acceptance. Such a life as this, wrote Aristotle
in the most Hegelian passage of his *Ethics,*

> will be higher than the human level: not in virtue of his humanity
> will a man achieve it, but in virtue of something within him that is
> divine; and by as much as this something is superior to his com-
> posite nature, by so much is its activity superior to the exercise of
> other good habits. If then the intellect is something divine in com-
> parison with man, so is the life of the intellect divine in compari-
> son with human life. Nor ought we to obey those who enjoin that
> a man should have a man's thoughts and a mortal the thoughts of
> mortality, but we ought so far as possible achieve immortality, and
> do all that man may live in accordance with the highest thing in
> him; for though this is small in bulk, in power and value it far
> surpasses all the rest.

Aristotle makes this ethical claim part of his defence of art
in the *Poetics,* where he argues against the Platonists that poetry
is indeed more philosophical than history and that its effect,
particularly in the case of high tragedy, is to purge us, through
vicariously experienced fear and pity, of our thought-suffocat-
ing passions. Thus purged, the human spirit can the more easily
rise to the life of thought thinking thought, transcending the
mortality of merely *historical* human existence. Centuries later,
the sages of judaism, Christianity, and Islam who most felt the
influence of Greek thought sought to identify their experience
of the actuality of divine life with the Aristotelian account of it;
but they hesitated to so much as entertain the notion that art —
the pursuit of artistic beauty — might be a valid way of ascent,
on a par with the saint's way or the theologian's way. It was Dante,
in his *Divine Comedy,* who insisted on it once again, and in terms
consistent with the Judaic-Christian experience of transcendent
Divinity. Hegel's aesthetic doctrine, particularly its interpretation of the medieval-romantic aesthetic achievement, presents

itself quite explicitly as a high philosophic justification of Dante's poetic experience and the Aristotelian adumbration of it in the *Poetics.*

In Hegel's words, art fulfills its supreme task "only when it has placed itself in the same sphere as religion and philosophy." And he says, further: "It is in works of art that nations have deposited their profoundest intuitions and ideas; art is thus often the key, and in many nations the sole key, to their philosophy and religion." The ultimate object of artistic activity, as Hegel conceives it, is to perfect human *making* on the same level that high religious experience perfects human *behaving* and high philosophic insight perfects human *explaining.* Making, behaving, and explaining — productive, practical, and theoretic activity in the meaning those terms have had from Aristotle to Kant — are for Hegel distinct lines of experience that rise, like meridians far removed from one another at the equator, to converge on a single point at the pole. The saint's line is *praxis,* the sage's way is *theoria,* and the artist's way is *poiesis;* but their convergence is three in one, absolutely: the highest good, the highest truth, and the highest beauty

With the *Philosophy of Fine* Art we get our first vision of the point of convergence, still at a great remove. Art, not less than religion and philosophy, says Hegel, is a "way of bringing to our minds and expressing the *Divine,* the deepest interests of mankind, and the most comprehensive truths of the spirit . . . . Art shares this vocation with religion and philosophy but in a special way, namely by displaying even the highest objectivity, bringing it thereby nearer to the senses, to feeling, and to nature's mode of appearance." The Divine is subjectively possessed in religion, and high philosophy comprehends that religious subjective possession with an objectivity that is beyond the range of the sensory; but the passage is initially made, in the historical experience of all peoples who make it, by way of the artistic imagination. In this respect, art is therefore, says Hegel, "by virtue of its power to create forms cognate with its own substance, the *first* interpreter of religious consciousness." What is "shown" by inspired art is worshipped in religion's love-filled heart. "Worship," writes Hegel, "does not belong to art as such. Worship arises from the fact that now by the subject's agency the heart is permeated with what art makes objective as externally perceptible, and the subject so identifies himself with this content that it is its inner presence in the ideas and depth of feeling that becomes the essential element."

Art and religion, together, have the whole divinity as content. They lack only that living integration in thought which comes with their convergence in the philosophic experience. In the process of convergence, the objectivity of art is retained, Hegel explains, except that its external sensuousness is exchanged "for the highest form of the objective, the form of thought." And the subjectivity of religion is similarly retained, but "purified into the subjectivity of thinking. For thinking on one side is the most inward, intimate subjectivity, while true thought, the idea, is at the same time the most real and the most objective universality which only in thinking can apprehend itself in the form of its own self."

Thus we have subject and object, religion and art, linked by a verb which expresses or rather *is* their oneness. And we have come around to Aristotle's thinking subject that actively or verbally thinks about thinking object. That is the perfection of life in its highest form, says Hegel.

The *Philosophy of Fine Art* is the bridge of easiest access into this high sphere where art, religion, and philosophy, as absolute moments of productive, practical, and theoretic mind, are one.

For Hegel, history is the evolution of Spirit, or self- consciousness, of self-awareness — the history of the gradual internalization of what at first was posited as external and absolute laws of human conduct. The Greeks with their absolute ethical laws, their undeviating moral judgments, could not possibly understand the Hegelian notion of Spirit, gradually unfolding in the human consciousness. For them — to illustrate quickly — Oedipus could never claim to be innocent, even though he was not personally responsible for his transgression. He says that himself in the play; guilt is not a matter of personal intention but an absolute fact based on an absolute act. For Oedipus and the Greeks, the completed deed determines guilt or innocence. The complex internal struggle of the soul for self-possession according to its own inner laws is meaningless to them. Not until Hamlet — who is the first great creation of the modern world in this sense — do we have an example of a soul caught in the effort to translate absolute moral law (the dictates of the Ghost who comes from an absolute God) into internal personal conviction. The whole play illustrates the dichotomy and ends with an assertion of personal righteousness over absolute external ethical law. Hamlet, in the end, kills Claudius because the King has proved he deserves to die — not because the Ghost has convinced Hamlet of that. It's the crowning irony of the play. The Ghost — the absolute moral law — never gets what he asks for. Hamlet acts on his own conviction and strength of soul.

That illustrates in a nutshell the basic difference between Greek and Shakespearean or modern tragedy. The modern world — which is the beginning of the Romantic era in a broad sense — is the world where Spirit prevails, unfolding itself in the search for self-awareness. Hamlet is the first and most striking expression in art of the shift from external absolutes to personal conviction of right.

Greek art, Hegel explains, had attained *adequate* representation, the perfect expression of the sensuous and the Ideal — of form and matter — of the balance between external values, the ethical code of human conduct and man's artistic impulse. For this reason, Hegel asserts that classical art is the most *beautiful* art the world has ever known, a total absorption of the highest religious and philosophical experience of an entire age in its artistic representations.

It was no doubt this kind of estimate that led A. C. Bradley, the great Hegelian Shakespearean critic, to mistake the ultimate significance of Hegel's praise of ancient classical art. Bradley took Hegel to mean — when he said that Greek art was the most *beautiful* the world has ever known — that it was the *highest* form of art. But Hegel clearly meant no such thing. When he praises the *Antigone,* for example, he is speaking within the context of that notion of classical art we have described. But elsewhere, and several times (not just once), he points out that art can go much further. Art can penetrate the inner world of man, his spiritual consciousness, and show the workings of his soul. And, in this context, *beauty is not the final word.* Hegel's conclusion with respect to this particular argument is stated very clearly: the highest form of tragic art is not found among the Greeks but among the Elizabethans — and the most glorious among them is Shakespeare.

Hegel's conclusion is clear enough to anyone who has read his pages. It accords with the notion that for the Greeks art and religion were intimately connected: Greek religion *is* their art. There is no other religion outside the artistic configuration of the gods. They are idealized human nature, idealized human conduct: the absolutes made flesh, or almost flesh. Defending this classical ideal of *making,* and yet touching on its limitations, Hegel writes:

Personification and anthropomorphism have often been decried as a degradation of the spiritual; but art, insofar as its end is to bring before perception the spiritual in sensuous form, must advance to such anthropomorphism, as it is only in its proper body that mind is adequately revealed to sense.

Of course, these notions develop among the Greeks; for Aristotle divinity is no longer simply humanized gods but those virtues in man which make him most human — his thinking — and therefore most divine. That divinity, which is the source of all beauty, truth, and goodness, for Aristotle is the proper object of art. And he saw it accomplished best in tragic drama. For the Greeks, divinity was seen most plainly in human nature at its best; and they found the most suitable means for expressing it. Hegel writes about sculpture especially — where the classical ideal of the *adequate* representation of sensuous matter and ideal is most obvious —

> A more spiritual religion can rest satisfied with the contemplation and devotion of the soul, so that the works of sculpture pass for it simply as so much luxury and superfluity. A religion so dependent on the sense vision as the Greek was must necessarily continue to create, inasmuch as for it this artistic production and invention is itself a religious activity and satisfaction, and for the people the sight of such works is not merely sight-seeing but is part of their religion and spiritual life. . . . Only on grounds such as these can we find a rational explanation, if we consider the great difficulties which the technique of sculpture implies, for the host of sculptured figures, this forest of statues of every kind, which in their thousands upon thousands were to be met with even in any one city, in Elis, in Athens, in Corinth, and even in towns of lesser importance, as also in the greater Greece beyond the Islands of the Cyclades.

The Symbolic art of the East eludes such artistic expression; it is inexpressible in truly sensuous terms. Later on, the art of the Judaic-Christian middle ages also found artistic expression inadequate for the transcendence of its content. And in Hegel's system, the Romantic age represents a new kind of artistic transcendence, the kind of experience in art which approximates in some ways the transcendence of religious mysticism and symbolic mystery.

In the *Aesthetics,* Hegel considers systematically and with an astonishing variety of examples the full implications of these notions. He deals with them in other settings too — in works like the *Philosophy of Religion,* the *History of Philosophy,* and even the *Philosophy of Right.* Aristotle had spoken eloquently for the Greek experience, but Hegel is the first to explore the total experience of art.

His major classification is in terms of symbolic, classical and romantic art — and these were inspired of course by Aristotle's sketchy but profound discussion early in the *Poetics* on the relationships of content, form, and medium. Aristotle, we know, was the first to explore these relationships head-on. In the area of poetry, these relationships determine the various genres, with respect to manner of imitation. But the objects of imitation for Aristotle also made a difference. These objects can be summed up as the "characters of men, as well as what they do and suffer" — and the different ways in which they are represented distinguish, for example, tragedy and comedy, epic and mock-epic, and so on.

The manner in which such representations are conceived is another point of difference. And here Aristotle focuses exclusively on poetry, distinguishing what we have come to call the three voices of poetry: the *Epic* (narrative), the *Lyric,* and the *Dramatic.* Aristotle indicates that this same kind of distinction applies to the other arts, but it is Hegel who examines the full implications of the parallels working out for us the fruitful notion of symbolic origins, classical perfection, and romantic transcendence in art — both poetic art and other arts. The distinctions as they apply to poetry are, for Hegel, the last step in a series or progression which reflects the full development of Spirit.

All art begins with Wonder, he reminds us, taking his cue from the Greeks. Art is the irresistible impulse to express the dilemma of man who recognizes somehow the "Mighty Presence" in and around him and the frustration of his physical dependence. Wonder, which is the beginning of all knowledge, is also the beginning of art, which "by virtue of its power to create forms cognate with its own substance," is the "first interpreter of religious consciousness." (This idea illuminates the commonplace about the religious origin of drama.)

At first, the effort to express the dilemma of divinity and man is frustratingly inadequate in that the mystery of nature, of the forces around us, of divinity, cannot be fully grasped. The forms of art, in the early stages, are monstrous shapes imbued with unnatural suggestiveness. Think of the Egyptian sphinx, the ancient Chinese and oriental art. At its worst, such art is a confusion of color, weird sounds and hieroglyphs; but at its best, it is awe-inspiring in its sublimity and mystery. Think of the pyramids, the ziggurats of Mesopotamia, the cliff-tombs, etc. At its best, such art, in which we see the inadequacy of matter and form, is represented by the architecture of the Greeks, where we immediately sense however a vital difference. The architecture of the Greeks, their form of symbolic art, is charged with a pregnant force. It is not the dead environment of the Egyptian tombs. The Greek temples are living enclosures; they call into being, as it were, the human form. And sculpture for the Greeks thus becomes the presence of Spirit in its human form. Hegel says that the sculptor's art is summoned into being by the symbolic representation of architecture. This is a provocative notion. Greek statuary brings into focus the *living* intelligence that gives to architecture its many-faceted symmetry .The Greek statues represent, therefore, the perfect adequacy of content and form — or, to use Hegel's phrase, "the highest excellence of which the sensuous embodiment of art is capable." In it, *mind* is reflected in its human idealized totality — a divine presence which is called forth by the *living* symbolic representation of Greek architecture.

In other words, although for Hegel certain periods fall into the symbolic, classical, and romantic classifications he has elaborated, in itself Greek art, the Greek experience, contains those classifications in its own brief development (brief by contrast with the totality of history). Greek architecture is the symbolic art made as classically adequate as such art can ever be; Greek sculpture is the classical art par excellence; and beyond these, we have painting, music, and poetry — all of which probe the depths of spirit, the inner man, moving inward to the core of being: the romantic arts.

The romantic arts, in their efforts to dematerialize themselves, may correctly be called art "transcending" itself.

Painting, whose medium is color or reflected light, destroys the mechanical and spatial qualities of the external environment. It creates a three-dimensional illusion on a plane surface, providing a "mirrored" view of the world. Painting can depict just about anything, so that the medium determines a much larger content for representation.

The second of the romantic arts, music, is the most immaterial. Here all spatial relationships are dissolved into temporal extension: sounds. The laws of musical composition suggest architectural configurations, but the result is the most elusive the most suggestive of all artistic representations. Music, according to Hegel, is the most inward of the arts and therefore the most romantic.

But it is with words, in the art of speech, that the human

voice best sings its emotional life. The art of poetry can do everything the other arts can do — and in a very special way. It can paint scenes, build architectural structures, describe statuary in motion, sing the innermost emotions of the soul in cadences that are musical, and with melodic inventiveness. Hegel writes about the human voice:

> With respect to the tones emitted, it may be regarded as the most complete instrument of all. It unifies the characteristics of both wind instrument and string. That is to say, we have here in one aspect of it a column of air which vibrates, and, further, by virtue of the muscles, the principle of a string under tension. Just as we saw that in the color inherent in the human skin, we had the most perfected presentment of color, so, too, we may affirm of the human voice that it contains the ideal compass of sound, all that in other instruments is differentiated into its several composite parts. We have here the perfect tone, which is capable of blending in the most facile and beautiful way with all other instruments. Add to this that the human voice . . . expresses the ideal character of the inner life, and most immediately directs such expression. In the case of all other instruments, on the contrary, we find that a material thing is set in vibration, which, in the use that is made of it, is placed in relation of indifference to and outside of the soul and its emotion. In the human song, however, it is the human body itself from which the soul breaks into utterance.

Song, or singing, would correspond to the lyrical impulse in its purest form. But in all that pertains to poetry, to the human voice as the vehicle of art, there is a very special quality. The difference lies in the medium of poetry. It is not marble or stone or brick; it is not color or line or light or sound. It is *words;* and *words* are a very special medium, because they come already imbued with *thought* and *rationality*. The medium of poetry is the least external, the most intimately human, the richest in possibilities. Words are the least sensuous means of expression, yet they can build for us an objective world which includes painting and sculpture, the whole spectrum of emotional lyrical life, musical suggestiveness, and architectural structure.

We witness, in this sequence of the arts — from the symbolic and classical to the romantic — a gradual dematerialization of the matter of art, so that with poetry we have the most immaterial and the most totally human of the arts. Poetry rests therefore on disciplining language to suggest the many-faceted possibilities already mentioned. Poetry contains in effect all the other arts; it can reproduce them in its own way through words alone. And because words are full of meaning and already shaped in the image of human thought, they are infinitely suggestive. Understandably therefore, for Hegel poetry is "the most universal and cosmopolitan instructor of the human race."

We should remind ourselves quickly here that this three-fold classification applies to the arts (by way of definition) but also to historical periods. Thus the Egyptian, Oriental, Near-Eastern art is symbolic (in the mutual inadequacy of matter and form); the Greek experience is classical (the perfect adequacy of sensuous and Ideal); the modern experience is romantic (the internalization of art and therefore a new transcendence).

Every age goes through these categories to some extent. The Greek experience, as we said, although generally classical (and in this respect its most characteristic art form is sculpture), has its symbolic expression in its architecture and its romantic expression in its lyrics and dramatic poetry.

But there is also a progression within the art of poetry, according to Hegel — and it recalls the progression from architecture to poetry in many ways. (T. S. Eliot will later pick up this argument, giving us the phrase "the three voices of poetry.") The medium of poetry, as we said, is the word — but more accurately, the *imagination*. And insofar as the imagination runs through all the other arts also, it follows that poetry in some way or other works through them.

The poetic imagination, the poetic voice, works through three main vehicles: the epic, the lyric, and the dramatic. The epic, or narrative, builds an architectural whole, provides a total picture of a people and age through some grand action with which they can identify. Hegel speaks about the lack of epic among the Chinese, he talks of the Hindu epics (Ramajana and Maha-Bharata), he refers to the Bible and the epic elements in it, and of course, talks at great length about the Greek epics. This is the external voice.

The lyric voice is the internal and personal voice of poetry. The lyric poet is all wrapped up in himself, in his own subjective emotional life. The objectivity of national consciousness (which characterizes the epic) disappears from the lyric, which is immediate, personal, and spontaneous.

The dramatic voice brings together, in effect, the subjective lyric and the objective narrative epic through an action which is independent, fully realized as an immediate fact depicted through independent figures placed in relationship with one another on stage. Such a totality includes the narrative element of the epic (with all its architectural structure) and the subjective personal element of the lyric (in the individual voices of characters expressing their innermost feelings). The dramatic voice contains the other two in a unique composite, which makes it the synthesis of the two and, in a very real sense, the most perfect form of poetry.

The distinctions described so far must be kept in mind in any discussion of Hegel's theory of tragedy.

Hegel's Theory of Tragedy

Tragedy becomes possible where the dilemma of divine and human is a balance of equal forces. It is no accident that where the supernatural overwhelms the soul, symbolic art prevails. Drama — and tragedy particularly — presupposes a genuine paradox. The Greeks were the first to exhibit this profound insight; and later, the Elizabethans. These are the only two genuine periods of "tragic" drama. And this too is no accident. The Athens of Pericles and the England of Elizabeth represented in each case a moment of balance — a civilization still fully subscribing to divine absolutes while exploring just as fully the prerogatives of reason and human values. The old has not been cast off; and the new is irresistibly seductive. It is the condition of Oedipus and Hamlet. They are the rational man, the inquisitive human animal who questions divine prerogatives while unconsciously still subscribing to them. It is the kind of environment which makes tragedy possible. And, again, it's no accident that we have not had genuine tragedy except in those two historical periods.

There is a difference of course between ancient and modern (or romantic) tragedy. Hegel delves into this in many works and in many startling ways. Ancient tragedy, which accepts the fundamental paradox as absolute values on both sides, is not interested in the translation of those values into personal feelings and responsibilities beyond those that reflect the confrontation of two opposites. In other words, the Greek tragic hero is all of "one piece" — there are no excursions into his innermost doubts and personal idiosyncrasies. He accepts or rejects certain values — not without a struggle, of course, but that struggle is determined and described solely in terms of the paradox, the ethical confrontation. The Greek tragedies were a real cathartic (Aristotle was absolutely right about this). Tragedy moves us to recognize ourselves in people totally different from us — and this is the source of the famous statement about pity and fear. We pity what is distant from us but which evokes our sympa-

thetic response as a fellow-human being; we fear what we *do*
associate with, as something that deep in the insight of the soul
can happen to us just as it is happening to that king or emperor,
or leader of men. Pity is the sympathetic but detached response;
fear is the immediate identification. Pity is the personal recognition; fear is the recognition of a situation.

Greek tragedy is rooted in this kind of confrontation; whatever greatness we encounter later, let's not underestimate for a
moment the awesome character of this kind of tragedy. It will
never cease to overwhelm us, instruct us, refine us in every way.
Those who still put forward simplistic judgments about the
Greeks not knowing how to develop character are way off base:
the Greek dramatists were not interested in the purely artistic
representation of personality on stage — no more than our dramatists today are, especially those of the "absurd." The Greek
tragic hero is deliberately delineated as he is, in the *single thrust
of the one great action* that determines his entire character. A magnificent and provocative artistic commitment; not at all an easy
task! The Italian Nobel Laureate in Drama, Luigi Pirandello,
forces us to consider that commitment in modern terms: what
one action, what one pose, what one point of view translated
into action tells us who and what a person is? Of course, that
person has many particular details about him, which may or may
not be interesting — biography is always fascinating because of
the clutter of details! — but can any one of us, for example, isolate the one single trait or action or situation which will provide
a stranger with the basic insight needed to understand a certain
person?

That was the Greek intention. Antigone, Oedipus, Orestes
were dramatically interesting in their one single and most characteristic action. What they were "behind the scenes," in their
ordinary humanity, in their everyday cleverness, did not interest
the Greeks. They depicted their tragic characters the way they
did, by *choice.* Not until Aristophanic comedy do we get all the
ordinary details — distorted to serve a special purpose, of course,
but clearly there. They proved it could be done, after all.

Hegel talks at length about these matters. He notes that
for the Greeks the tragic confrontation was all-important. The
lesson to be learned was a basic and recurring one: that in man's
willful decision to be true to his innermost convictions lies his
grandeur; but that his tragic insight depends on his knowledge
that his decision is subject to the absolute laws of the gods and
that the tragic hero recognizes the prerogatives of the gods in

the matter while insisting on his own thing. And in this confrontation, in this visual and dramatic explication of the paradox of human and divine, lies the greatness of Greek tragedy.

Hegel distinguishes at least three major categories of tragic conflict: the first is one in which the forces at odds are equally "justified" — that is, equally *right* (or, if one prefers, equally wrong) — never *good* or *bad.* The critics who persist on a good/ bad confrontation have understood nothing at all; they are simply imposing on Greek tragedy their own modern views. In this first confrontation, the neatest perhaps, the opposing forces or demands or values are both intrinsically worthy of respect. The law of family relationships, of family bonds, of united individuals who have a common background of blood ties, cannot be disobeyed lightly. The repercussions will eventually catch up with us. Today, psychologists tell us this in a different way; but we don't need psychologists to impress this truth upon us. You may not get along with your mother or father or brother; and you may have to leave them and seek your own destiny; but until those two facts are brought together again, until you realize that there is no real escape, that you must somehow come to grips with the differences and the difficulties without undermining the fact of the basic relationship, you cannot grow into anything worthwhile.

This is why so many young people say about slightly older ones that they have become "conservative." They too will have to become that, if they are to find their true stride. For the Greeks, family ties were sacred; but no less sacred (and this must be underscored, because even well-known and respected critics have misunderstood), no less worthy of respect and obedience were the laws which the king passed for the protection of the commonwealth. Ordinarily, the two go hand in hand. The tragic confrontation takes place when, in some peculiar situation, these two worthwhile laws come into opposition. The *Antigone,* says Hegel, is the most remarkable example of this kind of confrontation in tragedy. And within this context, he says, it is the most beautiful tragedy ever written. (Bradley's blunder in this matter has encouraged carelessness in other, lesser, writers who took their cue from him, not bothering to read Hegel for themselves.)

In a second kind of tragic conflict, the forces in opposition are not equally clear .The best example of this kind of tragic confrontation is the *Oedipus Tyrannus,* where unconscious forces come into play and obscure the validity of the two opposing and equal laws. (A lot of rubbish has been written about this play,

one critic going so far as to wonder why Aristotle used it as the
example of the greatest tragedy of his time. Hegel is very clear
and convincing on the subject, if allowed to present the full argument in his own voice.)

For the modern reader and critic, the play's difficulty seems
to be that the hero suffers for something he didn't want to happen. On the surface, that seems to be the case. And it is certainly
true, if we look at it from our own post-Hamlet world, from a
world of psychological penetration, of personal commitment, of
deep and individualized values. But was that the Greek world? Is
it fair to restructure, critically, a play like *Oedipus Tyrannus* according to our modern notions? Many critics do just that, conve-
niently ignoring the lines of the play itself, lines that warn us not
to be too hasty in judging the play in our image. After all, Oedipus himself never once offers the excuse that he didn't know
what he was doing. Jocasta does, interestingly enough; but Oedipus never does. And this should give us pause. Sophocles put
forward that kind of answer and rejected it. Critics cannot pick
it up as though it had never been considered.

Hegel says that the *Oedipus Tyrannus* is the best example
of the *second* kind of tragic conflict, where one of the forces in
opposition is masked as it were. Here's the rational man who
solves the riddle of the Sphinx and becomes King, marries the
Queen, and rules happily for many years — until the past catches
up with him. In the slow unfolding of a past which he had sewn
up and stored away, Oedipus comes to understand that he had
done one thing while thinking another. This partial truth had to
be corrected. He despised the oracle, scoffed at it openly, but
what exactly does that mean? Here's the son of a couple living in
Corinth who hears about a prophecy that he will kill his father
and marry his mother. Does he laugh it away? Again and again
in the play we are reminded that he cares nothing about prophecies, birds, omens, etc. But what he actually does is leave Corinth
to make sure the *prophecy* does not come about. It's like saying:
"I'm an atheist, but just to make sure that God won't punish me
for blaspheming I will go to confession." Oedipus reacts in much
the same way. If the oracles are untrustworthy, if he doesn't believe in them, why run away from them? Well, that's exactly what
the rational man, known far and wide for having solved the riddle
of the Sphinx, actually does: he runs away to avoid the terrible
prophecy about his fate. And in so doing, he ran headlong into
the consequences predicted. All this is implicit in what Hegel
says.

In this instance, Hegel doesn't stop to give us details or illustrations; the large picture speaks for itself. Taking our cue from him, we are bound to reach the same conclusion; to interpret the play as the tragedy of "humanity" or some such thing — as Bowra, Lucas and others have done — is at best sheer carelessness; at worst, utter stupidity.

The third kind of tragic conflict, says Hegel, is much more psychological and internal. Euripides is perhaps the best example of the elaboration of this kind of conflict. His interest in the more personal motivations of character and the peculiar circumstances that trigger the individual's responses anticipate — but are still a far cry from — modern tragedy, with its psychological penetration of character.

Not until we come to Elizabethan tragedy — and Shakespearean tragedy particularly — does tragedy take on a new aspect. With the modern concern with all the nuances of character, the idiosyncrasies of personality, the particular and peculiar quirks of individual behavior (even when they seem to have nothing in common with the large purpose and intention of a dramatic character), tragedy assumes a totally new and difference perspective. In Shakespeare's plays, it is not the tragic confrontation of two opposite, absolute, and equally justified ethical laws that constitutes the major interest but the personalities of the tragic protagonists, in all their peculiarities, so that the characterization becomes even more important than the conflict of ethical forces. Hamlet is the core of the play; we almost forget action as such. So much so (as T. S. Eliot reminds us), that we tend to look at Hamlet as a real person. Or take Lear. Or Othello. Or Macbeth. They are living people, fully developed characters full of quirks and interesting contradictions — even beyond the essential ones that shape the character dramatically and trigger events in the dramatic action. This is the most striking difference between ancient and modern tragedy.

Hegel describes it at length. He points out also that in Shakespearean tragedy (which is the modern form), *evil* comes into prominence, when it never figured in the ancient plays. The Greek tragic hero was never bad. He may have been misguided, but his error of judgment was never a malicious assertion of personal will. Even Agamemnon, who was forced to do a terrible thing — kill his own daughter to placate the gods of war and victory — was not an evil person. His responsibility was like that of a Chief of Staff, a war leader with several armies under his command, armies assembled and prepared to wage a certain war. Could such a man, in all responsible honesty, say to those waiting troops: go home, my daughter has to be saved. A daughter is precious, but an entire country and a civilization may — for some of us — be even more precious. There is in all things a gradation of values. Examples of this kind of thinking persist and can be found throughout the world — especially in the Middle East. It makes no difference that a country is small; the rationale is the same as that of a large world power and just as correct.

With Elizabethan and Shakespearean tragedy, evil comes into its own, but it is handled in such a marvelous way that the most villainous of Shakespeare's heroes become, as Hegel says, artists in their own right. This too is a provocative observation worth careful research in the plays themselves. Take Iago: his whole procedure is spellbinding. He deserves an Oscar three times around. He is absolutely superb in his understanding of human nature, in his artistry in phrasing the arguments that will lead to a certain conclusion, and in his ease and mastery of any and all situations, turning any moment to his advantage. He is an incredible magician, performing so deftly that he cannot be even vaguely suspected of anything other than friendship and good will. This is high art indeed.

Clearly, Shakespearean or modern tragedy is much more complex, more varied and difficult. The reason is that *personality,* the inner being coming to know itself in its most intimate complications, has become the central force of the modern world. Not surprising, therefore, to find that Shakespearean tragedy is full of passion, individual quirks, difficult confrontations (which for the Greeks were terrifyingly simple). Yet, in its bare and basic structure, Shakespearean tragedy accords with Greek tragedy (another point well worth probing with perverse resolution!). A. C. Bradley, in all good conscience, tried to salvage some kind of parallel between the two; but, although his instincts were right, his particular arguments were wrong. Still, he deserves large credit for coming closest (among those who have written on the subject) to understanding the full implications of the Hegelian ideas on tragedy. Even when he took issue with this or that, he was honest enough to recognize that his criticism did not in the least minimize the value of Hegel; and that, if anything, he (Bradley) was to blame for misinterpreting the Hegelian text.

One important observation, by way of conclusion, about Hegel's insightful analysis of the use of the simile, metaphor, and image in dramatic poetry.

Wolfgang Clemen, who wrote what is still the most important book on Shakespeare's imagery, certainly the most substantial one (and qualitatively different from Caroline Spurgeon's work, which must be regarded as the forerunner to a computerized listing of words and phrases — a necessary preliminary task but not a penetrating study), notes early in his book that the most enlightening pages ever written on dramatic imagery, metaphor, and simile are to be found in Hegel. Long before anyone else was talking about the dramatic language peculiar to tragedy, Hegel had in fact explored the matter with his usual precision and in some detail and — most remarkable — drawing all his illustrations from the plays of Shakespeare! The implications of this must surely impress the most sanguine critics of Hegel to reconsider their opposition to him and will perhaps encourage more Shakespeareans to read Hegel's pages. It is as though T. S. Eliot, or Henri Peyre, or Rene Wellek, writing about poetic language, had used illustrations exclusively from Dante. Many of us would understand their doing so, but we would also be surprised. The same kind of pleasant shock is produced by Hegel's pages on dramatic imagery, where the argument is enriched and illuminated by examples drawn solely from Shakespeare's plays.

Shakespearean scholarship has much to gain from the Hegelian analysis.

PART TWO
(51-96)

COMEDY, SOCIAL DRAMA, VERSE DRAMA

"Hegel's Theory of Comedy" first appeared in *Comedy*, ed. Maurice Charney, New York Literary Forum, New York 1978.

"Anne Paolucci's ingenious compilation of 'Hegel Theory of Comedy'" noted as one of the articles that "deserve special mention." (Choice, May 1979)

CHAPTER 3

HEGEL'S THEORY OF COMEDY

The comic, it has been said, is the ultimate refinement of art, the "purest" of the purely aesthetic artistic experiences, beyond which art has nowhere to go without ceasing to be art. Like religion and philosophy, art may indeed begin — as Aristotle alleged — with wonder; but its end comes with the excitement of self-confident or self-assuring laughter.

The end comes with the representation of persons, happenings, and/or things that are comical in themselves, that make us smile or laugh sympathetically, recognizing that they were intended to make us do so. We do not find such comic awareness where there has not been a self-conscious effort to make us experience it — and that is so because the genuinely comic has not, like the tragic, a non-intentional counterpart in the non-artistic sphere.

Of course the great difficulty — one might even venture to say, the traditional difficulty — in generalizing about comedy and the comic lies in the fact that we do not have, in this sphere, an Aristotelian legacy to defend or attack, supplement or amend. Of Aristotle's fragmentary *Poetics* it has been aptly said that it contains "a greater number of pregnant ideas on art than any other book."[1] On comedy and the comic, however, it is virtually silent, offering only the barest promise of a theory: not remotely enough to serve as a guide or challenge to subsequent criticism. Some modern critics rejoice in the fact that, with respect to comedy, there are "no authorities to get in the way; none of the age-old assumptions to overcome; few widely held prejudices to discard; and no attractive, but false, critical positions to mislead us." Yet there are also a variety of pitfalls yawning in the way of intelligent criticism here, not the least of which is the danger of entering upon a treadmill — the perspective from which always seems so various, so beautiful, so new, until its repetition becomes obvious. And the worst danger is, as Robert W. Corrigan observes in his excellent anthology *Comedy: Meaning and Form,* that, precisely for want of the kind of guidance that Aristotle provided with respect to tragedy, the modern unencumbered venturers in the sphere of comic theory too often run the "risk of missing the subject altogether."[2]

Had Aristotle left us a theory of comedy, we might at this point have presumed to introduce our subject with the directness of A. C. Bradley's lecture on "Hegel's Theory of Tragedy," which begins:

> Since Aristotle dealt with tragedy, and, as usual, drew the main features of his subject with those sure and simple strokes which no later hand has rivalled, the only philosopher who has treated it in a manner both original and searching is Hegel.[3]

Bradley held the Chair of Poetry at Oxford and was in the midst of delivering the lectures on Shakespearean tragedy that raised him to eminence as one of the greatest interpreters of Shakespeare when he sought to define his own theory of tragedy by comparing and contrasting it with Hegel's — "to the main ideas" of which, as he explained, "I owe so much that I am more inclined to dwell on their truth than to criticize what seem to be defects."[4] But with the true disciple's absolute preference for truth, Bradley gave himself fully, in that lecture on Hegel, to the task of criticism, seeking first to supplement and then to amend the Hegelian theory. At the close of the lecture, he said with candor:

> I leave it to students of Hegel to ask whether he would have accepted the criticisms and modifications I have suggested. Naturally I think he would, as I believe they rest on truth, and I am sure he had a habit of arriving at truth. But in any case their importance is trifling, compared with that of the theory which they attempt to strengthen and to which they owe their existence.[5]

Bradley, it has been noted, refrained altogether from theorizing about comedy.[6] Yet it is generally acknowledged that his "Rejection of Falstaff" in the *Oxford Lectures on Poetry* contains one of the profoundest treatments of humor in all literature and also that, as Professor E. F. Carritt has demonstrated at some length in his *Theory of Beauty,* the profoundest insights of that "inimitable essay" owe their being to Hegel's direct influence.[7] Bradley knew how to read and use Hegel. In his lecture on Hegel's theory of tragedy, he warns his audience repeatedly that the theory is part of an organic, philosophical whole, saying at one point: "I cannot possibly do justice in a sketch to a theory which fills many pages of the *Aesthetik;* which I must tear from its connections with the author's general view of poetry and with the rest of his philosophy," and at an other point: "His theory of tragedy is connected with his view of the function of negation in the universe. No statement therefore that ignores his meta-physics and his philosophy of religion can be more than a frag-mentary account of that theory."[8] Bradley's words apply with equal rigor to Hegel's theory of comedy, which, as we here pro-pose to show, is also part of Hegel's view of the function of nega-tion in the universe.

The Place of Comedy in the Hegelian System

An initial difficulty in studying Hegel's view on comedy lies in the fact that he traces, defines, and circles back to his subject in many different passages of many works. His main con-tribution to the development of a philosophic theory of comedy is, of course, to be sought in several hundred pages of his volu-minous lectures on *Aesthetics*. But there are also briefer discus-sions in almost all his other works, ranging from the early *Phe-nomenology of Mind* through the *Encyclopedia* to the posthumously published lectures on the *Philosophy of History,* the *Philosophy of Religion,* and the *History of Philosophy*. Even in his treatise on *Natural Law,* which is otherwise highly technical in its exposi-tion, Hegel manages to climax his discussion of the moral im-perative of practical reason with several pages on the nature of the comic spirit that serve, incidentally, to justify Dante's charac-terization of his great poem as a *commedia*.[9]

The point here is that to appreciate fully and correctly Hegel's view on any given subject, including comedy, one should have, ideally, a grasp of the large philosophical canvas. Short of such a grasp, the discussions on comedy, scattered as they are in so many different places, may seem fragmentary and abortive. Still, even a novice learns to appreciate individual insights quickly enough; and where the subject matter is familiar to him, he soon recognizes the validity of the Hegelian analysis and lingers over it with profit. For some, unfortunately, the experience of read-ing Hegel is nothing more than a series of such insights, a kalei-doscopic fragmentation that is never properly redeemed by the effort needed to understand the full implications of Hegel's in-tellectual world. Thus abstracted from their implied base, many of Hegel's observations often are interpreted as the very oppo-site of his intended meaning.

We cannot enter here on a discussion of the phenomeno-logical base of the Hegelian theory of knowledge and how it is shaped critically in Hegel's discussion of aesthetics. For our present purpose, it will suffice to point out that the Hegelian discussion of comedy contains the two characteristics of the Hegelian method generally: (1) firm adherence to the notion of

an organic logical necessity that directs the evolution of the Idea
in all its manifestations and (2) conviction that the historical process in which the Idea unfolds and reveals itself is a dialectic of
extremes, spiraling into and out of inherent contradictions. The
foci of *universal* and *particular* are linked under tension, as opposites, in the *individual,* the unity of which is thus what might
be characterized as an essentially *elliptical* unity; and the oscilla-
tions that result – the orbiting toward meaning through seemingly contradictory tendencies, swinging from peaks into valleys
(apogees and *perigees),* from dark ages into enlightenments
(aphelions and *perihelions)* – preclude the common view of a "progressive" linear thrust forward and upward toward "perfection."
And individual human experience here parallels the course of
historical cultural development. In each of us the Idea works
itself into light through a process of self-shattering inner rejection, which makes possible a spiritual fusion of the many self-
contradictory masks of willfulness each of us wears and sheds at
any one moment. In these terms, the Hegelian dialectic, with its
seeming paradoxes, is the very heartbeat of thought.

One need not revert to the clichés of the Hegelian manu-
als to grasp the importance of the sort of triads to which we have
alluded. From both a phenomenological and an historical perspective, each is a complete moment of awareness and becomes,
almost by necessary reaction, the first term of a new triad, and
so on. For instance, in the sphere of drama, both tragedy and
comedy are represented to us as a dialectical tension of opposites, with comedy triumphing in the life of thought only when
the tension of tragedy has become too much to bear and the
unity of the tragic personality is shattered so profoundly that art
can no longer piece it together. But more important than the
method of the dialectic as such is Hegel's application of it, in
which he brings to bear an incredible knowledge of specific facts
and thorough acquaintance with the individual works of particular authors.

For Hegel, comedy takes on crucial meaning and plays a
vital role as the "universal dissolvent" that clears the stage of
history of all the accumulated debris of anciens regimes or out-
worn conventions and standards. Its specific dramatic expression may be as varied as the number of comic poets; farce, sarcasm, ridicule, irony, all kinds of laughter and *humor* in the restricted modern sense, surface in comedy with the necessity to
clear away the one-sided insistence on prejudices of all kinds,
formal beliefs, and misdirected actions. Hegel notes parallels

between comedy and tragedy here. In both, a crucial opposition is set up between absolute and one-sided claims; but whereas in tragedy that one-sided insistence inspires awe because of the substantive and truly ethical content that is threatened (for example, *Antigone, Richard II*), in comedy such insistence is merely laughable and absurd because it is not the *substantive* content of true values that is at stake, but only the *excesses* and *contradictions* that have rendered the ethical content inoperative (for example, *The Clouds, Henry IV, Part I* and *Part II*).

Comedy, in other words, is the other side of the coin: the absolute standards of tragedy are undermined as society loosens up, comes to recognize and tolerate its idiosyncrasies, turns back upon itself, and reverses its former rigorous position — as indeed the Athenians did with respect to Socrates, after his death finally acknowledging their own fatal excesses with and through comedy. The rigorous confrontations of the tragedies of Aeschylus and Sophocles give way to the more immediate sensibilities of Euripides and finally to the laughter of Aristophanes. Comedy is the exhaustion of an age and clears the way for what follows; it is historically a *negative* force, the final statement of a given equation. In its individual dramatic expression, however, it appears as a *positive* force, an art form in its own right, beyond history, in which the comic poet traces the refracted, multifaceted reflections of his age, drawing upon his own personal and immediate experience, as well as the myriad situations and characterizations of his time, in order to expose sham and restore through ridicule and laughter a proper balance.

Through his genial description of human follies and hypocrisy, the comic writer is thus able to create an entire world, richer in its particulars than the world of tragedy, a world at once recognizable and renewed through a comic catharsis not altogether different from that of tragedy. What in tragedy produces catharsis through the immediacy of *fear* (identification with the notion of suffering and of man's vulnerability) and the distance of *pity* (recognition of special circumstances not applicable to all) surfaces in comedy as *laughter* (or, more precisely, the immediate response to the folly of excesses through which the audience expresses, often only visibly with a smile, its acceptance of the truth of the exaggerations depicted) and *ridicule* (the distance between the "knowing" spectator and the "foolish" protagonist). Comic catharsis, it may therefore be said, prepares our own hearts, as well as the stage of history, for the restoration of essential values in a new social structure.

Precisely because it exaggerates the oscillation between extremes that characterizes the Hegelian approach generally, the concept of comedy provides an excellent introduction to the Hegelian world. In this respect, the discussions of comic subject matter in the chapters of Hegel's *Aesthetics* that focus on the symbolic, classical, and romantic (modern) forms of art, together with the treatment of comedy as a sub-genre of the third or dramatic voice of poetry, are of central importance. Yet wherever the idea of the comic surfaces in his treatment of other subjects — phenomenology, psychology, economics, law, religion, politics, history — we get illuminating observations that bring the force of those other subjects to bear on comedy at the same time that they give us a broadened sense of the entire Hegelian canvas of thought through a mosaic of penetrating cumulative insights.

Briefly, therefore, but always with a masterful command of the large idea and particular details, Hegel explores for us, in a variety of contexts, the distinction between irony and the genuinely comic spirit; the determinant importance of content rather than form in distinguishing the varieties of comedy (and of the comic generally) in both its ancient and modern development; the nature of comic characterization, diction, thought, and feeling; the part that audiences are made to play in recognizing and responding to, and thereby completing, the different possible comic effects; and the ultimate moral and political as well as artistic function of comedy as it relates to tragedy, enriching his argument throughout with references and examples from Molière, Aristophanes, Plautus and Terence, ancient satyric drama, Spanish comedy, and Shakespeare — who is here exalted to the same position of absolute superiority that Hegel accords him with respect to tragedy. It is Shakespeare who emerges as the unassailable "master" of modern comedy, the dramatic poet who "outshines all others" in this field. Hegel's procedure in all of this is altogether empirical and inductive. He moves only very gradually from *particular* instances of works of art directly appreciated to the definition of *universal* principles, which then serve him as the basis for classification, analysis, and critical or reconsidered appreciation of *individual* works of art in their social and historical contexts, apart from which they lack genuine individuality in Hegel's sense of the term.

But before taking up the constituent themes of the Hegelian approach to comedy, we need to make a final introductory comment about comedy and tragedy and the function of negation in the Hegelian universe. The opposition in human relations that triggers comedy certainly bears a close resemblance to the conflict of substantive values found in tragedy; yet the comic resolution is both artistically and morally more demanding. Comic action is full of contingencies and accidents, conflicting motives, projects, ambitions, intrigues. Instead of the cataclysmic upheavals of necessity that bring the tragic opposition to resolution, comedy gives full rein to individual idiosyncrasies, particularized intentions, and quirks and habits and mannerisms in rich profusion. Yet it remains true at the same time to an unwavering serious purpose: its spiritually liberating task of exposing the world's follies through that proprium of man — which is his capacity (unknown to beasts below him and to angels above him) to laugh. In comedy, as in tragedy, we are offered assurance of the ultimate indestructibility of substantive values; but to give us that assurance, the characters of comedy do not have to suffer the kind of internal erosion that is exhibited in the protagonists of tragedy. The comic heroes, says Hegel, are free and invulnerable in themselves and can, therefore, focus on whatever stirs their fancy and pass judgment on all things without losing their equanimity.

Aesthetic Irony and the Comical

It deserves to be stressed, I think, that when Hegel first speaks of the comical in his lectures on aesthetics, it is to distinguish it sharply from aesthetic irony, with which it was then, as now, often confounded. Having traced the development of the modern concept of art through Kant, Schiller, Winckelmann, Schelling, etc., Hegel quite early in his lectures takes up the widely current notion of the artist's life as a life of ironic detachment, of self-conscious retreat from the present state of mind or heart into the depths of the infinite ego. It is that willful retreat, Friedrich von Schlegel held (following Fichte's lead), that makes possible the romantically modern "artist's life" — for which there is no ancient and certainly no medieval or even Renaissance precedent. "With respect to beauty and art," writes Hegel, Schlegel's idea "receives the meaning of living as an artist and forming one's life *artistically*. But according to the principle before us, I live as an artist essentially only when everything I do or say, with respect to any content whatever, remains for me a mere 'put-on' or show, assuming a shape which is wholly within my power." Others, looking on, may take that show seriously. But that means simply that those "others" are not yet free artists in their own right; that they are not yet able to "see in all that usually has value, dignity, and sanctity for mankind, simply a product of one's own power of caprice" — the power whereby a genuinely free artist "is able to set his seal on the value of such things and determine for himself whether or not they shall be of importance in his life" (B/124-125).[10]

The viewpoint of the man or woman skilled in living the ironical artist's life (Hegel observes, not without a touch of the same sort of irony) is, of course, the viewpoint of *Godlike geniality* or, more precisely, that of the divinely *creative* genius who, having liberated himself from art's ancient bondage of *mimesis*, or mere imitation, knows himself to be wholly free with respect to every possible content of his life and art. Confronted by any merely objective thing, he has an absolute confidence that he "can annihilate as well as create it" with equal ease. The one who has attained the standpoint of such Godlike geniality, writes Hegel,

> looks down in superiority on all other mortals, for they are pronounced *borné* and dull, inasmuch as law, morality, and so forth retain for them their fixed, obligatory, and essential validity. The individual who thus lives his artist's life does not, of course, on that account deny himself relations with others. Quite the contrary, he insists on having friends, mistresses, etc., but as genius he simply cannot permit any such relations to have a determinate bearing on the reality of his life and actions, or to retain any significance of universal value in their own right; his attitude toward all such relations is, in sum, ironical. (B/126)

Hegel observes that this irony was an "invention" of Friedrich von Schlegel, though he was by no means alone in its celebration. So long as the ego clings to such a standpoint, "everything appears to it as without worth and futile, excepting its own subjectivity" (B/127), which values itself most, of course, precisely when it has willfully emptied itself of all positive content and is thus, in its ironically hollow utterances, most like sounding brass or tinkling cymbal.

If, however, the ego is in time no longer able to *enjoy* simply its own emptiness in prolonged intimacy, a disquiet comes over it, and it becomes what Hegel calls the *"morbidly* beautiful soul" that yearns to fill its "abstract inwardness" with solid, substantial, essential interests, yet dares not act to satisfy that longing, dares not "do or touch anything for fear of surrendering what it has so long prized as its inner harmony." A *truly* beautiful soul, says Hegel, *acts* and is actual. The *morbidly* beautiful soul, on the other hand, lacks the strength to fill its dissatisfaction and empty longing with a content of substance. Taken abstractly, this sort of irony

> borders closely on the principle of comedy; yet, granting a mea-
> sure of affinity, the comic must be essentially distinguished from
> the ironical. For the comic must be limited to showing that what is
> brought to nothing is something inherently null, a false and self-
> contradictory phenomenon; for instance, a whim, a perversity, or
> particular caprice, set over against a mighty passion; or even a
> *supposedly* reliable principle or rigid maxim may be shown to be
> null. But it is quite another thing when what is to be shown as null
> is *in reality* substantive, moral, and true . . . . Therefore, in this dis-
> tinction between the ironical and the comic, what is essentially at
> issue is the content of what is to be brought to nothing. (B/128-
> 129)

By way of illustrating his meaning, Hegel observes that
there is nothing truly comic in attempts to show the nullity of,
say, a Cato, who "can live only as a Roman and republican."
Cato is not null in himself; and where art insists on the contrary,
it makes itself essentially null. Irony, in other words, tries to show
that worth itself (not merely pretended worth) is worthless and,
as a corollary, that the worthy are truly worthy — ironically —
only when, from their lofty station of ironic creative genius, they
reveal how profoundly aware they are of the worthlessness of
true worth. That is what makes them, in their own eyes, the "best
and the brightest" — the *schöne Seele* of the morbid variety, in
Hegel's sense. The treatment of fallen "heroes" of recent political history comes to mind in this connection, but perhaps the
most vivid example of the ironic creative genius who indulges
what is "best and brightest" in himself to the point of self-destruction is Shakespeare's Hamlet. Hegel's discussion here, together with his scattered references to that enigmatic and elusive masterpiece of dramatic characterization — ironically tragic,
not comic — deserves close and serious scrutiny .[11]

The Personae of Ancient and Modern Comedy

In his long discussion of the "independence of character"
of figures drawn from heroic ages, Hegel notes that only princes
can be represented as essentially tragic characters. With respect
to tragic willfulness — ancient, medieval, or modern — the mass
of common people can only be spectators, a chorus of onlook-
ers responding with conventional judgment. When epic or tragic
poetry reaches into that mass for its heroes and heroines, the
result — and it is usually fully intended — is invariable mock epic
and mock tragedy. The genres that can appropriately draw upon
the lower classes of civil society for their characters, writes Hegel,

are those of comedy and the comical in general. In comedy, he says, "individuals have the right to 'spread' themselves however they wish and can." In their willing, if not in their acting, "they can claim for themselves an independence" that is manifestly contradicted by their actual social condition and that is "immediately annihilated by themselves" in action. (K/192)

Comedy thus finds its proper subject matter in all that is petty, perverse, exaggerated, inflated, vain, ridiculous, foolish, and hypocritical, skirting around the positive core of substantive values but never probing it. Hegel stresses that these negative moments are found in both comedy and tragedy, but he notes also that what is negated in both is never anything substantively positive *as a whole*. In tragedy, the protagonist is always pressing a one-sided claim that cannot validate itself so long as it remains one-sided. In comedy, what is negated is always a vain and empty claim. The result, in one case no less than in the other, is thus the negation of a negation — a catharsis, in other words, that prepares the human heart, if not the times, for a positive reaffirmation of moral and cultural values. And that is quite the contrary of the ironic effect, where the intent is to triumph over "everything that is excellent and substantive." What distinguishes the comic from the tragic approach to this catharsis of negation is made most obvious, according to Hegel, in the treatment of the leading personages of the best ancient comedies — which are, of course, the plays of Aristophanes.

Introducing his most pointed discussion of the comic genius of Aristophanes, Hegel says: "What is comical is a personality or subject who makes his own actions contradictory and so brings them to nothing, while remaining tranquil and self-assured in the process." This is followed immediately by an extended observation to the effect that comedy, in fact, "has for its basis and starting point what tragedy may end with, namely an absolutely reconciled and cheerful heart." The possessor of that heart may repeatedly frustrate his own purposes by the means he uses to attain them; yet he does not on that account lose his "peace of mind." On the other hand, this is only possible if we are made to see that, for him, as well as for us, those purposes really have no substantive value. Then comes this classic Hegelian observation, which is supported, philosophically, by the full force of his view of the function of negation in the universe:

> In this matter we must be careful to distinguish whether the dramatis personae are comical in themselves or only in the eyes of the audience. The former case alone can be counted as really comi-

cal, and here Aristophanes was a master. On these lines, an individual is portrayed as comical in the strict sense only when it is
obvious that he is not serious at all about the seriousness of his
aim and will, so that this seriousness always carries with it, in the
eyes of the individual himself, its own destruction . . . . The comical therefore plays its part more often in people with lower aims,
who are what they are, and have not the least doubt about what
they are and what they are doing. But at the same time they reveal
themselves as having something higher in them because they are
not seriously tied to the finite world with which they are engaged
but are raised above it and remain firm in themselves and secure
in face of failure and loss. It is to this absolute freedom of spirit
which is utterly consoled in advance in every human undertaking,
to this world of private serenity, that Aristophanes conducts us. If
you have not read him, you can scarcely realize how men can take
things so easily. (K/1220-1221)

Hegel then proceeds to explain that, whereas true comedy draws
the interests that it exhibits in this way from the spheres of genuine morality, religion, and even art — that certainly was the practice in the old Greek comedy — it is never by virtue of acting
seriously that truly comic characters fail to realize such interests.
It is always by "subjective caprice, vulgar folly, and absurdity"
that the protagonists of comedy "bring to nought actions which
had a higher aim." (K/1221)

And here, especially, Hegel reminds us that "Aristophanes
had available to him rich and happy material partly in the Greek
gods and partly in the Athenians." The "humanized" Olympians
contain in their very concept a contrast between the divine and
the human that is essentially comical, particularly when they are
represented as acting on motives of manifestly human pride while
insisting on their "divine significance." But it is especially the
follies of the Athenian masses and their demogogic spokesmen,
the absurdities of the war against Sparta, the new morality of the
Sophists, and especially the new direction given to tragedy by
Euripides that Aristophanes likes to dissect. In all his best comic
portrayals — Socrates teaching Strepsiades and his son in *The
Clouds;* Dionysius descending to Hades to fetch up a tragedian
in *The Frogs;* the heroes and heroines of *The Knights, Ecclesiazusae,* and *Peace* — the keynote that resounds is the

self-confidence of all these figures; and it is all the more imper-
turbable, the more incapable they obviously are of accomplishing
their undertaking. The fools are such naive fools, and even the
more sensible of them also have such an air of contradiction with
what they are devoted to, that they never lose this naive personal
self-assurance, no matter how things go. It is the smiling blessed-

ness of the Olympian gods, their unimpaired equanimity which
comes home in men and can put up with anything. In all this
Aristophanes is obviously not a cold or malignant scoffer. He is a
man of most gifted mind, the best of citizens to whom the welfare
of Athens was always a serious matter. (K/1222)

Aristophanes does not, in fact,

turn into ridicule what is truly of ethical significance in the social
life of Athens, namely genuine philosophy, true religious faith,
but rather the spurious growth of the democracy, in which the
ancient faith and the former morality have disappeared; what he
exhibits, in other words, is sophistry, the whining and querulous-
ness of tragedy, the inconstant gossip, the love of litigation, and so
forth, and these are placed before us, as opposed to true political
life, religion, and art, in their suicidal folly. (O/iv,304)

The all-pervasive corruption in institutions and individuals is
contrasted, by Aristophanes, with the true values to which lip
service is given, so that what we have in that lip service finally "is
a mask concealing the fact that real truth and substance are no
longer there, but have been handed over to subjective caprice."

Aristophanes himself, however, belongs to the same movement of spirit that he criticizes, Hegel observes. And with that,
we are brought face to face with the ultimate negative significance of all genuine comedy. In unmasking the "subjective caprice" of the new philosophers, tragedians, rhetoricians, etc.,
Aristophanes is actually bringing to completion the very triumph
of what he unmasks. For all the profundity of its insights, there
is implicit in the Aristophanic comic sense "one of the greatest
symptoms of Greek corruption, and thus these pictures of a
wholly unperturbed sense of 'everything coming out right in the
end' are really the last great harvest of this gifted, civilized, and
ingenious Greek people." In this respect, the comic treatment
of Socrates — or what we might venture to call the Aristophanic
"rejection of Socrates" — is particularly significant, says Hegel.
And in his lectures on the *History of Philosophy*, as well as in those
on the *Philosophy of History*, Hegel dwells on that "rejection" to
trace in it the signs of inherently inevitable decay confronting
the Greek world of beauty, truth, and freedom. With Socrates,
tragedy indeed walks off the stage into the actuality of history;
but the Greek spirit can find in that moment a good-natured,
good-humored, purposeful redemption of its contradictions by
portraying Socrates himself as comically self-conscious in a
Falstaffian sense of the self-destructive side of his own philosophical method.[12]

But comedy in which the characters appear comical to

themselves as well as to others is not the only kind of comedy. Hegel notes that a second type eventually arose among the Greeks, in which characters are dramatically betrayed by their authors, with the result that they appear comical only to others. Aristophanes, the "comic author par excellence," adhered strictly, in all his plays, to his original principle. "But in the new comedy of Greece," writes Hegel, "and later in Plautus and Terence the opposite tendency was developed, and this has acquired such universal prominence in modern comedy that a multitude of our comic productions verges more or less on what is laughable in a purely prosaic sense and even on what is bitter and repugnant." Hegel is thinking of Molière here and, therefore, hastens to explain that when he uses the term *prosaic* comedy, he does not mean to suggest that such comedy is necessarily an inferior form of the genre. Writing particularly of Molière's best comedies, which are by no means "to be taken as farces," Hegel explains:

> There is a reason for prose here, namely that the characters are deadly serious in their aims. They pursue them therefore with all the fervor of this seriousness and when at the end they are deceived or have their aim frustrated by themselves, they cannot join in the laughter freely and with satisfaction but, duped, are the butt of the laughter of others, often mixed with malice. So, for example, Molière's Tartuffe, *le faux devot*, is unmasked as a downright villain, and this is not funny at all but a very serious matter; and the duping of the deceived Orgon leads to such painful misfortune that it can be assuaged only by a *deus ex machina* . . . . There is nothing really comical either about the odious *idèe fixe* of such rigid characters as Molière's miser whose absolutely serious involvement in his narrow passion inhibits any liberation of his mind from this restriction. (K/1233-1234)

Molière's departure from the Aristophanic model is intentional. But from the time of the New Comedy of Greece and its Roman imitators there has been another tendency of an inferior sort that has by no means always been pursued intentionally; and that is the tendency that results in the comedy of intrigue, for which Plautus and Terence provided what have remained the principal models. Hegel's discussion of the varieties of comic intrigues might easily have been illustrated out of Shakespeare, for here, too, Shakespeare is a master; but, no doubt, because he treats it as an inferior genre, he prefers to cite examples of what he calls the Spanish "mastery" of intrigue. Where the hand is not sure in fashioning comic characters — and that is rarely the case in Shakespeare — one turns for a substitute to ancient and fashionable models or works out ideas of one's own for "carrying out a well-constructed intrigue." Generalizing, Hegel observes that intrigue of a comic variety usually arises "from the fact that an individual tries to achieve his aims by deceiving other people." One variety of intrigue shows us the deceiver pretending to share the interests of other characters in the play and to be laboring to further them; but this "false furtherance" usually backfires, so that the deceiver finds himself caught in a trap that he has himself set. Another variety shows us the deceiver putting a "false face on himself in order to put others in a similar perplexity." But the variations on this sort of coming and going, in and out of deceptions, are virtually limitless.

Citing Spanish examples, which have much in them that is "attractive and excellent," Hegel is concerned however to stress that "intrigues and their complications" are not to be regarded as inherently comical, any more than the interests of love, honor, loyalty, etc., on which they are usually built are inherently comical. Tragedy makes use of the same interests and complications. But whereas in tragedy such interests are plainly substantive and "lead to the most profound collisions," in comedy, writes Hegel, they are, as motives, "clearly without substance from the start — as for example a prideful unwillingness to confess a long-felt love which at last finds itself just for that reason betrayed — and can therefore most appropriately be annulled in a comic fashion."

What makes the genuine comedy of intrigue comical is not plot as such, therefore, but the nature of the interests and values at stake and the characters of the chief personages involved. In modern comedy, the characters who "contrive and conduct intrigues are usually — like the slaves in Roman comedy — servants or chambermaids who have no respect for the aims of their masters, but further them or frustrate them as their own advantage dictates and only give us the laughable spectacle of masters being really the servants, or the servants masters." In most intrigues of this sort, "we ourselves, as spectators, are in on the secret; and because we are not in the least threatened by the deceits and betrayals, often pursued against the most estimable fathers, uncles, etc., we can readily laugh over every contradiction implicit or obvious in such treacheries." (K/1234-1235)

Hegel notes that this sort of modern comedy, for the most part, lacks anything even remotely resembling the "frank joviality that pervades the comedies of Aristophanes." What that frank joviality provides in the old Greek comedy is the possibility of a genuinely cathartic effect upon the observer. In modern comedies, the effect of intrigue is often altogether repulsive, particularly where the "cunning of servants, the deceitfulness of sons and wards, gains the victory over honest masters, fathers, and trustees who have not been actuated by prejudices and eccentricities." But just as we are being tempted to conclude that Hegel altogether prefers ancient Aristophanic comedy to anything the modern world has produced in the genre, we get this important reservation:

> Nevertheless, in contrast to this essentially prosaic way of treating comedy, the modern world has in fact developed a type of comedy which is truly comical and truly poetic. Here once again the keynote is good humor, assured and careless unconcerned gaiety despite all failure and misfortune; and with this, the exuberance and dash of what is at bottom pure tomfoolery and, in a word, fully-exploited self-assurance. As a result we have again here (but on a profounder level, in a more intimate depth of humor, the sweeping compass of which includes a much broader sector of human society as well as subject-matter) what Aristophanes achieved to perfection in his field in Greece. As a brilliant example of this sort of thing I will, though without going into detail, once again emphasize the name of Shakespeare. (K/1235-1236; O/iv, 348)

I have already suggested, with a reference to the Aristophanic "rejection of Socrates" in *The Clouds,* that the great parallel between Aristophanic comedy and modern comedy is to be sought in Shakespeare's comic treatment of Falstaff; and I have in mind particularly what A. C. Bradley has called, in his thoroughly Hegelian Oxford lecture on the subject, "The Rejection of Falstaff." When he says that the "bliss of freedom gained in humor is the essence of Falstaff" and that the main source of "our sympathetic delight" in the "immortal Falstaff" is his "humorous superiority to everything serious and the freedom of soul enjoyed in it,"[13] Bradley is echoing what Hegel says specifically about the heroes of Aristophanic comedy. But if we trouble ourselves to gather together all that Hegel says incidentally about Shakespeare's comic heroes, we get an even clearer impression of how much Bradley has gained from Hegel as an interpreter of Shakespearean comedy.

It is, for instance, in his general discussion of Shakespeare's capacity to represent his tragic heroes as poets in their own right — with a "free imaginative power" by means of which they are "enhanced above themselves" — that Hegel interrupts himself to make a similar observation about "Shakespeare's vulgar

characters, Stephano, Trinculo, Pistol, and the absolute hero of
them all, Falstaff," who, although they "remain sunk in their vulgarity, are at the same time shown to be men of intelligence with
a genius fit for anything, enabling them to have an entirely free
existence and to be, in short, what great men are." (K/585- 586)
Hegel uses almost the very same terms to characterize the comic
treatment of Cervantes's Don Quixote and the entire world of
Ariosto's *Orlando furioso*. In Hegel's assessment, Cervantes and
Ariosto rank beside, and just below, the creator of Falstaff as the
greatest comic geniuses of the modern world — in whose work
we can trace a romantic equivalent of the dissolution of Greek
society that made possible the plays of Aristophanes. (K/590-
592)

Tragedy, Comedy, and the "End" of Art

Though the principles of comic dissolution remain the
same, there is a world of difference between the values at stake
in Aristophanes' *The Knights, Peace, The Clouds, The Frogs, The
Birds, Ecclesiazusae*, etc., and those at stake in the comic master-
works of Ariosto, Cervantes, and Shakespeare. Comic dissolution follows tragedy's last effort to save the substantive values of
an age. As Hegel repeatedly expresses it, tragedy destroys the
individual in order to reconcile the substantive values that his
one-sided willfulness has brought into conflict. Comedy, on the
other hand, spares personality in the last resort, when its sacrifice can no longer suffice to reconcile and thus save the once
substantive values that society as a whole no longer has the will
to sustain. These two fundamental features of action — which
are tragic when personality sacrifices itself for serious things and
comic when it triumphs over the ruin of serious things that are
beyond salvation — provide, according to Hegel, the one truly
consistent basis for distinguishing the two major dramatic genres.
The characters in comedy also dissolve finally, but "it is in their
own laughter that they dissolve" and then only "after their laughter has dissolved everything else." (K/1199) Triumphing in its
own dissolution, subjective personality challenges art itself to
dare to represent that dissolution as defeat, without sacrificing
itself as art.

A. C. Bradley makes this very point in the concluding paragraphs of his lecture on Falstaff, and he does so in words that
clearly anticipate what T. S. Eliot will later venture to say about
Hamlet, namely, that here we must simply admit that "Shakespeare
tackled a problem which proved too much for him."[14] With his
Mona-Lisa remark about the Mona-Lisa character of Hamlet, Eliot

may have meant to suggest that Shakespeare there pressed the capacities of tragic art to their absolute limits and perhaps a little beyond. But we don't have to surmise Bradley's meaning where he says of Shakespeare that "in the creation of Falstaff he overreached himself" and that "he was caught up on the wind of his own genius, and carried so far that he could not descend to earth at the selected spot." That is a thoroughly Hegelian judgment, the rationality of which is supported by the entire *Aesthetics.* For Bradley, as for Hegel, Shakespeare's drive to overreach his own artistic genius, in Falstaff as well as in Hamlet, is by no means an artistic defect. Shakespeare, says Bradley, could easily have brought his high-flying Falstaff down to the ground at any selected spot; but, had he chosen to do so, we could hardly have regarded it an "achievement beyond the power of lesser men." Shakespeare's achievement, says Bradley, "was Falstaff himself, and the conception of that freedom of soul, a freedom illusory only in part, and attainable only by a mind which had received from Shakespeare's own the inexplicable touch of infinity which he bestowed on Hamlet and Macbeth and Cleopatra, but denied to Henry the Fifth."[15]

Hegel is Bradley's source for that insight and judgment, except that Hegel presses the argument at least one step further to conclude that we must look not to tragedy, even on the heights of *Hamlet,* but rather to comedy — comedy of the order of Shakespeare's Falstaff — for, the ultimate aesthetic catharsis, beyond which art is powerless to move us. Just after he has concluded his treatment of modern comedy, with the final tribute to Shakespeare that has already been cited ("Als glänzendes Beispiel dieser Sphäre will Ich zum Schluss auch hier noch einmal Shakespeare mehr nur nennen als näher charakterisieren"), Hegel brings the entire course of his lectures on aesthetics to a close in two brief paragraphs that sum up its argument and clearly define the place of comedy in the whole. "Now, with this development of the kinds of comedy," he writes,

> we have reached the real end of our inquiry. We began with symbolic art where personality struggles to find itself as form and content and to become objective to itself. We proceeded to the plastic art of Greece where the Divine, now conscious of itself, is presented to us in living individuals. We end with the romantic art of emotion and feeling where absolute subjective personality moves free in itself and in the spiritual world. Satisfied in itself, it no longer unites itself with anything objective and particularized and it brings the negative side of this dissolution into consciousness in the humor of comedy. Yet on this peak comedy leads at the same

time to the dissolution of art altogether. (K/1236)

One need not labor either the originality or the impressive consistency of that statement. No one reading Hegel's pages and coming to this final conclusion can doubt even for a moment what he considered to be the most profound (though possibly not the most aesthetically perfect) expression of art. It is that of romantic art, of art on the verge, and even beyond the verge, of transcending itself as art. To suggest that Hegel depreciates art in rising to this conclusion is to have misunderstood all that he has said about architecture, sculpture, painting, music, and epic and lyric poetry, as well as tragedy and comedy. What he means, of course, very simply, is that when artistic power has stormed the highest heights, when it has aimed to do and has done much more than reason can ask of it or allow it to do, it must say, finally, with Shakespeare's Prospero —

> This rough magic
> I here abjure . . . . I'll break my staff,
> Bury it certain fathoms in the earth,
> And deeper than did ever plummet sound,
> I'll drown my book. *(The Tempest,* 5.1. 50-57)

Conclusion

The foregoing pages have attempted to place the Hegelian theory of comedy in its proper perspective by identifying its characteristic property (in the peculiarly human capacity to smile and laugh), by distinguishing it from irony, by comparing its ancient and modern forms, and, in a more general way, by contrasting it with tragedy and relating it, in some measure, to the large Hegelian system. The subject, needless to say, deserves a great deal of expansion, far beyond what we have attempted here. An anthology of Hegel's writings on the subject, doing full justice to the wealth of illustrations he introduces, would closely match in size a volume like *Hegel on Tragedy,* which runs to 400 pages. The intention here, of course, has been to focus upon the underlying or, rather, organizing theory. Hegel's method (as we noted at the outset) is, however, essentially empirical and inductive, so that it would have done violence to his aesthetic attitude had we started out with a summation of principles taken out of context, abstracted from what is, in effect, a very large body of sensitively critical literary analysis and comparison, focused constantly on the content and forms of the individual works of art themselves. Still, by way of summary, I should like to set down what amounts to an outline of points essential to the Hegelian theory, some of which have had to be glossed over, if not altogether neglected, in the main discussion.

The comic attitude, it must be said, is an essentially artistic attitude that has no merely natural, non-artistic counterpart. As the inner force that enables us to smile, it works as a dissolvent with respect to everything in life that tends to keep us from smiling. The comic is not to be confounded, however, with the ironic. The difference consists in the fact that the truly comic attitude restricts itself to showing that what dissolves beneath its gaze is something inherently null, a false and contradictory thing, idea, situation, or character that has already spent its substance.

In comic art (as in symbolic, classical, and romantic art generally), therefore, it is the content, not the form, that is the determinant thing. The form of the individual work of art must not be something added to the content, externally, but precisely that form that the already artistically determined content requires for its full expression. This is, of course, contrary to the "new criticism" or Crocian view, according to which art is form and nothing but form. In the case of comedy, says Hegel, the determinant content is the triumph of subjective personality in situations of conflicting interests and values that lead, in the case of tragedy, to the destruction of personality.

From what has just been said, it follows that comedy can indulge itself best with characters that do not have the responsibilities of princes or statesmen. A prince who ought never to have been a prince can be comical, but it is better for comic effect to bring lower-class characters into play — characters who can "put on airs," spread themselves transparently. When they negate themselves, together with their apparent interests and values, such characters reveal the requisite negation of a negation, which is the essence of comedy. Hegel finds this kind of comic effect in Dutch and Flemish painting, too.

But the comic attitude is not a merely rational attitude; it is an overriding emotion, or *pathos* in the Greek sense. Pathos — overriding feeling — is the true domain of art, says Hegel. Comic as well as tragic characters succeed in drama only when they possess, or rather are possessed by, true pathos.

Genuine comedy first appeared, according to Hegel, when the Greeks, for whom beauty was truth and truth beauty, ceased to be satisfied emotionally with that ideal identity. The beauty of classical art lost its reason for being when the Greek spirit, within itself, came to experience an overwhelming disquiet and dissatisfaction. That was the mood — the critical, sophistic, Socratic mood — of the times that gave rise to Aristophanic comedy. Although he was himself full of the critical spirit of Socrates, as also of Euripides, the great Greek comic playwright carried the dissatisfaction of his age beyond itself in the same direction. Aristophanic comedy can, therefore, be characterized as the expression of dissatisfaction with dissatisfaction; with its "rejection" of Socrates and Euripides, and so on, it negates the negation, triumphing over it serenely in the process. But here Hegel is at pains to distinguish the genuinely comical from the satiric, which is bitter and critical without reconciliation, without redemption, and without poetry.

The world of true comedy is a world where subjective personality makes itself absolute master of all. It raises poetry to a peak of subjective self-confidence without objective support. It is art's last bloom. It smiles a self-assured smile, and then there is a fall into prose. Art loosens its hold on all that it has theretofore taken seriously, so that its *aesthesis* is then able to transform itself into religious *ecstasis* and, sometimes preferably, into scientific *sophia*.

Aristophanes gives us characters who are comic in and for themselves as well as for us. Later, Greek comedy and the Roman masters of the genre — Terence and Plautus — departed from his example. They could not rise to the poetry of true comedy and so contented themselves with characters that are laughable only for others, not themselves. They gave us slaves who trip up their masters, sons and daughters who deceive their fathers, humorously. But because the characters deceived are not essentially null, the laughter has to be pursued either in slapstick fashion or through the ins and outs of elaborate intrigues, more often than not contrived by deceived deceivers.

Although most of the modern world's comedy has been of this kind, it has, nevertheless, managed not merely to match, but even to surpass, the poetic mastery of Aristophanes in Shakespeare. The comic world of Shakespeare is more intense than that of Aristophanes because the truth of romantic art, to which it is prepared to sacrifice ideal artistic beauty, is higher than the truth of classical art. Shakespeare is the culmination of romantic art. In his *Hamlet,* he pushed the poetry of tragedy so far that those who apply ideals of classical beauty to its interpretation are tempted to judge it a failure; and in his comic characterization of Falstaff, he does the same — and more. In his high comedy, Shakespeare indeed validates Hegel's assertion that art's ultimate triumph consists in its own romantic effort to transcend itself as art.

NOTES

1. W. D. Ross, *Aristotle* (London, 1930), p. 290.

2. Robert W. Corrigan, ed., *Comedy: Meaning and Form* (San Francisco, 1965), p. 2.

3. A C. Bradley, "Hegel's Theory of Tragedy," *Oxford Lectures on Poetry* (Bloomington, Indiana, 1961), p. 69.

4. *Ibid.*, p. 81.

5. *Ibid.*, p. 92.

6. E. F. Carritt, *Theory of Beauty* (London, 1923), p. 312. Carritt says: "To the barrenness of most accounts of humour I have found three grateful exceptions; . . . Mr. A. C. Bradley's 'Rejection of Falstaff' . . . is a perfect illustration, by a concrete instance, of the truth; but he refrains from theorizing. The two theories are those of Hegel and Bergson."

7. *Ibid.*, p. 316.

8. Bradley, p. 69.

9. G. W. F. Hegel, *Natural Law,* trans. T. M. Knox, introduction by H. B. Acton (Philadelphia, 1975), pp. 104-108.

10. G. W. F. Hegel, *Aesthetics: Lectures on Fine Art;* trans. T. M. Knox, 2 vols. (Oxford, 1975); *The Philosophy of Fine Art,* trans. F. B. B. Osmaston, 4 vols. (London, 1920); *The Introduction to Hegel's Philosophy of Fine Art,* trans. Bernard Bosanquet (London, 1886). Quotations have been slightly adapted by the author in most cases, in accordance with the text of the German: *Asthetik,* ed. H. G. Hotho, 1842, and reedited by F. Bassenge, 2 vols. (Berlin, 1966). The references in the text are to the translation used as a 'base" *(K, 0,* or *B),* followed by page(s); for this initial reference (B/124-125), read, "Bosanquet translation, pp. 124-125."

11. Most of Hegel's comments on *Hamlet,* scattered throughout his works, are collected in *Hegel on Tragedy,* ed. (with an introduction) Anne and Henry Paolucci (New York: Anchor Books 1962; reissued New York: Harper Torchbook, 1974; reissued New York: Greenwood Press, 1978, hardcover; reissued New York/Smyrna, Delaware, 2001.) See Index under "Hamlet."

12. *Hegel on Tragedy,* "Socrates" in Index.

13. Bradley, "The Rejection of Falstaff," *Oxford Lectures on Poetry,* pp. 262 and 269.

14. T. S. Eliot, *Selected Essays* (London, 1932), p. 146.

15. Bradley, p. 273.

Chapter 4

Social Drama as Heir of Tragedy and Comedy; Theatre of the Absurd and the Break with the Past

Greek tragedy may be summed up as one aspect of man's exploration of divinity. In what Hegel calls the "uncritical wisdom of the chorus" we have the translation of "ethical maxims . . . and specific conceptions of duty and right" into the simple ideas of the Beautiful and Good. Shakespearean tragedy carries the process into other areas where we no longer have "religion for religion's sake, . . . the embodiment of human reconciliation in the unqualified religious sense, or of morality pure and simple. On the contrary, we are presented with individuals, conceived as dependent solely on themselves, possessed with individuality, and which they carry through as best satisfies them with the unmitigated consequences of passion . . . ." This same rational principle enters into history with Socrates, in whom Hegel recognizes not only the turning point in the history of thought but also the culminating moment of Greek tragedy and the appearance of comedy.

In asserting himself as a new oracle, Socrates paved the way for all the exaggerations which inevitably grow out of such a posture. He embodies in himself the very dilemma of subjectivity, which posits its internal certainty as universal truth. What is justified in Socrates degenerates all too easily, with time, into personal prejudice, obstinate assertion of private interest, individual arbitrary claims to absolute truth. And when this happens, a reaction sets in — a reaction which acts as a restorative for substantial values and sweeps away all the exaggerated claims.

That reaction to the excesses of Socratic subjectivity, says Hegel, comes with Aristophanes, who in all his plays poses precisely those excesses. What is undermined is not Socrates himself but, for example, the spurious growth of the democracy in its sophistry, in the querolousness of tragedy, in the love of litigation, and so on. In its true form, comedy never destroys the vital force of substantive being or personal life but through irony exposes the pretentious claims of a universal opposed to the private and arbitrary self. Through the universal dissolvent of laughter — always shared by the protagonist, in genuine comedy — the stage is cleared of all the accumulated debris, which Hegel describes as "the contingency of self-expression." The comic world is one "in which man has made himself in his conscious activity, complete master of . . . [the] essential content of his knowledge and achievement." The comic hero rises above his own contradictions and false assertiveness as the master of the situation, creating and dissolving action without being destroyed in the process.

Because in comedy the principle of subjectivity is asserted in all its freedom, the protagonist throughout remains unbroken, self-assured, self-reliant, serene and confident in exposing "the contradiction between that which is essentially true and its specific realization . . . ." In true comedy, "the purely *personal* experience" emerges as "infinite self-assuredness." And here too, as in the definition of tragedy, Hegel is very precise. There is much that casually passes as comedy, he reminds us; but the "subjective serenity" and serious purpose which characterizes genuine comedy are found only in Aristophanes and Shakespeare. He is as emphatic in his praise of Shakespearean comedy as he is in his praise of Shakespearean tragedy. Shakespeare is "the master, who . . . outshines all others in his field . . . ." By comparison, the comedies of Molière — for example — suggest a different kind of dramatic experience; for although we can justify their prosaic quality in the bitter earnestness of their aims and the pursuit of these — characteristics which save this kind of comedy from becoming mere farce — the characters of Molière appear ridiculous only to others and emerge as "disillusioned objects of a laughter foreign to themselves and generally damaging." At its very best, modern comedy — like Aristophanic comedy — "gives play on the stage to private interests and personalities of . . . social life . . . in their accidental vagaries, laughable features, abnormal habits and follies" but never insists on what is purely ridiculous or foolish or stupid or nonsensical as, for example, where the individual identifies his personal life seriously with false values such as avarice. The true comic character recognizes his own failings in the same way that the true tragic character comes to know his own limitations and rises above them: there is no real loss ultimately.

Genuine comedy, like genuine tragedy, insists on preserving substantive ends; but in the drama that follows Shakespeare, those substantive ends come through to us with "attenuated strength" in the expression of concrete civic or private rights — those of State, Church, family life in all its particularity; in conflicts of love, honor, duty, etc. German drama in particular centers around "the world of the citizen and family life" and represents "the triumph of *ordinary morality*" in terms of property, finance, status in the community, matters of love — virtue and duty always winning out. Where we have imitations of ancient tragedy, as among the French and Italians, we find specific passions like love, honor, fame, ambition, tyranny personified in an "abstract style of character-drawing." Goethe in his youth attempted to achieve something like Shakespeare's "natural truth and detailed characterization; but in the ideal force and exaltation of passion his rivalry collapses." In his *Faust,* however, Goethe succeeds in dramatizing the full "sphere of true particularity" which is the main attribute of modern social drama. In that work "the spirit of disillusion in the pursuit of science and . . . the vital resources of a worldly life and earthly enjoyment — in a word, the attempted mediation in the tragic manner of an individual's wisdom and strife with the Absolute in its essential significance and phenomenal manifestations, offers a breadth of content such as no other dramatic poet has hitherto ventured to include in one and the same composition." Schiller's *Carl Moor* has something of this same quality, according to Hegel.

The ethical absolutes of Greek and Shakespearean tragedy become in modern social drama the absolutes of a bourgeois society, the ideals of a civic community in which particular interests and duties are clearly defined as social ends. In this sense, modern social drama appears as an intermediate link between tragedy and comedy, a serious effort to translate universal values for a prosaic world turned in upon itself. Yet, its greatness ultimately is to be found not in the "recreation" or the "moral education of public taste" but in the expression or translation of these aims into something deeply personal. Hegel cites Schiller's praise of Goethe's *Iphigenia* in these terms: "the ethical content, the heart experience, the personal opinion is there made the object of the action and is as such visually reproduced." But where Goethe succeeds, others fail; in presenting the totality of individual experience against the canvas of social values and ideals, other dramatists — the young Goethe himself — often produce characters that are, Hegel says, "double men," as, for example, Weislingen, Fernando in *Stella,* Clavigo, or characters lacking any kind of "substantial" base and in whom "conversion" or resolution is utterly unconvincing, as those of Kotzebue and Iffland. But even where this difficulty of characterization is resolved and we *do* have organic, whole figures — as in Goethe's *Iphigenia* and his *Torquato Tasso* — we still do not have, Hegel says, "perfect examples of dramatic vitality and movement." And the reason for this is implicit in the nature of modern social drama "in which the element of subjectivity is steeped in the sensuousness of genuine social conditions and substantial characters, while the tragic steadfastness of volition and the depth of collisions is so far weakened and reduced that it becomes compatible with a reconciliation of interests and a harmonious union of ends and individuals."

In other words, the force of character is here felt in the immediacy of a particular set of events or conditions rooted in historical contingencies. The outcome of the dramatic action in such cases need not be destructive, Hegel tells us, and, in fact, the best kind of reconciliation is that in which a character transforms the conditions around him and restores the social values that had been threatened. It is precisely in the "conversion of a purely mechanical conception of Divine activity into the atmosphere of the subjective consciousness . . . of freedom and ethical beauty" that Hegel recognizes in Goethe's *Iphigenia* "a beauty that we cannot sufficiently admire." He returns to praise this particular work in many passages and quotes a number of lines from it to illustrate the genial manner in which Goethe translates divine imperatives into personal immediacy, the human reconciliation which springs from the tenderness of Iphigenia's faith, "the purity and ethical beauty of her inner life" which actually transforms her into "the divine personification and the protectress of the house."

In this kind of modern drama, the large canvas of world-history and universal ends gives way usually to particular national purpose and goals; just as reshaping the Greek story of Iphigenia, Goethe adapted it to the subjective imperatives of personal definition. Again, it is Goethe — according to Hegel — who demonstrates real genius in choosing in so many of his works the kind of historical material that lends itself to wider application. Within the narrow range of a given time and period and locale, he is able to suggest and mirror the facts of world history in their widest and most inclusive meaning. Hegel mentions *Hermann and Dorothea* as the idyllic expression of this juxtaposition; but his greatest praise is reserved for Goethe's *Götz*. In this early play, Goethe shows his astonishing grasp of the need for

choosing a certain kind of setting: the action of the play is rooted
in an historical period — Hegel explains — in which "knight-er-
rantry and the self-reliant individuality of the . . . nobility is being superseded by the new creation of an external and legally
constituted social order." We have before us, in other words,
that moment of transition when epic heroes, in their own definition of right and wrong, pave the way for the ethical formulations of a social order. The Middle Ages represent such a period
of transition, when heroic types once again assert themselves as
a law unto themselves and shape the new society that will embody their convictions. Of Goethe's choice of setting for *Götz*,
Hegel writes: "To have selected precisely this critical time,
where . . . the heroic characteristics of the Middle Ages and the
legalized fabric of modern society meet and collide, for the subject of his first artistic production shows much penetration . . . . For Götz and Sickingen are still heroes in the genuine sense, who are resolved to exercise their influence over circumstances, whether immediately affecting them or of wider
range, out of the resources of their own personalities, their courage, and their private sense of right."

Schiller too, according to Hegel, gravitates to this kind of
historical setting. His *Carl Moor* has precisely this kind of historical force: it depicts "a rebellion directed against the whole organic framework of civil society." Although Schiller's play exalts
the "robber-ideal" and contains "the germ of wrong which can
only lead to the criminal act on which it will fall to pieces," it
nevertheless insists on the heroic quality of the protagonist who
"has the courage to break the bonds which bind him to law and
order . . . [and] creates for himself a heroic situation, in which
he appears as the champion of right, and the self-constituted
avenger of wrong, injustice, and oppression." Here, as in *The
Bride of Messina*, right and law are expressed *not* as external commitment but as internal conviction translated into action, which
is meant to create a new social order. Hegel notes that "Don
Caesar is able to exclaim, and justly: 'there stands no higher
judge than myself!' And when he has to be punished he must
himself give judgment and execute it"; punishment is "wholly
dependent on himself." These heroic types are not the princes
and kings of tragedy, whose fall is also the disruption of entire
peoples, but new leaders of epic proportions seen in their struggle
against the bondage of old forms. Their personal ideals of honor
and loyalty and goodness shape their world and create new compelling values. Schiller's William Tell is an excellent example of

how such character remains true to his explicit purpose and yet redeems his subjective ideals in universal terms.

The focus in all such drama is on the individual sense of right and wrong as it finds proper expression within a given social structure. The subjective life of such personalities is elaborated along these lines and given consistency within the narrow scope of a more restricted action. Such characters are compelling in their personal insights into situations only if they are organically sound. Thus, old Attinghausen is perfectly consistent and believable when he "foretells the destiny of his country"; the "prophetic instinct" operating in him "is quite in the right place." Unlike the consistency of Schiller's characterizations, Kleist's Prince of Hamburg displays a kind of spiritual disease in the manner in which "magnetism, somnambulism, and sleepwalking are depicted" without "real causal effect." Hegel is especially hard on Kleist. "This Prince of Hamburg," he writes, "is a most pitiable exhibition of a general; he is distracted when he makes his military disposition, writes out his orders in a way none can decipher them, is engaged in the night previous to the battle with morbid forebodings, and acts on the day of the battle like a fool. And despite such duality, raggedness, and lack of harmony in such a character" writers like Kleist and Kotzebue, Hegel goes on to say, "imagine that they tread in the footsteps of Shakespeare. Wide indeed is the distance which separates them, for the characters of Shakespeare are essentially consequent in what they do. They remain staunch to their master passion, in what they are and in what confronts them; nothing makes them veer round but what is in strict accord with their rigidly determined character."

Schiller, in *Fiesco* and *Don Carlos,* succeeds superbly in delineating "characters of nobler significance and more substantive content, heroes . . . resolved to liberate their country, or assert the liberty of religious conviction." There is no vacillation in such characters. Carl Moor shows us a man who "rebels against the entire order of civic society and the collective condition of the world and the humanity of his time, and fortifies himself as such against the same." Wallenstein embodies a "far-reaching purpose, the unity and peace of Germany." Schiller's characters live up to the large implications of his political vision — a vision which is always expressed in its widest terms. Hegel notes, for example, how in *The Bride of Messina* Schiller is "at pains to shift the quarrel of the brothers on to still more fateful circumstances."

Throughout Hegel's analyses of German drama, we sense

the force of national purpose which dictates the kinds of sub-
ject-matter and character which best express that purpose. Germany was, in fact, the last great nation to emerge in Europe.
And in that moment of cultural and political self-determination,
it produced the equivalent of epic statements with a force just as
compelling as the more universal and rigorous necessity which
drove the Greeks to write their tragedies. In both, the principle
of freedom is the source of inspired action; and if the dramatic
canvas of German drama is more contained, more particularized, it is also a more perfect mirror of conditions and emotions
that are the basis of our modern world. A. C. Bradley's summary
of Hegel's view of modern German drama is a sound one and
worth recalling in this context. Hegel, writes Bradley,

> points out that [our] modern tragedy . . . shows a much greater
> variety. Subjects are taken, for example, from the quarrels of dy-
> nasties, of rivals for the throne, of kings and nobles, of state and
> church . . . . Schiller in his early works makes his characters de-
> fend the rights of nature against convention, or of freedom of
> thought against prescription — rights in their essence universal.
> Wallenstein aims at the unity and peace of Germany; Carl Moor
> attacks the whole arrangement of society; Faust seeks to attain in
> thought and action union with the Absolute. In such cases the end
> is more than personal; it represents a power claiming allegiance of
> the individual; but, on the other hand, it does not always or gener-
> ally represent a great *ethical* institution or bond like the family or
> state. We have passed into a wider world.

That wider world, with its unambiguous values and clear
priorities, remains essentially unchanged in the realistic theater
of the nineteenth and early twentieth century, where playwrights
like Ibsen, Strindberg, O'Neill, and Arthur Miller continued to
focus on social issues and social reform. In our own time, however, a major change has taken place. Forged in the existential
crucible that followed two world wars, our western theater
emerged, around the middle of the twentieth century, as the
fractured expression of shattered hopes. As in architecture, sculpture, painting, and music, literary expression struggled for new
definition among the ruins of earlier standards that reflected
staunch national commitment and clear moral values. Literature in all its forms threatened to exceed traditional limits as it
became absorbed into what the Hegelian poet-critic of Expressionism, Gottfried Benn, calls the "lyrical" voice, the subjective
voice of the modern world as it probes the depths of "spirit."

It might be worth pausing briefly to recall the impact Benn
had on the great poet-critic of our time, T. S. Eliot. Although

Eliot never admitted any direct Hegelian influence on his work, he was familiar with German philosophy long before reading Benn. At Oxford, where he completed his dissertation on German Idealism with F. H. Bradley, brother of the Shakespearean critic A. C. Bradley, and came into contact with other eminent Hegelians like Bernard Bosanquet, Eliot absorbed enough German philosophy and Hegelian ideas for us to recognize decidedly Hegelian influences, for example, in his provocative notion that *Hamlet* is the "Mona Lisa of literature" and, at the same time, an "artistic failure." His familiarity, direct or indirect, with Hegelian ideas may also have perfected Eliot in the use of paradoxes that verge on outrageous contradictions, such as the one just quoted. He was right of course, if we understand that paradox to mean, in Hegelian terms, that the protagonist of the play threatens to burst the dramatic bonds that contain him. (I have explored this topic elsewhere, examining the "double image" of Hamlet and the strange discontinuity of the soliloquies, as examples of a play threatening to break through traditional form, anticipating in fact, "Theater of the Absurd.") Erich Heller points out in his *Journey into the Interior,* that Eliot displays a keen insight in his judgment of the play but does not realize that what he condemns is, in fact, the great achievement of Romantic art — his own included. Eliot's discussion of Falstaff reflects the same Hegelian insights. More obvious, and adding support to the argument here put forth, is Eliot's acknowledged debt to Benn in his account of "The Three Voices of Poetry" — an account Benn, in turn, drew directly from Hegel's genial definition of the major literary genres.

The "lyrical" or subjective voice that, according to Hegel and Benn, has absorbed contemporary drama is first heard in such playwrights as Pirandello, Sartre, Camus, Samuel Beckett, Eugene Ionesco, all of whom seem without precedent, outside of any recognizable tradition. The break with the past is sharp and seemingly irreconcilable. For the early dramatists of the Absurd, realism no longer served either as subject matter or form. Or, rather, a new reality emerged: a fragmented world with individuals who expressed states of being, paradoxical insights, conflicting emotions rather than logical perceptions based on cause and effect, action and reaction. The play as play became a series of events eliciting what seemed to be unexpected responses. The language of the Absurd emerged as musical reprises, fugue-like repetitions, images and symbols, *non-sequitors,* paradoxical inversions.

In spite of its sharp break with traditional forms, however, Theater of the Absurd is in fact a new constructive challenge to what has come before. Its existential premise is a new source of vitality and hope; its rejection of established traditions is based on the need to express the inexpressible, to find a totally new kind of language that will do justice to the "subjective correlatives" that now demand attention. It is, paradoxically, a theater that tends toward *silence* rather than *statement,* as Vivian Mercier points out in *Beckett/Beckett.* In that book, Mercier insists that Theater of the Absurd must be seen as a dialectical movement of opposites in order to approximate "meaning." Chapter headings (like the title of the book itself) reflect this premise: "Thesis/ Antithesis," "Gentleman/Tramp," "Ireland/The World," and so on.

Much earlier, Robert Corrigan had reminded us that when accepted standards disintegrate "distinctions between tragedy and comedy break down as well." Tragedy, he tells us, "deals directly with the serious" and need not be considered in the same context as comedy; but, he adds quickly, that "when talking about comedy, we must always refer to the standards of seriousness which give it its essential definition." In Theater of the Absurd, tragedy and comedy combine in a new way. Redirected by the tragic and universal principle of an existential negativism, the contemporary theater has turned the large universe of both tragedy and comedy — as elaborated by the Greeks and Elizabethans — into a galaxy of microcosms, each infinitesimal part reflecting in its own way the whole. In that existential whole, the particularized complex of actions, reactions, intentions, follies, mistakes, obstinate self-interest which characterize comedy finds its way, sharpening the "self-conscious language" of comedy into an incisive instrument of skepticism.

CHAPTER 5

VERSE DRAMA: THE BURDEN OF THE SHAKESPEAREAN MODEL, WITH SPECIAL EMPHASIS ON THE 'BECKETS' OF TENNYSON AND T. S. ELIOT

Almost all the nineteenth-century poets we consider "major," as well as some "minor" ones, wrote verse drama. It was a grand effort — perhaps inevitable — of appreciative imitation, taking Shakespeare and other Elizabethan and Jacobean playwrights as models. Not many of the finished plays reached the stage; and those very few that did, failed to survive whatever measure of contemporary success they enjoyed. Today the eclipse of nineteenth century verse drama is virtually complete. Not one of the hundreds of such plays produced or published is included in either the dramatic or poetic heritage of the English-speaking people.

Was it all simply a poetic waste? Was all the time, thought, and imaginative energy expended on verse drama by men of unquestionable poetic genius just an exercise doomed to failure? As one tries to answer these questions definitively, a number of intriguing facets reveal themselves. Was it a mistake to be so appreciative of the Shakespearean model? Was failure even for poets of genius like Wordsworth, Coleridge, and Scott, Keats, Shelley, and Byron, Browning and Tennyson inevitable?

Denis Donoghue remarks that "for Shelley, as for so many nineteenth century poets, the limits of drama were set by his apprehension of Shakespeare. Like Coleridge, Schiller, and A. W. Schlegel, he practically equated drama with tragedy, and, in turn, tragedy with its Shakespearean manifestations." Clearly, the Romantic apotheosis of Shakespeare as the type of poetic genius makes obvious why the best romantic poets were drawn to him almost like moths to a flame. What is not quite obvious is why it should have led them to write tragedies, or for that matter, any sort of verse, in dramatic form. For that connection one must assume that, in the general contemporary conception,

Shakespeare was primarily a poet who happened to write in dramatic form. One needs to add the assumption that, from the nineteenth century literary perspective, Shakespeare was primarily a poet who happened to have written his best poetry in dramatic form. That the reverse might be true — that Shakespeare was essentially a dramatist working in a theatrical tradition which obliged him to use verse — was probably alien to the Romantic conception.

There is no doubt that Shakespeare was for the Romantics a poet to be studied, known, and responded to on the printed page rather than in stage representations. He had reached the heights of poetic excellence writing lyric, narrative, and dramatic poetry. Poets eager to reach those same heights might thus be tempted to follow his example, venturing at some point into tragic verse drama, even if their own poetic genius was epic or lyric rather than dramatic.

Still, this doesn't quite explain why a poet of genius, led by a false aesthetic to undervalue the essentially theatrical character of Shakespeare's tragic verse drama should necessarily fail, in following his example, to produce either memorable poetry or viable drama. The argument that those who wrote poetic drama in the nineteenth century were generally ignorant of stage mechanics and theatre techniques appears sound . . . until we recall that a number of them were avid, observant, and consistent theatre-goers and that Browning and Tennyson, notably, had the advice and counsel of two of the outstanding actor-managers of the century — Macready and Irving respectively. Nor is it sufficient explanation to say that Shakespeare had exhausted the possibilities of stageworthy verse drama in iambic pentameter. Even allowing for the symbiotic relationship existing between a structural type of the imagination and the cultural *gestalt* in which it is produced, history is too replete with examples of transplanted and reinvigorated forms to say that the interdependence is absolute. Finally, the fact that nineteenth-century poets often went so far as to reproduce the peripheral stage business of the Elizabethans (e.g. Tennyson's repartee among the Citizens and the Gentlemen in *Queen Mary*) is to be chastised as an error in taste rather than seen as a fundamental inability to create workable drama in the older form.

The failure of nineteenth-century poets to produce vital drama must ultimately be assigned to the very nature of Romantic poetry itself. The Wordsworthian theory of poetry fully comprehended the practice of the best poets of his age, and I think it is fair to say that the practice, not less than the theory, is essentially anti-dramatic, or, at any rate, non-dramatic. The ideal poet of Wordswvorthian theory transcends society; he has seen the Eternal , and Everlasting and returns to our shadowy social existence to address us, for our own good, with a personal authority like that of the Hebrew prophets sent by God .

The Romantic poets generally — not just Shelley of *The Defense of Poetry* and *The Ode to the West Wind* — conceived of themselves as "lamps" guiding humanity rather than as Shakespearean "mirrors" objectively reflecting it. Two major consequences of great importance resulted from the Romantic theories of the poet's nature and mission. The first is that it restricted (although this was hardly its intention) *all* poetry, in effect, to lyric, philosophic, or meditative verse. Poetry had to be, according to such theory, a kind of evangelic preaching. The utterance of the poet, like that of the evangelist minister, had the value of "truth" because he had personally experienced its truth for himself, not because it instructed his audience in the objectively validated truths of a received tradition. Even today, the value of Wordsworth's poetic utterances for readers appears to depend primarily on one's faith in the authenticity of the personal experiences he records. I mean specifically his experience of transcendental states of being and his sense of unity and continuance of existence beyond the transient and phenomenological.

This kind of personal expression in poetry, valued by the reader or hearer because it is authentically personal, is essentially *lyrical* expression as contrasted with narrative and dramatic expression. Under such a restricted conception of the nature and mission of poetry, verse narration in the epic tradition becomes virtually impossible. It becomes a task of prose, assuming an almost historical, anti-poetic realism, to fashion "objective worlds" for the imagination. The consummate objectivity of the world of the poetic drama — where an historical realism can't be faked — becomes literally inconceivable.

The second major consequence of the Romantic "poetics" surfaced soon enough as an almost instinctual recognition by the greatest poets of the age that the conditions they had imposed on themselves as ideal were self-contradictory and self-defeating. In fact, the history of poetry from Wordsworth, Coleridge, and Shelley to Yeats, Eliot, Pound, and Wallace Stevens can be said to be very much the history of the attempts of "romantic geniuses" possessed of creative imagination to es-

tablish an authority for their products separate from any authority based on their individual persons. The extreme of personal,
evangelical poetics generated the opposite.

At the height of the Romantic Era, the instinctive longing
to escape the burden of personality manifested itself more often
than not as a longing to die, a *Sehnsucht nach der Tode*. But it
manifested itself also in an apparently irresistible urge to pursue
the Shakespearean example all the way to the heights where the
Hamlets, Othellos, and Lears are heard speaking for themselves
as creatures of the dramatist's imaginative *impersonality*. The failure of this instinctive urge to achieve such impersonality, to die
to oneself by entering Shakespeare's precinct on his own level,
is related in a direct manner to the fact that Romantic poetry is,
by definition, *personal*. What we have, in effect, is a dialectic of
opposites: one extreme generates another.

T. S. Eliot's ultimate importance for historians of the future may very well be that he first demonstrated the method by
which poetry could again be made *impersonal* and *authoritarian*
aside from the poet. In his well-known essay, "The Three Voices
of Poetry," he provides a most valuable insight into the subject
under discussion here. The three "voices" of the poet are the
lyric, the epic, and the dramatic. In the lyric voice, the poet constructs in a way that reveals him as the *persona*. Anyone who
hears or overhears the poet-persona who speaks in this fashion
recognizes in that voice the personal response to existence. The
voice of the epic is one in which the persona of the poem is
abstracted, taken to be, in a real manner, the objective — if still
individually focused — spokesman for the cultural and historical
collective, the people, the nation, humanity. Milton's references
to his blindness in *Paradise* Lost, though praised by the Romantic critics — as was consistent with the theory of the value of the
individual — would, in the authentic epic tradition, have been
questioned as an excrescence, something not only unessential
but also distracting. The voice of the dramatic poet, finally, for
Eliot, is totally objective, impersonal, and separated from the
author. The "voice" of the poet is not heard at all; what is heard
are "voices," the created characters of the drama who exist con-
textually in their own right, speaking for themselves. As such the
voice of the poet-playwright has achieved impersonality, objectivity, and a kind of authority with the audience which has little
or no relationship to himself at all.

It was this "third voice" which the Romantic poets, for the
most part unconsciously, sought to achieve or find again — with

comparatively little success. The impulse to achieve success in drama, and to an almost equal extent in epic poetry, was aborted by the very nature of Romantic poetry. It resulted in efforts to escape from the *cul de sac* into which the Romantic theory of poetry had forced its practitioners; it meant, in other words, finding modes and structures and techniques by which the poet could reposition himself as individual persons vis-a-vis the work they produced. It meant establishing the validity of such work outside himself and, for want of a better term, as autonomous in itself. The three poets who concerned themselves most consistently with this problem were Keats, Browning, and Tennyson.

Keats in his brief creative life recognized perhaps before anyone else the essential problem to be solved: namely, that poetry could not survive if it was to rest merely on a subjective and personal authority. It must validate itself in some objective way; "truth" is impersonal, objective, available to all, like the Grecian urn, the Elgin marbles. These are not true or beautiful because they are by X or Y. The product is foremost; the person who produces it is secondary. This is the very opposite of the non-classical, evangelical attitude which validates a product by saying it is by Picasso or Rembrandt, or Beethoven, or Mozart, or Keats even: the person first, the product second. Keats remade himself as a poet on the basis of this insight. In his theory and gradually evolving practice, he worked to a position of objective impersonality. "Truth is Beauty, Beauty Truth" is a succinct expression of his goal. There is little doubt that by "Beauty" Keats meant something fairly close to Clive Bell's idea of "significant form," and there is less doubt that by "Truth" Keats meant the autonomous, objectified, impersonal structure usually identified as "a work of art." The task of the poet was to create such works, whose value and importance, both to the poet and to his audience, was that they were *true* and therefore beautiful in *themselves*. As such, their validity had, ultimately, nothing to do with any value put upon the individual creator nor with one's faith in his private experiences as the ground of authority.

The fundamental contribution of Keats to the history of nineteenth-century and modern poetry — and in fact to the whole complex problem of the relationship of the artist to society — is still coated over by the acceptance in our culture of the very Romantic idea he sought to invalidate by his radical rethinking of the relationship of the poet, the poem, and the public attributed to him in the Romantic context. The fact is that he insisted on the task of the artist to provide *true* creations whose authority resided in themselves and not in any regard for the author.

In Browning's case, there is no trace of ambiguity. One may characterize his entire productivity by the one word: "Impersonality." By nature, rather than by theoretical conclusions, Browning was protected against the Romantic imperative to speak out of the *personal*. His talent and particular personality cooperated to create and develop in the same impersonal way that Keats had recognized. The dramatic monologue is the unambiguous testimony of his poetic goal. Of all the important personalities of the nineteenth century, Browning is the most resistant to conformist theorizing. In a century of "prophets" and "seers," he held curiously aside as a person, concerning himself with the development of new forms and poetic techniques consistently in line with his instincts to objectify the poetic experience. *The Ring and the Book* is, after all, only one of a large number of approaches by Browning to the problem of a depersonalized validation of the poetic message. The dramatic monologue is the most successful of his attempts to achieve objectivity and objective authority for his production. To realize the difference between the Romantic and non-Romantic authority for poetic expression one must compare the significance of the "I" persona of, say, Wordsworth's "Resolution and Independence" with the "I" persona of Browning's "My Last Duchess." The difference is fundamental. The "I" of Wordsworth is, in the reader's mind, valued because it is an expression of the existential Wordsworth; the "I" of "My Last Duchess" is not to be taken as an expression of Browning's own voice. In Keats' terms, both poems are *true* but in very different ways. Browning worked to develop impersonal forms and structures to separate himself from his poems. Wordsworth, convinced of the authority which resided in him as the prophet or insightful voice, works to perfect the various modulations of that single voice.

Because of his personality, Tennyson had a more difficult job to do. His psychology urged him toward Romantic isolation and lyrical expression; his character, however, responded to the imperatives of communal, societal responsibilities. Basically a lyric poet, he tended toward Romantic criteria; personal expression proved to be the most congenial to his nature. Unlike Keats, whose move towards the objective and impersonal was founded purely on an aesthetic re-evaluation of the relationship of the poet to the work, and unlike Browning, whose impersonal forms and techniques appear to be clearly the product of his personality rather than of deeply felt theoretical conclusions, Tennyson seems to have sought impersonal techniques, forms, and subject matter, not only for aesthetic reasons but also because of his conception of the poet's moral and social responsibility to his audience.

These three poets attempted to achieve depersonalization of poetry in numerous ways. They used the older forms of poetry — the ballad, the sonnet, the iambic pentameter especially, but they utilized the Spenserian stanza and others as well. They developed new stanzaic forms — particularly Browning and Tennyson. They created new relationships between the poet, the poems, and the audience. The most successful of these inventions was the dramatic monologue, which, as a technique, might be combined with any of the above-mentioned structures. They enlarged the subject matter of poetry, primarily in terms of moving into the near or distant past, or across social and other lines in the present.

The range of experimentation in nineteenth-century poetry has been impressive. The poetic options were considerably increased for English poets by the end of the century. Moreover, the range of subject matter conventionalized for acceptance as poetically feasible was also increased. Tennyson is of central importance to the history of the development of nineteenth-century poetry not only for his contribution of important poems to the corpus of literature, but also because his career shows a generally consistent and deliberate movement from the pure subjectivity of the lyric through techniques and forms requiring more and more depersonalization, until at the end of his career he turned to drama — the most depersonalized of poetic forms. Unlike Milton, who gives the impression of discarding forms like cocoons once perfection has been achieved, Tennyson accommodated to and continued to cultivate the lyric, the epic, and in his final years the dramatic with undiminished facility. There is still discernible, however, the sequence which demonstrates that he progressed with a logical consistency from the "voice" of the lyric through the "voice" of the epic, to the "voice" of drama. His plays — especially the historical trilogy of *Becket, Queen Mary,* and *Harold* — have tremendous importance for the student of Tennyson and nineteenth-century poetry, an importance which has not yet been fully appreciated in any systematic way.

Tennyson's plays are important for two reasons. First, they form essential, chronologically terminal parts in the long sequence of productions in which he worked to overcome the problem of artistic isolation indigenous to the Romantic position. His plays represent his most sustained attempt to function in a mode which demanded objectivity and impersonal creation, in which success is achieved largely in the degree to which the creator is separated from the world of his autonomously acting and interacting creatures. As such, the dramas have great value for the student of Tennyson as a craftsman deeply involved with finding workable solutions to the problems of making poetry in his own age.

But beyond this interest in the dramas as solutions, or at least attempted solutions, to problems in aesthetics, there is another interest which is related to Tennyson as a social and political philosopher. The assumption is that Tennyson worked to achieve success in drama because he believed quite profoundly that he had something important to say which could only be said in dramatic form. His intense life-long commitment to poetry as an art was matched only by his equally intense belief in his responsibility as a poet to speak for and to his public. Hence, for Tennyson, solutions to the problems of poetry were not only important in terms of aesthetics but also in the implementation of his societal role.

That a poet of Tennyson's character and responsibility, both to his craft and to his role as he conceived it in society, should have devoted so much time and creative energy to the drama, should in itself support the impression that drama is indeed important to an understanding of his growth both as a poet and as a spokesman before his public.

With this summary in mind, we can begin to appreciate in the effort of T.S. Eliot to discipline himself in the traditional forms of the third or dramatic voice, as a means toward objective dialogue, impersonal representation, the recurrence of this impulse. What Eliot succeeds in doing in his plays is to extend the first voice into drama — and here we should remember the argument of Gottfried Benn, that the *lyric* impulse has absorbed *all* three voices in the modern period. In his excellent chapter on *Beckett*, Andrew Kennedy writes (*Six Dramatists in Search of a Language*) in a way that illuminates the argument of Benn. Kennedy makes no reference to Benn, but what he says is extremely important as a witness to the efficacy of that argument. The first excerpt summarizes the efforts of Eliot to forge a new language and contrasts him with Beckett.

> It was Eliot who in his early criticism had stressed the importance
> of "abstraction from actual life," of a dramatic language that con-

centrates or compresses expression; it was Eliot who wanted to create a verbal rhythm that would have the power of primitive — pre-rational — drama. (*Sweeney Agonistes* came perhaps nearest to embodying these aesthetic aims.) It is Beckett, however, who seems to have written all his plays, with all their differences, from a primary expressive urge tending to abstraction, to compression, and to the rhythms of a primitive — not just pre-rational but seemingly counter-rational — dramatic language. It is, further, Beckett who has pushed his dramatic language back to that "still point" — the world of perpetual solitude — which Eliot expressed only in his non-dramatic poetry. Eliot took pains to avoid, or to counterbalance, the pull towards subjectivity; his whole development as a dramatist might be seen as a conscious and progressive effort to "objectify" his dramatic language, in terms of situation and character; he was prepared to sacrifice expressive power for the sake of deliverance from a private language and the attendant danger of *statis* . . . .

By contrast, Beckett starts from an acceptance of that solipsistic condition. For him language is irredeemably private; words germinate in the skull of the speaker, at an inestimable distance from things and other persons, motive and argument, local time and place. "Art is the apotheosis of solitude" wrote Beckett in his early work on Proust; and this "creed" was not abandoned when he came to drama. From the start Beckett accepts the paradox of dramatic *statis*; movement in his plays is nearly always a succession of still points or a cyclic recurrence of verbal occasions. His dialogue . . . is a quasi-dialogue composed of counterpointed or subtly doubled monologues. (130-131)

What is especially interesting here — aside from the attempt to separate Eliot's effort from his results as a dramatist and the comparison with Beckett — are the interesting insights which result from the applications of Benn's formulations to Eliot's efforts in drama by a man who obviously has come to these conclusions without the aid of Benn. What Kennedy is saying here is that Beckett succeeds as a dramatist — and I would add, most of the Absurdists succeed in the same way — because he is consciously attempting to create drama in the only way possible for our age, that is, as a lyric expression which is an absolute and objective one in depicting the effort to delineate through verbal dialectic. Kennedy refers to *stasis* (static) at least twice in the passage quoted; and we should remember that the word is central in Benn's argument. Poetry in our time is a series of static points, absolute expressions of the subjective made objective. Kennedy recognizes that Eliot, in his early efforts to forge a new language for the lyric, succeeded when he wrote consciously in that voice; and he suggests that when Eliot tried to forge an objective new language for drama he failed because he did not realize that what he was expressing was a lyric dialogue of the kind that Benn tells us is characteristic of modern poetry generally. Where the dramatists like Beckett attempt consciously to forge a new language in those terms, they succeed. Drama in our age is the objective verbalization of the subjective dialogue. *Waiting for Godot* is one of the best examples of this, but if you want Modern British equivalents we can certainly mention Pinter or, in American terms, Edward Albee.

Further on, Kennedy writes:

> Beckett himself has deliberately refrained from theorising about drama or dramatic language, and we need only the minimum of theory — a brief look at some of Beckett's known critical positions — to sidelight the close study of the language of the plays. We need to understand, first of all, the extent of Beckett's dependence on words as a primary element in drama, despite his undisputed mastery of gesture, movement, and setting — the art of visual counterpoint. (The dustbins, the sand-mound, and the urns are containers for human voices — visual equivalents for Krapp's tapes.) In asserting the primacy of language, Beckett equates language and "content" and, ultimately, language and "reality." This amounts to something that might be called Beckett's verbalism — though one is not eager to add to the gluts of "isms." (133)

This amounts also to a brilliant explication of Benn's entire argument about language in an expressionistic context.

One last excerpt from Kennedy's book, where he reminds us of Eliot's indebtedness to F. H. Bradley — A. C. Bradley's brother — who was an Hegelian philosopher and from whom A. C. drew most of the ideas which are reflected in his Hegelian writings on tragedy and on Shakespeare in particular:

> It is as if the split between Appearance and Reality — crystallised in the young Eliot by his study of F. H. Bradley — had to express itself in dramatic and linguistic parallels: a doubleness of action on two levels of language where one level is speech-of-appearance which mocks or falsifies "real" speech. We may reflect that the appearance/reality dualism is eminently dramatic, even theatrical, and that there is much in the greatest drama — from *Hamlet* to *Ghosts* and *Six Characters in Search of an Author* — that works through the enactment of this vision. But no one before Eliot has come to drama with such a dualistic approach to language itself. And perhaps no one before has had to devote so much energy to converting an initial non-dramatic impulse — the impulse to purify the dialect of the tribe out of existence — into finding ways to dramatise speech-of-appearance. (110)

Eliot's comments about his own feelings of failure in his plays — notably with reference to the chorus in *Family Reunion* — take on very suggestive overtones in the context of Kennedy's critical examination of Eliot's search for language. Poetry, as Benn reminds us, is always an absolute and independent creation which lives outside the poet and society. All great poetry, in whatever voice, lives on in an absolute and independent way. What we have traced are the efforts, beginning with certain poets of the Romantic Age, to forge a new objective authority for the first voice; with Tennyson — who is the most musical of lyric poets — the effort extends into dramatic poetry, the third voice. But let me call attention in passing to "The Lotus Eaters" — where the musical or lyrical element reaches perfection is such lines as:

> There is sweet music here that softer falls
> Than petals from blown roses on the grass . . . .

And those marvelous lines which are also a "cadenza" in falling numbers of syllables:

> Here are cool mosses deep
> And through the moss the ivies creep
> And in the stream the long-leaved flowers weep
> And from the craggy ledge the poppies hang in sleep . . . .

First 6 then 8 then 10, then 12. The numbers increase, but the effect is of falling.

Eliot picks up that challenge and tries to forge a new language for drama along the lines of a modern poetics in which language becomes the single most important element; he succeeds in his lyrical work but he fails to understand that even drama has become part of that lyrical voice — as Benn describes it and as Beckett realizes it. What Eliot succeeds in doing in the lyrical vein falls short of perfection in his plays.

In other words, Benn's theory has been validated in the works of Joyce (that one-man revolution); of Eliot, the avant-garde creator of a new lyric language in "The Wasteland" and other poems; of Pinter, Beckett, Ionesco, and Edward Albee in their plays; all attest to the conscious revolution of language as the medium which absorbs everything else in our age. And in that total acceptance of the role of language as the means and the end of poetry in all its voices, the poet finds an objective form for *stasis*, for the unchanging inner experience which is not "communication" but "expression" of Absolute Spirit (to use Hegel's term).

What we see and what Benn has described to us is that the narrative and lyric voices of poetry are both present in the po-

etic world of drama, just as in the performance of plays the arts
of architecture, sculpture, painting, and music are present. With
its temple-like painted sets and its statuesque players whose
speech is musically cadenced, colorfully performed drama unites
all the other arts. Or, in Hegel's words:

> The point is that a truly dramatic use of language makes it impos-
> sible for the dramatist to depict in words what his characters look
> like, how they stand or move, or where they find themselves, in
> anything remotely approximating. the wealth of external detail that
> epic narration permits. If it is to attain full artistic actualisation,
> therefore, what it cannot supply with words drama must supply by
> other means, for which purpose it is obliged to call on the other
> arts for help. Briefly: for full theatrical presentation it needs a set
> which is in part architectural, in part natural, with both elements
> treated pictorially; and upon that set it must introduce manifestly
> statuesque figures whose changing facial expressions, postures, and
> movements are animated paintings and whose cadenced speech is
> the profoundest song of living thought and feeling.

But, historically considered, the drama, like the true epic,
has its specific time. Epic poetry is artificial when it does not
have for its world-content the first coming to maturity of a people
in a great uniting act that really makes them conscious of its
objective identity as a people. To tell the story of that great act
of the "birth of a nation" — the birth of maturity — in a self-
effacing way, is the artistic task of the epic poet. That can really
be performed only at a specific time. Similarly, the drama in its
greatness has its specific time. Lyric, on the contrary, has no
specific time, for it expresses individual subjectivity. And that is
present, ready for expression, at all times. The lyric has its seemingly narrative moments, as in the folk ballads, etc. And it is out
of such ballad impulses that the narrative epic emerges, when
the historical time is ripe. In the epic, the subjective element is
overcome. And it is that overcoming of the subjective that serves
to open up a world for poetry, as distinct from the prosaic world
in which lyric is first made possible. Lyric poetry has no world in
itself. It belongs, as individual expression, to the prosaic world.
That's why Hegel calls epic the first voice of poetry: the epic
voice makes the *world* of poetry for the people who have epics.
Thereafter, even lyric poetry has a poetic world in which to sing,
and dramatic poetry becomes possible. Hegel reminds us that
dramatic poetry *presupposes* the

> early times of the true epic and the first lyric outpourings of sub-
> jective feeling . . . . Like the epic, drama sets a complete action
> before us, as happening, indeed, before our very eyes; but, on the

other hand, it shows it to be an action rooted in the subjective feelings of characters who speak their minds to one another in our presence with lyric directness.

The lyric, which expresses its subjectivity even before there is an objective world of poetry, built imaginatively by the epic muse, sings after that world is built; and while it can be, and must be absorbed in the poetic fullness of great drama — which becomes possible only when a nation has become dramatically self-conscious through tragic confrontations in national goals and aims — lyric poetry survives the time of drama, even as it survives the time of epic.

PART THREE
(97-200)

SHAKESPEARE

"Bradley and Hegel on Shakespeare" was first published in *Comparative Literature*, Summer 1964. (Singled out as one of three articles in the short bibliography for the "Hegel" entry in *The Penguin Companion to Literature (Europe)*, ed. by Anthony Thorlby. Allen Lane, The Penguin Press.)

"Shakespeare Revisited: Hegel, A. C. Bradley, T. S. Eliot," in *Cultural Horizons, A Festschrift in Honor of Talat S. Halman*, ed. Jayne L. Warner. Syracuse University Press, Syracuse, New York, 2001.

"*Macbeth* and *Oedipus Rex*: A Study in Paradox" was first published in *Shakespeare Encomium*, Special Anniversary Issue, City College Papers I, CUNY Press, 1964.

"Marx, Money, and Shakespeare: The Hegelian Core of Marxist Shakespeare Criticism" was first published in *Mosaic*, Manitoba U. Press, 1977.

CHAPTER 6

BRADLEY AND HEGEL ON SHAKESPEARE

The refusal of critics to take seriously A. C. Bradley's emphatic acknowledgement of his debt to Hegel must appear as an embarrassing paradox to anyone examining the matter today. The growing interest in Hegel's writings has brought into focus what may prove to be the most interesting aspect of Bradley's work; and the shift in critical sensibilities, within the last fifty years, has cleared away what was purely transient and personal in Bradley's writing, reinforcing its vital core and thus preparing the way for a careful and sympathetic review of what he himself considered to be an important source of inspiration. The opening words of "Hegel's Theory of Tragedy" can leave no doubt as to Bradley's estimate of the German philosopher;

> Since Aristotle dealt with tragedy, and, as usual, drew the main features of his subject with those sure and simple strokes which no later hand has rivalled, the only philosopher who has treated it in a manner both original and searching is Hegel.[1]

Although his main purpose in the essay is to correct and supplement Hegel's views, especially as they apply to Shakespearean tragedy, Bradley reminds us that "to the main ideas I owe so much that I am more inclined to dwell on their truth than to criticize what seem to be defects."[2] He insists that, in spite of his criticism, "the central idea" of the Hegelian theory remains unshaken and, in fact, seems "to touch the essence of tragedy [3]

The importance Bradley attached to the reading of Hegel and his sincere effort to grasp the full implications of the Hegelian theory may be measured, to some extent, by comparing the essay as it appeared, in 1912, in the *Oxford Lectures on Poetry*,[4] with an earlier version in *The Hibbert Journal*.[5] The final version is decidedly less dogmatic and reflects a more appreciative estimate of Hegel's position. Any serious appraisal of Bradley's Hegelianism must take these two essays into account. Ultimately, however, it is Hegel's influence on Bradley's Shakespearean essays which must be examined. I need not labor the far-reaching effects of a thorough study of this kind. As Kenneth Muir has remarked: "Nearly all recent critics have been influenced by Bradley in one way or another, not least when they have reacted against his methods."[6] For those of us who still see in Bradley the most impressive single figure in Shakespearean criticism of the last hundred years, who still believe that "it is a rash man who rejects [his judgments] out of hand,"[7] who are convinced that the most cautious among us "diverge from him, as we often must, at our peril,"[8] a systematic analysis of Bradley's Hegelianism represents an important step forward in the field of Shakespearean studies.

The present article cannot go beyond some very preliminary observations suggested by the essay on Hegel. Since even these observations, however, must be restricted by the limited space at my disposal, I have chosen, in place of a general examination of the entire essay, an analysis of what I consider to be the most serious and basic objection raised by Bradley: his conviction that Hegel preferred Greek tragedy to Shakespearean and modern drama.[9] To do justice to the argument (even within the limits thus defined) and to trace effectively the source of Bradley's error, I shall begin by summarizing briefly Hegel's evaluation of the *Antigone,* correcting in the process the notion introduced by Bradley and repeated indiscriminately by many critics after him that Hegel considered that play the "perfect exemplar of tragedy"[10] and reminding the reader of the serious limitations which Hegel saw in ancient tragedy, before turning (in the last portion of the paper) to his evaluation of Shakespeare. Only by thus reviewing Hegel's basic distinctions between the ancient and modern world can we hope to understand Bradley's error and appreciate the judgment of Professor Carl Friedrich, who states emphatically that it is not Greek tragedy, ultimately, but the Shakespearean dramatic world which Hegel exalts as "the very pinnacle of aesthetic achievement."[11]

Bradley's misleading notions about Hegel's final estimate of Greek tragedy — and of the *Antigone* especially — is the result of his failure to grasp the full distinction between aesthetic and spiritual beauty (a distinction rooted in the Hegelian doctrine of the evolution of Spirit in time).[12] With regard to the *Antigone,* Bradley betrays also a certain carelessness in the reading of the Hegelian tests. Hegel's notorious statement comes, in fact, in the midst of a discussion of ancient tragedy and is meant to serve as an illustration of a particular type of conflict within the classical form. The Hegelian analysis is worth reviewing, not simply as an answer to the often repeated judgment introduced by Bradley, but also as evidence that, contrary to the opinion of many critics, Hegel did not set up a "single formula" for Greek tragedy, but — like Aristotle — recognized a variety of conflicts and resolutions.

The most arresting type of conflict in ancient tragedy, Hegel says, is that which deals with the body politic, that is, with "the opposition . . . between ethical life in its social universality and the family as the natural ground of moral relations."[13] Outstanding in this category are such plays as *Seven Against Thebes, Iphigenia in Aulis, Antigone, Agamemnon, Choephorae, Eumenides,* and the *Electra* of Sophocles. In all of these, there is a well-defined conflict between two sets of values, both of which deserve respect and obedience. There is a second type of conflict in which the opposition is not so sharp; greater alertness is required to recognize the contending forces, for they are not in obvious contrast. The *Oedipus Rex* and *Oedipus at Colonus* of Sophocles are, according to Hegel, the best illustrations of this second type. The substantive nature of these two types of conflict gives way, in a third type of content, to an interest in the emotional life of the protagonists; the plays of Euripides anticipate, in this respect, the deepening and growth of personality which characterize modern drama. There are countless other kinds of conflicts, Hegel reminds us, but these three are the most striking ones.

In enumerating the various ways in which such conflicts may be resolved, Hegel distinguishes two main types, but these are subdivided into four distinct categories. In the first type, the protagonists (each of whom embodies and recognizes in himself the authority of the power which threatens him) "are seized and broken by that very bond which is rooted in the compass of their own social existence"[14]; they are crushed, in other words, by the very forces immanent in their lives and against which they struggle. But the tragic issue is not always so destructive. There is a second type of reconciliation which does not necessitate the downfall of the hero. This kind of resolution may be effected through the intercession of a god *(Eumenides),* or — in less external fashion — as a last-minute surrender on the part of the protagonist of his one-sided point of view *(Philoctetes),* or — more intimately — as the reconciliation "of the soul itself, in which respect there is, in virtue of the personal significance, a real approach to our modern point of view" *(Oedipus at Colonus).*[15]

It is in connection with the first type of tragic content — where the protagonists "stand fundamentally under the power of that against which they battle"[16] and consequently are shattered in their attempt to disassociate themselves from it — that Hegel cites the well-known example of the *Antigone*:

> Of all that is noble in the ancient and modern world — I know pretty nearly all of it, and it is right and possible to know it — the *Antigone* appears to me, from this point of view, the most excellent, the most satisfying work of art.[17]

If we recall the context in which he is speaking, Hegel's generous praise will not be misconstrued; he is saying, in effect, that of all ancient and modern tragedies ever written within the framework of the particular content just described, Sophocles' *Antigone* is by far the best.

At least two other passages should be cited in this connection. In the *Lectures on the Philosophy of Religion,* the *Antigone* is again mentioned as the clearest embodiment of the divine forces of family and community life: "The collision between the two highest moral powers is set forth in a plastic fashion in that supreme and absolute example of tragedy, *Antigone.* "[18] And, writing in *The Philosophy of Fine Art* on the opposition between these divine powers, Hegel once again isolates the *Antigone* as "one of the most sublime, and in every respect most consummate works of art human effort ever produced."[19] All three passages contain significant qualifications; in each case, the *Antigone* appears as an illustration of a particular type of collision in ancient tragedy. But to understand fully Hegel's attitude toward the *Antigone* and the important distinction between ancient and modern tragedy, we must consider briefly the relationship of classical tragedy to art, generally.

It is on this crucial point that Bradley seems to have gone seriously astray. In the note appended to the 1912 essay, he came to the conclusion that the reason for Hegel's preference for Greek tragedy lay in the unswerving conviction that "Classical Art is Art *par excellence,*"[20] and that modern tragedies are nothing more than "declensions from the more ideal ancient form."[21] But anyone familiar with Hegel's historical outlook, with his view of history as the gradual unfolding of the human spirit and the realization of human freedom, cannot fail to see that Bradley's conclusions contradict the basic premises of the Hegelian scheme. Bradley seems to have missed the all-important distinction Hegel makes between the Greek and the Shakespearean world, between "classical" and "romantic" art.

The reciprocal inadequacy of content and form, which characterizes symbolic art, is overcome — according to Hegel —

in classical art. When the symbolic temple of architecture is ready, the classical hand of sculpture provides, in the idealized figure of man, an embodiment of divinity itself. In sculpture's perfect adequacy of content and form, the classical type of art, Hegel asserts, "attained the highest excellence of which the sensuous embodiment of art is capable." Indeed, Greek art generally, according to Hegel, reflects the same perfection. Hegel believed — to use Bradley's words — that "in Greece beauty held a position such as it never held before and will not hold again."[22] But he did not believe — as Bradley concluded he did — that classical art, as "Art *par excellence*," exhausts the aesthetic impulse. For Hegel, art can aim higher. It can attempt to express the inner, self-conscious life of divinity — characteristically, the task of painting, poetry and music; historically, the grand achievement of Shakespearean tragedy.[23]

In the attempt to express the inner life of spirit, which is the content of romantic art, the materials of three-dimensional space become inadequate. Color, sound, and thought now take the place of wood, marble, and stone, as the means by which the diversified interior life of spirit is expressed. In this sequence, tragedy represents the highest point of poetic achievement and romantic tragedy the fully conscious inner world of spirit, which has a "significance which goes beyond the classical form of art and its mode of expression." In the full coming to light of the inner world of man, romantic tragedy exhausts the aesthetic impulse and "must be considered as art transcending itself."[24] The purely sensuous embodiment of beauty here gives way to spiritual beauty, defying in a sense the very attempt at representation: "beauty is no longer an idealization in respect to objective form, but rather the ideal and essential configuration of the soul itself; it is in short a beauty of spiritual ideality . . . ."[25]

In the light of this sequence, it is hard to understand Bradley's conclusion that Hegel objected to romantic tragedy (a conclusion stretched to absurdity by more recent critics).[26] According to Bradley, Hegel saw in the boundless subjectivity of modern tragedy, in the emphasis on personal motives in action, in the introduction of "un-beautiful reality into the realm of Beauty," necessary characteristics but at the same time drawbacks.[27] On this score, however, Bernard Bosanquet has answered emphatically: "It has been said that Hegel's classification is a descending series. This is not so; the romantic arts are the culmination of art as such, though it is mere truth to say that they are not the culmination of beauty in the narrow sense."[28]

But it is Hegel himself who provides the most emphatic answer. The Greek consciousness, seen from "our profounder modern consciousness," is seriously limited in a number of ways. Above all, it fails to distinguish intention from actual deed:

> The plastic nature of the Greek . . . adheres to the bare fact which an individual has achieved, and refuses to face the division implied by the purely ideal attitude of the soul in the self-conscious life on the one hand and the objective significance of the fact accomplished on the other.[29]

As a result, the Greek tragic hero does not recognize personal guilt in his one-sided ethical claim; the "higher form of reconciliation," which requires that the hero himself "should have the consciousness of his wrongdoing," is not characteristically Greek. There are, Hegel admits, some faint traces of this type of inward change or conversion in Greek tragedy, but even in the most striking example — that of the *Oedipus at Colonus* — the internal reconciliation is merely hinted at and remains, basically, a kind of "outward purification." Ancient tragedy — including the *Antigone* — is, on the whole, deficient in this respect: "there remains here something unsolved in that the higher element does not appear as the infinitely spiritual power; we still have here an unsatisfied sorrow . . . ." Our profounder modern consciousness requires an awareness of personal guilt, an internal state of being which may be set apart and examined separately in and for itself. In the Christian scheme of things, reconciliation necessarily involves what we have come to recognize as "conscience":

> In the present day we demand more, since with us the idea of reconciliation is of a higher kind, and because we are conscious that this conversion can occur in the inner life, whereby that which is done can be rendered undone.
>
> The man who is "converted" gives up his one-sidedness; he has extirpated it himself in his will, which was the permanent seat of the deed, the place of its abode; that is, he destroys the act in its root. It is congenial to our way of feeling that tragedies should have conclusions which have in them the elements of reconciliation [i.e., "conversion"].[30]

The Greeks could not understand this kind of attitude. The full depth of subjectivity was never attained by them, and they never realized, therefore, true spiritual reconciliation.[31] The whole structure of personal morality is wanting:

> Classical art has not worked its way to the full contradiction which is fundamentally involved in the notion of the Absolute and overcome that contradiction. For this reason it does not recognize the

aspect which is in close relation to this contradiction, that is the essential obduracy of the subject as opposed to that which is ethical and of absolute significance, namely, sin and evil, no less than the waste of individual life in its own subjective aims, the dissolution and incontinence of that world which we may summarily describe as that of the entire sphere of its divisions, which is productive on the side both of sense and spirit of distortion, ugliness, and the repulsive. Classical art fails to cross the pure territory of the genuine Ideal.[32]

Among the Greeks, conscience — and all that is connected with it — has not yet "secured its rightful place."[33]

What Hegel saw in the art of Greece was not the perfect expression of art (as Bradley thought), but the perfect artistic balance between the sensuous and the Ideal. Classical art, for him, is indeed the most *beautiful* art the world has ever known, but that art "and its religion of beauty," Hegel concludes unequivocally, "does not . . . wholly satisfy the depths of Spirit."[34] In classical art, human individuality has not yet reached "the full height of spiritual attainment, where the subject draws the determination of his actions . . . from his own resources."[35]

It should not be difficult, at this point in the discussion, to anticipate where Hegel's preferences really lie. Having come this far, any attempt at "justifying" Hegel's supposed preference for Greek tragedy — and for the *Antigone* in particular — must appear shortsighted. For Hegel, the content of ancient tragedy could never fail to produce a sublime effect; but it is modern and Shakespearean tragedy which contain universal human interest:

A similar position of advantage, such as that we allow to Shakespeare, would be attributable to the tragedies of the ancients, if we did not, apart from our changed habits in respect to scenic reproduction and certain aspects of the national conciousness, make the further demand of a profounder psychological penetration and a greater breadth of particular characterization.[36]

The beauty of Greek tragedy lies in the striking embodiment of ethical forces as seen in an awe-inspiring dramatic action; but beyond that beauty, lies the profound inspiration of Shakespearean tragedy, the illumination of the internal world of man's soul, caught in all its magic fluidity.

The themes of romantic tragedy, as Hegel defines them, show clearly a shift from the unified dramatic action of the ancients to intimate psychological characterization. Personal fidelity, honor, and love furnish the broad subject matter of modern tragedy — subjects which make possible "every sort of action" and create "a wide expanse of contingent relations and conditions."[37] The awesome spectacle of the "rationality of destiny"[38] as it unfolds, in classical tragedy, in the conflict of equally compelling forces gives way, in romantic tragedy, to the spectacle of self-reflecting personality as it asserts itself against the world; external events merely supply the occasion for a conflict which is essentially personal and internal. Where ancient themes are used successfully by modern dramatists — as in the case of Goethe's *Iphigenia* — the materials are adapted to highlight the wealth and insight of personality.[39] As a rule, however, dramatic imitation of the ancients (especially in French and Italian, and to a lesser extent in Spanish drama) turns out to be nothing more than "personifications of specific passions" adorned by lavish displays of declamation and rhetoric, all of which resembles — Hegel observes — "the dramatic failures of Seneca" rather than "the dramatic masterpieces of the Greeks." Modern tragedy at its best is to be found, not among the French or Italians or Spanish or even among the Germans (although Goethe deserves high praise for his profound insights into character), but among the English, who "in their mastery of the exposition of fully developed characters and personality . . . are exceptionally distinguished." And, at the very pinnacle of this clearly articulated scale of dramatic achievement, "soaring above the rest at an almost unapproachable height, stands Shakespeare.[40]

The extraordinary achievement of Shakespeare — and, indeed, of romantic tragedy, generally — lies in richly suggestive characterization. The figures of Greek tragedy, Hegel reminds us again and again, are not defined very sharply; even the "heavenly" *Antigone* — "that noblest of figures that ever appeared on earth"[41] — remains at the end of the play what she was at the outset, for the Greek heroes are wholly identified with the forces which dominate the action. The possibilities for the development of character are limited by the emphasis on collisions of equally compelling moral values and the kind of reconciliation they call for; the outstanding feature of Greek tragedy is not personalities but the "substantive content of action."

In romantic and Shakespearean tragedy, on the other hand, the dramatic action as such is much less rigorous; the main interest is on the full prism of personality as it realizes itself and develops in the course of even the most arbitrary sequence of events.[42] From the modern point of view, which recognizes moral absolutes only insofar as they spring from individual conscience, Greek tragedy leaves something to be desired. The suggestive simplicity of the Sophoclean figures, for example, haunts us with the same quiet beauty found in Greek sculpture; but the characters of Shakespeare move the very depths of our soul with their intimate and complex emotional life — the true content of romantic art.

> In the finest figures of sculpture we behold a tranquil depth, which unfolds, as it were, the pregnant womb, from which all other potencies may be born. In contrast with sculpture it is yet of more vital importance to the arts of painting, music, and poetry, that they should display the inmost complexity of character, and real artists of every age have recognized this. In Shakespeare's *Romeo and Juliet*, for example, the most pathetic characteristic of Romeo is his love: but he is also placed before us under relations of the greatest contrast, whether it be in reference to his parents, his friends, his love troubles, or his affair of honour in which he fights with Tybalt, his attitude of deference and trust to the monk, nay, even on the verge of the grave his conversation with the apothecary, from whom he purchases the poison. Throughout he is the same worthy and noble man of deep emotions.[43]

And yet, if dramatic action in Shakespearean tragedy is less rigorous, less compelling in terms of "substantive" universal values, it is not therefore merely a convenient background for the delineation of character. The most arbitrary occurrences, even supernatural manifestations, are somehow transformed into compelling dramatic motivation. The "accidents" in *Romeo and Juliet* and *Hamlet*, for example, create an illusion of inevitability, since they are a reflection or, rather, a projection of the internal state of the main characters. What seem to be purely arbitrary events imposing themselves upon the individual are, in fact, echoes of his own inescapable will:

> the demand is direct and irresistible that the external accidents ought to accord with that which is identical with the spiritual nature of such noble characters. Only as thus regarded can we feel ourselves reconciled with the grievous end of Hamlet and Juliet. From a purely external point of view, the death of Hamlet appears as an accident occasioned by his duel with Laertes and the interchange of the daggers. But in the background of Hamlet's soul, death is already present from the first. The sandbank of finite condition will not content his spirit. As the focus of such mourning and weakness, such melancholy, such a loathing of all the conditions of life, we feel from the first that, hemmed within such an environment of horror, he is a lost man, whom the surfeit of the soul has well-nigh already done to death before death itself approaches him from without. The same thing may be observed in the case of Romeo and Juliet. The ground on which these tender blossoms have been planted is alien to their nature; we have no

alternative left us but to lament the pathetic transiency of such a beautiful love, which, as some tender rose in the vale of this world of accident, is broken by rude storms and tempests, and the frangible reckonings of noble and well-meaning devices.[44]

In a similar manner, the supernatural creatures in *Hamlet* and *Macbeth* are shown to be external expressions of desires and thought already present, in each case, in the hero's will:

> The witches in *Macbeth*, for example, appear as external powers, who foretell for Macbeth his future destiny. What they *do* foretell, however, is precisely that which is his own most secret wish, which is reflected back on him and declared in this, merely in appearance, external form. With a still closer regard to beauty, yet profounder insight, is the ghost in *Hamlet* treated as the purely objective embodiment of Hamlet's own intuitions. We find Hamlet in the first instance overpowered with a vague feeling that something horrible has taken place. His father's ghost then appears and gives definite form to these awful premonitions.[45]

The outside world, with all its arbitrary events and its variety of personalities, carries within itself the seeds of purposeful action; through its seeming confusion, character is gradually defined and the Shakespearean hero is forced to reveal himself in the fullness of his emotional life.

It is this emotional life, its rich and varied passions held together by steadfast will, that gives — according to Hegel — enduring, universal appeal to the characters of Shakespeare: "if the signet mark of Shakespeare is conspicuous on any one quality it is on the firm and decisive delineation of his characters, even when it is only the formal greatness and consistency of evil that is in question."[46] Greatness of soul impels them to assert themselves against others, according to the "formal necessity of their personality";[47] but they are able, also, to see themselves objectively, in the same way that an artist contemplates his own work. Their imaginative power and genius lift them "above that which their condition and definite purpose would make them."[48] By virtue of the intelligence and imagination conferred upon him by his creator, even a criminal figure like Macbeth emerges — no less than Falstaff, Lear, or Hamlet — as a free artist in his own right, capable of contemplating himself objectively as a work of art. Within the limitations of extreme evil and folly, such characters display in their overwhelming force of utterance, in the lightning rapidity of their images and similes, a vitality which awakens our wonder and admiration. The very language,

> here the barren child of no school, but the growth of genuine emotion and penetration into human personality, is such that, if

we take into account this extraordinary union of the directness of life itself and ideal greatness of soul, we shall find it hard indeed to point to a single other dramatic poet among the moderns whom we are entitled to rank in his company.[49]

The Shakespearean figure is, in this sense, a magnificent paradox; limited by the compelling force of his own personality, he is able nevertheless to rise above the particular circumstances of his life and thus gain insight into necessity. Shakespeare's clowns and fools "bubbling over with wit and the humour of genius"[50] manifest not only an awareness of their own limitations but also an extraordinary intelligence "whose genial quality is able to take in everything, to possess a large and open atmosphere of its own, and in short makes them all that great men are."[51] So too, Macbeth rises above his crimes and punishment by means of profound insight into human nature and his own soul; while recognizing in his bitter lot that "which his action merits,"[52] his vivid imagination sees far beyond the immediate circumstances of his guilt. This combination of subtlety and simplicity is most striking, perhaps, in the delineation of the "silent" soul — among the most delicate creations of all Shakespearean drama. Such natures seem unconscious of what they possess and may even appear quite ordinary on the surface; they reveal themselves, Hegel observes, only in flashes of "isolated, unrelated, naive, and involuntary expressions." Such is Juliet. To all appearances passive and submissive, she concentrates her personality, following her encounter with Romeo, in "one supreme form of emotion." Thus awakened, her true nature bursts forth from the "spring source of the soul" and comes to know itself in a brief but magnificent display of strength and beauty.[53]

The paradox of the *schöne Seele,* the beautiful soul who remains true to the "formal necessity" of personality while fully conscious of its limitations, is nowhere drawn more impressively than in the character of Hamlet. The substance of Hamlet's tragedy, Hegel points out, is deep within the personality of the hero. Anticipating Bradley's attempt to extend the analysis of Greek-type collisions to Shakespearean tragedy, Hegel distinguishes modern collisions from ancient ones by emphasizing the shift from external, substantive values to internal, personal ones — illustrating his point with references to the *Choephorae,* Sophocles' *Electra,* and *Hamlet.* The passage is worth quoting in full, not only for its interesting comparison of ancient and modern masters but also for its unambiguous answer to Bradley's attempt to "save" Hegel's analysis of ancient tragedy by "extending" it to

Shakespeare.

> In order to emphasize still more distinctly the difference which in
> this respect obtains between ancient and modern tragedy, I will
> merely refer the reader to Shakespeare's *Hamlet*. Here we find
> fundamentally a collision similar to that which is introduced by
> Aeschylus into his *Choephorae* and by Sophocles into his *Electra*.
> For Hamlet's father, too, and the King, as in these Greek plays, has
> been murdered, and his mother has wedded the murderer. That
> which, however, in the conception of the Greek dramatists pos-
> sesses a certain ethical justification — I mean the death of Aga-
> memnon — in the contrasted case of Shakespeare's play, can only
> be viewed as an atrocious crime, of which Hamlet's mother is in-
> nocent; so that the son is merely concerned in his vengeance to
> direct his attention to the fratricidal king, and there is nothing in
> the latter's character that possesses any real claim to his respect.
> The real collision, therefore, does not turn on the fact that the
> son, in giving effect to a rightful sense of vengeance, is himself
> forced to violate morality, but rather on the particular personality,
> the inner life of Hamlet, whose noble soul is not steeled to this
> kind of energetic activity, but, while full of contempt for the world
> and life, what between making up his mind and attempting to carry
> into effect or preparing to carry into effect its resolves, is bandied
> from pillar to post, and finally through his own procrastination
> and the external course of events meets his own doom.[54]

But, although he recognizes in Hamlet a finely strung nature "with emotions held in persistent reserve," unable to tear
itself from its "internal harmony," Hegel does not agree with
writers like Goethe, who see the play as the imposition of some
"supreme action on a soul whose growth was unadapted to its
execution." Shakespeare, he observes, "when referring to the
apparition of the ghost, contributes a far profounder trait of
character in explanation of this debated point. Hamlet delays,
because he does not right off wholly believe in the ghost."[55] Greatness of soul and firm and decisive purpose are as clear in the
delineation of Hamlet as they are in that of Macbeth or Juliet.
What has been loosely termed "mental indecision" is neither a
wavering of purpose nor a spiritual disease; Hamlet is in doubt
only "as to the way he shall carry out his purpose, not at all as to
what has to be done."[56] He is at once ready to seek revenge; "his
sense of duty is always before him reflecting the innermost crav-
ing of his heart." But his self-absorption, his overwhelming desire to justify to himself all that he does and thinks, makes him
misjudge the realities of life. He acts in a hurry "where he should
have been more circumspect," and "bows passively" to external
events where he should have risen to meet them. In the pent-up

energies of his spirit, he resembles Juliet more than any other
Shakespearean character. When the crisis comes, he too is helpless. The fatal issue of the drama is, in fact, realized — Hegel
insists — without any action on his part: "the fated *dénouement* of
the entire drama, including that of his own persistently self-re-
tiring personality," comes about as a result of "external incidents
and accidents."[57]

External determinations resolve the tragic action, but in
no other Shakespearean play are they so ineffectual in solving a
moral dilemma. The events that unfold — although reflecting very
often Hamlet's tragic self-mistrust — do not succeed in rooting
it out. Nothing in the action of the play brings him relief. His
hidden feelings flash out in "involuntary expressions" which light
up, momentarily, deeper doubts and fears. In him, Shakespeare
has embodied most successfully the profounder requirements
of the modern point of view, allowing us to gaze into the inexplicable paradox of human consciousness. There is nothing in all
ancient tragedy to compare with the figure of Hamlet; in fact,
there is nothing quite like it anywhere else in Shakespeare:

> He [Oedipus], who had the power to unlock the riddle of the sphinx,
> and he too who trusted with childlike confidence [Orestes],
> are . . . both sent to destruction through what the god reveals to
> them. The priestess, through whose mouth the beautiful god speaks
> [in the Delphic Oracle], is in nothing different from the equivocal
> sisters of fate [the witches in *Macbeth*], who drive their victim to
> crime by their promises, and who, by the double-tongued, equivo-
> cal character of what they gave out as a certainty, deceive the King
> when he relies upon the manifest and obvious meaning of what
> they say. There is a type of consciousness that is purer than the
> latter [Macbeth's] which believes in witches, and more sober, more
> thorough, and more solid than the former which puts its trust in
> the priestess and the beautiful god. This type of consciousness,
> therefore, lets his revenge tarry for the revelation which the spirit
> of his father makes regarding the crime that did him to death, and
> institutes other proofs in addition — for the reason that the spirit
> giving the revelation might possibly be the devil.[58]

In attempting to represent this profound self-consciousness, "with
all the intimate traits of its evolution" in "self-destructive conflict with circumstances,"[59] Shakespeare produced the supreme
masterpiece of all human art. In Hamlet, Hegel sees the fulfillment of ethical life, the compelling force, not of external, substantive values, but of individual conscience. In the *schöne Seele*
which proclaims its freedom in self- conscious personality, we
recognize the divinity within the temple of art.

Returning to "Hegel's Theory of Tragedy" from a careful reading of Hegel, one is likely to be all the more impressed by Bradley's clarity of exposition. His very errors take on new meaning. The attempt to enlarge the Hegelian theory to include Shakespearean tragedy, for example, calls attention to the underlying truth of his conviction that classical and romantic drama could not possibly be considered within the same critical framework, that some kind of adaptation was necessary in order to relate them. Throughout the essay, Bradley shows an unshakable commitment to do justice to Hegel's thought; even his most serious objections are phrased as tentative conclusions or purely personal opinions. It is clear that his estimate of the German philosopher as the most "original and searching" writer on tragedy, since Aristotle, was not meant as idle praise.

Nor will the serious student of the Hegelian writings on tragedy find such praise an exaggeration. Hegel can provide Shakespearean studies today with as strong an impetus as that which he gave to them, over half a century ago, through Bradley. And, for those interested in the broader philosophical and historical implications of dramatic poetry, there is much more. I will simply remind the reader, by way of conclusion, of Hegel's many provocative pages on social drama, his interesting examination of the meaning of "pity" and "fear" as used by Aristotle, his discussion of the *schöne Scele* and its place in modern tragedy, and his brilliant analysis of the emergence of the tragic hero in history, in the figure of Socrates — this last analysis, in my opinion, among the most inspiring accounts of the trial of Socrates and the dissolution of ancient tragedy under the penetrating attacks of Aristophanes.

NOTES

An earlier version of this essay appeared in *Comparative Literature*, Volume XVI, Number 3, Summer 1964.

1. Anne and Henry Paolucci, eds., *Hegel on Tragedy* (Doubleday, New York, 1962), p. 367. For the reader's convenience, quotations from Hegel will be drawn from this work. The original source will be given in parentheses. This important collection was reissued by Harper and Row, Greenwood Press, and most recently (2001) by Griffon House Publications, Smyrna, DE.

2. *Ibid.*, p. 377.

3. *Ibid.*, p. 380.

4. *Ibid.*, pp. 367-388.

5. A. C. Bradley, "Hegel's Theory of Tragedy " *The Hibbert Journal*, II

(1903-04), 662-680.

6. Kenneth Muir, "Fifty Years of Shakespearian Criticism: 1900-1950," *Shakespeare Survey,* IV (1951), 4.

7. Clifford Leech, "Studies in *Hamlet,* 1901-1955 " *Shakespeare Survey,* IX (1956), 3.

8. Muir, p. 4.

9. See *Hegel on Tragedy,* p. 388: "whether it is correct or no . . . the impression produced by the *Aesthetik* is a true one, and . . . Hegel did deliberately consider the ancIent form the more satisfactory."

10. *Ibid.,* p. 371.

11. Carl J. Friedrich, ed., *The Philosophy of Hegel* (New York, 1953), p. lix.

12. Bradley himself, it should be noted, emphasized the necessity for keeping the larger framework in mind: "no statement . . . which ignores [Hegel's] metaphysics and his philosophy of religion can be more than a fragmentary account of that theory." *Hegel on Tragedy,* pp. 367-368, note 2.

13. *Hegel on Tragedy,* p. 68 (*Fine Art,* IV) .For the full discussion here reviewed see *ibid.,* pp. 68-76 and 259-287 (*Phenomenology*).

14. *Hegel on Tragedy,* p. 73 (*FA.,* IV).

15. *Ibid.,* p. 75.

16. *Ibid.,* p. 73.

17. *Hegel on Tragedy,* p. xxvi (editors' translation) .

18. *Ibid.,* p. 325 (*Rel.,* II) .

19. *Ibid.,* p. 178 (*F.A.,* II) .

20. *Ibid.,* p. 387.

21. *Ibid.,* p. 381. Cf. "The Substance of Shakespearean Tragedy," *Shakespearean Tragedy* (London, 1950), p. 16: "Hegel's view of the tragic conflict . . . had its origin in reflections on Greek tragedy and, as Hegel was well aware, applies only imperfectly to the works of Shakespeare."

22. *Ibid.,* p. 387.

23. I have refrained from any discussion of the three romantic arts — painting, music, and poetry — since it would take us too far afield. I will simply mention Hegel's provocative analysis of what T. S. Eliot has popularized as "the three voices of poetry." I do not know whether Eliot had read *The Philosophy of Fine Art* when he came to formulate his ideas on the subject, but his arguments are strongly reminiscent of Hegel's. See *Hegel on Tragedy,* pp. xxii-xxiv.

24. *Hegel on Tragedy,* p. xxi.

25. George W. F. Hegel, *The Philosophy of Fine Art,* tr. F. P. B. Osmaston (London, 1920), II, 298.

26. See. for example, Israel Knox, *The Aesthetic Theories of Kant, Hegel*

and Schopenhauer (New York, 1936), pp. 109-111, 115, especially Knox's statement that Hegel "objects to Shakespeare's characters because they are vessels driven by passion and hate and love and doubt and fear and desire" (p. 115). Cf. *Hegel on Tragedy*, p. 91 *(F A.,* IV).

27. *Hegel on Tragedy*, p. 387.

28. *Ibid.*, p. xxiv.

29. *Ibid.*, p. 69 (*F.A.*, IV).

30. *Ibid.*, pp. 326-327 (*Rel.*, II).

31. George W. F. Hegel, *The Philosophy of History*, tr. J. Sibree (New York, 1899) , p. 250.

32. Hegel, *The Philosophy of Fine Art*, II, 181. See also *Hegel on Tragedy*, pp. 165-168 (*F.A.*, II).

33. *Hegel on Tragedy*, p. 171 (*F.A.*, II) .See also *ibid.*, pp. 69-71 (*F.A.*, IV) and the discussion on conscience and the *schöne Seele* of the modern world, *ibid.*, pp. 277-278 and George W. F. Hegel, *The Phenomenology of Mind*, tr. J. B. Baillie (London, 1931), pp. 642-679.

34. Hegel, *The Philosophy of Fine Art*, II, 180.

35. *Hegel on Tragedy*, p.171 (*F.A.*, II).

36. *Ibid.*, p. 25 (*F.A.*, IV).

37. *Hegel on Tragedy*, p. 84 (*F.A.*, IV). See also *ibid.*, p. 206 (*F.A.*, II).

38. *Ibid.*, p. 71 (*F.A.*, IV).

39. *Ibid.*, pp. 143-145 (*F.A.*, I) and p. 57 (*F.A.*, IV). See also *ibid.*, pp. 26-27, 33 (*F.A.*, IV).

40. *Ibid.*, p. 85 (*F.A.*, IV).

41. *Ibid.*, p. 360 (*Phil.*).

42. *Ibid.*, pp. 208-209 (*F.A.*, II). See also *ibid.*, pp. 202-203 (*F.A.*, II) and *ibid.*, pp. 79-80 (*F.A.*, IV).

43. *Ibid.*, pp. 156-157 (*F.A.*, I).

44. *Ibid.*, pp. 90-91 (*F.A.*, IV)

45. *Ibid.*, p. 146 (*F.A.*, I).

46. *Ibid.*, p. 162. See also *ibid.*, pp. 206-207, 215-217 (*F.A.*, II).

47. *Ibid.*, p. 88 (*F .A.*, IV) .See also *ibid.*, p. 21.

48. *Ibid.*, p. 216 (*F.A.*, II) .See also *The Phenomenology of Mind*, p. 708: "Spirit is *Artist.* "

49. *Ibid.*, p. 86 (*F.A.*, IV). For Hegel's provocative analysis of the function of the simile and image and of Shakespeare's excellent use of poetic language for dramatic effect, see *ibid.*, pp. 224-227, 228-231 (*F.A.*, II). Wolfgang H. Clemen isolates these pages for special notice in *The Development of Shakespeare's Imagery* (London, 1953), p. 14.

50. *Ibid.*, p. 158 (*F.A.*, I).

51. *Ibid.*, p. 216 (*F.A.*, II).

52. *Ibid.,* p. 90 (*F.A.,* IV).

53. *Ibid.,* pp. 210-212 *passim* (*F.A.,* II).

54. *Ibid.,* p. 83 (*FA.,* IV).

55. *Ibid.,* p. 147 (*F.A.,* I).

56. *Ibid.,* p. 162 (*F.A.,* I).

57. *Ibid.,* p. 214 (*F.A.,* II).

58. *Ibid.,* pp. 294-295 *(Phen.).*

59. *Ibid.,* p. 88 *(F.A.,* IV).

CHAPTER 7

SHAKESPEARE REVISITED: HEGEL, A. C. BRADLEY, T. S. ELIOT

Although Hegel has left his indelible mark on modern aesthetics and criticism in all the arts, his impact on American literary criticism, and on Shakespearean studies in particular, has been on the whole negligible. The neglect may be due in part to A. C. Bradley's fall from favor in the last two or three decades — although, as one Shakespearean scholar reminds us, "[n]early all recent critics have been influenced by Bradley, in one way or another, not least when they have reacted against his methods.[1]

Bradley's acknowledged debt to Hegel in his studies of Shakespearean tragedy may help explain the strange ambivalence of American Shakespeare critics, bred on pragmatism, toward his work. A similar case may be made for their reluctance to acknowledge T. S. Eliot's deep and continuing interest in philosophy and its impact on his literary criticism, especially where he compares and contrasts the achievement of Dante and Shakespeare as literary Titans. The truth is that Eliot, like A. C. Bradley before him, had turned to German Idealism as an answer to pragmatism as early as 1913, when he first read F. H. Bradley's famous work *Appearance and Reality.* Hardly a coincidence that the two leading literary critics of our century should have been influenced, directly or indirectly, by German Idealism, Hegel, and F. H. Bradley (A. C.'s older brother), who was one of the leading Oxford Hegelians in the early part of the century. But American scholars, while acknowledging their worth in other ways, have found it difficult to come to terms with the patent philosophical and ultimately Hegelian echoes in the dramatic criticism of A. C. Bradley and T. S. Eliot.

For whatever reasons, American literary critics have preferred the easy way out, ignoring Hegel or dismissing him whenever he claims attention. If he is mentioned at all, it is usually on grounds that are often based on prejudice or are patently absurd. An incredible example of such treatment is Israel Knox's pathetically ill-informed assertion that Hegel "objects to

Shakespeare's characters because they are vessels driven by passion and hate and love and doubt and fear and desire."[2] In marked contrast, one may cite the work of Wolfgang H. Clemen on *The Development of Shakespeare's Imagery.* Not only does Clemen recognize in Hegel's discussion on the function of metaphor, image, and simile in dramatic poetry a fertile field for study, but he also made excellent use of that discussion in his own work.[3] Let me add, parenthetically (and as a quick answer to Knox), that in that excellent discussion Hegel draws all his examples from the plays of Shakespeare.

In what follows I will summarize, first, Bradley's careful and appreciative interpretation of Hegel's view of tragedy in his well-known essay "Hegel's Theory of Tragedy," comparing briefly Bradley's crucial readings with Hegel's own words;[4] then touch briefly on some examples of Bradley's application of Hegel in his own writings on Shakespearean tragedy;[5] and, finally, give some examples (and possibly encourage others to explore my lead) to show that, although, unlike A. C. Bradley, Eliot never acknowledged any debt to Hegel and minimized his philosophical interests in German idealism, he echoes many Hegelian ideas in his literary criticism, particularly in his writings on Shakespeare. Throughout, I have also drawn from Hegel's own discussion on drama and art to clarify and illustrate the major points of my argument.

Bradley opens his essay, "Hegel's Theory of Tragedy," with these words of high praise:

> Since Aristotle dealt with tragedy, and, as usual, drew the main features of his subject with those sure and simple strokes which no later hand has rivalled, the only philosopher who has treated it in a manner both original and searching is Hegel. *[HT 367]*

No account of that theory which ignores Hegel's writings on the philosophy of religion or his metaphysics can be "more than a fragmentary account," Bradley cautions, and he does his best to do justice to Hegel in his own brief summary of the German philosopher's large and multi-faceted discussion. Even in his attempt to explain where, in his opinion, Hegel went wrong, he is respectful, almost apologetic.[6] In that spirit, he concludes with these words:

> I leave to students of Hegel to ask whether he would have accepted the criticisms and modifications I have suggested. Naturally I think he would, as I believe they rest on truth, and am sure he had a habit of arriving at truth. But in any case their importance is trifling, compared with that of the theory which they attempt to

strengthen and to which they owe their existence. [385]

In what follows, I have reviewed Bradley's major criticism of Hegel's theory of tragedy in that same spirit, to suggest what Hegel's reply would have been to Bradley's astute but often misleading observations.

In his essay on the subject, and more particularly in the appended "Note," Bradley more than once offers to answer a question which he himself raises: "Why did Hegel . . . so treat tragedy as to suggest the idea that the kind of tragedy which he personally preferred (let us for the sake of brevity call it 'ancient') is also the most adequate embodiment of the idea of tragedy?" Bradley is at pains to acknowledge that Hegel never himself explicitly expresses such a preference; and he adds, also, that, from the suggestion of such a preference, it would not follow that Hegel "thought the advantage was all on one side, or considered this or that ancient poet greater than this or that modern, or wished that modern poets had tried to write tragedies of the Greek type." Even so, Bradley's own impression is that "Hegel did deliberately consider the ancient form the more satisfactory" and even that the "ancient form" is the "typical form," and the modern rather a modification of it and not "an alternative embodiment." He bases such criticisms on his more fundamental assumption about Hegel's entire aesthetics; for Hegel taught, he assures us, "that, in a sense, Classical Art is Art *par excellence,* and that in Greece beauty held a position such as it never held before and will not hold again." (386-387)

The last judgment quoted is both correct and consistent with Hegel's dramatic theory, so long as we understand precisely what Hegel meant by the terms used, in the large contexts of his philosophy of religion and metaphysics, as well as his aesthetics. Hegel *did* say, and in many different ways both in his lectures on aesthetics[7] and elsewhere, that classical art is the most beautiful art the world has ever known. He *did* say that the *Antigone* of Sophocles is the best example of that classical beauty as it is expressed in Greek tragedy. But he did not conclude, as Bradley does, that "the ancient form" is the "more satisfactory."

Even a superficial knowledge of his basic philosophic premise of the evolution of the human Spirit and the change brought on by Christianity in the modern world should warn us that Hegel could not have considered Greek art satisfactory in *absolute* terms. The emergence of the modern consciousness in all its complexity, the open-ended search for individual identity, the notion of sin, guilt, and the possibility of personal redemption, reflect a spiritual reality not to be found in classical drama. The awesome tragedies of the Greeks which portrayed human beings pitted against the gods, or more correctly, against an invisible unrelenting fate, are indeed unforgettable as mutually destructive assertions of ethical absolutes, both of which are right (or, if one prefers, both of which are justified). In those confrontations, the Greeks created some of the most *beautiful* drama ever written. But, as Hegel goes on to say and in many different places and works, *Art can aim higher*. Conscience, the idiosyncratic personality, the often obsessive self-analysis we see, for example, in Hamlet's search for meaning, in Macbeth's despair as he faces the *secunda mors,* the death of the soul, in Lear's intense personal suffering, are profounder drama, not to be found among the Greeks.

For Hegel, Greek art as a whole represents the perfect balance between the informing principle and the raw material of art. The entire classical experience (as differentiated from both the earlier Symbolic period, where the raw matter overwhelms the informing idea, and the later Romantic period, where the idea or form seems to overwhelm the sensory medium of expression) is characterized by *a reciprocal adequacy of matter and form.*[8] Modern or Romantic art, like Symbolic art at the opposite end of the scale, is no longer that perfect adequacy of matter and form. In all its achievements, postclassical art depicts a world that threatens to exceed the very limits of art in its search for expression. In the case of tragedy, the modern or Romantic form (by which Hegel meant Shakespearean) does not depict awesome confrontations between absolute and often self-destructive ethical forces, as in the *Antigone* or *Oedipus Rex,* but a deeper struggle of the soul seeking definition and redemption in a Christian world and in its own terms. After Shakespeare, says Hegel, tragedy becomes increasingly mere social drama depicting community values, friendship, love, honor, trust, loyalty, family obligations, etc.

Because Shakespearean tragedy centers on the individual's self-absorption in his own inner being, action becomes a *function* of idiosyncratic character: the plot seems to spin around the often unpredictable protagonist and is directed by it. The Shakespearean plot seems in fact to unfold arbitrarily when compared to the earlier struggle of absolute ethical forces each insisting absolutely on its "right." The Shakespearean protagonist is no longer a spokesperson for divine values caught in an awesome confrontation but a personality in his own right. The modern protagonist at his very best, says Hegel, is a *schöne Seele,* a self-determined "beautiful soul" who seeks the rationale for his actions within himself. Hamlet, Romeo, even Macbeth and Brutus are such characters. Their Socratic insistence on setting up their own rules and laws, their own justification for what they do, is both sublime and dangerous. Often such characters not only ignore moral and ethical standards in their self-justifying insistence on what is right, but they also seem at times to exceed the dramatic mold itself. Hamlet defies both definition and ultimate form. He is larger than the play. We are often tempted to see him as a real person because he answers to what we recognize, in some way, deep inside ourselves. Moreover, in Romantic or Shakespearean tragedy, conscience, the notion of evil, personal redemption and forgiveness, Christian reconciliation (not necessarily connected with the sacrifice of death), and the dramatic exploration of personality in and for itself shape both action and character in seemingly arbitrary ways. In this context we can begin to grasp Hegel's statement about *art transcending itself*[9] in the modern world.

Among the Greeks, Hegel reminds us, conscience and all that is related to it has not yet "secured its rightful place." (171) As a result, the reciprocal adequacy of matter and form connected with the Greek experience, the perfect artistic balance between the sensuous and the Ideal, all of classical art in its splendid manifestations and its religion of beauty does not wholly satisfy the depths of Spirit. In classical art, human individuality has not yet reached "the full height of spiritual attainment, where the subject draws the determination of his actions . . . from his own resources." (171) Or, in even sharper terms, the vital difference between the Greek experience and the modern one — Hegel explains — is that

> . . . art became in Greece the highest expression for the Absolute, and Greek religion is the religion of art itself, whereas romantic art, which appeared later, although it is undoubtedly art, suggests a more exalted form of consciousness than art is in a position to supply. (166)

At the risk of laboring the obvious, let me point out that in limiting the Greek experience in this way, Hegel never minimizes its awesome effect, the powerful response elicited even at this distance in time by self-destructive confrontations between absolute ethical forces; just as in his discussion about modern tragedy he never minimizes the difficulties which arise in any open-ended philosophical and aesthetic effort to define the idiosyncratic and elusive personality, with all its contradictions, motivations, ambitions, public and private tensions. For Hegel, the content of ancient tragedy could never fail to produce an arresting effect; but it is modern or Shakespearean tragedy which contains universal human interest. He says, late in his lectures on aesthetics:

> A similar position of advantage, such as that we allow to Shakespeare, would be attributable to the tragedies of the ancients, if we did not, apart from our changed habits in respect to scenic reproduction and certain aspects of the national consciousness, make the further demand of a profounder psychological penetration and a greater breadth of particular characterization. (25)

Modern tragedy is (to use a phrase of Eliot's) the objective correlative for the internal world of consciousness as it comes to know itself. And at its best, modern tragedy is to be found not among the French, Spanish or Italians (who depict for the most part "personifications of specific passions" adorned with lavish displays of declamation and rhetoric — all of which, says Hegel, resemble the "dramatic failures of Seneca" rather than "the dramatic masterpieces of the Greeks"), not even among the Germans (although Goethe deserves high praise, says Hegel, for his profound insights into character), but *among the English* who "in their mastery of the exposition of fully developed characters and personality . . . are exceptionally distinguished." And at the very pinnacle of this clearly articulated scale of dramatic achievement, says Hegel, "soaring above the rest at an almost unapproachable height, stands Shakespeare." (85)

Hegel's unqualified praise of Shakespeare could not be clearer. In that tragic world of seemingly arbitrary events, confusion, and unexpected happenings, the protagonist reveals himself in the fullness of his emotional life. As Hegel puts it:

> if the signet mark of Shakespeare is conspicuous on any one quality it is on the firm and decisive delineation of his characters, even when it is only the formal greatness and consistency of evil that is in question. [162; see also 206-207, 215-217]

There is, even in characters like Macbeth, Hegel argues, a greatness of soul which impels them to assert themselves against others, according to the "formal necessity of their personality." (88, 21) But they are also able to see themselves objectively, in the same way as an artist contemplates his own work. Their imaginative power and genius lift them "above that which their condition and definitive purpose would make them." (216; ["Spirit is *Artist,*" he writes somewhere in the *Phenomenology*]). Even a crimi-

nal type like Macbeth must emerge in his self-righteous excesses —
no less than a Falstaff, a Lear, a Brutus, or a Hamlet — as a free
artist in his own right, capable of seeing himself objectively as a
work of art. Bradley, we know, followed this fertile line of inquiry with much success in his time.

Hegel never shies away from the implications of the character as "villain" in Shakespeare. Indeed, it is a major and continuing source of intriguing speculation for him (as it continues
to be for critics today). Within the limitations of extreme evil
and folly, Shakespeare — Hegel asserts — is able to sustain the
heroic core of character, the greatness of even a soul like
Macbeth's. Very often that paradoxical display is expressed in
the character's "overwhelming force of utterance," in the "lightning rapidity" of images and similes, a vitality which awakens
our wonder and admiration, even as we recoil from the horrible
deeds we learn about or actually witness. But Hegel carries the
discussion about Shakespeare's language much further.
Shakespeare's linguistic mastery helps define the playwright's
genius, according to Hegel. In terms that cannot possibly be
misunderstood, he once again gives incontrovertible proof of
where his preference lies:

> [the very language] here the barren child of no school, but the
> growth of genuine emotion and penetration into human personal-
> ity, is such that, if we take into account this extraordinary union of
> the directness of life itself and ideal greatness of soul, we shall find
> it hard indeed to point to a single other dramatic poet among the
> moderns whom we are entitled to rank in his company. (86)

This brief summary suffices to make clear that while for
Hegel the *Antigone* of Sophocles was indeed the most *beautiful*
tragedy every written, the one that best reflects our modern existential self-awareness is to be found in Shakespeare. In attempting to represent profound self-consciousness with all the intimate traits of its evolution Shakespeare has indeed produced,
says Hegel, the supreme masterpiece of all human art: *Hamlet*.
We see in all the ambiguities and unresolved questions of that
play the fulfillment of ethical life, the compelling force not of
external substantive values but of individual conscience, the *schöne
Seele* proclaiming its freedom through self-conscious assertive
personality, with all its doubts and ambiguities.

Whatever the reasons for Bradley's honest misreading of
Hegel's preferences and their impact on the distinctions he made
between ancient and modern art — preferences and distinctions
upheld without contradiction in many different contexts through-

out Hegel's writings — Bradley was never tempted to repudiate Hegel because of the difficulties he had encountered in trying to grasp those crucial arguments. Hegel's insights are clearly evident in Bradley's own critical writings both in his *Oxford Lectures on Poetry* and in *Shakespearean Tragedy*. In "The Substance of Tragedy," for example, he asserts unequivocally that "deeds are the predominant factor" in any Shakespearean action and that "[t]he centre of the tragedy, therefore, may be said with equal truth to lie in action issuing from character, or in character issuing in action."[10] We grow more and more convinced, says Bradley, as a Shakespearean tragedy approaches its close, that "the calamities and catastrophes follow inevitably from the deeds of men, and that the main source of these deeds is character."[11] Where "abnormal conditions" (insanity, Lady Macbeth's sleepwalking, etc.) are introduced into the action, they "are never introduced as the origin of deeds of any dramatic moment." *(ST* 13) And where the supernatural is introduced, it "is always placed in the closest relation with character." (14) His discussion about the role of accidents and chance, especially in *Romeo and Juliet* and *Hamlet,* are particularly suggestive of Hegel's pages on the subject.

In his intriguing question, in that same essay, as to whether "action" in Shakespearean tragedy can properly be described as a "conflict," Bradley recalls Hegel, directly.

> The frequent use of this idea in discussions on tragedy is ultimately due, I suppose, to the influence of Hegel's theory on the subject, certainly the most important theory since Aristotle's. But Hegel's view of the tragic conflict is not only unfamiliar to English readers and difficult to expound shortly, but it had its origin in reflections on Greek tragedy and, as Hegel was well aware, applies only imperfectly to the works of Shakespeare. [16]

He refers the reader to his essay on Hegel for further clarification and explanation; but the discussion which follows is itself an Hegelian reading of the nature of tragic action in plays like *Macbeth* and *Hamlet.* Conflict in the usual sense, he explains, cannot properly describe the kind of dramatic action where the outer struggle invariably is translated into an inner struggle, where a "spiritual force" acts upon the human spirit, for good or evil, transforming the protagonist before our eyes. On this important point he concludes, with Hegel, that

> the notion of tragedy as a conflict emphasises the fact that action is the centre of the story, while the concentration of interest, in the greater plays, on the inward struggle emphasises the fact that

this action is essentially the expression of character. [19]

A struggle of this kind often brings forth *evil* and a sense of *waste.* (19-23) In depicting a world struggling for perfection, "but bringing to birth, together with glorious good, an evil which it is able to overcome only by self-torture and self-waste" (39), Shakespeare, Bradley observes, was suggesting not only the Christian Fall from grace but also the possibility of personal redemption. Hegel looms large in this entire discussion, in which Bradley enlarges on Hegel's exploration of the idiosyncratic character and the emergence of *evil* and *waste* in modern tragedy — Shakespeare in particular. He is clearly present, also, in the individual essays that follow, where the idea of "reconciliation" is expanded within the context of individual plays.

In his long critical analysis of *Hamlet* and the essays on *King Lear, Othello,* and *Macbeth (ST),* as well as in "The Rejection of Falstaff" and "Antony and Cleopatra" *(OLP),* Bradley's Hegelian reading is clearly in evidence. I can't possibly do justice here to the two major essays on *Hamlet* (covering a total of almost 100 pages: *(ST* 79-128; 129-174), but a few of the highlights will leave no doubt as to the impact of Hegel on Bradley's thinking on this subject.

In Bradley's view, *Hamlet* represents a transition to those plays in which the "more pervading effect of beauty gives place to what may almost be called explosions of sublimity or pathos." *(ST* 88) It is — and in this sense it resembles *Julius Caesar* — a play in which evil is minimized, where the "villain" is "a small one." (82). Hamlet himself is the sum and substance of the play; without him the tragedy is merely "the symbol of extreme absurdity." (90) He takes time to summarize the various theories about Hamlet's seeming delay in avenging the murdered king, discarding them finally with the practical observation that "no theory will hold water which finds the cause of Hamlet's delay merely, or mainly, or even to any considerable extent, in external difficulties." (94) What Hamlet wanted was "public justice" (94), but he never mentions a plan that will bring this about. Throughout, he must "convince *himself . . .* that the Ghost had spoken the truth." (96)

Hamlet himself, Bradley points out, never suggests anywhere in the play that he has not accepted the mandate of the ghost. (99) His delay does not evoke a sentimental sensitive Werther; such a view evokes "pity not unmingled with contempt. Whatever else he is, he is no *hero"* in this view of things. (101-102) Nor is the delay the result of "reflection" or irresolution

(104). We are not dealing here with "a condition of excessive but useless mental activity . . . but rather one of dull, apathetic, brooding gloom, in which Hamlet, so far from analyzing his duty, is not thinking of it at all." (126) Hamlet himself, Bradley insists, seems not to understand the reason for the delay. In his profound psychological awareness of the discrepancy between his accepted task and his failure to realize it, Hamlet reminds us "of the soul's infinity, and the sense of the doom which not only circumscribes that infinity but appears to be its offspring." (128)

I should add that in the course of his detailed analysis Bradley reminds us that Hamlet is quite capable of acting, often impulsively, on the basis of his own inner conviction of right and wrong, with scarcely any trace of remorse or regret. The *schöne Seele* of Hegel, the beautiful soul that answers only to its own internal Socratic certainty, is responsible in some way for at least eight deaths. But even this seeming contradiction is resolved if we grasp, as Bradley did, that Hamlet can accept his task only in his own terms. The delphic pronouncement of the Ghost, at the beginning of the play, is finally understood as part of what Hegel calls the *completed deed,* fully realized.

In Falstaff, Bradley (with Hegel's arguments clearly before him) sees not only the comic counterpart of the great figures of tragedy, but also the kind of protagonist who, like Hamlet, directs events and shapes dramatic action accordingly. Hamlet's insistent probing for elusive purpose makes him the center of interest, whatever the circumstances or events, just as Falstaff emerges as the indomitable spirit of *Henry IV,* accepting whatever happens and turning it to his advantage.

In the genial characterization of Falstaff, Shakespeare, according to Bradley, "created so extraordinary a being, and fixed him so firmly on his intellectual throne, that when he sought to dethrone him he could not." *(OLP* 259) We laugh with Falstaff, but he is never "a mere *object* of mirth." (261) He lies but rarely expects to be believed. "He abandons a statement or contradicts it the moment it is made." (264) We delight in Falstaff, in "his humorous superiority to everything serious, and the freedom of soul enjoyed in it." (269) We see the comic aspects of his misdeeds without judging their moral implications. This, says Bradley, echoing Hegel, "is the very spirit of comedy; [270] . . . [i]t is in this character, and not in the judgment he brings upon Falstaff's head, that Shakespeare asserts his supremacy ." The achievement was Falstaff himself and the conception of that "freedom of soul, a freedom illusory only in part, and attainable only by a mind which had received from Shakespeare's own the inexplicable touch of infinity which he bestowed on Hamlet and Macbeth and Cleopatra, but denied to Henry the Fifth." (273)[12]

Bradley gives us a powerful Hegelian reading of both the function of true comedy and the nature of the protagonist in that kind of setting. For Hegel, one of the central distinctions of genuine comedy, both ancient and modern, is "whether the individuals in the play are aware that they are comic, or are so merely from the spectator's point of view" *(HT* 76-77); "whether the folly and restricted outlook of the characters appears ridiculous to others only, or also to themselves; whether . . . the comic figures are an object of laughter only for the audience, or also for themselves." (93) Bradley, like Hegel, clearly saw Falstaff in such a light and saw him so *consistently.* He insisted, as Hegel did, on the indissoluble link between the comic Falstaff who drinks and cavorts with Prince Hal and the Falstaff who is rejected by King Henry V. In both roles, Falstaff emerges as the irresistible comic spirit whose whims direct the dramatic action.

In the world of comedy, that action is fragmented, its purpose uncertain; its citizens are "egotistical, litigious, . . . frivolously arrogant . . . boastful, vain." It is a world "of ends that have become self-destructive because they are inherently without substance" and that "dissolves itself in the folly of its substanceless deeds." In genuine comedy (and for Hegel only Aristophanes and Shakespeare fit the bill, as he makes very clear in his many comparisons between French, Spanish, and other modern examples and in his distinctions between comedy and farce), the stage is swept clear of the trivial and the unsubstantial. Society is reconstituted through self-directed criticism and the catharsis of laughter. In the reconstituted purposeful forward-looking new brave world of *Henry V*, comedy can play no major role, a Falstaff cannot flourish. But where he does flourish, says Hegel, Falstaff emerges as the perfect counterpart to the great figures of tragedy. Both are free spirits whose actions necessarily presuppose either a lively sense of individual freedom and independence, or at least a willful determination to accept responsibility for what they do or suffer to be done to them.

> In tragedy individuals either destroy themselves in the one-sided nobility of their character and aims or they are brought finally to accept in total resignation what they had earlier opposed with all their hearts; in comedy, instead, what we witness is a triumph of subjective personality in individuals who, in the midst of their own laughter, which dissolves everything, including themselves, man-

age to remain self-assured.[13]

In this context, Bradley seems to have had no difficulty accepting, on the one hand, Hegel's unqualified assertion that what Aristophanes created "in the ancient world and in his own field" was "beyond all rivalry," and, on the other hand, his final and absolute judgment on the matter. There is nothing in Bradley's detailed Hegelian study of Falstaff and Shakespearean comedy generally to suggest the kind of problems he saw in Hegel's pages on modern tragedy. And yet Hegel's conclusion about ancient and modern comedy is perfectly consistent with his ultimate judgment about tragedy.

> . . . the modem world, too, has elaborated a world of comedy which is both truly comic and poetical in its nature. The fundamental note here again is the cheerfulness of disposition, the inexhaustible resources of fun, no matter what may be the nature of miscarriage or bad luck, the exuberance and dash of what is at bottom nothing better than pure tomfoolery, and, in a word, exploited self-assurance. We have here as a result, in yet profounder expatiation, and yet more intense display of humour, whether the sphere of it be more restrictied or capacious, and whether the mode of it be more or less important, what runs on parallel lines with that which Aristophanes in the ancient world and in his own field created beyond all rivalry. As the master, who in a similar way outshines all others in his field, . . . I will . . . once again emphasize the name of William Shakespeare. [*HT* 95-96; *Knox* 1235-1236]

Bradley sees in the two major figures of *Antony and Cleopatra* another striking example of characters that are larger than life. He notes, by way of introduction, that the play's 42 scenes do not suggest a tragic conflict in terms we can easily relate to, nor do they produce the same compelling effect as other major Shakespearean tragedies. The two main figures, rather than the scattered events of the action, absorb us in this play. Like Hamlet and Falstaff, Antony and Cleopatra seem to exist beyond dramatic conventions; they dominate and overwhelm the action from beginning to end. And yet, the final outcome, Bradley concedes, although perhaps not tragic in the familiar rigorous sense, nevertheless creates a strong impression of tragic "reconciliation."

> The peculiar effect of the drama depends partly . . . on the absence of decidedly tragic scenes and events in its first half; but it depends quite as much on this emphasis [of reconciliation]. [*OLP* 292]

This impression, he explains, is unusually strong — stronger for many readers than "the fear and grief and pity with which they contemplate the tragic error and the advance of doom." (292)

Here Shakespeare has given us characters that rise above the terrifying forces of tragedy, whose impact seems somehow to leave them intact even in death. Like Hamlet and Falstaff, Antony and Cleopatra exert an attraction beyond anything suggested simply by the tragic events that claim them. In Hegelian terms, and as Bradley describes them, they transcend the dramatic mold created for them.

It is this notion of modern tragedy *transcending* itself, while somehow *remaining* art in that very transcendence, that best illustrates Bradley's profound debt to Hegel in his reading of Shakespeare. Two striking examples are offered in the lectures on *King Lear.* "How is it," Bradley asks at one point, "that this defective drama so overpowers us that we are either unconscious of its blemishes or regard them as almost irrelevant?" *(ST* 261) And at the close of the first lecture, he presents us with an utterly Hegelian paradox of artistic self-transcendence, identifying what he calls the "keynote" of the tragedy:

> Its final and total result is one in which pity and terror, carried perhaps to the extreme limits of art, are so blended with a sense of law and beauty that we feel at last, not depression and much less despair, but a consciousness of greatness in pain, and of solemnity in the mystery we cannot fathom. [279]

I have done no more than scratch the surface of this intriguing subject. But if indeed "it is a rash man who rejects [Bradley's judgments] out of hand,"[14] if indeed we "diverge from him, as we often must, at our peril,"[15] then a systematic analysis of Bradley's Hegelianism, as it comes through in his writings on Shakespeare, represents an important mandate for all those interested in Shakespeare studies.[16]

Eliot as a reader if not a disciple of Hegel may seem at first harder to validate. He never acknowledged directly, as A. C. Bradley did, his debt to Hegel, and rarely mentions any solid connection with the German philosopher. But the influence of F. H. Bradley on his development as a poet and critic can hardly continue to be ignored at this distance in time. Recent studies have made eminently clear that a firm and lasting connection exists and deserves to be explored between Eliot's writings and his philosophical interests, some of which proved deep and lasting.

Eliot's formal interest in philosophy, as we had occasion to mention earlier, can be traced back to his graduate days at Harvard. In his search for answers to then-current pragmatic trends, which he could not bring himself to accept, he soon gravi-

tated to Professor Josiah Royce's seminar and the philosophy of
F. H. Bradley, especially the latter's major work, *Appearance and
Reality*.[17] Bradley was the leading exponent of German Idealism
and Hegelian philosophy at Oxford — part of that extraordinary
group among whom we must include not only his brother A. C.
Bradley, but also Bernard Bosanquet (who translated into English the long Introduction to Hegel's *Philosophy of Fine Art*[18]). It
was at Oxford, in 1916, that Eliot submitted a final version of a
dissertation on Bradley, which he had virtually completed while
at Harvard. For whatever reasons, the work was not published
until almost half a century later.[19] For years critics have minimized or ignored Bradley's influence (or that of any philosophical writer) on Eliot's literary criticism. Louis Freed gives a thorough account of this long-prevailing attitude in his useful book
T. S. Eliot: The Critic as Philosopher,[20] where he himself argues
convincingly against the common assumption that Eliot's critical discipline does not have a firm philosophical base. Against
writers like John Crowe Ransom, for whom Eliot's critical work
is marked by a "theoretical innocence" in which philosophy plays
no part; or John D. Margolis, who in his book, *T. S. Eliot's Intellectual Development*, relegates Bradley to a footnote; or Frank
Kermode, who in his Introduction to the *Selected Prose of T. S.
Eliot* (1975) never once mentions Eliot's published work on Bradley, Freed sets up others who in some way have taken on the
challenge of exploring the relationship between Eliot and Bradley and, in a few scattered instances (though rarely in a substantive way), the connection between Eliot and Hegel.

Freed states his own unambiguous position in the first page
of his Introduction:

> Eliot, as critic, is still regarded as a mere *littérateur*, and his relation
> to Bradley is treated as just another fact to be filed under "sources
> and influences," useful perhaps as a footnote. Yet Eliot's critical
> prose is largely unintelligible apart from his philosophy, and in
> order to direct attention to this fact I have tried to show that com-
> mentators who ignore or discount the philosophy cannot as a rule
> find a meaning for Eliot's language. [xv]

He reminds us of Anne C. Bolgan's study of Eliot's dissertation,[21]
in which she sets down her specific objective

> to assert that every major critical concept which appears in Mr.
> Eliot's literary criticism — many of which initiated such stubborn
> controversies — emerges from his radical absorption in and criti-
> cism of Bradley's philosophy, and the content of my dissertation is
> but a demonstration of the way in which these notions and con-
> cepts originate in Bradley, are digested and recorded by Eliot as

he writes his own Ph.D. dissertation between 1914 and 1916 and reappear beginning a year or two later, now in new, full, literary dress in Mr. Eliot's reviews and essays. [44]

Freed, predictably, is convinced of Bolgan's assertion, although — like Bolgan's dissertation mentor, Northrop Frye — he doesn't seem to have found anything more specific to recommend in Bolgan's work. He notes that some writers like Kristian Smidt acknowledge Bradley's influence on Eliot while insisting that Eliot's critical writing lacks a theoretical basis. He cites Austin Warren, who dismisses Bradley, "the British neo-Hegelian, . . . on whom Eliot wrote a Harvard dissertation [sic]," by attributing to him a "cautious and elegant" prose style, which may have had a certain influence on Eliot's own writing. He quotes Hugh Kenner's view that "though Bradley's mind lies behind certain statements of Eliot's, the critical work is not a theory of poetry but a collection of incidental remarks and *ad hoc* writings . . ." (xvi); "the critical prose was empirical." (26) Perhaps the most interesting work he cites is Mowbray Allan's 1974 study, *T. S. Eliot's Impersonal Theory of Poetry,* in which Allan not only accepts the influence of Bradley on Eliot but actually talks of an Hegelian base to Eliot's criticism.

> In the "Conclusion" we are told that Eliot's critical theory is remarkably Hegelian, though "of course, the influence of Hegel would be mostly indirect, through Bradley." Further, "We may say, then, that if Eliot's critical theory is in the Romantic tradition, his critical practice is *an effort to escape from that theory* — that is, from subjectivism." [65]

But as Freed correctly observes: "Allan seems bent on blurring his own argument, and even on discounting it." Freed's own conclusion to his "Brief Review" of critical opinion about Eliot and Bradley ends with a quotation from Graham Hough, who says of Allan that he "makes a good case" for the thesis that Bradley's influence is without question "the strongest and most continuous guiding thread" in Eliot's own critical writing. (65)

More recent studies clearly support the thesis that Eliot was deeply influenced throughout his life by his philosophical studies. One of the best arguments along these lines is to be found in Richard Shusterman's "Eliot as Philosopher"[22] where we are told in no uncertain terms that "T .S. Eliot began his career by training as a professional philosopher rather than a poet or critic" and that he "pursued philosophical questions throughout his career." (31) Rejecting earlier criticism of Eliot's non-philosophical critical base, and the frequent assertion by critics of his non-dependence on Bradley, Shusterman asserts emphatically that "Eliot's criticism both early and late is thoroughly Bradleyan in character" and cites, as perhaps "the most important" connection, Bradley's "Hegelian holism . . . ." (33) Other recent critics on the subject have come to the subject with a certain bias, focusing more often than not on Eliot's struggle with idealism in order to dismiss it as an influence, at times quoting Eliot's own criticism of Bradley, at least once citing his rejection of the "absolutism" of Bradley and other German idealists, including Hegel.

Jewel Spears Brooker's *Mastery and Escape: T. S. Eliot and the Dialectic of Modernism,* is an illuminating book-length analysis of historical, religious, and philosophical questions that deserve to be explored by all critics of Eliot's work.[23] (Brooker provides the reader with a real bonus in those chapters where she seeks out philosophical and other influences in such major poems as *Gerontion, The Waste Land* and *Four Quartets.*) This author has no difficulty with the view that "Eliot found in Bradley a doctrine that, at least on the intellectual level, explains away the fragmentation and chaos that seem to characterize contemporary culture;" (135) but, following earlier leads, she is careful to distinguish between Bradley's British-Hegelianism and Hegel's own position, a distinction made by other critics as well, in their effort to explain Eliot's ultimate rejection of Bradley. "Bradley believed with Hegel," she explains, "that reality is an all-encompassing unity; but he disagreed with Hegel's first principle, that is, with the notion that the real is of the nature of thought, that it is intellectual — to use a Hegelian vocabulary, that the real is the rational." (176)[24] She further explores the distinction in a later chapter on "F. H. Bradley's Doctrine of Experience in T. S. Eliot's *The Waste Land* and *Four Quartets*" (191-206) where, in addition to clarifying the philosophical notions themselves, she attempts to apply them to Eliot's major poems. She concludes about *Four Quartets,* for example: "While [it] cannot be reduced to a versification of Bradley, Eliot's great philosophical poem is deeply indebted to Bradley's ideas." (206) Late in the book, in the course of appraising Jeffrey Perl's *Skepticism and Modern Enmity: Before and After Eliot* (John Hopkins Press, 1989), Brooker reminds us of Eliot's genial habit of writing in paradoxes, of saying a thing and its opposite in the same breath, and getting away with it — a subject that deserves the attention of all students of Eliot's prose style, especially (from our point of view) in its relation to A. C. Bradley's habit of spiraling to conclusions and Hegel's own expert handling of seemingly paradoxical arguments. There is no doubt that in using dialectical inversions and apparent contradictions, Eliot (like A.C. Bradley before him) hit on an ideal format for critical explication — an approach which may well be traced back to Hegel himself. Brooker's suggestion (and Perl's) could prove a fertile source of new insights in any reassessment of a critical prose that has often been mistakenly described as arbitrary and personal. Brooker herself suggests a wider application of this notion, crediting Perl for showing "that Eliot was philosophically not at all self-contradictory." (209)

Writing in 1992 on Eliot's critique of F. H. Bradley, Manju Jain joins those critics who emphasize Eliot's prejudicial view of metaphysical systems, quoting Eliot's own words where he "criticized not only Bradley but also Hegel and Spinoza for being romantic, in that they produced the 'one man' philosophy — a system, a world-view, which was a projection of the personality of its author."[25] Like other critics who have made a point of noting Eliot's wide-sweeping rejection of "systems," Jain does not comment on the validity of such a position. Eliot himself may have been sincere in putting down F. H. Bradley, Spinoza, Hegel, and others for their "systems" — after all, he himself struggled for years to find a truth that was compelling, objective, and explicit; but most writers who indulge in the popular bias against "systems" do so irrationally. In literary criticism contradictions are blatant: Marxists who denounce Hegel can somehow enthusiastically adopt "economic determinism" or simplistic and dead-end Freudian correspondences as their premise or analytical base. All critics have a "system" (if only their own small ones): the real question is: what system or theory holds together the greatest number of phenomena (or facts, as the Greek astronomers and our contemporary scientists would say) in a consistent and effortless way? This question is relevant in any discussion dealing with Hegel's influence on literary or any other form of criticism.

The confusion persists as writers try to bring together statements that are not easily assimilated without some effort at interpretation and analysis. In his book-length study, *T. S. Eliot and American Philosophy,* Jain writes that "far from being peripheral to an understanding of his *oeuvre,* Eliot's study of philosophy played a crucial role in nourishing his creative imagination and critical intellect."[26] But he agrees with Richard Wolheim that "any attempt . . . to deduce from [*Knowledge and Experience*] Eliot's own philosophy, or to trace connections between his thesis and his poetry and literary criticism, is a hazardous enterprise which must necessarily be tentative" (205). He cites Eliot himself, who cautions the reader "against the tendency to overestimate [Bradley's] debt to Hegel." (230)

In fact, most readers and critics have not in the least been tempted to overestimate Eliot's debt to Bradley or to Hegel. Where Bradleyan or Hegelian connections are made, they are usually glossed over quickly or worded in philosophical abstractions. John Kwan-Terry's attempt to establish a connection between Eliot and Hegel is a good example of such well-intentioned but abortive efforts. In his essay "Time, History and the Problematic of Truth: A Reading of *Four Quartets,*" Kwan-Terry quotes Geoffrey Hartman's explanation of the function of Romantic Art as

> analogous to that of religion. The traditional scheme of Eden, fall, and redemption merges with the new tradition of nature, fall, and imagination; while the last term in both involves a kind of return to the first . . .

and then goes on to explain:

> . . . if self-consciousness marks a fall from nature, then the only kind of return that would not be a regression to the immediacy of mere consciousness would be the return by way of still another turn of the self-consciousness. "Anti-self-consciousness," as Hartman terms it, is not un-selfconsciousness but rather self-consciousness of self-consciousness, the self-directed negation of the negativity of self-consciousness. As Hegel puts it in his interpretation of the Fall quoted by Hartman, "the hand that inflicts the wound is also the hand that heals it" or, as Eliot puts it in Part IV of "East Coker": "The wounded surgeon plies the steel/That questions the distempered part;/Beneath the bleeding hands we feel/ The sharp compassion of the healer's art/Resolving the enigma of the fever chart. (*FQ* 29)[27]

Part of the difficulty is Eliot's reluctance to acknowledge any debt to Bradley or to Hegel. It should be clear, however, even after this short and by no means exhaustive review of some of the critical literature on the subject, that the influence of Bradley on Eliot was pervasive and, moreover, that Eliot had probably read much more of Hegel than he would have his readers believe — a notion supported by Eliot's provocative admission, in the April 1935 issue of *The Criterion:* "I wish that I had taken Hegel more seriously in my youth, but like many people, I was caught napping."[28] Clearly, he had read some Hegel, but — in his own mature opinion — not enough. How much further he may subsequently have gone in his reading of Hegel can only be determined by a close scrutiny of his mature poetry and prose.

But even those critics who have explored to some extent and for different reasons the connection between Eliot, Bradley and Hegel, have yet to focus on this intriguing possibility in any systematic way.

There is one important connection with Hegel that Eliot himself acknowledges and which can serve us as an indicator of what waits to be discovered. In "Three Voices of Poetry," Eliot cites as his source for the definitions he puts forward of the literary genres the German expressionist poet and critic Gottfried Benn:

> It is in this sense [the voice of the poet talking to himself or nobody] that the German poet Gottfried Benn, in a very interesting lecture entitled *Probleme der Lyrik,* thinks of lyric as the poetry of the first voice . . . . [106][29]

Eliot's discussion leaves no doubt concerning his careful reading of Benn and the thorough use he made of his source.[30] What should be particularly noted in this context is that Benn, in his turn, had drawn his ideas directly from Hegel, whom he had studied with profit.

Directly or indirectly, Hegel seems to have furnished Eliot with some of his most brilliant critical statements (as well as his critical style). I will limit myself to just one example of what I have come to recognize as Eliot's stunning display of Hegelian virtuosity: his pages on *Hamlet.*[31] He concedes early on that certain problems of consistency and interpretation may be traced back to difficulties inherited in "the 'intractable' material of the old play [*The Spanish Tragedy,* by Thomas Kyd]." He argues: "Of the intractability there can be no doubt. So far from being Shakespeare's masterpiece, the play is most certainly an artistic failure." The play is "puzzling and disquieting as is none of the others. Of all the plays it is the longest and is possibly the one on which Shakespeare spent most pains; and yet he has left in it superfluous and inconsistent scenes which even hasty revision should have noticed." He ends that passage with the observation that

> probably more people have thought *Hamlet* a work of art because they found it interesting, than have found it interesting because it is a work of art. It is the "Mona Lisa" of literature. [123-124]

An artistic failure. The Mona Lisa of Literature. How does one reconcile these two seemingly contradictory statements?

One's first reaction (always a dangerous temptation where Eliot is involved) is to deny at least the first statement. *He's wrong,* one is tempted to say in response to such a judgment — until one realizes with a shock of discovery that Eliot has hit on a provocative conclusion through a pedestrian argument. Whether *The Spanish Tragedy* was a source for *Hamlet* we'll never really know; nor does it really matter. Arguments relating to the "intractable material" of the earlier play can never be conclusive, since Kyd's play has not come down to us. The end result is Shakespeare's, and whatever he accepted for himself as the final product must be judged in those terms. If we are justified in paying tribute to his genius in transforming as he did the raw materials of Holinshed, Stow, Plutarch, North, Italian short stories, etc., into powerful and compressed drama, on what grounds do we exclude *Hamlet* as it has come down to us? The play must be judged as it stands, without any trimming. Still, in what has become a popular exercise in open-ended guesswork, Eliot has as much right to indulge an opinion about undigested or "intractable" source materials as the next critic — and ultimately be dismissed with all the others. Of real interest, on the other hand, is the dialectical statement which illuminates the elusive pattern of his thought — a pattern which is his unmistakable stylistic *signature,* as well as a discursive habit.

The full implication of Eliot's genial conclusion about *Hamlet* can be grasped only by recalling the Hegelian notion of modern art having reached that point where it threatens to exceed its conventions, when we see *art transcending itself.* In discussing Shakespearean tragedy (which, as we saw, he equates with modern or Romantic art), Hegel explores every aspect of the reconstituted tragic hero, especially in his role as *schöne Seele,* the Socratic conscience seeking self-definition. Hegel cites Hamlet as one of the best examples of the "beautiful soul" searching for meaning and internal conviction in his own consciousness. We saw how the action of the play centers about that idiosyncratic character in search of definition, how in these terms the plot becomes a function of character. For Hegel, Hamlet is the *schöne Seele* par excellence, the Romantic hero trying to articulate the profoundest depths of the modern spiritual journey into the interior. In such a play, events have a minimal dramatic impact, the main protagonist is the center of attention, whatever he turns to becomes important. In such a play, not only does the hero shape the course of events, but he often remains curiously detached from the consequences of those events, although he is carried along by them.

To rephrase Eliot's pronouncement in this light, we might say that *Hamlet* the play is in Hegelian terms an artistic failure

precisely because it is the Mona Lisa of literature. The protagonist takes on a life of his own, tempting readers and critics alike
into identifying with him — something, by the way, which Eliot
himself warns us against. The play lacks what Eliot calls "artistic
'inevitability'," that "complete adequacy of the external to the
emotion," which we find in plays like *Macbeth*. "[T]his is precisely what is deficient in *Hamlet,*" Eliot tells us. "Hamlet (the
man) is dominated by an emotion which is inexpressible, because it is in *excess* of the facts as they appear." In *Hamlet,* the
"objective correlative . . . a set of objects, a situation, a chain of
events which shall be the formula of that particular emotion" is
missing. (124-125) Eliot may have had in mind what A. C. Bradley had earlier said about an "artistic flaw" in *King Lear*. That
play, Bradley had argued, "is admittedly one of the world's greatest poems," and yet it leaves us with a "total and final impression" that it is "composed almost wholly of painful feelings —
utter depression, or indignant rebellion, or appalled despair."
No other of the world's comparably great poems, he assures us,
"produces on the whole this effect, and we regard it as a very
serious flaw in any considerable work of art that this should be
its ultimate effect." A parenthetical, utterly Hegelian note makes
the meaning precise: "A flaw, I mean, in a work of art considered not as a moral or theological document but as a work of
art — an aesthetic flaw." (277-278 and n. 1)

Charles Warren informs us, in an interesting observation
in his *T. S. Eliot on Shakespeare,*[32] that Eliot was well acquainted
with A. C. Bradley's work (3) and at one time had recommended
"*Four Tragedies of Shakespeare* (sic) in the syllabus for his Elizabethan extension course, calling the book 'an excellent study.'"
But, Warren goes on,

> at the end of the essay on "Swinburne as Critic" Eliot questions
> whether Bradley is one of those critics "interested in extracting
> something from their subject which is not fairly in it" and in a
> "London Letter" of 1922 he calls *Four Tragedies* a "needless luxury"
> and ranks Bradley with those gentlemanly critics who lack "punch."
> [16]

This reminder of Eliot's estimate of A. C. Bradley's *Shakespearean
Tragedy* is significant for it not only proves that Eliot was familiar
with Bradley's work (not really surprising given his long preoc-
cupation with the writings of F. H. Bradley) but also establishes
a new line of influence, even if only indirectly, back to Hegel. To
Eliot's provocative analysis of *Hamlet,* Warren — like so many
other Shakespearean critics — has nothing new to add.

By contrast to Warren and others we have surveyed in this brief summary, Erich Heller is both refreshing and instructive in his comments on Eliot's treatment of Shakespeare's *Hamlet.* In his influential *The Artist's Journey into the Interior,* Heller says of Eliot's conclusion about *Hamlet* that the argument suffices "in all its strange wrong-headedness, to prove this poet's great critical intelligence. It reads as if T. S. Eliot had studied Hegel's theory of the difference between Classical and Romantic art . . . and then decided both to profit from it and to ignore it."[33] Further on, he enlarges on that comment with this illuminating summary:

> Clearly, T. S. Eliot knew what he was saying when he judged *Hamlet* an artistic failure because the hero's emotion exceeded his concrete situation or the "objective correlative." It is the more surprising that Eliot judged as he judged; for what he condemned is the occasion itself of Romantic art, including his own . . . . Perhaps he did not mean it. Mean what? It is the persistent and most troublesome question of the Romantic mind. For having lost its world, it can never do what it means; and what it means cannot be done. [136]

He concludes with this thoroughly Hegelian interpretation of Eliot's comments:

> Where T. S. Eliot diagnoses the "artistic failure" of the play, there lies in truth its achievement. Shakespeare, favored by his age . . . succeeded with *Hamlet* where Goethe . . . had to fail with *Torquato Tasso;* in creating, paradoxically speaking, the "objective correlative" for a subjectivity Romantically deprived of any adequate "objective correlative." [139]

By way of conclusion and as an important final appraisal of Hegel's abiding and profound interest in Shakespeare, I would like to quote from a critic who has shaped the thinking of literary experts and comparatists for well over half a century: Rene Wellek. In *A History of Modern Criticism,* Wellek writes:

> Hegel shows a remarkable grasp of the role of linguistic features (diction, word order, sentence structure) in poetry and elequently expounds the effects and charms of versification and rhyme. He makes the true observation that a "genuine artistic talent moves in his sensuous materials as in his most proper native element, which lifts and carries it rather than hinders and oppresses." He suggests that verse is implicated in the rhythm of the ideas, that it is a "music which, though in a distant way, echoes the dark yet definite course and character of the representations." He asserts the need for rhythm but not for exact measure in poetry and described well the clash between the metrical pattern and the rhythm of prose

which "gives the whole a new peculiar life."[34]

In the light of what has been put forth in this paper, I would suggest that Eliot no less than A. C. Bradley owes a great debt to Hegel and that the two are related as literary critics by virtue of that debt. Without laboring the point, let me conclude by saying unequivocally that Hegel considered Shakespeare the greatest dramatist of all time and *Hamlet* the profoundest tragedy ever written; that he saw in the tragedies of Shakespeare the grandest expression of the modern search for personal redemption in a Christian world; and that he recognized in the language of those plays the most powerful and wide-reaching dramatic expression ever conceived. He also, very simply, loved theater and made every effort to see English productions of Shakespeare whenever they came into Germany. His notebooks and journals carry descriptions of the mannerisms of English actors, their stage presence and style of delivery, and other details of performance. In that light, also, and in his infinitely suggestive pages on dramatic theory and practice, especially Shakespearean tragedy and comedy, he can redirect us, through Eliot and A. C. Bradley, to a rich lode of new critical possibilities

NOTES

1. Kenneth Muir, "Fifty Years of Shakespeare Criticism: 1900-1955," *Shakespeare Survey,* IV (1951) 4. See also: Augustus Ralli, *A History of Shakespeare Criticism,* vol. 2 (London: Oxford UP, 1932) 200ff.; F. E. Holliday, *Shakespeare and His Critics* (London: Gerald Ducksworth and Co., 1949) 264; Arthur M. Eastman, *A Short History of Shakespearean Criticism* (New York: Random House, 1968), Chapter 9, "Bradley," 186-204.

2. Israel Knox, *The Aesthetic Theories of Kant, Hegel and Schopenhauer* (New York, 1936), 109-111. Cf. Anne Paolucci/Henry Paolucci, eds., *Hegel on Tragedy* (New York: Doubleday Co. [Anchor Book], 1962; rpt. New York: Harper & Row [Torchbook], 1975; rpt. Greenwood P [hb only] Westport, Conn., 1978); rpt Griffon House Publications, 2001, 91.

3. Wolfgang H. Clemen, *The Development of Shakespeare's Imagery* (New York: Hill & Wang, 1953) 14.

4. A. C. Bradley, "Hegel's Theory of Tragedy," *Oxford Lectures on Poetry* (Bloomington, Indiana University Press, 1961) 69-95. The essay was reprinted in Anne Paolucci/Henry Paolucci, *Hegel on Tragedy,* 367-388. Unless otherwise noted, references to Bradley's essay and to Hegel are from *Hegel on Tragedy* and appear in parentheses in the text as (*HT,* p#.), in brackets [ ] at the end of indented quotations, or simply as (p.#).

5. Over 30 years ago I published an article on Bradley in which I first tried to correct a serious misreading of his interpretation of Hegel's

notion of "beauty" as it applies to Greek and modern tragedy. I had hoped at that time that Shakespeare critics particularly would be prodded into looking again at the plays with Bradley's pervasive Hegelianism in mind. This did not happen. See: Anne Paolucci, "Bradley and Hegel on Shakespeare," *Comparative Literature*, Vol. XVI, No.3, Summer 1964, 211-225, and Chapter 6 in the present volume.

6. The importance Bradley attached to the reading of Hegel and his sincere effort to grasp the full implications of the Hegelian theory may be measured, to some extent, by comparing the essay as it appeared in 1912, in the *Oxford Lectures on Poetry*, with an earlier version in *The Hibbert Journal* (II, 1903-1904, 662-680). The later version is decidedly less dogmatic and reflects a more appreciative estimate of Hegel's position. Any serious appraisal of Bradley's Hegelianism must take these two essays into account.

7. For passages on drama drawn from a wide variety of Hegelian texts, including *The Philosophy of Fine Art*, see Anne Paolucci/Henry Paolucci, *Hegel on Tragedy*. The Introduction (xi-xxxi) to this collection, which draws from a number of English translations of Hegel's works, including the *Phenomenology*, *The Philosophy of History*, etc., as well as *The Philosophy of Fine Art*, sums up many of the points discussed here on Hegel's views of Greek and Shakespeare tragedy. Also worth consulting is the translation of Hegel's *The Philosophy of Fine Art* ,4 vols. (London, 1920) by F. P. B. Osmaston; G. W. F. Hegel, *Aesthetics*, 2 vols., tr. T. M. Knox (Oxford: At the Clarendon Press, 1975); *Hegel on the Arts*, abridged and edited by Henry Paolucci (Frederick Ungar Publishing Co., New York, 1979 [hd and p], reprinted by Griffon House Publications, 2001.)

8. Hegel uses the same designations to describe the arts themselves. In ARCHITECTURE (the most "symbolic" of the arts) the raw matter is clearly identifiable — stone, brick, marble, etc., not fully transformed; in SCULPTURE (the "classical" form of art) the informing idea transforms the raw material into an identifiable human representation; in PAINTING (which together with music and poetry represents the romantic form) the medium is of a different kind — color — and form is expressed in a two dimensional representation on canvas); in MUSIC the medium — sound — is no longer spatial; in POETRY the medium is symbols represented by words, and these are the means for trasmitting ideas, (the most characteristically human form of expression). Among the literary genres, Hegel singles out drama as the highest form, since it contains all the other arts as well as the other genres. (See Chapter 2 in this volume.) For an application of Hegel's "dematerialization of the arts" to a reading of Dante's *Purgatorio*, see Anne Paolucci, "Art and Nature in the *Purgatorio*," *Italica* (Special issue: "Homage to Dante"), Vol. XLII, March 1965, No.1, 42-60. See Chapter 20 in this volume.

9. The importance of Hegel's phrase has gained recognition in recent years in studies dealing with Theater of the Absurd. One excellent example of how the idea seems to have suggested itself to some critics is Vivian Mercier's *Beckett/Beckett* (New York: Oxford UP, 1977). In my own work on Shakespeare, Pirandello, Edward Albee, Arthur Miller,

and Theater of the Absurd, I have made conscious use of this and other related ideas, applying the Hegelian notions to a variety of texts.

10. *Shakespearean Tragedy* (London, Macmillan and Co., 1950) 12. References to essays in this collection will appear in parentheses in the text as (*ST*, p#.) or simply as (p.#).

11. See also: Michael Taylor, "Bradley and Shakespearean Tragedy," *Modern Language Review*, Vol. 68, Number 4, October 1973, 734-740, especially, 737ff.

12. Of course Bradley's discussion of Falstaff and Shakespearean comedy generally should also be reviewed against Hegel's long passages on comedy, which he views as the reaction of a society to the excesses that threaten it. Aristophanic and Shakespearean comedy, according to Hegel, are the only two examples of how laughter can demolish the exaggerated and misdirected values of a people. The protagonist of this kind of profound and all-encompassing comic attack is never an object of ridicule, never laughed at by the audience (as in the farces of Molière, Hegel points out), but a character we can identify and laugh with. See Anne Paolucci, "Hegel's Theory of Comedy," *Comedy: New Perpectives*, ed. Maurice Charney, New York: New York Literary Forum, Vol. 1, Spring 1978, 89-108 and Chapter 3 in this volume; See also: E. F. Carritt, *Theory of Beauty* (London, 1923), especially: "To the barrenness of most accounts of humour I have found three grateful exceptions; . . . Mr. A. C. Bradley's 'Rejection of Falstaff . . . is a perfect illustration, by a concrete instance, of the truth; but he refrains from theorizing. The two theories are those of Hegel and Bergson." (312) See also: Anne Paolucci, "Comedyand Paradox in Pirandello's Plays (A Hegelian Perspective)," *Luigi Pirandello*, ed. with an Introduction by Harold Bloom (Chelsea House Publishers, NY and Philadelphia, 1989) 47-66. See Chapter 15 in this volume.

13. Henry Paolucci, *Hegel on the Arts*, 181. See also T. M. Knox, *Aesthetics*, Vol. II, 1199; Anne Paolucci/Henry Paolucci, *Hegel on Tragedy*, 51-52.

14. Clifford Leech, "Studies in Hamlet, 1901-1955," *Shakespeare Survey*, IX (1956) 3.

15. Muir, 4.

16. See also: Katherine Cooke, *A. C. Bradley and his Influence on Twentieth-century Shakespeare Criticism* (Oxford UP, 1972); "Introduction," *Hegel on the Arts*, vii-xxi, esp. x-xi, xvii-xviii.

17. A. David Moody, ed. *The Cambridge Companion to T. S. Eliot* (Cambridge UP, 1994) xv.

18. Bernard Bosanquet, tr. *The Introduction to Hegel's Philosophy of Fine Art* (London, 1886).

19. *Knowledge and Experience in the Philosophy of F. H. Bradley* (London: 1964). The 1916 dissertation was titled "Experience and the Objects of Knowledge in the Philosophy of F. H. Bradley."

20. Lewis Freed, *T. S. Eliot: The Critic as Philosopher* (West Lafayette, Indiana: Purdue UP, 1979), especially "Introduction" (xv-xix) and Ch. 3, "Eliot and Bradley: A Brief Review" (44-65). See also: Northrop Frye, *T S. Eliot* (Edinburgh: Oliver & Boyd, 1963), 43-45; John D. Margolis, *T. S. Eliot's Intellectual Development, 1922-1939* (Chicago: University of Chicago P, 1972) 14n.

21. Anne C. Bolgan, "What the Thunder Really Said: Mr. Eliot's Philosophical Writings" (Toronto, 1960). The dissertation later was published under the title *What the Thunder Really Said: A Retrospective Essay on the Making of 'The Waste Land'* (1973).

22. Moody, 31-47.

23. Jewel Spears Brooker, *Mastery and Escape: T. S. Eliot and the Dialectic of Modernism* (Amherst: U Mass. P, 1994). Of special interest for this discussion is the last section of the book, "Mastery and Escape: Eliot's Dialectical Imagination," 165-206.

24. See especially the section on "T. S. Eliot and the Revolt Against Dualism: His Dissertation on F. H. Bradley in its Intellectual Context," 172-190.

25. Manju Jain, " ' . . .that magnificent vision, into the apparent chaos,' T. S. Eliot's Critique of F. H. Bradley," *New Essays on T. S. Eliot*, eds. Vinod Sena and Rajiva Verma (Oxford UP, 1992), 68.

26. Manju Jain, *T. S. Eliot and American Philosophy* (Cambridge UP, 1992), x.

27. John Kwan-Terry, "Time, History and the Problematic of Truth: A Reading of *Four Quartets*," in *New Essays on T. S. Eliot*, eds. Vinod Sena and Rajiva Verma (Delhi, Oxford UP, 1992), 176-177. See also, Geoffrey Hartman, "Romanticism and Anti-Self-Consciousness," in *Romanticism and Conscsiousness*, ed. Harold Bloom (New York, 1970) 49, 54, etc.

28. T .S. Eliot, *The Criterion*, XIV , Apri; 1935, 433.

29. "The Three Voices of Poetry," *On Poetry and Poets* {New York: Noonday Press, 1961) 96-112, especially pp. 106-107, where Benn is cited and discussed.

30. See also: Henry Paolucci, "The Poetics of Aristotle and Hegel," *Hegel in Comparative Literature* (*Review of National Literatures*), Vol. I, No.2, Fall 1970, 190; (rpt in Henry Paolucci: *Selected Writings*, Griffon House Publications, Smyrna, DE, 2000); Anne Paolucci, "The Monologue Art of German Expressionism and Anglo-American Modernism, *German Expressionism* (*Review of National Literatures*) ed. Victor Lange (New York: Council on National Literatures, 1979) 10-24; See also Eliot, "The Three Voices of Poetry" {1961) 112.

31. T. S. Eliot, "Hamlet and His Problems," *Selected Essays* (New York: Harcourt, Brace and Company, 1950) 121-126.

32. Charles Warren, *T. S. Eliot on Shakespeare*. Studies in Modern Literature, No.66. {Ann Arbor/London, UMI Research Press, 1987).

33. Erich Heller, *The Artist's journey Into the Interior* (New York, 1965)

130. See also: Anne Paolucci/Henry Paolucci, "Poet-Critics on the Frontiers of Literature: A. D. Hope, T. S. Eliot, and William Carlos Williams," *Australia* (*Review of National Literatures*), ed. L. A. C. Dobrez (New York: Council on National Literatures, 1982) 146-191, especially p. 181.

34. Rene Wellek, *A History of Modern Criticism, 1750-1950*, Vol. II, The Romantic Age (New Haven: Yale UP, 1955), p. 323. See also: H. Paolucci, "The Poetics of Aristotle and Hegel," in *RNL* (1970) 189.

CHAPTER 8

MACBETH AND OEDIPUS REX;
A STUDY IN PARADOX

The names of Sophocles and Shakespeare — the greatest of ancient and the greatest of modern tragedians — have been linked so often in dramatic criticism that one is apt to wonder whether any conceivable connection between them can have remained unexplored. Comparative analysis seems to have been exhaustive; and yet, a review of the main currents of criticism dealing with these two dramatists leaves one with the decided impression that the currents have run almost exclusively in one direction. Bent on tracing the differences, critics by and large have tended to overlook the similarities. It has, in fact, become a commonplace to say that Shakespearean tragedy is really a new dramatic form, that the clearly defined ethical values embodied in the action of Sophoclean tragedy have been replaced, in Shakespeare's tragedies, by the internal conscious life of personality, with all its quirks and idiosyncrasies, and that even where modern dramatists have treated classical themes — as Goethe in his *Iphigenia* — the result is a probing psychological study rather than the spectacle of contending ethical forces. In the light of such conclusions, attempts to establish parallels may seem an impertinence.

The difficulty looms especially large in the case of the plays linked together here. What can the beautifully restrained movement of *Oedipus Rex* conceivably have in common with the violent action of *Macbeth*? Where in Sophocles' play can we find so much as a trace of that "prodigious energy" of evil, which — according to Bradley — characterizes the Shakespearean tragedy?[1] Where does Oedipus betray anything like the ambition, cruelty, and introspection of Macbeth? If comparisons must be drawn, might not Shakespeare's *Julius Caesar* serve as a more likely parallel? Its stoic restraint, the delicate balance of opposing forces, its rhetorical grandeur[2] and dramatic economy recall at once the marvelous simplicity of Sophoclean tragedy. In his rigorous sense of duty and justice, the noble Brutus bears a striking resemblance to Oedipus: both commit "crimes" for reasons hard to condemn; both are lacking in what may be described as evil purpose; both suggest intense emotions held in check, intentions buried in the self-righteous soul, an aversion to anything ignoble and selfish.

No such obvious parallels are to be found in *Macbeth* and *Oedipus Rex*. Their heroes appear to us, at first, as worlds apart in their motivations. But there are parallels; indeed, the apparent differences resolve, on closer examination, into significant paradoxes. The resemblances between the two plays are not to be sought in isolated elements of structure and characterization but in the central themes that sustain the dramatic action. In each the unifying principle is a paradox which manifests itself variously in the shifting attitude of the hero toward the supernatural, the ambiguous nature of those mysterious forces which seem to inspire him to action, the dramatic function of the prophecies, the elaborate play of contrasts and the use of dramatic juxtaposition, the changing role of the woman who shares the hero's tragic fate, the two-fold movement of the action — and, finally, in the poetic language of contradiction. For *Macbeth,* surely, is the finest example in modern drama of that awe-inspiring irony which has come to be associated almost exclusively with *Oedipus Rex*.

The most fruitful subject for comparative study of the two plays is, unquestionably, the nature of the prophecies and the response of the hero to them. In a brilliant passage in the *Phenomenology,* where he sums up the difference between ancient and modern tragedy, Hegel — for example — notes that

> the priestess, through whose mouth the beautiful god speaks [in the Delphic Oracle], is in nothing different from the equivocal sisters of fate [the witches in *Macbeth*],[3] who drive their victim by their promises, and who, by the double-tongued, equivocal character of what they gave out as a certainty, deceive the king when he relies upon the manifest and obvious meaning of what they say.[4]

On the surface, it must be admitted, the prophecies in the two plays resist comparison. In *Oedipus Rex* they appear to be objective oracular utterances heard distinctly but, as it were, from an awesome distance; in *Macbeth* they seem to be more immediate and personal but, at the same time, less clearly defined.[5]

Creon returns from Delphi with the straightforward message:

> The god commands us to expel from the land of Thebes
> An old defilement that it seems we shelter.[6]

Iocaste gives this literal report of the prediction concerning her husband and son:

> An oracle was reported to Laios once
> (I will not say from Phoibos himself but from
> His appointed ministers, at any rate)
> That his doom would be death at the hands of his own son —
> His son, born of his flesh and mine! (36)

Oedipus recalls Apollo's unmistakable warning that

> . . . I should lie with my own mother, breed
> Children from whom all men would turn their eyes;
> And that I should be my father's murderer. (41)

Iocaste underscores the clear words of the oracle when she points out that it would be impossible ever to show

> . . . that Laios' death
> Fulfilled the oracle; for Apollo said
> My child was doomed to kill him; and my child —
> Poor baby — it was my child that died first. (43)

Oedipus reviews the god's unambiguous words again in the presence of the Messenger:

> Apollo said through his prophet that I was the man
> Who should marry his mother, shed his father's blood
> With his own hands. (50)

The shepherd who finally unravels the terrible story says simply:

> It was said that the boy would kill his own father. (62)

Only once is the literal statement violated, when Oedipus, learning that Polybus has died a natural death, interprets the original prophecy and introduces the error on which the whole play rests:

> They prophesied that I should kill Polybus,
> Kill my own father; but he is dead and buried,
> And I am here — l never touched him, never,
> Unless he died of grief for my departure,
> And thus, in a sense, through me. No, Polybus
> Has packed the oracles off with him underground. (48)

The ambiguity in the prophecies of *Oedipus Rex* lies, obviously, not in the utterances themselves, but in the limited awareness on the part of Oedipus — and others — of the surrounding circumstances and of the past.

In *Macbeth*, on the other hand, the ambiguity lies to a large extent in the prophecies themselves. I do not mean to suggest that they are not literally true; but there is in them an unmistakable intention to deceive — as in the paradoxical words directed to Banquo:

> 1 Witch. Lesser than Macbeth and greater.
> 2 Witch. Not so happy, yet much happier.

3 Witch. Thou shalt get kings, though thou be none.

(I, iii, 65-67)[7]

The witches, and the apparitions they call upon, seem intent on bolstering Macbeth's ego, appealing to his daring and courage to predispose him to realize his ruthless ambition:

> Be bloody, bold, and resolute; laugh to scorn
> The pow'r of man, for none of woman born
> Shall harm Macbeth.   (IV, i, 79-81)

> Be lion-mettled, proud, and take no care
> Who chafes, who frets, or where conspirers are.
> Macbeth shall never vanquish'd be until
> Great Birnam Wood to high Dunsinane Hill
> Shall come against him.   (IV, i, 90-94)

The very first utterances of the witches — the most direct and simple statements of past, present, and future facts — contain an ambiguity in the subtle suggestion that *both* the two new titles with which they hail Macbeth will come to him in the natural course of things.

There is no parallel in the oracles of *Oedipus Rex* for this element of intentional equivocation aimed at spurring Macbeth on and giving him a false sense of confidence. Except for this suggestion of deception, however, the witches' prophecies resemble closely those in *Oedipus Rex*. In both cases, the hero accepts and acts upon a *partial* truth as though it were a *whole* truth, and the entire action is nothing more than the gradual unfolding of all the implications of that full truth. By rolling back time, as it were, Oedipus exposes at last the full meaning of the prophecies; just as Macbeth, in tracking down the victories predicted for him, discovers in the end that they spell out his doom.

The "equivocal character" of the prophecies is curiously reflected in what appears to be a wavering on the part of both Oedipus and Macbeth toward them and in the heroes' constantly shifting response to the supernatural agencies that make them known.

Oedipus, it will be recalled, fluctuates all through the play between rational self-sufficiency and confidence, on the one hand, and fear of the gods, on the other. When the evidence seems to lean in his favor, he scorns the omens, insults Tiresias and Creon, scoffs at the rituals and ceremonies connected with the reading of the future; but when he is impotent against the force of circumstances, when he finds himself powerless, for example, against the plague which is destroying Thebes, when the weight of the facts about his life becomes unbearable and the mysterious voice within him urges caution, then he is all too ready to fall back on the methods of the seer and the priests.[8] But this wavering is only apparent. In reality, Oedipus has admitted the power of the gods in the very attempt to flee the prophecies, for in leaving Corinth he was in fact affirming his acceptance of the Delphic utterance and placing himself — unconsciously, of course — under the shadow of the oracle. It is this knowledge, brought to the surface of consciousness through rational arguments and evidence, that frees him at last from superstitious bondage to the gods.

In Macbeth's case, the shift from acceptance to rejection of the prophecies is not drawn so sharply as the reversal reflected in the attitude of Oedipus; but there is, from the very beginning, an interesting parallel. We have seen that what appears to be a "rejection" of the oracle in Oedipus' flight from Corinth turns out to be an affirmation of its power; in a similar way, what appears to be "acceptance" of the witches' prophecies on Macbeth's part turns out to be — on closer analysis — something quite different.

First of all, we should remind ourselves that Macbeth — as Bradley has observed — is no mere spectator. The encounter with the "weird sisters" and the hero's response to them is simply the acknowledgment of a deep-rooted psychological disorder which Macbeth is acutely conscious of but which he only vaguely understands.

> The words of the Witches are fatal to the hero only because there is in him something which leaps into light at the sound of them; but they are at the same time the witness of forces which never cease to work in the world around him, and, on the instant of his surrender to them, entangle him inextricably in the web of Fate.[9]

This recognition, though only imperfectly understood by Macbeth himself, immediately establishes a relationship between the external and internal reality, the witches and the hero, in the same way that Oedipus' decision to flee the oracle established an inextricable bond between himself and Apollo. Macbeth's "acceptance" of the prophecies, like Oedipus' "rejection" of the oracle is, in other words, the unconscious recognition of an identity between an objective utterance coming from the outside and the subjective voice or inner consciousness of the hero. The point cannot be stressed enough, for it serves to explain the apparent contradiction and wavering we have noted already in the case of Oedipus, and which may be discerned also in the case of

Macbeth.

On at least two occasions, Macbeth rejects the prophecies of the witches by initiating action which directly contradicts those prophecies. He is told to beware of Macduff, but even as he listens he decides to seek him out and kill him. Even more striking is his determination to kill Fleance in an effort to destroy the source of what the witches (those same witches who had hailed him King of Scotland and whose utterances he appears to value) had predicted would be a long line of Scottish sovereigns.[10]

This apparent contradiction, which seems to be at the root of both characterizations, cannot be resolved so long as we see in the oracle or in the witches' utterances a categorical imperative, a tyrannical "law" against which the hero strives vainly. In an obvious sense, of course, both Oedipus and Macbeth are crushed by the unrelenting force of destiny; but that is only part of the picture. Both absorb only what they are psychologically and emotionally prepared to absorb at any one moment; and the whole play, in each case, is simply the transformation, or rather, the *internalization* of what at first appears only as something external. This point is beautifully illustrated in *Oedipus Rex,* where — in the very first scene of the play — Tiresias accuses Oedipus, in the most obvious, blunt terms:

> I say that you are the murderer whom you seek.
> ....
> I say that you live in hideous love with her
> Who is nearest you in blood. (19)

For Oedipus, however, the accusation remains a mere riddle. It takes the remainder of the play for him to absorb fully the truth of those statements and to accept them as his own. When he does, he is literally transformed into the image of Tiresias — the accuser — just as Macbeth comes to reveal his true image, finally, through the same demonic power which characterizes the witches and isolates them from the world of humanity.[11] This gradual internalization of the oracular *dictum* is illustrated in *Macbeth* in the hero's response to the two parts of the witches' prophecy. The negative portion of that prophecy is not questioned immediately — it is directed, in fact, to Banquo; the positive part of the prophecy at first overshadows the reference to Banquo, and the action that follows traces — as R. G. Moulton has pointed out — an upward movement in the fortunes of Macbeth, which corresponds exactly to the first half of the play. But, at a certain moment, the implications of the Banquo prophecy begin to stir within him; he seeks out the witches, who con-

firm his worst suspicions. The action that follows traces a complete reversal of fortune, bringing into sharp focus what had
been announced briefly but clearly at the beginning,

> Macbeth's series of successes is unbroken till it ends in the murder
> of Banquo; his series of failures is unbroken from its commence-
> ment in the escape of Fleance.[12]

This dialectical movement, which in time brings into prominence
the negative part of the witches' prophecy, corresponds exactly
to the gradual recognition by Oedipus of Tiresias' devastating
utterance. In both plays, we are conscious of what Moulton has
called "Oracular Action," in which Destiny or Providence is seen
"working from mystery to clearness," from an objective authoritarian statement to a subjective reality defined through human
actions.[13]

This seeming contradiction suggested by the wavering attitude of the hero toward the prophecies has other, deeper, implications. Both Oedipus and Macbeth display a striking reli-
ance on their own powers and manifest great daring and personal courage. Both reflect a willful and determined effort to
fulfill their plans — plans, it is important to stress, that they themselves have defined. And yet, in some strange way, both heroes,
operating on their own initiative, fulfill a plan which is *not* their
own. Oedipus, determined to prove the truth of his own rational insight, succeeds instead in proving — through reason — the
truth of divine insight and the failure of human logic. Macbeth
too fulfills the prophecies while acting, to all appearances, completely on his own. Fleance, whom he is bent on killing, escapes,
thus affirming the validity of the predictions and tightening the
mysterious bond between the weird spokesmen of the future
and the human instrument through which fate has chosen to
realize its purpose. Even when the full force of the prophecies
has become clear to him, Macbeth acts decisively and boldly,
buckling on his armor and going forth willfully to carry out the
very destruction predicted for him.

> "Fear not till Birnam wood
> Do come to Dunsinane!" and now a wood
> Comes toward Dunsinane. Arm, arm, and out!
> If this which he avouches does appear,
> There is nor flying hence nor tarrying here.   (V, v, 44-48)
>
>   I will not yield,
> To kiss the ground before young Malcolm's feet
> And to be baited with the rabble's curse.
> Though Birnam Wood be come to Dunsinane,
> And thou oppos'd, being of no woman born,

> Yet I will try the last. Before my body
> I throw my warlike shield. Lay on, Macduff,
> And damn'd be him that first cries 'Hold, enough!'
>
> (V, viii, 27-34)

What we see in this apparent movement between acceptance and rejection of the prophecies, between self-determined
action and inflexible predetermined ends, is of course the dilemma of human freedom and divine necessity or fate. Oedipus
runs headlong into his awful destiny even as he seeks to escape
it, confident of his rational understanding; Macbeth brings about
the predictions of the witches through his own independent actions. Human volition, while remaining utterly free, thus becomes
the instrument for realizing a mysterious, higher plan. "The supernatural has no power over men except by their own consent."[14]

There are other interesting parallels between the prophecies in the two plays. In *Oedipus Rex,* the oracle has foretold
the most horrible actions on the part of the hero, but Oedipus
interprets them in such a way that he seems to have turned the
"evil" prophecy into an actual "good." The witches in *Macbeth,*
on the other hand, predict an apparent "good" which Macbeth
proceeds to translate into evil deeds.[15] In both cases, moreover,
the hero himself later takes the initiative and seeks out the prophetic intermediaries. Oedipus sends to Delphi, at the beginning of the play, and calls upon Tiresias for help in his effort to
put an end to the plague which is ravaging Thebes, thus triggering the chain reaction leading to the truth about his past and, in
so doing, relating the earlier prophecies to the new ones. Macbeth
arrogantly demands a second interview with the witches, after
the murder of Duncan, and in discovering more about the fate
of Banquo's posterity, initiates a new, negative sequence of events
which destroys his earlier advantage; the two contradictory prophecies, like the oracular utterances, are seen, ultimately, as one
consistent revelation.

But perhaps the most significant parallel to emerge from
the paradoxical juxtaposition of human volition acting on its
own initiative and divine purpose or fate is the hero's assumption of responsibility. I have dealt at greater length, elsewhere,
with the question of Oedipus' apparent innocence;[16] here, I would
simply remind the reader that in spite of valiant efforts by overly
sympathetic critics to rationalize away Oedipus' responsibility
for his deeds, he himself refuses to do so, embarrassing his zeal-
ous apologists by assuming the full burden of blame. Coming to

know the truth, he cries out — in language not unlike that of
Macbeth as he prepares to go forth to battle after Lady Macbeth's
suicide —

> Blind I was, and can not tell why;
> Asleep, for you had given ease of breath;
> A fool, while the false yea:rs went by. (65)

And, reviewing the entire sequence of events, at the very end of
the play, he concludes:

> For the love of God, conceal me
> Somewhere far from Thebes; or kill me; or hurl me
> Into the sea, away from men's eyes for ever.
>
> Come lead me. You need not fear to touch me.
> Of all men, I alone can bear this guilt. (72)

As P. H. Frye has observed, Sophocles "never thought of denying Oedipus' responsibilty".[17] For the Greeks, an act could not
be separated from its consequences; the two were one thing —
what Hegel has called the "completed deed."[18] Intentions could
not change the ethical significance of an action. In Oedipus'
case, moreover, the crime actually is a clear reflection of the
character and temperament of the hero, whose every deed is a
proud assertion of self-confidence. As Frye points out:

> [Oedipus] has the temerity to act by his own lights with infatuate
> confidence in the clarity of his own vision — he, the puppet of des-
> tiny, blindfold from birth. who has never taken a step with a full
> sense of the conditions and consequences of his action. It is this
> pretender to clairvoyance, this dabbler in enigmas, the reader of
> the riddling Sphinx whom Sophocles represents as pretending light-
> heartedly to unravel the mystery of his own being.[19]

In Macbeth's case, of course, we cannot for a moment plead
the same extenuating circumstances which critics have put forward in their attempts to clear Oedipus of blame. Macbeth's
intentions match his deeds, and both are vicious. And yet — if
we are to make a point of consistency — he, no less than Oedipus, might understandably put forward the prophecies to excul-
pate himself. He does in fact remark, at one point:

> . . . be these juggling fiends no more believ'd,
> That palter with us in a double sense,
> That keep the word of promise to our ear
> And break it to our hope! (V, viii, 19-22)

— but it is nothing more than a bitter comment on his own sus-
ceptibility. He does not thereby excuse his conduct.[20] Like, Oedipus, he knows and admits the full extent of his transgressions:

> I have supp'd full with horrors.

> Direness, familiar to my slaughterous thoughts,
> Cannot once start me.   (V, v, 13-15)

In his final encounter with Macduff, he confesses his crimes:

> Of all men else I have avoided thee.
> But get thee back! My soul is too much charg'd
> With blood of thine already.   (V, viii, 4-6)

In assuming responsibility for their deeds, Oedipus and Macbeth are, in fact, asserting that man is free to act as he chooses and to direct his will. It may seem purely academic to suggest that without such freedom there would be no tragedy; but the fact remains that tragedy does insist on the condition of human freedom. Aristotle (who must be reckoned with, still, in these matters) made it the central point in his consideration of the tragic hero and the tragic conflict; and, closer to our own time, Hegel has affirmed its importance in both ancient and modern tragedy. The psychological resolution in *Oedipus Rex* and *Macbeth* lies precisely in the realization on the part of the hero that freedom — to use Spinoza's phrase — is insight into necessity. Both come to understand that puny man, who thinks himself free, is in reality fettered by another, greater, power. For Macbeth that power is a cold, indifferent, wholly arbitrary force. It sets the stage for our antics but remains itself unfathomable:

> Life's but a walking shadow, a poor player,
> That struts and frets his hour upon the stage
> And then is heard no more. It is a tale
> Told by an idiot, full of sound and fury,
> Signifying nothing.   (V, v, 24-28)

For Oedipus, it is the power of Nemesis and justice, an ethical force which — though not identical with it — is recognizable as a human moral absolute. It gives meaning to the drama in which he has been caught up and turns retribution into justice:

> . . . [God's] command is plain: the patricide
> Must be destroyed. I am that evil man. (74)

He himself carries out punishment upon himself. "O fearful act!" cries the Choragos on seeing the blinded, broken man emerge from the palace —

> What god was it drove you to rake black night across your eyes?

The answer is not only a declaration of reconstituted faith, but also an assertion of freedom gained through insight:

> Apollo. Apollo. Dear
> Children, the god was Apollo. (69)

Oedipus and Macbeth are most free — and most eloquent — when they come to know their limitations.

An interesting commentary on the attitude of Oedipus and Macbeth toward the prophecies, the gods, and fate, is the manner in which Iocaste and Lady Macbeth respond to the supernatural and the reversal they undergo from complete self-confidence to despair. Iocaste wavers toward the oracle in very much the same way as Oedipus. In the early scenes, she is even more skeptical than the king about trusting it:

> If it is a question of soothsayers, I tell you
> That you will find no man whose craft gives knowledge
> Of the unknowable. (36)
> . . . where oracles are concerned,
> I would not waste a second thought on any. (43)

She visits the altar of Apollo, at one point, presumably to ask the god to rid Oedipus of his foolish premonition of disaster; but with the coming of the Messenger from Corinth and the announcement of Polybus' death, she exults with her former assurance:

> O riddlers of God's will, where are you now!
> This was the man whom Oedipus, long ago,
> Feared so, fled so, in dread of destroying him —
> But it was another fate by which he died. (47)

She greets Oedipus with undisguised contempt for the oracle:

> Listen to what this man says, and then tell me
> What has become of the solemn prophecies. (47)

But throughout the swift denouement which follows the Messenger's well-meaning revelation that Polybus was not Oedipus' father, she is strangely silent, speaking again only when the pieces of the riddle are about to fall into place — and then only to keep Oedipus from continuing the interrogation. When she realizes the hopelessness of preventing him from discovering what she has already fathomed, she rushes into the palace where she commits suicide.

In her strong will, her desire to help and protect her husband, her common-sense attitude all through the early part of the play, Lady Macbeth bears a striking resemblance to Iocaste. She too provides her husband with moral support at those moments when he is uncertain and indecisive. Shakespeare, of course, draws the dramatic and psychological implications of the situation much more fully than does Sophocles. Lady Macbeth takes the initiative at once, with the reading of Macbeth's letter, and concentrates all her energies into urging Macbeth to accomplish those things which she knows are dear to him. She is dauntless in the face of obstacles, battering Macbeth's weakness,

shaming him into doing what in fact he has already realized in
his imagination and will. She scoffs at his vivid fears, at his powerful hallucinations, at the trance-like effect which the simple
tolling of a bell has upon him. She scorns the suggestion of any
supernatural power watching and judging his actions. The witches
themselves are scarcely mentioned;[21] they are remembered at
the very end of her soliloquy almost as an after thought:

> Hie thee hither,
> That I may pour my spirits in thine ear
> And chastise with the valour of my tongue
> All that impedes thee from the golden round
> Which fate and metaphysical aid doth seem
> To have thee crown'd withal.   (I, v, 26-31)

Like Iocaste, Lady Macbeth relies on her own powers, on the
efficacy of the human and the rational, in getting things done.
She is contemptuous of what is outside the scope of human understanding. For Macbeth to waste time worrying about the voice
he heard cry out "Sleep no more!" (II, ii, 41) is "brainsickly"
(46); the sleeping and the dead are but "pictures" —

> 'Tis the eye of childhood
> That fears a painted devil. (54-55)

The banquet scene calls forth all her energies in one last test of
emotional strength. She rises impressively to the occasion, shield-
ing Macbeth's weakness from the guests and urging him to courage and manliness. At this point — as though to underscore the
high pitch reached in this display of public endurance —
Shakespeare removes her from the action, bringing her back
into it after a considerable lapse of time and then only for the
brief sleepwalking scene. This long absence, like Iocaste's "on-
stage" silence, is eloquent. And her words, when she finally does
speak again, betray — as in Iocaste's case — the reversal which
has taken place. "A little water clears us of this deed" (67) she
had mocked, after Duncan's murder; now, in her fitful sleep,
that simple phrase takes on terrible significance:

> Yet here's a spot.   (V, i, 35)
>
> Out, damned spot! out, I say! (38)
>
> What, will these hands ne'er be clean? (48-49)
>
> Here's the smell of the blood still. All
> the perfumes of Arabia will not sweeten this
> little hand. Oh, oh, oh! (56-58)
>
> Wash your hands. . . . (68)

This unconscious confession provides a kind of temporary relief — something which Iocaste is denied. In the end, however, the powers she had scoffed at and ignored seize and break her in exactly the same way that they destroy Iocaste; in their suicide, both of them prove that their human confidence, their more than womanly strength, were mere illusions. Their violent end is the last impressive commentary on the course of action defined by Oedipus and Macbeth. It illustrates vividly that the one-sided exclusive claim of reason and common-sense will be destroyed by the inevitable swing to the opposite extreme; with the one-sided, exclusive counterclaim of the gods and conscience, the cycle is completed and moral balance restored.

The psychological reversals, the paradox of human will and predetermined fate, the contradiction implied by the simultaneous acceptance and rejection of the prophecies, are reinforced in both plays through skillful dramatic juxtaposition and, on the level of language, through unintentional irony. In *Oedipus Rex,* we watch in terrible fascination as, one after the other, Creon, Tiresias, Iocaste, the Messenger from Corinth, and the old shepherd make their appearance on stage — as if drawn by some invisible magnetic force — each bringing with him a piece of the riddle Oedipus is bent on solving. This awesome procession has no rest until the pieces are all there before us and the answer clear. But the movement of the action is not a simple linear progression; the cumulative effect of the "evidence" produced is intensified by a spiral-like motion, the result of alternating reactions of hope and despair. Creon brings the explanation of the oracle and thereby gives Oedipus something substantial to work with in his efforts to rid Thebes of the plague; Tiresias brings about a sharp but momentary set-back in his unexpected interpretation of that message; Iocaste restores the confidence of the king in one detail but arouses a painful doubt in his mind with regard to another; the Messenger restores Oedipus' confidence by bringing news of Polybus' natural death but destroys it almost immediately with the well-meaning revelation that Polybus was not really the king's father; the shepherd, finally, brings the full truth to light.

Shakespeare's use of dramatic juxtaposition — what one critic has aptly called "dramatic abruption"[22] — is no less impressive. Ross hails Macbeth Thane of Cawdor just after the witches have greeted the hero with that title and while Macbeth is still adjusting himself to the strange greeting; the messenger comes to Lady Macbeth with news of Duncan's imminent arrival even as she gives voice to the horrible plan she has conceived, independently of Macbeth, for getting rid of the king; Banquo's ghost appears immediately following the murder and — as it were — at Macbeth's invitation; the Porter scene, coming upon Duncan's murder, intensifies the dramatic tension with its grotesque parody of reality, particularly with the reference to "hell-gate." This last scene, representing among other things the intrusion of external upon internal reality, of the normal activity of the outside world upon the nightmarish happenings within the castle, is — as De Quincey has beautifully illustrated in his essay on the passage — the most perfect expression of dramatic economy and irony in the entire play.[23] The dramatic effect of juxtaposition is heightened, moreover — as in *Oedipus Rex* — by a skillful alternating of emotional extremes. Macbeth broods about how he can get the crown, even as he accepts the title of Cawdor; having attained the crown, all he can think of is his "rival" Banquo; having destroyed Banquo, he discovers a new threat in Macduff and wreaks his irrational vengeance on the family left behind; he prepares to go forth into battle still certain of his invulnerability, even as he mourns Lady Macbeth's death. Both plays rely on a cumulative, spiral-like movement for compression; both employ dramatic juxtaposition to its fullest, setting up tensions between appearance and reality through sharp, even abrupt, movement of action.

At least two other points relating to dramatic construction deserve to be mentioned. One is the use of prophecies at the very beginning of the action — a device which suggests at once a sense of fatality, of mysterious forces competing with the human will. The other is a paradoxical movement in opposite directions. In Sophocles' play this may be seen in the simultaneous forward and backward movement of the action. The swift progression toward a denouement is also a moving *back;* what is revealed in the end is what had been buried in time, long before. The whole play traces, as it were, a full circle, coming to rest where it began. *Macbeth* displays a similar peculiarity in the double, pendulum-like swing in opposite directions which defines the change of roles of the two chief protagonists. Lady Macbeth, at the end of the play, represents the realized potential of the early Macbeth; while Macbeth recalls in the Medusa-like firmness of the later portrayal, the inflexible will of the early Lady Macbeth. It is as though the threads of one characterization had been confounded, at a certain moment, with those of the other. The callous Macbeth of the end of the play is, in a sense, a commentary on the unswerving strength of will we see in Lady Macbeth right through the banquet scene; the distraught woman of the sleepwalking scene is, in the same sense, a reflection of the vivid internal life which characterizes Macbeth all through the early scenes.

These features of construction and movement all serve to bring into relief the contradiction implicit in the theme itself, reminding us — in the strange coincidences suggested by the juxtaposition of people and events, in the dramatic use of prophecies at the beginning, in the repeated alternating shift from hope to despair and back, in the Janus-like movement in two directions at once — of the paradox which is the problem of human conduct. But it is through verbal irony that the paradox is made vivid and immediate to us.

The dramatic effectiveness of this literary device, in *Oedipus Rex,* is at once apparent even to the most casual reader. Bradley, understandably, refers to it when he notes that in no other play of Shakespeare's is there so much irony as there is in *Macbeth:*

> I do not refer to irony in the ordinary sense; to speeches, for example, where the speaker is intentionally ironical, like that of Lennox in III, vi. I refer to irony on the part of the author himself, to ironical juxtaposition of persons and events, and especially to the "Sophoclean irony" by which a speaker is made to use words bearing to the audience, in addition to his own meaning, a further and ominous sense, hidden from himself and, usually, from the other persons on the stage.[24]

Macbeth is indeed "an extended metaphor of contradiction,"[25] the closest approximation to *Oedipus Rex* in its careful and sustained use of verbal irony.

In both plays, interestingly enough, verbal irony seems to be concentrated in the early part of the dramatic action. Oedipus is hailed by the Priest, at the very beginning of the play, as the "wisest in the ways of God," the "Liberator" of Thebes (5). He himself promises — in the new crisis that has developed — once more to "bring what is dark to light" and commits himself irrevocably to Laios' cause:

> By avenging the murdered king I protect myself. (9)

> Thus I associate myself with the oracle
> And take the side of the murdered king. (13)

> And as for me, this curse applies no less
> If it should turn out that the culprit is my guest here,
> Sharing my hearth. (13)

> I say I take the son's part, just as though

> I were his son, to press the fight for him
> And see it won! (14)

And in his sympathy for the suffering Thebans, he utters these ominous words:

> Sick as you are, not one is as sick as I. (5)

As the play progresses and contradiction gradually gives way to a single, transparent truth, verbal irony disappears

The same pattern may be observed in *Macbeth*. The confounding of opposites is perhaps the most striking feature of Act One. The most famous example, of course, is the Witches' "Fair is foul, and foul is fair" (1, i, 10), echoed by Macbeth's "So foul and fair a day I have not seen (1, iii, 38) — an innocent comment on the weather, which sets up psychological reverberations pregnant with meaning. It is Duncan, however, who indulges in unconscious irony most frequently in the first act. This is understandable when we realize that the king is, in a sense, a kind of Oedipus-figure; he remains throughout his brief appearance ignorant of the truth and fully confident in his powers of judgment, especially where they concern Macbeth.

> No more that Thane of Cawdor shall deceive
> Our bosom interest. Go pronounce his present death
> And with his former title greet Macbeth.   (I, ii, 63-65)

> > There's no art
> To find the mind's construction in the face.
> He was a gentleman on whom I built
> An absolute trust.
> > O worthiest cousin. . . .   (I, iv, 11-14)

> I have begun to plant thee and will labour
> To make thee full of growing.   (I, iv, 28-29)

> This castle hath a pleasant seat. The air
> Nimbly and sweetly recommends itself
> Unto our gentle senses.   (I, vi, 1-3)

> The love that follows us sometime is our trouble,
> Which still we thank as love.   (I, VI, 11-12)

Of course, verbal irony is by no means limited to Act One. Some of the most memorable lines of this kind occur later in the play — Lady Macbeth's casual reference to madness, in II, ii, 34, for example, her calm suggestion to Macbeth.

> > Go get some water
> And wash this filthy witness from your hand,   (II, ii, 46-47)

her confident explanation that

> > The sleeping and the dead
> Are but as pictures   (II, ii, 53-54)

are powerfully recalled in the inversions of the sleepwalking scene. Her final utterance, with its precise equation of contradictory terms —

What's done cannot be undone —   (V, i, 75)

is the emphatic resolution of unintentional irony into a single, positive, truth.

The impact of irony is intensified in both plays through constant references to light and sight, night and blindness. In *Oedipus Rex,* the figure of Tiresias, the blind prophet dedicated to the service of the god of light, is the powerful embodiment of both ironic juxtaposition and the moral implications of sight. The symbolism thus suggested is further elaborated in the contrast between the helpless blind man who possesses insight and truth and the seeing king who is blindly confident in the light of reason. The interplay between the two extremes is constantly before us. In one of his earliest speeches, Oedipus thus expresses his compassion for the people of Thebes:

I was not sleeping, you are not waking me. (5)

When Creon names Laios for the first time, Oedipus answers:

I learned of him from others; I never saw him. (7)

He promises to bring "what is dark to light" (9) and calls upon the blind seer to help him search out the murderer of Laios.

This encounter is perhaps the most impressive scene in the play, with regard to imagery of sight. Turning to Tiresias, Oedipus asks:

Why are your eyes so cold? (16)

In the quarrel that follows, he rages:

     . . . if you had eyes,
I'd say the crime was yours, and yours alone. (18)

You sightless, witless, senseless, mad old man! (19)

You child of endless night! You can not hurt me
Or any other man who sees the sun. (20)

Why, he is no more clairvoyant than I am! (20)

In the exchange, Tiresias responds in kind:

    You are blind to the evil. (19)

    You mock my blindness, do you?
But I say that you, with both your eyes, are blind:
You do not even know the blind wrongs
That you have done [your father and mother] , on earth
and in the world below.
But the double lash of your parents' curse will whip you
Out of this land some day, with only night

Upon your precious eyes. (21-22)

This two-part verbal fugue reaches its dramatic climax, later, with Oedipus' self-inflicted blindness. The confident, rational king is in the end transformed into a blind seer, very much in the image of Tiresias.

Shakespeare's treatment of light and sight imagery is, as one might expect, much more elaborate. The whole play is engulfed in black, murky night or unnaturally dark day (Duncan's arrival at Macbeth's castle in what appears to be bright, Spring-like sunshine is the notable exception), relieved — as Bradley points out — by lurid flashes of color, suggested by Macbeth's hallucinations, blood imagery, fire, torches, tapers.[26] In this setting, even the stars seem excessively bright. Macbeth apostrophizes:

Stars, hide your fires!
Let not light see my black and deep desires.   (I, iv, 50-51)

His wish is echoed, unconsciously, by Lady Macbeth:

Come, thick night,
And pall thee in the dunnest smoke of hell,
That my keen knife see not the wound it makes,
Nor heaven peep through the blanket of the dark
To cry, "Hold, hold!"   (I, v, 51-55)

Their exhortations are answered. "The moon is down," Fleance observes at the beginning of Act Two, and Banquo comments:

There's husbandry in heaven;
Their candles are all out.   (II, i, 2-5)

Dark night "strangles the traveling lamp" (II, iv, 7); light "thickens" (III, ii, 50); Banquo calls for a light, just before the murderers strike; one of the killers cries "A light, a light!" and immediately after the murder of Banquo, another asks, "Who did strike out the light?" (III, iii, 9-19 *passim*)

As in *Oedipus Rex,* images of sight and eyes are used to heighten the moral implications suggested by the absence of light and sun. Reflecting on the effect of Duncan's murder and the pity it will arouse in people's hearts, Macbeth imagines the winds proclaiming the murder thus:

. . . pity, like a naked new-born babe,
Striding the blast, or heaven's cherubin, hors'd
Upon the sightless couriers of the air,
Shall blow the horrid deed in every eye,
That tears shall drown the wind.   (I, vii, 21-25)

"Mine eyes are made the fools o' th' other senses," (II, i, 44) he comments when he tries unsuccessfully to grasp the bloody dag-

ger before him. He exhorts Banquo's murderers to secret effi-
ciency, having to mask — he says — "the business from the common eye" (III, i, 125). In the same mood, he calls upon "seeling
night" to "Scarf up the tender eye of pitiful day." (III, ii, 46-47)
His bloody hands seem to turn against him to "pluck out" his
eyes (II, ii, 59); the vision of Banquo's royal posterity sears his
eyeballs —

> Start, eyes!
> What, will the line stretch out to th' crack of doom?
> (IV, i, 116-117)

> Horrible sight! Now I see 'tis true. . . .   (IV, i, 122)

Macduff cries out, on discovering the murdered Duncan:

> . . . destroy your sight
> With a new Gorgon.   (II, iii, 76-77)

But perhaps the most Sophoclean use of light and sight imagery
is the brief exchange between the Doctor and Gentlewoman,
who are witnesses to Lady Macbeth's sleepwalking.

> Doct. How came she by that light?

> Gent. Why, it stood by her. She has light by her continually.
> 'Tis her command.

> Doct. You see her eyes are open.

> Gent. Ay; but their sense is shut.   (V, i, 25-29)

In her "blindness," ironically, Lady Macbeth has come to know
the truth; her unnatural sleep is actually the painful awakening
to reality. The reversals suggested in this brief scene are strongly
reminiscent of the last scenes of *Oedipus Rex*.

There can be no doubt that — in spite of important changes
in the manner of characterization,[27] in spite of a more elaborate
dramatic structure and a richer poetic language — "*Macbeth* is in
many respects the most classical of all Shakespeare's plays"[28] and
invites serious comparison with *Oedipus Rex*. Of course, such
comparisons will be impossible so long as we view Oedipus simply as "the victim of destiny" (taking issue with Aristotle, in the
bargain, for having selected *Oedipus Rex* "out of the many hundreds of Greek tragedies known to him" as the "best-constructed"
of them all)[29] and Macbeth as the embodiment of willful evil. So
long as we see in Sophocles' tragedy only the one-sided rule of
Fate and in *Macbeth* nothing more than the free exercise of human egoism;[30] if the only significant thing the two plays have in
common is — as one critic has suggested — the fact that the murders take place off-stage; if the best we can do is to say that
Macbeth "was bound to kill Duncan in exactly the same way that
Oedipus was bound to kill his father,"[31] all attempts at serious

comparison must fail. If, on the other hand, we approach *Macbeth,* as well as *Oedipus Rex,* as an inspired effort to probe "the problem of predestination and free will"[32] — admitting at the outset that the answer must contain both premises intact — we can begin to appreciate the paradox which shaped both plays and suggested the marvelous contrasts, contradictions, and irony common to both. Virgil K. Whitaker has summed up the basis for comparison emphatically and convincingly:

> . . . *Macbeth* seems to me Shakespeare's greatest monument to the
> ethical system that his age inherited from Western Christianity
> and the classical world, and to which it gave a new and vital expres-
> sion. For that tradition *Macbeth* is what the *Oedipus Rex* was for the
> Greek — an almost perfect dramatic embodiment.[33]

In no other Shakespearean tragedy is the problem of human conduct so clearly set forth and the illusion of self-sufficiency so beautifully illustrated. Like *Oedipus Rex, Macbeth* impresses us with the hero's almost compulsive drive toward self-annihilation,[34] while insisting all through on the integrity of the human will. They are the most powerful reminders in all dramatic literature of the simultaneous vanity and glory of life and the delicate balance which must be maintained between the two extremes. The Shakespearean solution is identical to that of Sophocles in its emphatic statement that to insist on one extreme to the exclusion of the other is to destroy both.

NOTES

An earlier version of this essay appeared in *Shakespeare Encomium,* The City College Papers, I. 1964.

1. A. C. Bradley, *Shakespearean Tragedy* (Cleveland and New York, 1955), p. 264.

2. The speech of Brutus and the oration of Antony are the most eloquent reminders of Shakespeare's conscious striving for classical effect. (See Milton Boone Kennedy, *The Oration in Shakespeare* [Chapel Hill, 1942], p. 141.)

3. Bradley — who acknowledges the direct influence of Hegel on his discussion of Macbeth (p. 348 n. 1) — may have had this passage in mind when he observed that Shakespeare's meaning would be perverted if we insisted on identifying the witches with Greek goddesses or "fates." But Hegel was not insisting on such an identity; he was merely noting the similarity in the manner in which the supernatural agents communicate with the hero, in each case. Bradley himself ultimately concludes that the weird sisters do, in fact, reflect the workings of Fate. (See especially pp. 272-273, 277.)

4. Anne and Henry Paolucci, *Hegel on Tragedy* (New York, 1962), etc., p. 294.

5. Part of the explanation, I think, lies in the fact that in Sophocles' play Apollo — the god of light — is immediately recognizable as the trustworthy voice of truth, whereas in Shakespeare's play the witches, while displaying knowledge of the future, suggest in their deformity and ugliness some evil purpose which is never actually explained.

6. Sophocles, *The Oedipus Cycle*, trans. Dudley Fitts and Robert Fitzgerald (New York, 1949), p. 7. Hereafter, page references will be given in the text itself.

7. All quotations from *Macbeth* are from George L. Kittredge, ed. *The Complete Works of Shakespeare* (Boston and New York, 1936).

8. For a full discussion of this ambivalence on the part of Oedipus, see A. Paolucci, "The Oracles are Dumb or Cheat: A Study of the Meaning of *Oedipus Rex*," *Classical Journal*, March 1963, pp. 241-247. (See Chapter 19 in this volume.)

9. Bradley, p. 277.

10. See Cleanth Brooks' comments on Macbeth's attempt to conquer the future ("The Naked Babe and the Cloak of Manliness," *The Tragedy of Macbeth*, ed. Sylvan Barnet, New York, 1963, pp. 214-217).

11. See William Rosen, *Shakespeare and the Craft of Tragedy* (Cambridge, Mass., 1960), pp. 84-85.

12. Richard G. Moulton, *Shakespeare as a Dramatic Artist* (Oxford, 1893), p. 127.

13. *Ibid,* p. 131. For the full discussion of "Oracular Action" and its relation to irony, see pp. 131-143.

14. Richard G. Moulton, *Shakespeare as a Dramatic Thinker* (New York, 1924), p. 304.

15. Croce, for example, identifies the "evil" in the play with the "greatness" prophesied by the witches. See Alessandro De Stefani, ed. *La Tragedia di Macbeth* (Torino, 1922) , p. 477.

16. See A. Paolucci, "The Oracles are Dumb or Cheat . . . ," Chapter 19 in this volume.

17. Prosser Hall Frye, *Romance and Tragedy* (Lincoln, 1961), p. 173.

18. Anne and Henry Paolucci, *Hegel on Tragedy*, p. 279.

19. Frye, p. 141.

20. See Bradley, p. 274.

21. See Cleanth Brooks, *op. cit.*, p. 215, and Mary McCarthy's comments about Lady Macbeth in the article reprinted in the Signet edition of *Macbeth* ed. Sylvan Barnet (New York, 1963), p. 230.

22. G. R. Elliott, *Dramatic Providence in Macbeth* (Princeton, 1960), p. 13.

23. Thomas De Quincey, "On the Knocking on the Gate in *Macbeth*," *Shakespeare Criticism: A Selection*, ed. D. Nichol Smith (London, 1949), p. 331.

24. Bradley, p. 270. See also J. A. K. Thomson, *Shakespeare and the Classics* (London, 1952), p. 119.

25. Brents Stirling, *Unity in Shakespearian Tragedy* (New York, 1956), p. 145. See also Moulton, *Shakespeare as a Dramatic Artist*, pp. 341 ff.

26. See Bradley, pp. 266-269.

27. There is, for example, no growth or development of character in Greek tragedy as there is in Shakespearean and modern tragedy.

28. Thomson, p. .119.

29. *Ibid.,* p. 244.

30. For a subtle variation of this position, see Tom F. Driver, *The Sense of History in Greek and Shakespearean Drama* (New York, 1960), pp. 166-167: "In the *Oedipus Tyrannus* the future is closed. One might almost say that it does not exist." In Macbeth, instead, "essentially . . . the future is open . . . . Oedipus has the freedom, therefore, only to discover the past, and as the past is that in which freedom is not even conceivable, he has only the ironical freedom to discover his lack of it."

31. Thomson, pp. 248-250.

32. Theodore Spencer, *Shakespeare and the Nature of Man* (New York, 1951), p. 157.

33. Virgil K. Whitaker, *Shakespeare's Use of Learning* (San Marino, Cal., 1953), p. 299.

34. See Stirling, p. 140 n. 3.

CHAPTER 9

MIRRORED USURPATION: HAMLET'S TRAGIC BURDEN

Critics are like astronomers posting a new theory of celestial mechanics: their task is not to get at the metaphysical substance of reality so much as to account for the observable facts — for what visibly and audibly happens in a given work. The Greeks had a phrase for this positing of hypotheses: *sozein ta phainomena,* to save the phenomena, the observable facts. It's a method that frees the inquirer of the burden of metaphysics. One begins with a flash of insight, usually accompanied by an overwhelming certainty — subjective certainty — that the key has indeed been found, and then, after applying the key to a particular sphere of experience, it is put to the test of observation to see how far and with what economy of thought it saves the phenomena — in this particular case, the text of *Hamlet.* What I have described is true of all literary criticism, of course; but it applies in a very special way to *Hamlet* because the textual realities of this particular play lend themselves to paradoxical conclusions, just as astronomical facts, observable phenomena in the heavens, lend themselves to a Ptolemaic or Copernican or Einsteinian interpretation; the Copernican theory was, for Galileo, absolute truth; but the Einsteinians have reminded us of the Greek insight into the matter; and practical navigation undermines our subjective certainty by insisting on a Ptolemaic approach to all its calculations. Theoretically, of course, that theory that accounts for the most phenomena and accounts for them most economically is obviously the one to be preferred.

In the case of Shakespeare's *Hamlet,* some critics have argues that the relevant "facts" to be explained critically were too much for Shakespeare himself to handle and so they are not in the play. Others have said that, because Shakespeare borrowed from other plays on the same or similar themes, and borrowed hastily, there are scraps and patches throughout that really don't belong there and in respect to which our model-theory should serve not to help explain but simply to "explain away." Still others have said that Shakespeare probably doesn't take seriously what some of his characters think — even so central a character as Hamlet — and that we must not therefore accept as fact, for purposes of scientific explanation, what we are led to believe are facts only on the say-so of a character, even if the character be, like Hamlet, at the center of the dramatic action. My own hypothetical theory-model is: Can the action of the play be accounted for on the assumption that Claudius's murderous and adulterous usurpation of his brother's rights to throne and queen (to say nothing of usurped rights to young Hamlet's filial loyalty) is what has wrenched the time out of joint and forced Hamlet, for the sake of justice (and as the most innocent living victim of such usurpation), to set it right? That is obviously what happens in *Hamlet* — if we start at the end and work our way forward. In the end, Claudius is killed — twice over — and the head of the new political administration accepts young Hamlet's version of the necessity of his regicide and step-patricide. To bring us to that end, Hamlet has twisted and turned, fretted and squirmed a long way around. But, in his way, he had put his uncle on trial, through the intervening acts and scenes, and had taken the original indictment against the man precisely as charged by the Ghost of the slain King.

Still, we don't start at the end in the play itself. And we certainly don't start *ab ovo* either, with Leda's famous egg, back to the large beginning of things. We start in the middle; and this is truer in Hamlet's case than in any other of Shakespeare's major tragic heroes. As Bradley observes, Hamlet is "the only one of his heroes whom [Shakespeare] has not allowed us to see in the days when life smiled on him." In the play, Hamlet's life is burdened — his character is on trial, from beginning to end; and when the trial ends, when the burden is lifted, his life ceases and the rest, as he says, "is silence."

Where we start in the play we get a view of what is to happen through the wrong end of the telescope, so to speak. With the ghost's charge, usurpation is presented to us directly as the major theme or motive. But as we move on, a marked gap develops between Hamlet and the Ghost. The Ghost charges usurpation and calls for justice; and, on his terms, justice is given him by the play's end. In effect the Ghost says: You, my son, are my rightful heir. My throne which was to be yours, my wife who is your mother — these have been wrenched from you. Remember me and do what must be done.

And yet, as we follow what happens in *Hamlet,* instead of peering through from the end to the beginning or from the beginning to the end, we find that Hamlet himself becomes what we are attempting to be: an experimental scientist, applying the hypothetical method of the theory-model. Everything will make sense if what the Ghost says and what Hamlet is powerfully disposed to believe are indeed true. Usurpation is indeed the theme, but if the facts are not as the Ghost claims and charges, then Hamlet is already in his heart guilty of precisely the kind of usurpation that has been charged in his heart against Claudius. If the Ghost's story is true, Claudius is guilty of a host of usurpations — having taken all sorts of things, by force and fraud that he has no right to. But what if the Ghost's story is *not* true? We know from the beginning that, for all his inner conviction that the truth is so, Hamlet has at his soul's center not quite a *doubt* but a *counterfact* lodged there as a kind of irritant. He knows that he is capable of destroying enemies ruthlessly. If, for instance, Claudius were a loving brother who lovingly married his brother's widowed Queen, to become a loving stepfather to Prince Hamlet — if such were the real Claudius and Hamlet were an ambitious Machiavellian aspirant to the power of the throne, what case might he make to others and perhaps even to himself, to justify denunciation of his uncle as a usurper and thereby oust him and take his place? If Claudius is not a criminal usurper, then what Hamlet has a mind to do makes him the usurper par excellence.

In this respect, Hamlet is indeed the mirror image of his uncle. In the end, as we have it, even on the Ghost's terms, Hamlet is no less a regicide than Claudius has been accused of being. And what additional slaughter and insult and treachery have attended Hamlet's act of killing a king! If Claudius is not guilty as charged, Hamlet is a villain of the same stamp and worse.

Is the whole usurpation motive Hamlet's hallucination? Does he project his own usurper's ambition, self-righteously giving himself a ghost's warrant, even as Macbeth projects his regicidal ambition demonically giving himself a witches' brew of prophecies?

In his dedicatory letter to *What Happens in Hamlet* J. Dover Wilson recalls that Gregg had made precisely that case in an article titled "Hamlet's Hallucination." When Wilson saw the piece, he realized in a flash — as he says — that "he had been born to answer it." Wilson could not accept Gregg's explanation of the "facts" by "explaining them away" as hallucinations on the part of Hamlet.

For both Gregg and Wilson, interestingly enough, the central business of *Hamlet* is, in effect, a piece of experimental science. The Ghost, we may say, has advanced an hypothesis to explain the phenomena. The reality is hard to establish and interrogate experimentally in a direct manner. So Hamlet (the true Baconian, in this respect) undertakes to make a laboratory-model of "reality" by means of which to conduct a controlled experiment; it is to be a model play, so concocted that, if it works, reality itself will blench to see itself mirrored in miniature. But Claudius views the model and doesn't blench. Is it then a false model? Has the Ghost misrepresented whatever ghosts can know? Is the Ghost and all it says Hamlet's hallucination?

Gregg says: Yes. The model came first, he says; Hamlet subconsciously remembers the play; and then (designing usurpation in his overwrought mind) he projects an alleged reality (with the Ghost as the link) to match the "model" play.

Wilson, on the other hand, rejects this. Too easy, he says. His own method is: 1. to determine, respectfully, the "factual" text; 2. to assume that Shakespeare knows his business better than his critics; 3. to assume — like the experimental scientist studying the seemingly indeterminate multiplicity of natural phenomena — that there is reason in it, dramatic reason in this case, in Hamlet's case, that can account for all if we but have the patience to search it out. First of all, we cannot dismiss certain things as "hallucinations" or leftovers from other plays or depths of experience that proved to be too much for Shakespeare's dramatic art.

Wilson opens the chapter on the "Tragic Burden" of Hamlet with the caption

> The time is out of joint. O cursed spite
> That ever I was born to set it right

— accepting the facts as Hamlet sets them forth. The hero's burden, as Wilson defines it, is threefold: there are two facts respecting the out-of-jointness of the time: Gertrude's sin and the state of Denmark; the third is the task — what Hamlet must do to set things right.

About the state of Denmark, Wilson contends — as we know — that the constitutional system Shakespeare represents for us as the play's political setting is "modeled" after or applicable to England's, and that Elizabethan audiences saw it as such. Wilson thus raises the question: "Shakespeare has etched this background in strokes masterly but few, for he would not detract from the main human interest. What was his model?" And then, sifting through the textual evidence, he answers: "Hamlet is an English prince, the court of Elsinore is modeled upon the English court, and the Danish constitution that of England under the Virgin Queen." Read in this light, he goes on to say, scene 2 of Act I is seen clearly to represent "a meeting of the Privy Council such as Queen Elizabeth constantly attended." That may seem, says Wilson, a trivial point; yet it raises a consideration of central importance for the play: "for if Shakespeare and his audience thought of the constitution of Denmark in English terms, then Hamlet was the rightful heir to the throne and Claudius a usurper."

Wilson argues that Claudius is a usurper not for having taken the throne by murdering the king his brother, but that an English audience would see that legally there is "something amiss here; brothers do not succeed brothers, unless there is a failure in the direct line of succession," which is father to first-born son. Why do the few references to usurpation on Hamlet's part come late in the play? Because, says Wilson, there was no need to stress that all too obvious element, which hangs over *all* that happens in *Hamlet*: and also because for Hamlet "the degrading incestuous marriage of his mother" is a "wrong which quite overshadows the other in his thoughts."

Wilson insists that "ursurpation is one of the main factors in the plot of *Hamlet*," that "as an aid to the operation of the plot it is second only in importance to a true understanding of the Ghost." And Wilson clearly means in this that Hamlet has thus a *legal* grievance against Claudius, apart from whether or not Claudius has murdered the former king. Why don't other critics see this, as the old ones through Johnson did? Because it was established at one point — "corroborated with all the weight" of Blackstone's legal authority — that Denmark in those times had an elective monarchy, and that, as a consequence, "Hamlet, though perhaps disappointed, had no legal grievance against Claudius." That would appear to be the position in the Brudermord version of the story, where Hamlet complains to Horatio that "while I was in Germany [Claudius] had himself quickly crowned king in Denmark; but with a show of right he has made over to me the crown of Norway and appealed to the election of the states."

Wilson, however, argues that the words "with a show of right" here afford "cold comfort to the followers of Blackstone" because they "indicate that Hamlet regarded the act as a usurpation; while that the matter is referred to at all proves that he was suffering from a sense of injustice." The throne of Elizabeth and James, too, is in a technical sense "elective." James "owed his crown to the deliberate choice of the Council, while the Council saw to it that he had the 'dying voice' of Elizabeth, as Fortinbras has that of Hamlet." Wilson says that Fortinbras' succession is "secured" at the close of the play in accordance with the "English constitutional theory of the age." At the close of his discussion of the "burden of usurpation," Wilson thus sums up what he thinks he has established *at the very least*:

> The election in Denmark, as even Blackstone admitted, was in practice limited to members of the blood royal; in other words, on the death of King Hamlet the choice lay between his son and his brother. In the eyes of such spectators [as might know the state system of Denmark], therefore, Hamlet's disappointment would seem just as keen and his ambitious designs just as natural, as if the succession was legal according to the principle of primogeniture. However it be looked at, the elective throne in Shakespeare's Denmark is a mirage.

Wilson's insistence on usurpation — or rather on Hamlet's *legal* grievance against Claudius' accession to the throne as a just grievance against usurpation — serves to illuminate an even profounder depth of Hamlet's tragic dilemma. Why does Hamlet not press his *just* grievance? Wilson is correct in saying that Hamlet has usurpation on his mind. We sense from the outset that it hangs over all he does and says, even in his soliloquies. But he will not clearly say it. Why? Wilson points to the answer where, after noting that "Hamlet . . . is not unmindful of it," he adds: ". . . still more important, Claudius is not unmindful either. In short, Hamlet's ambitious designs, or what his uncle takes so to be, form, not of course the most important, but a leading element in the relations between the two men throughout the play." Wilson then goes on to suggest that, if we suppress the usurpation-motive underlying what Claudius perceives to be "Hamlet's ambitious designs," we must "miss half the meaning of what happens in acts 2 and 3."

Though Wilson intends to prove something else, what his argument really helps to demonstrate is Hamlet's fear that all he has designed to do — because Claudius is an adulterous murderous regicide — he may seem to be doing and may in fact be doing because he wants the throne for himself, even if Claudius is *not* a murderer; he wants the throne because it is his by right, even if the members of the Privy Council, who "elect" Claudius don't recognize that right as legal (any more than modern audiences and critics are inclined to do).

That he may himself be just an ambitious would-be usurper looking for an excuse — listening to ghosts as well as to his own soul, in its deepest depths, for an excuse — is indeed a large part of Hamlet's tragic burden. But if Hamlet needed no excuse, if he had a right to succession by primogeniture, if there were *no sense* in which Claudius could legally be king, there could be, *pace Wilson, no* tragedy, much less *great* tragedy. The tragedy of Hamlet is indeed a tragedy of usurpation: Hamlet must know that Claudius is a usurper by virtue of his having murdered the king or he is himself guilty in his heart of murderous usurpation. That mirror-usurpation takes us to the center of Hamlet's soul, which center is the *will's necessity for choice*, which can only end when the will ceases to will, and the rest is silence.

On this theme, as on so many other themes, Hegel — A.C. Bradley's master in dramatic criticism — can be very instructive. Hegel was able to write with original insight about political tragedies like *Hamlet, Othello, Lear,* and *Macbeth,* to say nothing of the *Oedipus Rex* and Orestes plays of antiquity, because like Aristotle, he was also a giant among political thinkers. No one who reads his pages on the great Shakespearean plays and on the nature of the content that can support political tragedies, can come away without clarified insight. Hegel knows what's at stake when seats of power are vacated. And we should not be surprised to find in A. C. Bradley where such insight might point us in the case of Hamlet and the rights of primogeniture. Bradley, for instance, has a clear grasp of the burden of usurpation and thus insightfully links it with the "burden of Gertrude's sin": "the Queen was not a bad hearted woman, not at all the woman to think little of murder. But she had a soft animal nature, and was very dull and very shallow. She loved to be happy, like a sheep in the sun; and, to do her justice, it pleased her to see others happy, like more sheep in the sun. . . . It was pleasant to sit upon the throne and see smiling faces round her, and foolish and unkind in Hamlet to persist in grieving for his father instead or marrying Ophelia and making everything comfortable. She was fond of Ophelia and genuinely attached to her son (though willing to see her lover exclude him from the throne); and, no doubt, she considered equality of rank a mere trifle compared with the claims of love."

Gertrude knows nothing of the murder, but, if Hamlet has been excluded from what is rightly his by Claudius' coronation, then it has been done in such a way that Gertrude can expect her son to be of good cheer about it: he is still next in line, as far as she is concerned. From Bradley's point or view, Hamlet and Claudius are driven to meet and die at one another's hand, though they seek not to meet. "These two" writes Bradley, "the one by shrinking from his appointed task, and the other by efforts growing ever more feverish to rid himself of his enemy, seem to be bent on avoiding one another. But they cannot. Through devious paths, the very paths they take in order to escape, something is pushing them silently step-by-step towards one another, until they meet and it puts the sword into Hamlet's hand. He must die, for he needed this compulsion before he could fulfill the demand of destiny. And the king too, turn and twist as he may, must reach the appointed goal, and is only hastening to it by the windings which seem to lead nowhere." Bradley warns us that "concentration on the character of the hero" is apt to distract our attention from this convergence of the action on an appointed goal; but the fact is that in "no other tragedy of Shakespeare's, not even in *Macbeth,* is this aspect so impressive."

What Hamlet and Claudius are destined to do, because of their relationship to the throne, is to settle their claims to it, which are not settled obviously by law. And that is the point to be made against Wilson's thesis. If the law were wholly on Hamlet's side, Claudius could not have aspired to be king by marrying the new king's widowed mother. For had the law of primogeniture been fixed, young Hamlet would have been king, not prince, when his mother remarried. And there could not have been a tragedy of usurped succession, only a lustful murder, perhaps.

Hegel has written at length on the matter of kingly succession as a theme for tragedy. He confirms Wilson's view that, when the action of a play is drawn from another time and country the playwright's immediate task is to make it *present* for his audience. "History is only ours," he writes, "when it belongs to the nation to which we belong, or when we can look on the present in general as a consequence of a chain of events in which the characters or deeds or events represented form an essential link. After all, the mere connection with the same land and people as ours does not suffice in the last resort, the past even of one's own people must stand in closer connection with our present situation, life, and existence." If Shakespeare has done his job well, the court at Elsinore *will* be linked, in the audience's mind, with Elizabeth's and James' court. Shakespeare's tragedy does indeed illuminate the political reality of succession in the Elizabethan age. But precisely how?

To be of tragic use, the "burden of usurpation" must be conditioned — says Hegel — so as *not* to be an explicitly regulated and established right. "Otherwise," he explains, "the conflict at once becomes one of a totally different sort. I mean that if the succession is not yet established by positive laws and their valid organization, then it cannot be regarded as absolutely wrong if it is all one whether the elder or the younger brother or some other relative of the royal house is to rule. Now, since ruling is something qualitative, and not quantitative like money and goods, which, owing to their nature can be divided with perfect justice, it follows that dissention and strife are present at once in the case of such unregulated succession."

That, Hegel observes, is the situation in the Oedipus cycle, where the Theban pair, Eteocles and Polynices, "confront one another with the same rights and claims" to the succession, since primogeniture has not been established. Rival (because not yet positively determined) claims of brothers especially — but not exclusively — have supplied material for art in all ages and lands: in the Bible's Cain and Abel, in the Persian *Shahnameh*, in the *Braut von Messina*, etc. and Hegel very interestingly cites Shakespeare's *Macbeth,* where Macbeth is in Claudius' position, legally, with respect to usurpation, though he has not married a widowed queen. Hegel notes that in Shakespeare's *Macbeth* —

> Duncan is King, Macbeth is his next eldest relative and is therefore strictly heir to the throne even in preference to Duncan's sons. And so the first inducement to Macbeth's crime is the wrong done to him by the King in naming his own son as his successor. This justification of Macbeth, drawn from [Holinshed's] *Chronicles*, is altogether omitted by Shakespeare, because his only aim was to bring out the dreadfulness of Macbeth's passion, in order to make a bow to King James who must have been interested in seeing Macbeth represented as a criminal. Thus, according to Shakespeare's treatment of the subject, there is no reason why Macbeth did not murder Duncan's sons too, but let them escape.

It is noteworthy that Wilson too alludes to what a King James audience might prefer to see in Hamlet's relation to Claudius. It is important to note also that Macbeth — after he has attained the third of the honors prophesized by the witches — regards Banquo somewhat as Claudius regards Hamlet. Banquo has been told by the same witches that he will be father to a line of kings, and Macbeth fears, like Claudius, that violence may be done him to insure the desired succession. Macbeth's right to the kingship, like Claudius', is not otherwise defective than by proof that murder had been committed to realize it. Shakespeare, however, for dramatic (as well as political) reasons, boldly disallows any textual legitimazation of Macbeth's claim to succession,

as he could easily have done, but does not do, in the case of
Claudius. In the Introduction to the "New Shakespeare" *Macbeth*,
J. Dover Wilson in fact calls attention to Shakespeare's depar-
tures from Holinshed in these words: ". . . he suppressed every
hint of a Macbeth who 'set his whole intention to maintayne
justice,' 'to punishe all enormities and abuses,' and to furnish
the realm with 'commendable lawes,' traces of the vigorous and
firm ruler which had survived the tides of denigration . . . while
he was careful to exclude also suggestions likewise still discernible in Holinshed, that Macbeth possessed some claim to the
throne. Shakespeare's Macbeth is a mere usurper (5.8.55) an
'untitled tyrant' (4.3.104), who, after the murder of Duncan respects neither justice nor mercy." Wilson says that in the case of
Macbeth "there are good dramatic reasons for the change,"
though there are also political reasons, and that, indeed, "the
process of defamation begun in the thirteenth century culminates in this play by a 'servant' of King James and a writer for the
King's company." But it is also true, Wilson goes on to say, that
because the king's "servant" in this case happens to be Shakespeare, the tyrant-usurper is endowed with "enough nobility and
'human kindness' to claim our pity."

It is to be recalled, of course, that Shakespeare clearly indicates in *Macbeth* that succession is by no means *fixed* on the
primogenital line. After saying that he has begun to "plant"
Macbeth and make him "full of growing," King Duncan says:

> Sons, kinsmen, thanes,
> And you whose places are the nearest, know,
> We will establish our estate upon
> Our eldest, Malcolm, whom we name hereafter
> The Prince of Cumberland . . . . (I. 4. 35-39)

To fix the succession on his firstborn is the King's desire, not his
obligation, and not the firstborn's right. Macbeth's aside is clear
enough, despite Shakespeare's excision of Holinshed's explicit
word on the matter of Macbeth's right:

> *Macbeth.* The Prince of Cumberland!, that is a step
> On which I must fall down or else o'er leap,
> For in my way it lies. (I. 4. 48-50)

In his note on "Prince of Cumberland" Wilson observes
that Duncan's naming of his firstborn son violated "the old custom of succession . . . though Shakespeare knew nothing about
it." In his discussion of that old custom (*Macbeth*, Intro. p. viii),
Wilson writes words in 1947 which he ought to have recalled for
his 1950 edition of *What Happens in Hamlet*, for they are highly

relevant and strongly sustain the Hegelian view of what the state
of succession must be if it is to provide material for tragic treatment. Wilson writes:

> Out of the nine kings who reigned between 943 and 1040 all but
> two were killed, either in feud or directly by their successors. And
> this state of affairs was the result, not so much of the general bar-
> barism of the age, as of the ancient law or custom of alternate or
> collateral succession, which preceded the law of primogeniture in
> Scotland, Ireland and some other parts of Europe during the Dark
> Ages, and meant that, on the decease of a king, his crown passed,
> not to the direct descendant, but to the brother or cousin or even
> remoter collateral who seemed the strongest person within a cer-
> tain family group.

Wilson pursues at length the reasons why, in Shakespeare's time,
the fall of Macbeth should seem to serve as a "peculiarly appropriate starting point for the chronicle of a great line of kings."
But the matter is far more consequential for the light it throws
on the burden of usurpation in *Hamlet*.

The powers that move Hamlet and Caludius as rivals for
the royal succession in Denmark — with the fact of murder, to
which, apart from Hamlet and his father's Ghost no one in the
play bears witness, excluded from consideration — belong very
clearly to the kind of powers which Hegel enumerates and discusses in his account of the "Universal Powers over Action" with
special reference to tragedy. All such powers, having to do with
"family, country, state, church, fame, friendship, class, dignity,
and, in the romantic world especially, honor and love, etc.," may
have varying degrees of validity, "but all are inherently rational."
Yet, if they are to serve the needs of dramatic action, Hegel
adds,

> they should not appear merely as rights in a positive legislative
> order, (a) . . . the form of positive legislation contradicts the Con-
> cept and the shape of the Ideal, and (b) the content of positive
> rights may constitute what is absolutely unjust, no matter how far
> it has assumed the form of law. But the relationships just men-
> tioned are not something merely fixed externally; they are the ab-
> solutely substantial forces which . . . remain now precisely also as
> the impetus in action . . . . Of this kind, for example, are the inter-
> ests and aims which fight in the *Antigone* of Sophocles.

What is essential is that there be no *legal* criterion that settles the
right in an external way, just as there must be no external force
which the human will cannot resist when it acts on an indeterminate right. And Hegel here links Macbeth and Hamlet for illustration of his point:

In this matter, in particular, the artist must go straight for the fact that freedom and independence of decision are continually reserved for man. Of this Shakespeare has afforded the finest examples. In *Macbeth* for instance, the witches appear as external powers determining Macbeth's fate in advance. Yet what they declare is his most secret and private wish which comes home to him and is revealed to him in this only apparently external way. Finer and deeper still, the appearance of the ghost in *Hamlet* is treated just as an objective form of Hamlet's inner presentiment. With his dim feeling that something dreadful must have happened, we see Hamlet come on the scene; now his father's ghost appears to him and reveals to him the whole crime. After this monitory disclosure we expect that Hamlet will at once punish the deed by force and we regard his revenge as completely justified. But he hesitates and hesitates . . . . Hamlet hesitates because he does not blindly believe the ghost . . . . The apparition does not command a helpless Hamlet; Hamlet doubts, and, by arrangements of his own, will get certainty for himself, before he embarks on action.

Hegel's point is that the Ghost gives Hamlet too obvious a reason for doing what Hamlet, in his "beautiful soul," would not have determined to do, and that is to challenge openly Claudius' right of succession even though he has a perhaps better right of his own, as firstborn son. If Claudius is rightly king, then Hamlet's determination to oust him, except on the Ghost's indictment, can easily become a usurper's determination. And then, if the Ghost's indictment weren't true, if it were merely an excuse for action otherwise motivated by ambition . . . well, it is burning doubt. If all that sets the time out of joint is the fact of Claudius' succession to the throne that could by equal right, but not greater right, have been Hamlet's, then the curse to set it right is an interested party's curse, a curse of ambition, the result of which will be a murderous, matricidal usurpation more heinous than the usurpation charged to Claudius.

Hamlet cannot free himself from this hard "fact" which makes him the mirror-image of Claudius as a potentential usurper. And it is precisely because he will not free himself of it that he is, in the end, truly, the noblest spirit of them all. Till the very end, he concentrates his spirit in the point of freedom where nothing external can bind, where the necessity for choice remains infinite. That moment can be, according to Hegel, the profoundest depth of spiritual evil, if the soul hugs itself in it. Hugs is Hegel's term. The temptation to hug itself in the eternal necessity for choice is the dilemma, in Hegel's ethical and dramatic universe, of the *schöne Seele* – the beautiful soul.

T.S. Eliot puts his Becket into that moment in *Murder in the Cathedral*. Becket finds himself facing freely desired, freely elected martyrdom. There is the necessity for choice, no doubt, but Becket senses that he must not hug it, but must rather give it away, give it up. But, give it up for what, or to what? The religious answer, for Becket, is to pull the moment inside out: to *will freely* that, not my will but Thy will done; to be free in willing God's will. That is what, in Dante's world, makes heaven heaven. In hell, the common denominator is eternally willing one's own will without hope: *vivemo in disio sensa speme*. In heaven it is: I will that Thy will be done on earth (and in hell) as well as in heaven. Or as Piccarda says in the lowest heaven of the inconstant moon: heaven is heaven because all in it, in whatever heavenly level, have their peace which passeth understanding in the same form: *e la sua voluntade é nostra pace*: our willng his will is our peace.

Bradley on such grounds suggests that, when Hamlet finally says "the rest is silence," we expect more, even if he does not. It is enough for him to have stopped hugging the necessity for choice. For him, in answer to the question of the great soliloquy, it is enough, at last, to die. He had *said* he would willingly die — three times, indeed, in a quibbling angry response to Polonius, who had said: ". . . I most humbly take my leave of you"; to which Hamlet replied:

You cannot, sir, take from me anything that
I will more willingly part withal: except my life, except my life,
except my life.

That extravagant response, like the great soliloquy itself, is a hugging of the necessity for choice. Hamlet does not know till he has actually done it that all of life can indeed be concentrated in one point of will that lets go of itself in saying: "The rest is silence." We hear him utter the words. It is done for him. But *we*, as Bradley says, expect something more. Release of the will, so beautifully and freely, and then silence, are not enough. Shakespeare wants us, as Bradley suggests, to require something more, a "godlike reason" for what happens in *Hamlet*. We get it in Horatio's response.

At the end of the *Divine Comedy*, Dante — most willful Dante — is overwhelmed in his will which begins to turn as upon a great wheel, turned by the Love which moves the sun and the other stars. The "flights of Angels that sing thee to thy rest" — to the peace which transcends all understanding — are for Dante circular flights on love's outermost wheel.

As Bradley concludes, in the "unburdening" paragraph of his lectures on *Hamlet*:

> If these various peculiarities of the tragedy are considered, it will be agreed that, while *Hamlet* certainly cannot be called in the specific sense a "religious drama," there is in it nevertheless both a freer use of popular religious ideas, and a more decided, though always imaginative, intimation of a supreme power concerned in human evil and good, than can be found in any other of Shakespeare's tragedies. And this is one of the causes of the special popularity of this play, just as *Macbeth*, the tragedy which in this respect most nearly approached it, has also the next place to it in general esteem.

Have we here a final solution to the Hamlet enigma? Mirrored usurpation? Hardly. As we said at the beginning it is a question of saving the phenomena with maximum economy of means. One hypothesis gives way to another — and the play remains the thing. Hegel was fond of the image, and perhaps Bradley took the hypothetical-method idea from his favorite theoretician of tragedy, where he says in the opening paragraph of his second lecture on *Hamlet*:

> The only way, if there is any way, in which a conception of Hamlet's character could be proved true, would be to show that it, and it alone, explains all the relevant facts presented by the text of the drama. To attempt such a demonstration here would obviously be impossible, even if I felt certain of the interpretation of all the facts.

CHAPTER 10

MARX, MONEY, AND SHAKESPEARE: THE HEGELIAN CORE IN MARXIST SHAKESPEARE CRITICISM

> "Marx would recite *Faust* and *The Divine Comedy,* and he and Jenny would take turns at Shakespeare, which they had learned so to love from her father."
>
> Edmund Wilson (1940)

> "In matters of literary taste, Marx was by no means a Marxist."
>
> Peter Demetz (1959)

Socialist-Realism and Shakespearean Humanism

Nothing could be more Hegelian, Rene Wellek reminds us in *Theory of Literature* (written with Austin Warren), than to insist that "literature occurs only in a social context, as part of a culture, in a milieu." For Wellek it seems impossible "to accept a view constituting any particular activity" — whether it be something biological or racial, as in the theory of Taine, or economic, as in the theory of Marx — "the 'starter' of all the others." For a moment he is tempted to suggest, as the Marxists often do, that Hegel also ascribed the whole business to the "initiative" of some narrowly-conceived idea, but he restrains himself. The Hegelian approach to literature, Wellek is aware, is obviously comprehensive enough to include a host of particular "starters," of which the biological and the economic are but two. As an example of the excessive narrowness of some Marxist criticism, he cites these words of the Russian Marxist Anatoly Lunacharsky: "Shakespeare's tragic outlook on the world was consequential upon his being the dramatic expression of the feudal aristocracy, which in Elizabeth's day had lost their former dominant position.[1]

Wellek notes that such a judgment manifestly fails to "deal concretely with either the ascertainable content of Shakespeare's

plays, his professed opinions on social questions (obvious from
the chronicle plays), or his social status as a writer." This is not
to argue that we can presume to "dismiss the economic approach
to literature" on the strength or weakness of such a quotation. It
is introduced, apparently, so that Wellek can proceed to distinguish between the true Marxist and the "vulgar" Marxist economic approach. Marx, he says, clearly perceived the "oblique-
ness of the relationship between literature and society." He saw
that contradictions between "productive forces," "social relations," and "consciousness" ("'moments' in his Hegelian terminology") made a narrow deterministic account of artistic phenomena superficial. Marx, especially in his early writings — we
are once again told — was at pains to avoid any such superficiality; and it is only in the rare moments when he looks ahead to
what "might be" in the coming perfected communist society that
the master himself lapses into such uncritical views as to suggest
that, with the final contradictions of the dictatorship of the proletariat resolved, "everybody could be an excellent, even original painter." Wellek cites these words from *Die Deutsche Ideologie:*
"In a Communist society there are no painters, but at most men
who, among other things, also paint."

It is against such tasteless logical extremism that the most
serious Marxist critics have labored, and Wellek cites in this respect the work of A. A. Smirnov in the field of Shakespeare criticism. Yet, in attempting to rescue Shakespeare from "vulgar
Marxism" Smirnov perhaps goes too far. Writing from a twentieth-century point of view — says Wellek — Smirnov (as also V.
Grib) sought to

> rescue tlhe bourgeois writer by a recognition of his universal hu-
> manity. Thus Smirnov comes to the conclusion that Shakespeare
> was the "humanist ideologist of the bourgeoisie, the exponent of
> the program advanced by them when, in the name of humanity,
> they first challenged the feudal order." But the concept of human-
> ism, of the universality of art, surrenders the central doctrine of
> Marxism, which is essentially relativistic.

Wellek goes on to isolate what he considers to be the fundamental weakness of the Marxist approach to literature:

> Marxist criticism is at its best when it expresses the implied, or
> latent, social implications of a writer's work. . . . [Yet it] never an-
> swers the question of the degree of dependence of literature on
> society. Hence many of the basic problems have scarcely begun to
> be studied. . . . Though some kind of dependence of literary ide-
> ologies and themes on social circumstances seems obvious, the
> social origins of forms and styles, genres and actual literary norms

have rarely been established.[2]

In his *Marx, Engels, and the Poets: Origins of Marxist Literary Criticism,* Peter Demetz, who was a pupil of Rene Wellek, contrasts the work of Smirnov on Shakespeare with the "coarse simplifications" of the American Marxist Donald Morrow in his pamphlet *Where Shakespeare Stood* (1935). Morrow had declared flatly that Shakespeare stood "with the commercial class" and that "any play he wrote was a blow against feudal aspirations." Trying to avoid and correct such "meaningless oversimplifications," Smirnov had stressed that "even Shakespeare vacillated," that even his allegiance to the bourgeois class "was not free of flaws and suffered at times from the counter currents of the age." Smirnov distinguished three periods in Shakespeare's dramatic development: an initial period (1590-1600) of optimism, when he seems unaware of the inherent social contradictions of his age; a second one (1601-09), when he "reflects the slow disintegration of Elizabethan society in somber tragedies"; and a third period (1609-11), when he "finally feels himself forced by the anti-aristocratic tendencies of bourgeois Puritanism to make his peace with the aristocracy that supported the theater and thus he falls victim to the reactionary and royalist taste of his lords and patrons."[3]

Demetz doesn't single out for special notice what is perhaps the most interesting piece of criticism in Smirnov's *Shakespeare: A Marxist Interpretation* (New York, 1936), namely the treatment of *Hamlet.* In Smirnov's view, Hamlet the protagonist is not to be taken as representative of earlier Danish times, but as a character of Elizabethan England around whom Shakespeare constructs a pseudo-fictive framework that is actually a representation of the "socio-economic dilemma with which Shakespeare correctly felt his own person to be confronted." Feudalism was in a corruptive phase of decline, and Shakespeare regarded that corruption with disgust. But, as he was a "true humanist," he also regarded with disgust the rapidly rising force of bourgeois society with its philistinism and its creed of money above courage and honor and all the other virtues of medieval chivalry. Hamlet expresses Shakespeare's double disgust. He is a humanist; he sympathizes with the passing feudal age, though he knows it to be but a corrupt caricature of what once had been. He knows that there is no staying the rise of bourgeois society; yet facing that rise, as a humanist, he is paralyzed morally because he is "able to discover in his situation no humanist alternative."

Smirnov's point is clearly that subjective or psychological interpretations of Hamlet's "delay" miss the mark. An objective explanation, he argues, is provided by Marxist socio-economic analysis. In his *Aesthetics: A Study of the Fine Arts in Theory and Practice*, James K. Feibleman discusses Smirnov's view at some length, only to reject it finally on the grounds that a "solution to the shortcomings of theories which are excessively subjective assuredly cannot consist in a theory which overlooks the subjective realm altogether." Feibleman notes that it is not only Marxists who have sought to counter the traditional current of subjective criticism of *Hamlet* by attempting to identify objective grounds for Hamlet's delay. He cites K. Werder, *Vorlesungen über Shakespeares Hamlet* (Berlin, 1875), where it is argued that what the ghost requires of Hamlet "simply was not *possible*, and this for reasons entirely *objective.*" Given the circumstance of Hamlet's time, the murder of Claudius "followed by Hamlet's seizing of the throne would have been condoned neither by the courtiers nor by the masses of the people" unless he could give greater proof that Claudius had murdered his brother than the testimony of a ghost could offer. Feibleman also cites J. Dover Wilson's *What Happens in Hamlet* (New York, 1935) on the same theme, chiding him too, for suggesting that Hamlet is to be viewed as Shakespeare's contemporary confronting an objective situation that is essentially Elizabethan English, not medieval Danish; but he fails to note that Wilson draws a conclusion directly opposed to Werder's and Smirnov's, contending that external circumstances in fact press Hamlet to *act* not to *delay,* for he is patently the rightful heir to his father's throne and could therefore justify removing his uncle without having to charge him with fratricidal usurpation. According to Wilson, Hamlet's delay is therefore *entirely* a matter of character, not of objective circumstances.[4]

Although not focused on *Hamlet,* Georg Lukács' well-known tribute to Shakespeare has a bearing on Smirnov's view. Lukács agrees that Shakespeare lived in a "great transitional age," an age which experienced the "crisis and break-up of the feudal system." In Shakespeare, he says, "a whole set of the inner contradictions of feudalism, pointing inevitably to its dissolution, emerge with the greatest clarity." What could be more *Marxist,* as an explanation of Shakespeare, than talk of contradictions, dissolutions, break-ups in the social order? But Lukács runs the risk of leaving Marx far behind and of plunging irretrievably back into Hegel when he proceeds to write:

However, what interested . . . Shakespeare above all {was] not so-much the complex, actual historical causality responsible for the decline of feudalism, as the human collisions which sprang neces-sarily and typically from the contradictions of this decline, as the forceful interesting types among the older, declining human stock of feudalism and the new type of hero, the humanist noble or ruler. Shakespeare's cycle of historical plays, in particular, is full of collisions of this kind. With brilliant clarity and discernment he views the welter of contradictions which had filled the uneven but fatal path of feudal crisis over centuries. Shakespeare never simpli-fies this process down to a mechanical contrast between the "old" and the "new." He sees the triumphant humanist character of the rising new world, but also sees it causing the breakdown of a patri-archal society humanly and morally better in many respects and more closely bound to the interests of the people.

There is a *safe*, Marxist coloring in these words (one must play it safe in the Communist world of entrenched mediocrity when one Hegelizes) and here Lukács seizes the occasion to pit money against humanism in a thoroughly Marxist and still Hegelian vein:

Shakespeare sees the triumph of humanism, but also foresees the rule of money in this advancing new world, the oppression and exploitation of masses, a world of rampant egoism and ruthless greed. In particular, the types representing the social-moral, hu-man-moral decay of feudalism are portrayed in his historical plays with incomparable power and realism and sharply opposed to the old unworldly still unproblematic and uncorrupted, nobility. (Shakespeare feels a keen and personal sympathy for this latter type, at times idealizes him, but as a great, clear-sighted poet re-gards his doom as inevitable.) His clear eye for the social-moral features which emerge from this violent historical crisis allows Shakespeare to create historical dramas of great historical authen-ticity and fidelity, even though he has not yet experienced history as history in the sense of the nineteenth century, in the sense of the conception which we have analyzed in the work of Scott.[5]

That statement answers, of course, the question originally posed. Although the times were not *really* ripe, in a deterministic sense, for the kind of historical drama Shakespeare wrote, Shakespeare's "clear eye" supplied the deficiency. Or, to coin a phrase:

The poet's eye, in a fine frenzy rolling,
Doth glance from heaven to earth, from earth to heaven;
And, as imagination bodies forth
The forms of things unknown, the poet's pen
Turns them to shapes, and gives to airy nothing
A local habitation and a name.

(A Midsummer Night's Dream, V, 1, 12-17)

This idea of poetry may be a bit too far-fetched for any Marxist who must (if he is to retain even a semblance of materialist orthodoxy) abjure such "rough magic" — drown it, in fact, with Prospero's book, "deeper than did ever plummet sound."

The Marxist "Locus Classicus": Timon's Gold

The major genuinely *Marxist* contribution to Shakespeare criticism remains Marx's commentary in the posthumously published *Economic-Philosophic Manuscripts* (1844) on two passages from *Timon of Athens*. When he wrote that brief commentary, Marx was twenty-six; and almost all scholars who have had anything to say about the passages agree in linking them with Marx's published responses (perhaps under the influence of Moses Hess as well as Hegel) to Bruno Bauer's essay on the Jewish problem. In his own essay "On the Jewish Question" (1843) Marx had said that "Money is the jealous one God of Israel beside which no other god may stand. Money dethrones all the gods of man and turns them into commodities. . . . Money is the alienated, independently constituted value of all things. Money is the alienated essence of man's work and his being. This alien being dominates him and he worships it. The god of the Jews . . . is only an illusory bill of exchange. . . . The *chimerical* nationality of the Jew is the nationality of the trader, and above all of the financier."[6] In the passage of the 1844 *Manuscripts,* where he cites Shakespeare, Marx does not discuss the Jews. His concern is with the conceptual significance of money — which he calls the *"pimp* between man's needs and the object, between his life and his means of life." And he argues: "But *that which* mediates *my* life for me, also *mediates* the existence of other people *for me.* For me it is the *other* person."[7] To illustrate his meaning, he cites for commentary three poetic passages: one from Goethe's *Faust* and two from Shakespeare's *Timon.*

"Shakespeare's *Timon,*" Professor Demetz aptly observes, "provides Marx with a wealth of paradoxes which he used to define his idea of monetary perversion more precisely; and in unfolding his bitter vision of the mythic power of money, Marx combines the core of his earlier 'Judaic' theory with a series of violent contrasts that derive from Shakespeare's text."[8] But before taking up Marx's commentary on the passages from Shakespeare (and Goethe), it is important to note that Marx's discussion of money, both in the *Manuscripts* of 1844 and in his published criticism of Bruno Bauer's treatment of the Jewish question, derive directly from his reading of Hegel's *Philosophy of Right,* about which he had written and published an introductory critique in 1843.

Except for the use of the word "pimp" at the outset, the exposition with which Marx introduces the poetic quotations from Goethe and Shakespeare is essentially Hegelian — though Marx's intent was no doubt to stand the whole business on its head. Early in the *Philosophy of Right*, Hegel thus distinguishes — in terms of English political economy — two basic kinds of exchange: "(a) exchange of a thing pure and simple, i.e. exchange of one specific thing for another of the same kind, (b) purchase or sale (*emptio, venditio*); exchange of a specific thing for one characterized as universal, one which counts as value alone and which lacks the other specific character, utility — i.e. for money."[9]

Elsewhere in the *Philosophy of Right*, Hegel rounds out the subject noting first of all that the *specific utility* of a thing can be generalized for exchange because, "being quantitatively determinate it is . . . comparable with the specific utility of other things of like utility. Similarly, the specific need, which it satisfies is at the same time need in general and thus is comparable on its particular side with other needs. . . . As full owner of the thing, I am *eo ipso* owner of its value as well as its use."[10] To clarify his meaning, Hegel adds:

> The value of a thing may be heterogeneous; it depends on need. But if you want to express the value of a thing not in a specific case but in the abstract, then it is money which expresses this. Money represents any and every thing, though since it does not portray the need itself but is only the symbol of it, it is itself controlled by the specific value of the commodity. Money, as an abstraction, merely expresses this value. It is possible in principle to be the owner of a thing without at the same time being the owner of its value. . . . But since this form of property is not in accordance with the concept of property, such restrictions on ownership (feudal tenure, testamentary trust) are mostly in course of disappearing.[11]

The foregoing passages are from the early part of the *Philosophy of Right*, where the focus is on "abstract right." Later in the volume, in the chapters on the state, Hegel notes that if its institutions of public administration are to be supported equitably (in common, by all), a state must "tax" for its maintenance not by drawing on specific citizens for specific things but with a generalized levy. As he explains:

> In the state it may happen, to begin with, that the numerous aptitudes, possessions, pursuits, and talents of its members, together with the infinitely varied richness of life intrinsic to these — all of which are at the same time linked with their owner's mentality — are not subject to direct levy by the state. It lays claim only to a

single form of riches, namely, money. [Hegel will later take up the duty to defend the commonwealth]. . . . In fact, however, money is not one particular type of wealth amongst others, but the universal form of all types so far as they are expressed in an external embodiment and so can be taken as "things." Only by being translated into terms of this extreme culmination of externality can services exacted by the state be fixed quantitatively, and so justly and equitably.

Hegel reminds us that in Plato's *Republic*, where money is not used, the Guardians impose *particular* services upon individuals in particular classes. Similarly in the feudal era, services required of vassals were *particularized*, so as to fix people in particular castes. In earlier times:

> The same particular character pertains to tasks imposed in the East and in Egypt in connection with colossal architectural undertakings, and so forth. In these circumstances the principle of subjective freedom is lacking, i.e. the principle that the individual's substantive activity — which in any case becomes something particular in content in services like those mentioned — shall be mediated through his particular volition. This is a right which can be secured only when the demand for services takes the form of a demand for something of universal value, and it is this right which has brought with it this conversion of the state's demands into demands for cash.[12]

In an explanatory note to this paragraph, Hegel adds — with respect to "constitutional" rights and obligations of citizens in a free society:

> Services are now almost entirely reduced to money payments, and military service is now almost the only personal one exacted. In the past, far more claims were made directly on a man's own person, and he used to be called upon for work according to his ability. In our day, the state purchases what it requires. This may at first sight seem an abstract, heartless, and dead state of affairs, and for the state to be satisfied with indirect services may also look like decadence in the state. But the principle of the modern state requires that the whole of the individual's activity shall be mediated through his will. By means of money, however, the justice of equality can be achieved much more efficiently. Otherwise, if the assessment depended on concrete ability, a talented man would be more heavily taxed than an untalented one. But nowadays respect for subjective freedom is publicly recognized precisely in the fact that the state lays hold of a man by that which is capable of being held [namely external goods, and especially money, not talent or ability].[13]

Marx was familiar with all these passages. They were for

him an essential part of the system of Hegelian thought which he was early bent on turning upside down evaluatively in order to establish the new socio-economic principle: "From each according to his ability, to each according to his need." That principle, as Marx himself applies it, obliges revolutionary bureaucrats to seize talent and ability directly and put it to work for the cause. First, according to Marx, it will be done by the proletariat dictatorship with absolute coercion, forcing the former ruling classes to pay with their best abilities. Only after those classes are literally worn out of existence, will the surviving populace be properly disposed to give, without manifest coercion, according to ability in keeping with the new Marxian sense of equity.

These Hegelian passages are crucial for understanding Marx's use of "high art" to help him invert their significance. Having said that money, precisely because it generalizes services, is the *pimp* "between man's need and the object, between his life and the means of life"; having insisted that money thus becomes for *me,* the "other person" who can help to satisfy my need, Marx proceeds to cite his two great literary authorities: Mephistopheles, the devil of Goethe's *Faust,* and Shakespeare's Timon. He first cites *Faust* I, 3 (Faust's study):

> What, man! confound it, hands and feet
> And head and backside all are ours!
> And what we take while life is sweet,
> Is that to be declared not ours?
> Six stallions, say, I can afford,
> Is not their strength my property?
> I tear along, a sporting lord,
> As if their legs belonged to me.

Mephistopheles' image does not quite tell it all — for property has indeed always meant the *means* for the pursuit of happiness, the props to sustain the pursuit, from the self-possessed smile that properly moves hearts, to the physical city that makes possible a civilized pursuit of happiness. Marx needs, rather, a misanthrope to make his point, so he hastens to cite Timon:

> Gold? Yellow, glittering, precious gold? No. Gods,
> I am no idle votarist! . . .
> Thus much of this will make black white, foul fair,
> Wrong right, base noble, old young, coward valiant.
> . . . Why, this
> Will lug your priests and servants from your sides,
> Pluck stout men's pillows from beneath their heads:
> This yellow slave
> Will knit and break religions, bless the accursed;

> Make the hoar leprosy adored, place thieves
> And give them title, knee and approbation
> With senators on the bench: This it is
> That makes the wappen'd widow wed again;
> She, whom the spital-house and ulcerous sores
> Would cast the gorge at, this embalms and spices
> To the April day again. . . . Damned earth,
> Thou common whore of mankind, that putt'st odds
> Among the rout of nations.

And so later:

> O thou sweet king-killer, and dear divorce
> 'Twixt natural son and sire! thou bright defiler
> Of Hymen's purest bed! thou valiant Mars!
> Thou ever young, fresh, loved and delicate wooer,
> Whose blush doth thaw the consecrated snow
> That lies on Dian's lap! Thou visible God!
> That solder'st close impossibilities,
> And makest them kiss! That speak'st with every tongue,
> To every purpose! O thou touch of hearts!
> Think, thy slave man rebels, and by thy virtue
> Set them into confounding odds, that beasts
> May have the world in empire!

Marx immediately comments, in what is his single (though admittedly characteristically Marxian) contribution to serious Shakespeare criticism: "Shakespeare excellently depicts the nature of *money*." But before examining the passages from *Timon*, he would have us consider the meaning or implications of the passage from *Faust*. It is the devil, of course — Marx stresses— who urges us to assume such a *positive* attitude toward money — a selfishly, demoniacally positive attitude. He explains, typically:

> That which is for me through the medium of *money* — *that* for which I can pay (i.e., which money can buy) — that am *I*, the possessor of the money. The extent of the power of money is the extent of my power. Money's properties are my properties and essential powers — the properties and powers of its possessor. Thus, what I *am* and *am capable* of is by no means determined by my individuality. I am ugly, but I can buy for myself the most *beautiful* of women. Therefore I am not *ugly*, for the effect of *ugliness* – *its* deterrent power — is nullified by money. I, in my character as an individual, am *lame*, but money furnishes me with twenty-four feet. Therefore I am not lame. I am bad, dishonest, unscrupulous, stupid; but money is honoured, and therefore so is its possessor. Money is the supreme good therefore its possessor is good. Money, besides, saves me the trouble of being dishonest: I am therefore presumed honest, I am *stupid*, but money is the *real mind* of all

things and how then should its possessor be stupid? Besides, he can buy talented people for himself, and is he who has power over the talented not more talented than the talented? Do not I, who thanks to money am capable of *all* that the human heart longs for, possess all the human capabilities? Does not my money therefore transform all my incapacities into their contrary?

If *money* is the bond binding me to *human* life, binding society to me, binding me and nature and man, is not money the bond of all *bonds*? Can it not dissolve and bind all ties? Is it not, therefore, the universal agent of *divorce*? It is the true *agent of divorce* as well as the true binding agent — the *galvano-chemical* power of Society.

It is of course the devil-misanthrope that thinks there is no difference between an ugly and lame rich man and a handsome and whole rich man. In retrospect, it is obvious that a totalitarian dictatorship of the proletariat, with or without money, is very capable of exercising "power over the talented," forcing them, according to their abilities to satisfy the needs of the untalented, as prescribed by the proletarian party dictatorship. Moreover, if money *could* relieve the burdens of extreme ugliness or of being otherwise helplessly lame, would it be the whore that Marx, on Timon's lead, makes of it, in expounding Shakespeare's meaning? On Timon's misanthropic invectives, Marx is brief and to the point:

Shakespeare stresses especially two properties of money:
(1) It is the visible divinity — the transformation of all human and natural properties into their contraries, the universal confounding and overturning of things: it makes brothers of impossibilities.
(2) It is the common whore, the common pimp of people and nations.

The overturning and confounding of all human and natural qualities, the fraternisation of impossibilities — the *divine* power of money — lies in its *character* as men's estranged, alienating and self-disposing *species-nature*. Money is the alienated *ability of mankind.*

That which I am unable to do as a *man,* and of which therefore all my individual essential powers are incapable, I am able to do by means of *money.* Money thus turns each of these powers into something which in itself it is not — turns it, that is, into its *contrary.*[14]

Marx's view, directly opposed to Hegel's, seems to be that only money, not an oriental despotism or dictatorship of the proletariat, can gain control over the ability of mankind. A critic of nineteenth-century English political economy who was not also a misanthrope might more reasonably have said that money has in fact made it unnecessary to use talented people directly for the labors of building pyramids, or Great Walls, or — in our own time — city subways and highways. At any rate, on the strength of his comments on the passages from *Timon,* Marx has earned a place in Francelia Butler's *The Strange Critical Fortunes of Shakespeare's 'Timon of Athens,'* (1966) where the passage is cited at length.

In his lectures on the *Philosophy of Fine Art* (upon which A. C. Bradley drew so heavily and appreciatively for his Shakespeare studies — not only the tragedies but the histories and comedies as well, most notably the rejection of Falstaff), Hegel speaks only briefly of Timon's character. But he does so in the midst of a long discussion of *pathos* as the "proper center, the true domain, of art," where he insists that "neither in comedy nor in tragedy may the 'pathos' be mere folly and subjective caprice."[15] J. C. Maxwell, incidentally, makes the same point in his Introduction to the Cambridge edition of *Timon,* where he chides critics who advance the view, articulated in "its most extreme form by O. J. Campbell,"that Shakespeare has set Timon before us "merely for derision." Maxwell thus sums up his "reading" of *Timon* in this regard:

> At a highly abstract level, it is easier to summarize without serious distortion than any other of the plays. To say that it is a study of a potentially noble but unbalanced and prodigal nature, corrupted by a usurious and materialistic society with its flattery, and thrown off his balance and plunged into an equally extreme and indiscriminate misanthropy when the loss of his wealth discovers the falsehood of his friends — to say this is probably a less hopelessly inadequate account of "what the play is about" than could be given for any other important play of Shakespeare.[16]

Hegel says with comparable brevity:

> In Shakespeare, e.g. Timon is a misanthrope for purely external reasons; his friends have taken his dinners, squandered his property, and when he now needs money for himself, they desert him. This makes him a passionate misanthrope. This is intelligible, but not a "pathos" inherently justified.[17]

Hegel's point is that one need not, from the experiences Timon has had, become the misanthrope Timon becomes, though it is understandable. Marx, on the contrary, suggests that money — which is to say, exchangeable capital — suffices of itself (once one has understood the truth about it) to make any reasonable, sensitive man a misanthrope. Money's very existence, according to Marx, is objective proof that the "ability of mankind" has been alienated, to the advantage of all the ugly, lame, and stupidly dishonest, ignoble people who need it to buy what they haven't got and want.

Dwelling on the theme in *To the Finland Station*, Edmund

Wilson notes that Marx had had precisely such an impression of what Western society is all about through his personal experience of it in Germany, France, and England. Wilson presumes, however, to view it as a typically Jewish experience in an essentially hostile Christendom — an experience having demonstrably very little to do with the actualities of English political economy. And he argues on that presumption that in the process of becoming the great revolutionary critic of moneyed society, Marx simply "substituted for the plight of the Jew the plight of the proletariat.[18] Throughout his revolutionary career, says Wilson, the "proletariat remains for [Marx] something in the nature of a philosophical abstraction." What is real in his life that *corresponds* to that abstraction is something that is not in the least proletarian. Briefly: "The primary emotional motivation in the role which he assigns to the proletariat seems to have been borrowed from his position as a Jew."

Marx, according to Wilson, had early assumed a posture toward the so-called Jewish question which led him to conclude that the "special position of the Jew was vitally involved with money-lending and banking, and that it would be impossible for him to disassociate himself from these until the system of which they were a part should be abolished." The "animus and rebellion" due to long-suffered social disabilities as well as the moral insight and world vision of the Messianic biblical tradition that were Marx's legacy as a Jew were — as Wilson expresses it — "transferred in all their formidable power to an imaginary proletariat" concerning the reality of which Marx knew substantially nothing.[19]

European proletarian and Jew had both, indeed, been "disfranchised and shut off from society." But there, though Marx failed to see it, the similarity ended. From his rabbinical forbears, Marx had inherited a "tradition of spiritual authority" which could not permit him to imagine that the proletariat of the West would be easily satisfied with a simple bettering of its material circumstances, that it would want for itself precisely what the bourgeoisie wanted. In Wilson's words: "When a proletarian gave an indication of wanting what the bourgeoisie wanted, Marx regarded him as a renegade and pervert, a miserable victim of petty bourgeois ideas."[20]

If Wilson's assessment of his plight is correct, then Marx was certainly the very sort of man, in Western capitalist society, whom we might expect to identify himself most *pathetically* (in Hegel's sense) with Shakespeare's Timon. Had he been a rich man, Marx would probably have been lavishly generous — perhaps even more lavishly generous than his bourgeois-capitalist patron Engels would always prove to be. Lacking the means himself, and having instead to depend upon the generosity of another, Marx could understandably imagine how eager an entire class of have-nots might be to seize by violence if need be the means of buying the talents of the talented for their own use. Yet, in retrospect, it may yet come to seem that Engels had more of Timon in his heart than Marx. At least, as Plutarch tells the tale, Marx might more aptly have identified himself with the part assigned to Alcibiades. According to Plutarch, Timon lived at the time of the war between Sparta and Athens, and he was mocked in the comedies of Aristophanes and others, where he was called a "viper and malicious man unto mankind." Timon, says Plutarch,

> used to shun all other men's companies but the company of young Alcibiades, a bold and insolent youth, who he would greatly feast and make much of, and kissed him very gladly. Apemantus, wondering at it, asked him the cause what he meant to make so much of that young man alone, and to hate all others: Timon answered him, "I do it," he said, "because I know that one day he shall do great mischief unto the Athenians."[21]

That might well have been Engels' bourgeois-misanthropic attitude in his life-long patronage of Marx. Certainly it has been the attitude of many wealthy families since, in the West, in supporting revolutionary parties and causes.

In the scene in *Timon,* from which Marx cites his favorite passages, it is with Alcibiades that Timon speaks in the intervening dialogue. Alcibiades, not knowing that Timon has found gold, offers him some in taking leave:

> *Alc.* Why, fare thee well;
> Here is some gold for thee.
> *Tim.* Keep it, I cannot eat it.
> *Alc.* When I have laid proud Athens on a heap. . . .
> (IV, 3, 100-104)

Learning that Alcibiades schemes to ruin Athens, Timon interrupts to reveal that he has found much gold which he can give the bold adventurer in support of his destructive design. Alcibiades, Timon concludes, was born to "conquer my country." He is pleased to finance the "conquest" provided it is sufficiently destructive. "Make large confusion," he says, "and, thy fury spent,/Confounded be thyself. Speak not, be gone" (IV, 3, 128-9). Timon curses Alcibiades for having spoken well of him. Perhaps it is the feeling that Engels in the secret depths of his bourgeois soul felt for the destructive revolutionary Marx, who promised to bring ruin not to Engels' country merely, but to all of Western Christendom.

From Misanthropy Back to Hegel

Misanthropy can be fiercely poetic; yet it often props itself up defensively on a moralizing prosaic vision of the world as it yet might be if men could somehow cease to be men and become angels. Two years after he had cited Goethe's Mephistopheles and Shakespeare's "Loup-garou, or the man hater"[22] as authorities on the social omnipotence of money, Marx indulged himself with Engels in just such a vision of mankind freed at last from the curse of bourgeois greed. The. result was that notorious paragraph of *Die Deutsche Ideologie* that reads:

> In communist society, where no one has an exclusive sphere of activity, but can perfect himself in any branch that pleases him, society regulates general production and thus makes it possible for me to do one thing today and another tomorrow, hunt in the morning, fish in the afternoon, raise cattle in the evening and go in for criticism after dinner, as I please, without ever becoming either hunter, fisherman, or critic.[23]

In addition to going in for criticism after dinner, the liberated "species-man" of perfected communist society can, of course, also paint or compose music or write poetry — if he pleases — without becoming either painter, composer, or poet. Marxist apologists eager to claim something more for art in the communist future have been tempted to argue that the representation of that future in *Die Deutsche Ideologie* was not intended to be taken seriously, that Marx and Engels were in fact offering a sympathetic parody of the anarchist ideal that underlies the fierce polemic of Max Stirner's *Der Einzige und sein Eigentum (The Ego and Its Own)* of 1844 which, at least in its attitude toward money as the reigning god of the bourgeois epoch, anticipated Marx's inversion of Hegel.

Yet there is no escaping the fact that, beyond its revolutionary appeal (which it must share with many other movements, racial, national, and religious, as well as economic), Marxism is bound to offer its mass-supporters, whether in the crowded cities or on the dwindling farms and expanding campuses of modern society, the promise of a problem-free future, sans greed, sans class oppression, sans bigotry, sans war, sans everything that has ever in the past excited human imagination to high poetic expression. Even after he has pleaded through a whole book for a return to the young Marx, and to Hegel, for aesthetic renewal, Henri Arvon cannot hold back on the sort of promise Marxism is bound to give of happy times to come. "In throwing its doors wide open to the visions of a better future and the dreams of freedom that have always comforted mankind throughout the centuries," writes Arvon in the concluding paragraph of his book on the subject —

> Marxist esthetics will cease. to be the tool of oppression and obscurantism that it has been ever since Socialist Realism became official Soviet policy, and will finally be able to play its real role within a firmly established Socialist society, that of keeping consciences that are drowsy by nature on the alert, of spurring men on toward the ever-widening horiron of the future, of revealing to men the ever-changing and permanent meaning of their existence.[24]

Even when its political masters in the party *apparat* are relatively benign, if it is to remain meaningfully Marxist in any intelligible sense, Marxist criticism must follow Marx's own example in judging contemporary writers in terms of their political attitudes; and it is bound also to join Engels in urging Marxist writers to plant partisan-literary time bombs in the hands of unsuspecting bourgeois readers, in preparation for the inevitable time when there will be nothing left for art to do than to celebrate past exploits of the workers in the long struggle to recover "their status as human beings" — a struggle. which, in Engels' words, belongs "to history and must therefore lay claim to a place in the domain of realism."[25]

It is no wonder that the best students of living literature among the Marxists of recent years have tended, where they could get away with it, to saturate their criticism with a mood of (if not always an explicit doctrinal commitment to) an existential sort of social despair that envisions no Marxist heavenly denouement on earth. Jan Kott surely ranks high among Marxists of that new variety who have concerned themselves with Shakespeare. As Richard C. Clark has noted in "Shakespeare's Contemporary Relevance — From Klein to Kott to Knight," Professor Kott's widely praised book *Shakespeare Our Contemporary* gives us a Shakespeare who is the epitome not of socialist realism in the Marxist sense, but of political realism in the existential sense. In Kott's view (as Professor Clark sums it up), Shakespeare enables us to see that "no matter how humanitarian the program, politics is nothing more than the lust for power, that the world is a storm, and that history and nature are cruel."[26] *Coriolanus,* says Kott, in a thoroughly Marxist vein, "is a modern play." Its hero is crushed by history, "but it is not royal history any more. It is the history of a city divided into plebeians and patricians. It is the history of class struggle." Bertolt Brecht, Kott notes, "saw it as a drama of the people betrayed by their fascist leader." But it cannot (the existentialist in Kott hastens to add) be thus simply categorized. And he proceeds to ascribe to Shakespeare's past audiences the variety of impressions that would justify an existentialist interpretation: "The play annoyed those who believed in the masses, and those who despised them; those who recognized the purpose and didactics of history, and those who laughed at it; those who saw mankind as a mound of termites, and those who saw only lone individual termites painfully experiencing the tragedy of existence. Coriolanus did not fit in with any historical or philosophical conception current in the eighteenth and nineteenth centuries."[27]

Hailing Kott as "a revolutionary in at least two senses of the word," Benedict Nightingale writing for *The Guardian* especially raises him for having taken a view of Shakespeare as our contemporary which "has startled the universities as much as it has delighted the producers; and his life has been a constant fight against oppressors. He suffered under Stalin, and refuses to talk about it. He suffered during the war, and brushes it off by saying that, well, everyone had troubles then, didn't they? He lost his father to the Nazis and, since he is Jewish, occupied Poland was particularly dangerous. He edited an underground newspaper and was arrested several times; once he was sentenced to death, but reprieved." According to Nightingale, Kott acknowledges that the "cruelties and atrocities he saw during the war have affected his view of life, and hence his writing." The consequence is that, while still a Marxist "revolutionary," he has "no illusions." In his words: "Life is cruel, cruel, and hopeless. The only hope is to know that it is hopeless. The only dignity of man is in his consciousness of things." And it is to this, Nightingale concludes, that we must ascribe Kott's "love for Shakespeare: supremely conscious, according to Kott, of the blackness of things."[28]

The final chapter, or appendix of Kott's book is titled "Shakespeare — Cruel and True." It is a review of Peter Brook's production of *Titus Andronicus,* with the Shakespeare Memorial Theatre Company in Warsaw, June 1957. Kott there says that he had just re-read the play and found it ridiculous. Yet the Brook production, with Laurence Olivier in the title role, proved to be a moving experience, thrilling and even overpowering. Kott's analysis of the production, which made use of film techniques

on stage, is brilliantly suggestive and free of bureaucratic or ideological subservience — even, perhaps, in its final paragraph, where
he gives us a measure of the grand sweep of his world of performing arts. *"Titus Andronicus,"* he writes, "has revealed to me
a Shakespeare I dreamed of but have never before seen on the
stage. I count this performance among five great theatrical experiences of my life, with Leon Schiller's production of
Mickiewicz's *Forefathers' Eve* seen in childhood; with Jouvet whom
I had seen before the war in *Doctor Knock;* with Brecht's *Mutter
Courage* at Berliner Ensemble; with the Chinese Opera at Pe-
king."[29]

To "use" Shakespeare as a contemporary expression of
partisan discontent against all statecraft (till the Marxist prophecy of an eventual withering away of the triumphant communist
state is realized) is of course not the worst thing that can be, or
has been done, with England's national poet. Certainly it is a
way of treating him sympathetically in cosmopolitan circles without having to brand him as, in Shaw's sense, an ideological reactionary. But the result of the kind of contemporary use Kott
makes of Shakespeare is at best a mixture of falsehood with truth
— a mixture, as Sir Francis Bacon roundly phrased it, "like alloy
in coin of gold or silver, which may make the metal work the
better" in certain capitals of the world, but "embaseth it." Ours
is *not* an age for Shakespearean tragedy; on both sides of the
iron curtain, intelligent men and women know it to be an age of
prosaic comfort and prosaic conformity even in the organization and expression of discontents. The world may again see a
truly heroic age worthy of another Homer, or a time of genuinely tragic spiritual division, where nothing can stand authori-
tatively as law. But that can hardly occur while the major communist states of our time continue to indoctrinate their citizens
with a Marxism steeped in Hegel; for, as our own John Dewey
knew so well, wherever Hegel is taught, life is still being lived in
that characteristically Western contemplative dusk when Miner-
va's owl takes its flight.

"The great periods of tragedy," wrote Georg Lukács in
The Historical Novel, "coincide with the great historical revolu-
tions in human society."[30] And the fact is that there have been
really only two great periods of tragedy — one of which produced Aeschylus and Sophocles, the other Shakespeare. According to Hegel, it was not a change in the methods of production
but an awakened "consciousness of freedom," in both instances,
that made tragedy possible. It is only after hundreds of pages of

historical, logical, and phenomenological as well as ethical and political discussion of "personality" as the most adequate expression (on a political as well as individual level) of the actuality of freedom that Hegel links freedom and personality as the essential constituents of an environment in which the third or dramatic voice of poetry can make itself heard.

According to Hegel, the Greek world with its many city-states confronting one another as recognizable "peers" in the drama of history, and the age of England's Queen Elizabeth with its emerging system of nation-states destined to parallel the Greek experience on a grander scale, appear to be in retrospect a pair of great stages: rationally worked-over historical "sets" on the boards of which, in shared recognition of their prerogatives as free men and women, a great variety of "personalities of the drama" could make their entrances, fret and strut an hour, and then, because of the trans-historical power of art, pass into the seemingly deathless remembrance of civilized mankind.

Marxism and almost all the other *isms* of our time demand of literature what the author of "Dover Beach" so poignantly demanded of it in the Victorian era — that it be a criticism of life. For, in a critical age, that is how readers read, and they cannot do otherwise. In the opening pages of his lectures on the *Philosophy of Fine Art,* Hegel makes the point most emphatically. Critical-minded times cannot give us true epics or tragedies. They can give us some varieties of comedy and unheroic tales of common life that are more criticism than art. And they can give us very personal expression of an infinite variety of lyric feelings. But criticism, too, has its rights and values. If we cannot write like Homer, Aeschylus, Dante, and Shakespeare, we can be thrilled by them; and it is a compelling task of criticism to explain why that is so. Marx raised the question in his introduction to the *Critique of Political Economy;* in Hegel's *Philosophy of Fine Art* we get a thorough explanation, passing all the arts in review, with an overwhelming mass of particular illustrations, detailed analyses and evaluative interpretations, and culminating in the judgment that, so far as the dramatic delineation of characters is concerned, the highest mastery was attained, not by the Greeks, but by the English playwrights of the Renaissance; and that among those modern masters, "soaring above the rest at an almost unapproachable height, stands Shakespeare."[31]

NOTES

An earlier version of this essay appeared in *Mosaic,* X/3, 1977.

1. René Wellek and Austin Warren, *Theory of Literature* (New York, 1947), pp. 101-2.

2. *Ibid.*, pp. 103-5.

3. Peter Demetz, *Marx, Engels, and the Poets: Origins of Marxist Literary Criticism* (Chicago, 1967), pp. 152-3.

4. James K. Feibleman, *Aesthetics* (New York, 1968), pp.275-9.

5. Maynard Solomon, ed., *Marxism and Art* (New York, 1973), p. 401.

6. Robert Tucker, ed., *The Marx-Engels Reader* (New York, 1972), pp. 48-9; cf. David McLellan; *The Young Hegelians and Karl Marx* (New York, 1969) p. 157, and Demetz, p.156.

7. Solomon, p. 44.

8. Demetz p. 156.

9. Georg W. F. Hegel, *The Philosophy of Right*, trans. by T. M. Knox (Oxford, 1953), pp. 62-3.

10. *Ibid.*, p.51.

11. *Ibid.*, p. 240.

12. *Ibid.*, pp. 194-5.

13. *Ibid.*, 291-2.

14. Solomon, pp. 44-6.

15. Georg W. F. Hegel, *Aesthetics: Lectures on Fine Art* trans by T M Knox (Oxford 1975), pp. 232-3.

16. William Shakespeare, *The Life of Timon of Athens*, ed. by J. Dover Wilson and J. C. Maxwell (Cambridge, 1957), pp. xxv, xli-xlii.

17. Hegel, *Aesthetics*, p. 233.

18. Edmund Wilson, *To the Finland Station* (New York 1953), p. 307.

19. *Ibid.*, pp. 145-6.

20. *Ibid.*, pp. 320-2.

21. Shakespeare, *Timon* p. xv.

22. Geoffrey Bullough, ed. *Narrative and Dramatic Sources of Shakespeare*, Vol. VI (London, 1966), p. 255.

23. Cited in McLellan, p. 132.

24. Henri Arvon, *Marxist Esthetics* (Ithaca New York 1970) p. 117.

25. Demetz, p. 132.

26. Richard C Clark "Shakespeare's Contemporary Relevance — From Klein to Kott to Knight," *Shakespeare and England (Review of National Literatures)* Vol. III, No. 2, Fall 1972, p. 186.

27. Jan Kott, *Shakespeare Our Contemporary* (New York, 1964), pp. 139, 133-5.

28. Clark, pp. 186-7.

29. Kott, p. 236.

30. Cited in Demetz, p. 212.

31. See *Hegel on Tragedy*, ed Anne and Henry Paolucci (New York, 1962; reissued 1974, 1975, 2001).

PART FOUR
(201-246)

DRAMA'S REDEMPTION OF THE ABSURD

"Shakespeare and the Genius of the Absurd" was first published in *Comparative Drama*, Fall 1973.

CHAPTER 11

FROM THE TITAN OF AESCHYLUS TO ALBEE'S *TINY ALICE*

> *Credo quia absurdum.*
>
> (Anonymous)
>
> "I can't believe *that!*" said Alice. "Can't you? "the Queen said in a pitying tone. "Try again: draw a long breath, and shut your eyes." Alice laughed. "There's no use trying," she said. "One *can't* believe impossible things."
>
> (Charles Dodgson)
>
> Comedy is a narrow escape into faith.
>
> (Christopher Fry)

As the old dramatic masks plainly show in their grimaces and laughter, tragedy and comedy have a common origin. The pain of life, its puzzling perplexity or absurdity, calls them both into being. That does not mean that tragedy and comedy have the same content. On the contrary, each offers us a distinctive experience of pain. In tragedy, we experience it painfully, as pain; whereas in comedy, as Christopher Fry has aptly characterized it, "pain is a fool, suffered gladly."

But whether suffered painfully or gladly, the pain that dramatic art offers us is a vicarious and cathartic pain. We are made to experience the puzzling perplexity or absurdity of life aesthetically in order, somehow, to find in it a redemption of the absurd. In his extensive reinterpretation of the Aristotelian doctrine of the aesthetic catharsis, Hegel reminds us that tragic and comic *effects* are possible in all the arts, and certainly in epic and lyric poetry as well as in the two chief genres of dramatic poetry. Yet it is in dramatic poetry alone, he insists, that art can bring its tragic and comic effects to complete development so as to vie with philosophy, and even religion, in confronting the absurd and redeeming it.

According to Albert Camus, father of modern artistic existentialism, the human situation is not accidentally, and certainly not only apparently, but *essentially* absurd: absurd to the core; and art's obligation, when it acts for humanity, is to recognize that absurdity for what it is and to face up to it tirelessly, with a Promethean determination and defiance. We today, of course, know what Promethean determination and defiance are, largely from Goethe, or Shelley, or Karl Marx, rather than from Hesiod or Aeschylus; which is to say, we know the triumphantly iconoclastic Prometheus rather than the semi-comic or truly tragic Titan of the great Greek poets and philosophers. Goethe's Prometheus cries out self-confidently against all "authoritarian religion and political absolutism":

> I know nothing poorer under the sun that you gods!
> . . . Your majesty would starve were not children and beggars
> Hopeful fools. . . .
> Didst thou really think that I should hate life . . .
> Because not all my dream-blossoms ripened?
> Here I sit, form men after my image,
> A race resembling me,
> To bear, to weep, enjoy, rejoice
> Careless of you as I myself.

In the opening stanzas of Shelley's *Prometheus Unbound,* the Titan, still pinned to the Icy Rocks of the Caucasus, gives us this existentialist cry:

> Ah me! alas, pain, pain ever, for ever!
> No change, no pause, no hope! Yet I endure.

At the play's close, however, the Titan is unbound and triumphant; and a heroic Demogorgon thus draws the existentialist (not to say cabalist) moral of the tale of tireless defiance and resistance:

> To suffer woes which Hope thinks infinite;
> To forgive wrongs darker than death or night;
>   To defy Power, which seems omnipotent;
> To love, and bear; to hope till Hope creates
> From its own wreck the thing it contemplates:
>   Neither to change, nor falter, nor repent;
> This, like thy glory, Titan, is to be
> Good, great and joyous, beautiful and free;
> This is alone Life, Joy, Empire, and Victory.

And the young Marx, about to launch himself upon a career of what he called "ruthless criticism of everything existing," thus writes in the foreword to his doctoral thesis:

> Prometheus's admission: "In sooth all gods I hate" is [true phil-

osophy's] own admission, its own motto against all gods, heavenly and earthly, who do not acknowledge the consciousness of man as the supreme divinity. There must be no god on a level with it. And to the wretched March hares who exult over the apparent deterioration of philosophy's social position it again answers, as Prometheus did to Hermes, the messenger of the gods: "I shall never exchange my fetters for slavish servility. 'Tis better to be chained to the rock than bound to the service of Zeus." Prometheus is the noblest of saints and martyrs in the calendar of philosophy.

In this modern Goethe-Shelley-Marx vision of the Titan who stands up for man against the gods and who hopes till hope creates from its own wreck the thing it contemplates, the dramatic puzzle of the old Prometheus is, unhappily, resolved in a way that (as I shall try to show) makes genuine drama impossible. The old Prometheus of Hesiod and Aeschylus sets us on the dividing line between the pain of tragedy and the pain of comedy. Hegel's dialectical treatment of the common origins of tragedy and comedy helps to clarify the matter. But before I get to Hegel, let me dwell for a moment on the insightful analysis of the mystery of *Prometheus Bound* that C. J. Herington offers us in his introduction to the translation of Aeschylus's play, which he and James Scully have lately published.

"The long history of the interpretation of the *Prometheus Bound*," writes Professor Herington, "is almost the history of a mirror. Romantics, liberals, and socialists, gazing into these disturbing depths, have found there an Aeschylean justification of romanticism, liberalism, and socialism, respectively. Authoritarians on the contrary, from the medieval Byzantines onwards, have emphasized with approval the crushing punishment ultimately accorded the rebel against the Supreme Authority. In a word: *Tell me what you are, and I will tell you what you think of the* Prometheus Bound."

In reading the text today, it is certainly tempting, Professor Herington acknowledges, to "come to rest in that sublime and appalling concept: *God is a Tyrant,* bent on suppressing mankind's benefactor, and on preventing the awakening of humanity!" Prometheus is readily perceivable as an imprisoned dissident and the techniques employed by the Zeus regime can certainly be said to foreshadow the "methods of twentieth-century totalitarianism." The "political offender" is isolated, chained, tortured psychologically as well as physically, and generally abused by callous male and female police-agents; and there is even a seemingly disinterested professorial or expert examiner whose task it is to talk the prisoner into betraying himself.

The trouble with this interpretation — what we might call the "neat black uniforms and jackboots" view of *Prometheus Bound* — is that it just doesn't begin to do justice to all that is actually revealed about the protagonist in the play. We find on closer reading, says Professor Herington, that Prometheus "appears to be deliberately represented as an unstable compound of mortal Sufferer and immortal prophet." Proud defiance repeatedly gives way to sheer panic; and there is overwhelming textual evidence that "almost all the odious characteristics attributed to Zeus (mostly by Prometheus) — stubbornness, anger, rashness, harshness — are also attributed to Prometheus himself by other characters, including sympathizers like the chorus." We have here, in other words, no "simplistic opposition between blameless and incurable wickedness," writes Herington: "Rather we are at a nightmare stage of this universe, in which the true nature of any character, at any level, is hopelessly elusive." And the most partisan reader is bound to recognize, finally, that just as there is "a strain of Zeus in Prometheus," there is also a strain of Prometheus in mighty Zeus himself who, indeed, knows better than all the other Greek divinities what sort of blind necessity or fate holds ultimate sway over all that has come into being out of the original chaos. Aeschylus's *Promethus Bound*, was originally part of a tragic trilogy. We have only meager fragments of the other two plays and cannot, therefore, reconstruct the design of the whole. Still, according to Herington, who has studied them carefully, the fragments seem to support the view that the same sort of pattern we find in other trilogies — a pattern of arousing moral support first for one side and then for the other in order to prepare for the negation of one-sided sympathy in a higher synthesis — served to link the plays of the *Prometheia* together. "It thus seems likely," Herington concludes, "that to the thesis of the *Prometheus Bound*, 'Zeus is a Tyrant!,' the *Unbound* responded with the antithesis, 'Zeus is a Savior!', and that in the light of this response a synthesis became possible: the reconciliation of the almighty powers of Zeus with the civilizing intelligence of Prometheus."

With that suggestion, we are brought at once — by way of contemporary literary criticism rather than speculative philosophy — into the very center of Hegel's theory of dramatic catharsis as a redemption of the absurd which, by the dialectic of its own inner logic, divides itself into the dramatic genres of tragedy and comedy. "In tragedy," says Hegel, "the eternal substance of things emerges victorious in a reconciling way. The conflicting individuals are stripped of their one-sidedness, while the positive elements in their willfulness . . . are harmonized. . . . In tragedy the individuals either destroy themselves through the one-sidedness of their otherwise solid will and character, or they must resignedly accept what they have opposed even in a most serious way." That alternative to total self-destruction — a resigned acceptance of what has been seriously opposed — is what we find in *Oedipus at Colonos*, for instance, after Antigone and Creon have destroyed themselves in their one-sided willfulness. Resigned acceptance of what one has opposed is, of course, a sacrifice of personality — a tragic sacrifice — in the profoundest spiritual sense. Where both antagonist and protagonist are immortal, as in the case of the Zeus-Prometheus confrontation of Aeschylus, tragedy is possible only on the pattern of resigned abandonment of willful one-sidedness *on both sides* of the opposition.

What cannot be in the least tragic, from this point of view, is the Goethe-Shelley-Marx conception of the Prometheus-Zeus confrontation. If what must triumph in the end is Prometheus' will — of an absolutely moral resistance-fighter pitted against jackboot omnipotence — we have absurdity indeed, but no possibility of tragic redemption. Shelley's way out of the absurdity in his *Prometheus Unbound* is to confess at the close that Zeus has been presented as omnipotent in the course of the play only for dramatic effect — for he is really *not* omnipotent at all. The key phrases in the Demogorgon's rhetorical closing speech make the pseudo-tragic character of the representation only too clear:

To suffer woes which Hope *thinks* infinite. . . .
To defy Power, which *seems* omnipotent. . . .

The whole point of genuinely Promethean defiance is that it is to be sustained in suffering woes that *are* infinite, against Power that *is indeed* omnipotent. And that is precisely the existentialist context of absurdity — beyond practical redemption — demanded by Albert Camus' interpretation of the "Myth of Sisyphus." What would a Prometheus be like if, without sacrificing his one-sided, self-righteous willfulness, he went on sulking impotently against omnipotence *forever*, always looking for some occasion to "get even"? We don't have to speculate here, for we have the answer, quite unambiguously, where Promethus himself is brought on stage to give it to us in the climax of Aristophanes' comic masterpiece, *The Birds*.

For Hegel, that comic answer is not an accident. Having sought the essence of tragedy in a reconciliation of opposites that requires a sacrifice of one-sided personality or willfulness on both sides, Hegel sees in comedy a redemption of the absurd that leaves personality intact. "In comedy," he writes, "it is subjectivity, or personality, which in its infinite assurance retains the upper hand. . . . There comes before our contemplation, in the laughter in which the characters dissolve everything, the victory of their own subjective personality which, through it all, persists self-assured." And, even more to the point of our discussion of drama as a redemption of the absurd, Hegel says:

> What is comical is a personality or subject who makes his own actions contradictory and so brings them to nothing, while remaining tranquil and self-assured in the process. Therefore comedy has for its basis and starting-point what tragedy may end with, namely a reconciled and cheerful heart. . . . But this subjective self-assurance in a self-contradictory [or absurd] situation is only possible if the aims, and so with them the characters in question, either have no real substance in themselves or, if they have, then their essentiality has been pursued in a shape that really contradicts itself; so that finally it is only what is inherently null and indifferent that comes to grief, and the individual remains firm on his feet and undisturbed.

Aristophanes is, for Hegel, the ancient, and Shakespeare the modern master of such comedy. To recognize true comedy, Hegel goes on, "we must be very careful to distinguish whether the dramatic personae are comical in themselves or only in the eyes of the audience. The former case alone can be counted as really comical." In their self-dissolution, genuinely comical characters —

> have not the least doubt about what they are and what they are doing. But at the same time they reveal themselves as having something higher in them because they are not seriously tied to the finite world with which they are engaged but are raised above it and remain firm in themselves and secure in face of failure and loss. It is to this absolute freedom of spirit which is utterly consoled in advance in every human undertaking — to this world of private serenity — that Aristophanes conducts us. If you have not read him, you can scarcely realize how men [and, of course, the humanized gods of comedy also] can take things so easily.

I can't begin to do justice here to the fullness of Hegel's discussion of dramatic literature as a redemption of the absurd, for more than a thousand pages of his published writings and lectures are devoted to the theme, which he approaches from every conceivable avenue of interest, starting with his early *Phenomenology of Mind* and running through his lectures on the *Philosophy of History*, the *Philosophy of Religion*, and the *History of Philosophy*, as well as through his *Aesthetics*, which is our main source. What makes his treatment of the theme very contemporary in its relevance is precisely his use of the ambiguities of the Prometheus legend to get at the heart of the matter. Before Aeschylus undertook to make a tragedy out of Prometheus' plight, the fire-bearing Titan was regarded by the Greeks generally — even by Hesiod in the *Theogony* and *Works and Days* — as a semi-comic figure. Professor Herington makes the point: you simply *don't trick Zeus* and get away with it; Prometheus, as a sort of impudent wag, was therefore properly put down. Hegel discusses the matter at some length, to trace the emergence first of a tragic interpretation of his plight and then of a genuinely comic, rather than merely semi-comic interpretation.

Drawing not only on what the Greek epic, lyric, and dramatic poets say about Prometheus but also on what the Greek historians, literary scholars, and philosophers say, Hegel gives us a rather complete account of the materials that make up the fullness of the Promethean legend.

Is the confrontation of Prometheus and Zeus a confrontation between blameless virtue and incurable wickedness, as the Goethe-Shelley-Marx representations insist; is it even a confrontation — headed for reconciliation — of the civilizing intelligence of Prometheus and the almighty power of Zeus, as Professor Herington suggests? *Is* Prometheus a mythological expression of civilizing intelligence?

Hegel reviews the evidence. Although he is a Titan of the pre-Olympian generation of gods, Prometheus appears at first as siding with the new gods; then he appears as a benefactor of men who otherwise have no concern in the relations of the new gods with the Titans; he brings fire to men and therefore the possibility of developing technological skills, etc. For this act, Zeus punishes Prometheus, until at last Hercules releases him from his agony. That, briefly, is the central thread of the legend, from Hesiod through Aeschylus, Aristophanes, and beyond, into the literary critics and philosophers — however variously the details about character, motivation, etc. may be developed or interpreted. At a first glance, there is nothing "titanic," Hegel emphasizes, about what Prometheus is accused of having done; and therefore, at a certain point in the development of the legend, it begins to strike some people as rather absurd, and certainly illogical, that Zeus, chief of the spiritual gods of civilizing truth and beauty, should have chosen to punish Prometheus perpetually for having given mankind a truly civilizing spiritual gift.

"Yet on close inspection," Hegel writes, "the illogicality of Zeus' act disappears" — or, at any rate, a "few passages from Plato seem to suffice for a wholly satisfactory answer." Hegel then cites at length the account of the Prometheus myth that Plato gives us in the *Protagoras*, where that greatest of the Sophists, who gets the better of Socrates, defends the ideal of democratic government. If ever there was a likely partisan of the Goethe-Shelley-Marx view of Prometheus in antiquity, it ought to have been Protagoras the great Democrat. Yet it is Protagoras who justifies as absolutely ethical, moral, civilizing, and spiritual the punishment that Zeus assigns to Prometheus.

Plato's Protagoras reminds us that originally the Olympian gods had assigned Prometheus and his brother Epimetheus the task of supplying all the newly conceived animals, including man, with all the natural gifts needed for life. Epimetheus — the naturalist sort of in charge of endangered species — blunders; he gives away all the natural gifts before he gets to man and so man, as an animal, is left physically naked without protection or means to defend himself against weather or the violence of other animals. A redistribution of natural gifts is out of the question because all the animals — including man — must begin at once to populate the world. Prometheus, desperately good-intentioned, does what he can. As a mere Titan, he has no access to the truly spiritual heights of Olympus. And so he contents himself with stealing what he can of the *lowest* of the spiritual arts — the arts that have to do with developing and applying fire-power — from a marginal workshop of the gods, and these arts he gives to mankind, without authorization, to compensate for his brother's mistake.

Those workshop arts that Promethus steals were indeed to have been distributed on earth, according to Zeus' plan; but only *after* the highest spiritual gifts of *political virtue* had been received by mankind directly from the hand of Zeus himself. Paraphrasing the words of Plato's Protagoras, Hegel reminds us that fire and the technology that makes use of it "are nothing ethical in themselves. . . . Such skills, in the first instance, appear solely in the service of selfishness and private utility without having any bearing on the public side of life." The recipients of Prometheus' gifts used them, indeed, to protect themselves against other animals, and collected themselves in towns to do so more effectively; but, as Protagoras says, "for want of political skill, they injured one another until they were forced to scatter again," so that Zeus was sorely tempted to give up on them.

The Promethean fire-gifts had upset the spiritual priorities, so to speak. Without political virtue, men do themselves much more harm than good with such gifts (as many are arguing quite convincingly today). The worst of it is that, in the kinds of wants that fire or energy-developing arts can satisfy, there is really "never any sense of satiety; on the contrary, the need is always growing and the care is ever new." Zeus accordingly imposed on Prometheus a punishment to match the offense. Just as man's need for fire-making technology is endless, so Premetheus is to be endlessly chained to his rock, where a vulture constantly gnaws at his liver, which always grows again — a pain which like the human need for energy "never ceases."

To counteract the destructive force of fire technology, which gift he cannot take back, Zeus sends Hermes down to earth to distribute justice and a sense of respect for one's fellows among men. "Shall I distribute them as the arts are distributed," asks Hermes; "— to a favored few only, one skilled individual having enough medicine or any other art for many unskilled ones?" No, says Zeus — and here we get an expression of the sense of spiritual priorities that Prometheus lacked — "No. I should like all men to share in the sense of justice and respect for one's fellows; for commonwealths cannot exist, if only few share in these virtues, as in the arts."

But why then is Prometheus freed in the end by Hercules, and with the consent of Zeus? That takes us to the "tragedy" of Zeus and the Olympian gods generally. Hercules, the mortal who *earned* Olympian spiritual immortality, is greater than Prometheus, who remains a non-spiritual Titan. And Hercules, it is said, is destined to succeed to the prerogatives of Zeus, if only he can resist conspiring to overthrow Zeus by force. Zeus knows his limits, even while exercising his Olympian hegemony. He knows that above him and his kind *fate* rules. What Epimetheus did was spiritually wrong, but fated; and so was what Prometheus did. Compared with fate, the Olympian gods are themselves such stuff as dreams are made on and their little life is rounded in a sleep. It will take more than a Prometheus or a Zeus to solve the riddle of life, to redeem its sublime absurdity. Zeus knows this; and when Prometheus learns it, they are reconciled. But in the end, to show his recognition of the "spiritual" justness of Zeus' response to his theft, the Titan still keeps — or rather wears — his chains symbolically in the form of a garland.

What would Prometheus be and remain if he could never be brought to see the truth about himself and Zeus? Would he be what Goethe, Shelley, and Marx make of him? Certainly the ancient Greeks never indulged themselves in any such heroic, not to say satanic vision of their fire-bearing Titan. Had Prometheus not found a redemptive catharsis for the absurdity of his tragic plight in the Aeschylean tragedy that has come down to us, his only proper escape would have had to be an escape into comedy — which he in fact makes, with genuinely comic self-confidence, in the comic world of Aristophanes.

Although Prometheus makes only a relatively brief appearance in *The Birds* of Aristophanes, that comedy is nevertheless essentially Promethean from beginning to end. There, the Athenians Euelpidas and Pisthetaerus, who come on stage in the opening scene (like the protagonists of *Waiting for Godot*), concoct in our presence a very Promethean plan to bring the Olympian gods to heel. They will organize the birds, so to speak, by bringing them human know-how which, coupled with their natural capacity to fly, will enable them to build a god-defying "Cuckoobirdland in the Clouds." This Cuckoobirdland will be a benefaction to mankind, of course, because there will be open immigration into it for all human beings who have Cuckoobirdish Promethean tendencies. Once their airy Commonwealth has been built, its denizens, whether feather-bodied or feather-brained, will obviously be in a powerful position. Located between earth and heaven, they can easily bottleneck the religious sacrifices ascending from below, and thereby starve the gods into submission, since the gods — as all Protheans know — have only the odors of superstitious sacrifices to feed on.

But what about Olympian wrath and the terrible divine omnipotence? It is at this point in the argument of the play that the true Prometheus — who has tragically defied divine omnipotence — comes on the scene with a timely warning. He enters all wrapped up, so that his face is hidden. "Dear me," he says, "I hope Zeus won't see me here. . . . Look behind me, will you? Is there a god in sight?" In Aeschylus' characterization, where defiance alternates with sheer panic, Prometheus at one point cannot contain the cry. "*I'm afraid* whatever happens." Aristophanes here gives us clearly, a comic equivalent of the mood of that line. When the Cuckoobirdland hosts assure their visitor that there are no gods behind him, he uncovers and is recognized. "Prometheus!" someone cries. "Shh," he says, "you musn't call out my name. You'll ruin me if Zeus finds out I'm here. Before I tell you how things are up there, just hold this parasol above my head, to keep the gods from catching sight of me."

Prometheus, we learn, has come with a benefaction, which,

under the circumstances, he evidently considers to be even more useful than his old gift of fire. It is a warning, and its message amounts simply to this: Defiance of the gods is futile, to say the least, so long as they have omnipotence or Absolute Sovereignty on their side. The bottleneck of the sacrificial odors is indeed having the intended effect. The barbarous hordes of gods above are starving, howling like Illyrians, and threatening to levy war against Zeus. "Good!," cry the Cuckoolanders. And they like the tidings even better when they learn that the Olympians are sending envoys to negotiate peace. Not so fast — Prometheus warns. Those Olympians will put one over on you, if they can. Whatever they agree to will mean nothing, he tells the Athenian chief of Cuckoobirdland, unless Zeus actually transfers his sceptre to you and gives you Sovereignty herself in marriage. Who is Sovereignty? Prometheus is asked. Back in the days when he stole the gift of fire from the workshop of the gods, Prometheus unhappily could not have had the least idea of what sovereignty — the ultimate political virtue — was. Now, in his comic epiphany, he knows. Sovereignty, he replies, is

> The sweet girl who keeps Zeus' thunderbolt,
> Etcetera, his statesmanship, his navyyards,
> His law and order, sheriffs, jury fees,
> His wisdom, his paperpushers, and his cash.

You mean — someone asks him — she runs the whole establishment? Yes, he replies:

> Take Sovereignty away from Zeus, and all is yours.
> That's why I came — to give you this advice.
> For since time was, I've been the friend of man.

In the grand literature of Greece that ends with Aristophanes, such are the final words of immortal Prometheus: Take Sovereignty away from Zeus, and all is yours. One of Falstaff's friends might have said as much to Falstaff, to forestall the awful rejection that becomes inevitable when Prince Hal becomes England's sovereign Henry V. Or Falstaff, in comic sublimity, might have said it to himself.

The Prometheus of Aristophanes is worthy of the Prometheus of Aeschylus, for it is the same absurdity that is redeemed in both.

But it is our contemporary drama, starting with Pirandello's *Six Characters in Search of an Author,* that has come to focus with tremendous vitality on the absurd. If it is true, as I have been suggesting, that Western drama was in its origins, and has remained essentially, a defiant confrontation of the absurd, followed always by a tragic, and then by a comic "redemption" of the absurd, then it may well be that (for all the complaints of critics) we may be approaching the dawn of a third great age of dramatic literature. The age of Shakespeare, with its Hamlet and Falstaff, was the second great age; that of the Greek tragedians and Aristophanes, the first. The danger now is that, having grasped the essential absurdity of the human situation, with all its dramatic implications, our age — tempted by the heroic but false image of Prometheus — will approach absurdity not tragically or comically but *absurdly* — which is to say self-righteously, thereby making genuinely literary expression impossible.

Not long after the appearance of Camus' *Resistance, Rebellion, and Death* (which contained, among other things, his "Myth of Sisyphus" and his Nobel-prize speech on the "role of the artist in society"), a great American contemporary philosopher, William Ernest Hocking, published an article on the "International Role of Art in Revolutionary Times," in which he thus generalized on the meaning of modern art's avant-garde absorption in the absurd:

> Art must find human experience where it is: in an era of hardness, art must speak for the hard. In sympathy for confusion, modern art must echo confusion. It thus assumes the first half of the artist's task, that of knowing the burden, in order to prepare for the second half, that of lifting the burden. Has "modern art" perhaps *failed to reach its second half?*
>
> As of today, all human life stands in the shadow of the cruel and the meaningless. The quest for sense in the world process encounters a blank factuality no where better expressed than in the words of Sartre and Camus. . . . Camus rejects revolution and equally rejects exploit; for he has a new answer to the exploiter — a personal revolt, which asserts equality with the tyrant and restores the solidarity of mutual respect.

Absurdity and revolt against absurdity. The dialectic of the affirmation of personality, in its one-sided everlasting Promethean defiance — the everlasting Nay, the *non serviam* of Joyce's *Portrait of the Artist as a Young Man*. Generalizing on the experience, Hocking continues:

> Let us say that the mission of art is the Redemption of the Absurd, overcoming the irrational brute-fact-aspect of existence, not by legality or other-worldly hopes, but by the immediate attraction of a vision of human nobility in creating solidarity. The mission of art is to evoke images that universally persuade, and thus create the will to unite.

Behind those words, for me, are the tragic and comic images of Prometheus in Aeschylus and Aristophanes. Literature is a gift of fire that can have comic as well as tragic consequences. Hocking reminds us that there is such a thing as "bad art, which can undo the best work of lawmakers." Confucius, Plato, Tolstoy acknowledge that truth; and social moralists have always, accordingly, sought to "control art in the interest of social progress." That surely lies behind every use of literature for or against omnipotent Zeus, for or against Promethean defiance. Such use of art by public-minded people is, of course, an admission of its power. "But Camus sees clearly," Hocking concluded, "that while art, for every reformer, is on trial, it can only exist as free, never as the instrument of a specific polity or diplomacy. As the voice of human hope, art precedes diplomacy and makes diplomacy possible." In other words, the limit of the social utility of art *as art* is the redemptive catharsis. It is an old lesson, but nonetheless true for being old.

For me it is the lesson of Pirandello's theater and also of the plays (of which we have by no means had the last) of Edward Albee: — Focus unflinchingly on the irrational brute-fact-aspect of the human condition; revolt against it unto death, if need be; and, in death or new life, with tragic serenity or comic self-assurance, redeem the absurd. But for the time being, we are once again at a "nightmare stage of this universe, in which the true nature of any [experience or] character, on any level, is hopelessly elusive." It is no time, as Robert Corrigan points out in his excellent anthology on comedy, for clear "distinctions between tragedy and comedy." Indeed, when accepted standards of human conduct disintegrate, the confines of the two dramatic genres are inevitably obliterated. The artistic consciousness itself demands this if dramatic renewal is to be rendered possible.

Such is the key, I think, to a correct understanding of what Pirandello is up to when he attempts to force us, aesthetically, to experience the same disturbingly absurd human situations both tragically and comically at the same time. In my book on *Pierandello's Theater*, which I subtitled *The Recovery of the Modern Stage for Dramatic Art*, I tried to show that Pirandello very deliberately undertook to take his audience through the pattern of a dramatic trilogy that would be simultaneously a tragic and comic redemption of the absurd. In my book on the plays of Edward Albee *(From Tension to Tonic)*, I supported no comparable thesis; but, in retrospect I have become increasingly more persuaded that there is really no other course for our contemporary dramatists to follow if they are to remain genuine dramatists.

Back in 1951, Christopher Fry (whom I cited in the caption) put it this way: "I know that when I set about writing a comedy the idea presents itself to me first of all as a tragedy." In so saying, he apparently meant that, in developing his originally tragic idea, he found himself brought to a point where a tragic catharsis ought to have been possible but was not in fact possible for him. That I take to be the significance of his powerfully suggestive judgment: "comedy is an escape, not from truth but from despair: a narrow escape into faith." It's a judgment that clearly links itself with Dante's controversial justification, in his letter to Can Grande, for calling his great poem a *Commedia*. For Dante too there was a narrow escape into faith, an escape not from truth but from despair. In the opening lines of the *Commedia*, Dante thus describes the sensation of his narrow escape from the dark of spiritual death: "And as one cast forth gasping from the sea upon the shore turns toward the fearful water and looks upon it, so my soul, which was still fleeing, turned to look back upon the course where no man may remain and live."

The "comic relief" Pirandello offers us in his best plays — always in a tragically-menacing context — belongs to the same general order of comic relief that Dante gives us in his *Inferno*. Every one of the damned in Dante's hell is an existential Sisyphus; for having chosen "something less than the infinite," as Joseph Mazzeo has aptly phrased it, each of the damned gets in return "the finite eternalized." That is the effect of Pirandello's so-called theater plays. The notorious six characters, you will recall, are destined to play out their parts forever — repeating their sins and perpetuating their identities like Dante's damned — until they have found the author they are looking for. I have said "like Dante's damned"; but their plight is also like that of Prometheus, serving as a perpetual meal for Zeus' vulture, and of Sisyphus too, with his perpetually rolling stone. Pirandello does virtually the same thing, but with remarkable variety in his other two "theater" plays, *Each in His Own Way* and *Tonight We Improvise*, where the plays on stage repeatedly spill over into the real audience.

But it is in his masterpiece, *Enrico IV*, that Pirandello gives us his most rapidly-alternating currents of tragic tension ad comic relief. Here the protagonist makes his life a stubbornly persisted-in put-on play, of which he is stage designer, director, and producer, as well as author, and for which he has apparently been "blocking parts," as directors say, for six characters who have not been searching for an author but who nevertheless let themselves be maneuvered into joining the protagonist's cast of players just in time for a long-delayed denoument. In the course of that denoument, tragic and comic roles are reversed, and so are the paintings and human beings and the 20th and the 11th centuries. Everyone in this pseudo-11th century emperor's palace is forced to be himself by playing someone else; but it is real *masquerade* not real *life* that is being masqueraded. All of this serves to "humor" us — players and audience alike — in our short-sightedness and inflated self-esteem: even Henry under the cover of his imperial madness is not spared. But through it all we are led to self-identification and catharsis. The reversal of roles reminds us that the Pirandellian characters are never fools (unless we are prepared to call ourselves that); even when he gives us servants deceiving their masters, Pirandello — like Shakespeare — never resorts to caricature. The laughter provoked by the human frailties we witness is a self-conscious laughter. It is also therapeutic in reminding us that there is foolish potential in all of us.

In his last, unfinished, play — the large myth of *The Mountain Giants* — Pirandello puts the very notions of art, and particularly of the playwright's art, on dramatic trial. What is dramatic inspiration? What compels a poet to hear the third voice of poetry after he has heard the narrative and lyric first and second voices? How does art breathe independent will and intelligence into airy nothings to which imagination gives a local habitation and a name?' Pirandello's answer consists in conjuring up another conjurer, like Prospero; and this conjurer, in turn, dramatizes for us the labors of the Platonic demiurge in the process of creation, seen through a mythological prism which defracts our vision into tragedy, death, orgiastic frenzy, and a crowd of puppets waiting to be brought to life by the ancient magic of "two boards and a passion."

The chapter on Pirandello in Robert Brustein's *Theater of Revolt* sums up adequately, I think, what must be regarded as the Pirandellian contribution to the development of the modern theater. Supporting the prior judgments of Arthur Livingston, Eric Bentley, and Francis Fergusson, Brustein recognizes as Pirandello's "most original achievement in his experimental plays . . . the dramatization of the very act of creation." Pirandello's dramatis personae, he says, are living signatures of his artistry, "being both his product and his process." We get a flat assertion that "Pirandello's influence on the drama of the twentieth century is immeasurable." Some who have felt his influence were perhaps better artists, better practitioners of the craft "dramatized" in his plays, but there is no doubt in Brustein's view that even "a partial list of influences marks Pirandello as the most seminal dramatist of our time."

Brustein reminds us that "in his agony over the nature of existence," Pirandello anticipates the existential drama of the absurd in Sartre and Camus; that he anticipates Beckett with his "insights into the disintegration of personality," and Ionesco, with his "unremitting war on language, theory, concepts, and the collective mind." The author of *Theater of Revolt* goes on to specify how much of the dramatic approaches of O'Neill, Wilder, Pinter, Albee, Anouilh, Giraudoux, Genet, and even Jack Gelber, is to be found in the Pirandellian theater. And we can certainly agree that in all these contemporary and later playwrights, the dramatic dialectic defined by Pirandello finds an impressively valid extension into new areas. The existential themes become in many cases large allegorical statements, in which the particularized character nevertheless survives; philosophical attitudes prevail but without damage to the psychological mechanisms introduced by Pirandello; the tragic Promethean elements of the existential experience take on a stark simplicity not unlike that of ancient tragedy, while always and throughout, comedy emerges with a variety of moods and absurd possibilities as rich as the external network of events and characters described by Hegel as the "freedom" and "liberating" spirit of genuine comedy.

Following the existential catharsis according to individual preferences but still bound to the revolutionary insights of Pirandello, the playwrights of the "absurd" have produced the most important single body of plays after Pirandello. By way of conclusion, I will focus on two works — one of Beckett's and one of Albee's. They serve particularly well in this context because, though related in many of their dramatic habits, they are also, from another point of view, diametrically opposed. Both trace the large philosophical and religious implications of the absurd, both shape a new language to serve their new purpose, both make excellent use of symbol and allegory. Beckett, however, prefers a world stripped of particulars wherever possible, while Albee works in most instances in and through a familiar realism, converting it before our very eyes into something mysterious and disturbing, as though the known were being viewed through the wrong end of a telescope.

Inevitably, Beckett's *Waiting for Godot* and Albee's *Tiny Alice* suggest themselves for analysis in this kind of discussion.

Both plays are religious allegories reversed; both examine in depth the nature and attitudes of human hope and despair; both exploit the Promethean principle, which redeems the existential question ultimately, but without a trace of the "titanism" of the Prometheus of Goethe, Shelley, or Marx. Both carry out a controlled experiment, as it were, to determine the existence of the invisible God; both describe the isolation of the individual as a kind of hell; both provide through comedy the "distance" for proper appraisal of the situation; both fashion a language of their own, dictated by the profound questions that shape the play and the necessity for ironic awareness. Both, in other words, illustrate the view of life consonant with Hegel's notion of the freedom of art and the purifying effect of comedy as the restorative of a given age.

I have already discussed briefly Pirandello's *The Mountain Giants*, in which he seeks to dramatize the creative process itself. I recall it here only to stress that it serves, I think, as an excellent transition to the "absurd," for although Pirandello had already explored the many effects of the phenomenological question at the root of his dramatic vision, *The Mountain Giants* leaps over that rich experience and settles into a symbolic world not very different qualitatively from that of W*aiting for Godot* and *Tiny Alice.*

For Beckett and Albee — as for so many playwrights of this school — the allegorical mythological idiom becomes a constant. Both enrich it through musical effects, which carry their own hidden theme. In Beckett, the rigorous simplicity of the allegorical structure is redeemed by a fugue-like insistence on lines, phrases, and words which give the play the flavor of a litany. *Waiting for Godot* begins, as I noted in passing, earlier, very much like *The Birds* of Aristophanes — but it soon runs off on an original course of its own, though precisely where, who can presume to say? Godot is contacted; Godot sends messages; Godot will/ will not/may never come; Godot may in fact not exist at all; Godot remains a presence, invisible. The spiraling to some kind of a new beginning—nothing actually happens but everything is changed—has a mesmerizing effect. The protagonists circle toward built-in convictions in a dialectic of external efforts to grasp things as they appear to be, working forward and backward to some kind of Oedipal revelation. Their world is, in fact, a circumscribed circle, limited but also protective. Impostors are exterminated and the magic circle is kept inviolate for Godot. The contrasts are so stark that they border often on farce; and the pathos which is the burden of the play, gives rise to sustained humor throughout. Are the intruders perhaps Godot in his comic disguises? Are the protagonists themselves complementary images of the invisible god made flesh, with all the weaknesses and humor of human beings? Is the child who delivers the message the only true believer or just a joke? Becket's *Waiting for Godot* combines in the simplest conceivable dramatic formula evidence of the phenomenological/religious/psychological/social exhaustion of our age, with an impact as forceful and humorous as that of Shakespeare's Falstaff or Pirandello's mad emperor.

Like Beckett, Albee employs a religious myth as the starting point of *Tiny Alice* using familiar analogies, symbolical concentration and reversal of religious dogma, an insistent and devastating skepticism in a topological structure which is almost Dantesque. Like Beckett, Albee employs suggestive paradox as the means for dramatizing the reduction to absurdity (*reductio ad absurdum*) of expended values. Albee goes much further than Beckett in this; the Chinese-box arrangement in *Tiny Alice*, for example, is at once a clear visual symbol of eternity and an effective immediate stage prop, suggesting both an infinitesimal macrocosm and an equally open-ended microcosm. The play is indeed an infinite moment, the eternal present, in which characters take on the appearance of an internal, psychological shape. *Tiny Alice* is the Promethean heart of darkness in each of us, the very pulse of the existential dilemma.

Rote-like persistence sustains the unexamined faith of Brother Julian. His certainty about God is questioned and the examination of conscience which follows reveals his self-delusion. But was he lured by Miss Alice into stripping his mask of faith, or was he in some way aware of his deficiencies? The Hamlet-like burden which he carries is indeed his own; Miss Alice simply is the instrument which helps him to exorcise the dead Christ in himself. The climax of the play — the counterpoint "cappella" duet between Miss Alice and Brother Julian — together with Julian's passionate monologue at the end, when he calls upon the invisible god to cover him mercifully with darkness, are two of the most moving and beautiful passages in all the literature of the "absurd."

Albee, like Beckett, has fashioned a dramatic medium all his own and — unlike most of the other playwrights of this group — he refashions that medium from scratch with every new play. The symbolism and religious inversions of trinity, holy virtues, love, faith, salvation through suffering, redemption, and resurrection, appear as early as *The Zoo Story,* but in the early one-act play, Albee works gracefully and with incredible agility through a realism so immediate and unambiguous, that one is hardly aware at the end that he has witnessed a total transformation or translation of that familiar world. In *Tiny Alice* he begins at the opposite end, with an allegory so transparently clear that we are drawn without the least difficulty into the "penetration of character" — moving from a literal surface experience to an internal landscape at once recognizable and compelling. One should mention at least *Who's Afraid of Virginia Woolf?* and *Seascape* as vivid examples of realism penetrated by and transformed into another kind of experience.

Pirandello is the turning point in the history of dramatic literature in our time. In the intrinsic relationships of the Hegelian dialectic, his theater and that of the "absurd" can be said to be a new intermixture of tragic tension and insight and comic relief and self-assurance; and having come this far, we are reminded that the first great expression of that condition in the modern world was Shakespeare's Hamlet, the enigma and answer for our time. Hamlet's world is a universe of paradoxes, comic and absurd in its existential insistence on a simultaneous vision, a kaleidoscopic view of the vanity and glory in man. In his search for integral personality and new values, Hamlet destroys the world around him while remaining indestructible in the process. He is Promethean in his self-righteousness, wailing against times so out of joint that his mother can have married his father's regicidal and fratricidal usurping murderer. And yet, in the very midst of his Baconian experimental play within a play which is supposed to catch the conscience of his uncle and prove him a murderer, Hamlet sees the significance of his experiment suddenly turn against himself: he sees on the strength of the evidence of his own experiment that there is a streak of Claudius in Hamlet, and a streak of Hamlet in Claudius. Claudius and Hamlet are mortal and they can both therefore die — and must die, tragically — for what they have so one-sidedly willed and done. Had they both been immortal, their relation would have had to be somewhat like that of Prometheus and Zeus in Aristophanes' *The Birds* — which is to say, comical to the core.

It is no accident that Shakespeare, the greatest tragic poet of the modern world, should have been (as Hegel reminds us) also its greatest comic poet, creator of Falstaff as well as Hamlet. And, if it is true that Hamlet in his tragedy often wears a comic

— an ironically comic — mask that serves to teach us how to laugh at the tragic in ourselves, it is not less true that Falstaff in his comedy brings us, at the moment of his rejection by Prince Hal when he becomes England's sovereign, to the edge of profound tragedy.

Hamlet and Falstaff, the large Promethean image redefined by Aristophanes, the wide spectrum of juxtaposed opposites in the theater of Beckett, Albee, Pirandello, and others, provide the narrow escape into a faithful redemption of the absurd, where the masks of tragedy and comedy — our capacities to cry and laugh — become one.

Chapter 12

Avant-garde Anticipation of the Absurd

In one of his most famous pieces of literary criticism, entitled "The New Theater and the Old" ("teatro nuovo e teatro vecchio"), Pirandello tells the story of a poor peasant who couldn't read and who was startled to learn that, without his glasses, his learned parish priest couldn't read either. The priest had said that he couldn't read because he had left his glasses at home. Spurring his wit (as Pirandello says) "the peasant conceived the fancy idea that knowing how to read depended on having a pair of eyeglasses."

Off to the city the old man went, and, at an optometrist's shop demanded a pair of reading glasses. When none that he tried enabled him to read, the optometrist, losing patience, asked: "But, tell me, *can* you read?" To which the peasant answered: 'That's a good one! If I could read, why would I have come to you?"

Learning how to write plays by imitating what others have done, says Pirandello, is like putting on another's glasses in the expectation that it will enable you to read. In his Italy, he said, the so-called dramatists had purchased the glasses of Terence and Plautus for centuries; and then, when a new source became available through Paris, they began to purchase those. Machiavelli was a notable exception; and later, in some measure so was Goldoni. They too borrowed glasses, but they knew how to read and had much of their own to say, dramatically.

But Pirandello's point is precisely that the distinction between new and old theater (which is the essential presupposition for an avant-garde) is a false distinction. Speaking of the newness of Goldoni, he says:

> When this fresh expression of life burst on the mummified stage of the Italian theater and restored to it breath, warmth, and movement, they spoke of a reform. It was the new theater. Today, can we say that it is old theater because the spiritual attitude from which it grew is in itself superseded by the change of values with the passing of time?

223

In art what was created new remains new forever. Goldoni had witty, lively eyes with which he saw anew and created the new.

Any new writer today who copies and does not create, that is, who wears glasses, although in the latest style, and claims that with them he sees the liveliest problems and newest values in his time, if he wears glasses, will copy and will create old theater.

The new theater and the old. It is always the same question: of eyes and eyeglasses; of the work of creation and the exercise of copying.

Pirandello then sums up Lessing's fable of the ape who had said boastfully to a fox: "Can you name an animal so clever and shrewd that I, if I wished, could not imitate?" To which the fox rejoined: "And can you name an animal foolish and stupid enough to want to imitate you?"

Of course there is a paradox here, the essential paradox of the avant-garde. "Don't imitate!" is always avant-garde advice. But it is, of course, always much too late for such advice. After a history of drama that comes to us across two and a half millenia, "don't imitate" can only mean "don't imitate those who imitate; but rather, imitate those who don't imitate." "Do what the non-imitators do" means, after all, "imitate the non-imitators." There is no avoiding the paradox. The one thing worse that imagining that reading glasses can teach you to read is imagining that plucking your eyes out might conceivably supply the defect. Which is not to say that plucking one's eyes out cannot serve a high dramatic end. The eyes of Oedipus plucked out are indeed, at Colonus, a redemption of the absurd such as our age has been taught — precisely by the experience of the modern avant-garde theater — to long for.

In the late nineteenth century, the quest for a new theater went hand in hand, as most critics agree, with a longing for utterly realistic representation of the contemporary condition of man. And yet the theater turned almost at once to non-realistic means — to avant-garde means — of doing so, means made possible by the revolutionary advances of modern technology. Robert Brustein calls this period of drama, in retrospect, Theater of Revolt — which he contrasts with Theater of Communion. The latter, according to Brustein, is that of the past, "dominated by Sophocles, Shakespeare, and Racine, where traditional myths were enacted before an audience of believers against the background of a shifting but still coherent universe." Brustein thus lumps together all the works of a 2000-year theatrical past — ranging from the fifth century B. C. to the sixteenth and seventeenth centuries A.D., with the infinite divide of the Christian experience thoroughly ignored — in order to distinguish his new theater from a uniform old. He writes:

> By theater of revolt I mean the theater of the great insurgent dramatists, where myths of rebellion are enacted before a dwindling number of spectators in a flux of vacancy, bafflement, and accident. I have described these two theaters metaphorically in order to make two points rapidly: (1) that the traditional and the modern theaters are clearly distinguishable from each other in regard to the function of their dramatists, the engagement of their audiences, and the nature of the worlds they imply and invoke, and (2) that the playwrights of the modern theater form a movement just as distinctive as the various schools of the past. Ibsen, Strinberg, Chekov, Shaw, Brecht, Pirandello, O'Neill, and Genet — to name the dramatists discussed at length in this book — are all highly individualistic artists. Yet they share one thing in common which separates them from their predecessors and links them to each other. This is their attitude of revolt. . . .

Revolt, Brustein goes on to explain, against community, convention, custom in a reassertion of individuality — as if such revolt had not been the very essence of Greek tragedy (think of Aeschylus' Prometheus, Sophocles' Antigone!); and as if (after the Christian redemption of the absurd had grown obscure) it had not been also the very essence of Shakespearean tragedy in Othello, Macbeth, Lear, and Hamlet.

Pirandello, who is one of Brustein's playwrights of revolt, clearly saw the chasm of subject matter and of subjective consciousness that yawns between a Sophocles and a Shakespeare — a chasm as deep as the profoundest depths of conscience plummeted by the Judaic-Christian experience. The Greeks had an absurdity of the human personality to redeem, and they redeemed it dramatically. Christendom, in the time of the Renaissance and Reformation, ruptured its faithful confidence in a new sense of absurdity that called into being a distinctively new theater. What is the difference between the drama of the Greeks and that of Shakespeare? In his novel *The Late Mattia Pascal*, Pirandello gives us this impressive image:

> The tragedy of Orestes in a puppet theater!. . . . Now listen to this crazy notion that just came to me! Let's suppose that at the very climax, when the puppet who represents Orestes is about to take his revenge on Aegisthus and his mother for his father's death, a great hole were suddenly torn in the paper sky of the theater, what would happen?. . . . Orestes would still be bent on revenge, he would still be impatient to bring it about, but his eyes in that instant would be directed up there, to that ripped sky, where all kinds of evil influences would now filter down into the scene, and

he would become Hamlet. The whole difference, Signor Meis, between ancient and modern tragedy is just that, believe me: a hole in the paper sky.

Western drama, we may say, was in its origins, and has remained essentially, a drama of revolt in face of the absurd, followed always by a redemption of the absurd. Camus did not write his *Myth of Sisyphus* until 1942 and his Nobel Prize speech on the "role of the artist in society" was not made generally available until its inclusion in *Resistance, Rebellion and Death* (published in 1957). But as Lev Braun notes in his *Witness of Decline: Albert Camus: Moralist of the Absurd* (1974), the spirit of Camus' resistance, rebellion, and death can perhaps best be summarized in these words of Betrand Russell's *Free Man's Worship* (1903):

> Brief and powerless is man's life; on him and all his race the slow, sure doom falls pitiless and dark. Blind to good and evil, reckless of destruction, omnipotent matter rose on its relentless wave; for Man, condemned today to lose his dearest, tomorrow himself to pass through the gate of darkness, it remains only to cherish, ere yet the blow falls, the lofty thought that ennobles his little days; disdaining the coward's terrors of the slave of Fate, to worship at the shrine that his own hands have built; undismayed by the empire of chance, to preserve a mind free from the wanton tyranny that rules his outward life; proudly defiant of the irresistible forces that tolerate, for a moment, his knowledge and his condemnation, to sustain alone, a wary but unyielding Atlas, the world that his own ideals have fashioned despite the trembling march of unconscious power.

That is clearly the attitude of Prometheus and also of Macbeth after his vision of despair. The dilemma of the absurd has twice before ushered in a great age of dramatic literature.

Not long after Camus' *Myth of Sisyphus* and his Nobel Prize speech were published, the American philosopher William Ernest Hocking — student and then peer of William James and Josiah Royce — wrote an article entitled 'The International Role of Art in Revolutionary Times," in which he thus generalizes on the meaning of art's avant-garde absorption with the absurd in our time:

> Art must find human experience where it is: in an era of hardness, art must speak for the hard. In sympathy for confusion, modern art must echo confusion. It thus assumes the first half of the artist's task, that of knowing the burden, in order to prepare for the second half — that of lifting the burden. Has "modern" art perhaps *failed to reach its second half?*
>
> As of today, all human life stands in the shadow of the cruel and the meaningless. The quest for sense in the world-process en-

counters a blank factuality nowhere better expressed than in the works of Sartre and Camus. . . . Camus rejects revolution and equally rejects exploit; for he has a new answer to the exploiter — a personal revolt, which asserts equality with the tyrant and restores the solidarity of mutual respect.

Absurdity and revolt against absurdity: that is the dialectic of the affirmation of personality, of free personality — the everlasting *Nay,* the *non serviam* of Joyce, which is at once an everlasting *Yea.* Generalizing the experience, Hocking continues:

. . . let us say that the mission of art is the Redemption of the Absurd, overcoming the irrational brute-fact aspect of existence, not by legality or other-worldly hopes, but by the immediate attraction of a vision of human nobility in creating solidarity. The mission of art is to evoke images that universally persuade, and thus create the will to unite.

Hocking reminds us of how Plato and Confucius "both recognized that there is such a thing as bad art, which can undo the best work of law makers." Tolstoy shared the view. Social moralists have always, accordingly, sought to "control art in the interest of social progress." And Hocking concludes:

This sense of danger is an admission of [art's] power. But Camus sees clearly that while art, for every reformer, is on trial, it can only exist as free, never as the instrument of a specific polity or diplomacy. As the voice of human hope, art precedes diplomacy, and makes diplomacy possible.

That philosophic view of a contemporary of Pirandello sums up quite clearly Pirandello's own view of the mission of dramatic art. Focus unflinchingly on the irrational brute-fact aspect of the human condition; revolt against it unto death if need be; and in death of new life, redeem the absurd.

We must not forget that the great Greek dramatists wrote trilogies of absurdity, revolt, and redemption. Oedipus Rex, who flies absurdly from a prospect of killing his father and marrying his mother, only to fall into that very cruel and meaningless fate, is absurdity itself. Antigone is pure revolt against the absurd. And Oedipus in Colonus is the redemption. Shakespeare's plays too constitute a trilogy, rising from the brute fact of history through the tragic revolt of his great heroes to the redemption of his *Tempest* and related plays.

Pirandello too deliberately undertook to complete such a trilogy .The theme of the absurd in the so-called "theater plays" — *Six Characters in Search of an Author, Each in His Own Way, Tonight We Improvise* — can be traced from person to person to non-person in the de-personalization or dissolution of the *dramatis persona.*

The plays of revolt shatter the mirror that the theater plays have held up to life. And that shattered mirror gives infinite reflections of self in such plays as *At the Exit, It is So (If You Think So), As Well as Before, Better than Before, The Life I Gave You.* Revolt culminates in Pirandello's counterpart to Hamlet — the creative madness of *Henry IV.*

Pirandello's plays of redemption, or of art transcending itself, are *The New Colony, Lazarus,* and *The Mountain Giants.* These three so-called "myth plays" taken with several others (notably *Diana and Tuda* and *When Someone is Somebody*) can indeed stand alone as distinctive works of art; and yet, like Shakespeare's *Tempest* and even more like his *Henry VIII,* they reveal their full dramatic significance only to those who know the whole dramatic world of which they are the culminating achievement.

In using the term "redemption of the absurd," with Hocking, to signify the completion of art's mission, I am of course saying an old thing in a new way. One needs to recall that (as I have already suggested) in Greek drama the tragic catharsis was by no means complete in the first or second work of a trilogy. Before Sophocles produced his Oedipus trilogy, Aeschylus had already set the pattern. His *Prometheus Bound* needs not only a Prometheus unbound to complete its dramatic effect but also a play establishing Prometheus in Attica, as a benignant deity. In the Agamemnon-Cheophori- Eumenides trilogy, the cycle is not complete until Orestes is tried in a rational court and acquitted by a vote of Athena which puts the family curse to rest.

In his last plays, the author of *Six Characters* and of *Henry IV* is in effect drawing the chief meridians of his theatrical world upward to converge at a single point or pole. This whole business of life can be for us all no more than a tale told by an idiot unless we get deep enough below the surface of conventional values to the substantive core. What blind Oedipus "saw" at Colonus, what Orestes experienced in Athena's court of ultimate appeal, what Shakespeare reveals to us in the magic art of Prospero and in Cranmer's prophecy at the christening of the child destined to become Queen Elizabeth — such is the substance of Pirandello's myth plays. In them he gathers up all that he had already dramatized, into a new synthesis, to show us its social, religious, and artistic reality, in its rightness, its holiness, and its beauty.

The chapter on Pirandello in Brustein's *Theater of Revolt* sums up quite adequately, I think, what must now be regarded as permanent acquisitions for contemporary Pirandellian criticism, particularly insofar as that criticism has a bearing on Pirandello's contribution to the stylistic traits and themes, etc. of the avant-garde theater.

Supporting the judgments of Arthur Livingston, Eric Bentley, and Francis Fergusson, Brustein recognizes in Pirandello's "most original achievement in his experimental plays . . . the dramatization of the very act of creation." Pirandello's *dramatis personae,* he says, are living signatures of his artistry, "being both his product and his process." Brustein asserts flatly that "Pirandello's influence on the drama of the twentieth century is immeasurable." Some who have felt his influence were perhaps better artists, greater practitioners of the art "dramatized" in his plays, but there is no doubt in Brustein's mind that even a "partial list of influences marks Pirandello as the most seminal dramatist of our time." Summing up his judgment, the author of *Theater of Revolt* writes:

> In his agony over the nature of existence, he anticipates Sartre and Camus; in his insights into the disintegration of personality and the isolation of man, he anticipates Samuel Beckett; in his unremitting war on language, theory, concepts, and the collective mind, he anticipates Eugene Ionesco; in his approach to the conflict of truth and illusion, he anticipates Eugene O'Neill (and later, Harold Pinter and Edward Albee); in his experiments with the theatre, he anticipates a host of experimental dramatists, including Thornton Wilder and Jack Gelber; in his use of the interplay between actors and characters, he anticipates Jean Anouilh; in his view of the tension between public mask and private face, he anticipates Jean Giraudoux and in his concept of man as a role-playing animal, he anticipates Jean Genet.

Beyond his vast seminal importance, Pirandello has of course also left us a body of extraordinary plays, which, as Brustein readily admits, "continue to live with the same urgency as when they were first written."

Francis Fergusson is at pains to emphasize that the twentieth century has produced some superb playwrights but he goes on to say that the art of drama simply has "no place of its own in contemporary life." When we try to take our best playwrights together, he says, "we cannot tell what to make of them," for we have no conception, valid for our time, of the dramatic art in general.

It is from such a perspective that Pirandello's efforts to give us an "empty stage" — a stage for genuinely dramatic art, no longer confused with lyric poetry or editorializing, pure music or gossip — reveals its most impressive aspect. In Fergusson's apt phrase, Pirandello's dramatic art has literally invaded a stage long possessed by craftsmen of marvelous skills who have at best a mistaken "idea of theater." For Pirandello, between 1916 and 1921, when the "third voice" of poetry was forcing itself irresistibly on his mind's ear, the stage of his time seemed no place at all for living characters. Almost cynically, he concocted the idea of invading that stage with his *Six Characters in Search of an Author* to cast the rascals out. Can real characters find in the contemporary stage successful playwrights worthy of them? For that is the real point of Pirandello's *tour de force*. Here is a family of characters to mirror our contemporary state of mind and heart back to us. They have come out of the creative imagination of a man who writes novels and short stories to be marketed in bookseller's stalls. But they are searching for an author who can give their drama a fitting stage, a proper "place of its own in contemporary life." Those who grossly buy and sell mere entertainment in drama's temple, says Pirandello, are to be cast out, and so his six characters move in to overturn "the tables of the moneychangers and the seats of them that sold doves" and all the other props of those who make the temple of dramatic art a den of commercial swindlers.

What Pirandello achieved by his disdainful invasion of the theater as he found it was, in Fergusson's words, "the restoration of the ancient magic of 'two boards and a passion,' frankly placed in the glare of the stage light and the eye of the audience." It is the "empty stage" of purest theatrical potency. Pirandello did not, for he could not by himself, put on that stage a completely satisfying theater for our time, mirroring to its own age and body their true form and pressure. But for all who "search for a search," the author of *Six Characters*, of *Henry IV,* and of *The Mountain Giants* has shown where the search must begin and to what end. He is, in other words, precisely what our Livingstons, Pitöeffs, Sartres, Bentleys and Brusteins — to name but a few — have acknowledged him to be: the playwrights' playwright *par excellence* of the contemporary theater.

Pirandello argues that we have the playwrights for genuine theater plays, either actually or potentially, and there is always, in civilized societies, a potentially fitting audience. It is the place where the two must meet that is usually unavailable for the purpose. When a true playwright finds a proper stage, the thing can be done as it should be done; his audience, however sparse, can be made to share, through the dramatic catharsis, in the highest spiritual experience of which the theater is capable. And when the audience is few, it can be said of those few (as of Henry V's soldiers at Agincourt) so much the worse (the words are Pirandello's) for whoever stayed away; "he missed the chance to participate in an experience of spiritual life actually and wholly realized within the circle of the community of which he is a part, and there can be nothing to boast in his having turned his back on it."

CHAPTER 13

SHAKESPEARE AND THE
GENIUS OF THE ABSURD

Literary masterpieces, Benedetto Croce was fond of repeating, defy comparison; each is an organic whole, best experienced in its uniqueness, as we experience individual personality. Still, critics persist in their bad habits — as Croce himself
persisted in comparing great authors — in spite of the warning.
And this is perhaps as it should be because, although greatness
in literature cannot be measured by purely literary standards (as
T. S. Eliot insisted), many other constituents of literary value
can be measured, and the comparative study of literary works is
at least to that extent justified. Shakespeare's dramatic genius
certainly towers above the dramatists of our age, even as it soared
above the best efforts of his own contemporaries. But it is not
too far-fetched — not inexcusably absurd — to suggest that in his
treatment of character, in his rich use of symbolic overtones, in
his paradoxical juxtaposition of certain themes, in his subtle allegorical shadings, Shakespeare "anticipates" the dramatic habits and practice of contemporary dramatists such as Camus,
Ionesco, Beckett, and Albee (who, in my opinion, is the best —
though certainly not the most absurdist — of our playwrights of
the Absurd). Macbeth's castle, for instance, like the replica of
the mansion in Albee's *Tiny Alice,* reverberates with dark-light
images that serve to intensify the turns of dramatic action; Albee's
manic-depressive characterization of Brother Julian in that play
is built, like Shakespeare's characterization of Hamlet, around
the painful surfacing of deep and mysterious motives; in both
plays, paradoxical extremes produce a Sophoclean irony, and
past and future merge in the obsessive verbalization of actions
and intentions. Dramatic art has undergone many transformations since Shakespeare's time; yet with the Absurd, there is at
least an apparent spiraling back over old ground. From the new
perspective of contemporary drama we may gain a new appreciation of some of the oldest techniques of the playwright's art.
    We can begin to assess how far the history of dramatic art
has spiraled back on itself by recalling briefly the nature of the

recent shift from realism to the Absurd. The Ibsen-like realism of an earlier age professed to depict things as they are, to hold a mirror up to nature. But that mirror of realism is carefully "programmed"; it is highly selective to begin with. The realistic writer does not simply record events as they happen, in the sequence of actual experience. He chooses those things that will enable him to create the illusion of so-called reality. All art is selective in this way, of course; it recreates the complex organic totality of life by holding a mirror to things we recognize and accept.

The mirroring of complexity through organic simplicity is, in a sense, the definition of art. What differs from age to age is the quality of the mirror. Realism holds a smooth mirror up to nature; the Absurd holds a "magic" mirror, which distorts and exaggerates familiar things in order to shock us into a new evaluation of experience. The crazy mirror of the Absurd breaks up familiar patterns and forces us to accept a new dimension and a new kind of communication. It insists on the language of existential doubt within a framework of skepticism. In this kind of experience, the direct and powerful statements of "realism" are no longer adequate. Purposeful action inspired by clear-cut values, logical categories, the familiar patterns of human behavior as defined by the scientific method and unassailable reason are replaced, in the Absurd, by kaleidoscopic insights, fragmentation of intentions and deeds, levels of awareness, a distortion of the very mechanics of apprehension.

The historical transformation that has taken place in dramatic characterization reinforces the point. The single unswerving ethical thrust of the Greek tragic figures — all of one piece and wholly taken with their single-minded purpose — gives way in Elizabethan drama to a rich variety of personality with all its quirks and particularity; and this, in turn, becomes in the realistic drama of Ibsen, Strindberg, and O'Neill a kind of psychological probing, the ultimate end of which is self-consciousness and self-knowledge. Until this point there is — in spite of the shift in focus — an insistence on maintaining the organic wholeness of character. With the Absurd, this organic wholeness gives way to a splintering of personality which often appears as an unresolved dichotomy of purpose. This new vision of dramatic personality may best be described as the "dissolution" of character; its corollary is the "dissolution" of action. The plot of an Absurd play is apt to be rather sketchy; it is more like a commentary on the eternal moment which is captured and explicated. It is no accident that so many Absurd plays find their best expression in

symbols and allegorical suggestion. By stripping familiar sur-
roundings and reducing organic wholeness to states of mind,
fears and doubts, desires, opposing and often contradictory
impulses, the theater of the Absurd succeeds in creating before
our eyes a dissolving reality which is forever on the verge of
extinction. The first modern dramatist to explore the full implications of this new convention was Luigi Pirandello; but it was
Shakespeare who led the way.

In Pirandello's plays, the dissolution of character — together
with the dissolution of action and language — becomes almost
an obsession. But Pirandello never destroys the wholeness of
dramatic organic experience in the traditional sense.[1] Later dramatists like Ionesco push the dissolution of character, action,
and language to the very brink of incommunicability. Albee and
Beckett insist on the delicate balance between the demands of
conventional theater and the innovations of the Absurd. The
tension created by this juxtaposition, in my opinion, makes these
two dramatists the best representatives of the contemporary theater. Instead of repudiating the demands of the stage, they have
succeeded in translating them into their terms. Like Shakespeare,
they turn the very limitations of theater to advantage.

The world of the Absurd is a static world where, paradoxically, a great deal happens. It is a seemingly erratic and irrational world, and yet we recognize instinctively a circling around
the core of meaning, a spiraling around key symbols that take
on the force of refrains. The idea of the Absurd is best summed
up, we are told, in Camus' essay "The Myth of Sisyphus."[2] The
stone will never get pushed up to the top of the hill. But Sisyphus
seeks his meaning, absurdly, in the effort. It is like the labors of
the Biblical Cain, who builds a place of safety and rest for himself in the land of wandering, where to rest is to wander. It is like
the contrast between Dante's vision of the stars — with which
each of the three canticles of *TheDivine Comedy* ends — and
Giacomo Leopardi's stars in his famous poem, "Canto Notturno."
They are the same stars; but for Dante they most perfectly show
the meaningfulness of the universe, whereas for Leopardi's shepherd nothing could be more futile, not the labors of Sisyphus,
not the escapist curse of Cain.

As a moral or religious idea, the absurd of the theater of
the Absurd is very old and very central. But we get it obliquely in
the best plays. Dramatic theme is a matter of intuition and recognition, rather than statement — very like the intuitive insight
experienced by Hamlet as he hears the ghost of his father tell

how he was killed by Claudius. Character, in this new dramatic framework, follows the same pattern: personality is seen, as it were, from within, as a mosaic of impulses and feelings.

The Shakespearean play which offers the most suggestive comparisons in this context is, of course, *Hamlet*. As Robert Hapgood points out in his article, "*Hamlet* nearly Absurd":

> . . . Hamlet's critique of human action and communication is surely as thoroughgoing as that of any modern work — so modern that one way to place Shakespeare's view is to put it in the context of absurdist theatre. Certainly, the allusion to *Hamlet* in *Waiting for Godot* seems very much at home. Indeed, Vladimir's remark in the course of "raising Pozzo" — "But that is not the question. What are we doing here, that is the question" — helps to confirm that the whole sequence parodies Hamlet's rhythm of arrested action, including as it does: 1. the intense declaration of purpose. . . . 2. the arrestment of action — involving deflection. . . . 3. the final, sudden, almost inadvertent success that seems to come of itself. . . .[3]

In the most modern of his heroes, Shakespeare almost lets go of dramatic personality as understood from the time of the Greeks, threatening to reduce organic characterization to irreconcilable levels of consciousness. Perhaps this is the reason why so much criticism has sought to find in the character of Hamlet the symptoms of psychological disease. It is a temptation that must be resisted if we want to take Hamlet seriously, as a responsible agent of his fate. As Shakespeare conceived him, he assumes the full responsibility for his deeds and is perfectly aware of what he does. The contradictory motives which come to the surface are simply that — not symptoms of disease. He reflects the doubts in all of us.

The most interesting single element in this context is the soliloquies. They stand out from the surrounding action like islands of internal life, describing for us an internal condition of the soul and defining a personality which seems at odds with the Hamlet of the outer action of the play. We seem to be circling around a core of meaning on two separate levels, and we see the hero as a "double" image. The Hamlet of the soliloquies is driven by a kind of "floating anxiety" which is never fully understood or defined; the Hamlet of the outer action is energetic and ready for action — all but the one deed which the ghost has asked him to perform. Again and again, we sense in the Hamlet of the soliloquies a psychological paralysis, an indulgence in philosophical and spiritual meditation — the meaning of life, the place of men in the cosmic picture, the purpose of heroic commitment, the questioning of providential design, the self-consciousness of

the soul faced with doubt, the alternating rejection and acceptance of a divine dictum, the obsession with logic and rational-
ization as a substitute for straightforward direct commitment.
We see the world from the eyes of this Hamlet as though through
the wrong end of a telescopic lens. Everything is removed and
distant. There is a stoic quality reflected in the soliloquies, a
dissolving of time and place into some distant eternal setting.
This special quality of the soliloquies impresses itself upon us
when we realize that most of them can be interchanged without
doing serious damage to the continuity of the action.

The outer action suggests the manic side of the picture (I
am using the word "manic" only as a descriptive shorthand). In
the outer action or plot of the play, Hamlet emerges as a shrewd
Machiavellian realist, a man who can size up quickly the treachery of his erstwhile friends and who, like Cesare Borgia confronted with the betrayal of his captains, is quick to mete out
punishment of the same kind, luring them into a false sense of
security while plotting their death. He kills Polonius thinking it
is Claudius — but this does not explain the psychological indif-
ference to the deed, any more than the suspicion that Rosencrantz
and Guildenstern have been plotting with Claudius against him
can justify their execution. The Hamlet of the outer action makes
impossible demands of his mother and repudiates the girl who
was to be his bride, for no apparent reason. This same Hamlet
can, at the end of the play, fight and kill — not as the fulfillment
of the Ghost's request, but as a lashing out against those who
would kill him. This Hamlet does not procrastinate, does not
brood about what is to be done, does not have pangs of conscience about what he does. We see in this mosaic of arbitrary
events, a kind of destiny working itself out through the heter-
onomy of human intentions.

Action dissipates into a series of isolated confrontations.
And the hero of this action emerges as a double image: the Machiavellian worldly realist and what Hegel calls the *schöne Seele* —
the beautiful soul who justifies self-righteously his deeds in the
Socratic certainty of his inner convictions. We tend to identify
with the latter more easily, since it reflects the atomistic ethical
condition of our age. It is significant, however, that at the end of
the play, when time has run out, Hamlet no longer recalls the
task set for him by his father's ghost. Although he had acknowledged the responsibility to avenge the King's murder and had
promised to do so, that promise is all but forgotten in the last
confrontation with the King, when Hamlet is prompted to ac-

tion by Claudius' personal attack against him. Hamlet kills
Claudius for new reasons and remembers the Ghost only at the
moment of his own death. These two images, seen as the distortion of a magic mirror, remain unresolved. We see in Hamlet
the beginning of that dissolution of character which is the trade-
mark of the Absurd.

Like Brother Julian in Albee's *Tiny Alice*, Hamlet will not
bring himself to admit his profound skepticism about divine
prerogatives and about the request made by the agent of divinity. He does suggest, at a certain point, that the Ghost may be an
agent of the Devil — but everything before and after that statement indicates that he does not take that possibility seriously.
He cannot ever accept a divine command, although he would
like to and is eager to avenge the Ghost. He vows at the outset to
avenge his father's death, but with each succeeding soliloquy he
moves further and further away from that original intention.
His verbalizing is a sign of his doubt; we sense it with his very
first reaction: instead of going about the business asked of him,
he takes out his notebook and jots down a Machiavellian observation about how a man can smile and still be a villain. He is
torn between doing what his sense of honor tells him he must
do and accepting the task as a divine command. Like Julian in
Albee's play, he claims to have accepted the divinity outside him
and professes a kind of faith; but everything he says and does
proves the opposite. The Ghost, in this context, is — like the
giant replica of the mansion in *Tiny Alice* — the symbolic embodiment of an empty faith. Like the replica, the Ghost forces
that empty faith to the surface of consciousness, in slow stages.
Both these "props" (and I use the word in the best possible sense)
hang over the action of the play in each case, constant reminders of the ynacknowledged lie within the hero. Julian ultimately
confesses his dark despair and accepts the unknown divinity he
has courted unconsciously; Hamlet recognizes the lie within himself in his efforts to explicate the divinity that shapes our ends —
he picks away at the doubt inside him with compulsive determination, but the wound will not heal. In their search for spiritual
certainty and the conviction that comes with it, both Julian and
Hamlet are destroyed.

Perhaps the most interesting thing about this double image we have described is the ease with which the reader accepts
it and identifies with it. We tend to forget altogether the image
of the outer action and remember and identify exclusively with
the *schöne Seele*, the beautiful soul of the soliloquies. We accept

the existential questioning without insisting on answers, recognizing in the Socratic grandeur of the struggle toward freedom and light the redeeming feature of human weakness. It is this aspect of the characterization which attracts us. As Martin Esslin observes in *The Theatre of the Absurd*, "there is in Shakespeare a very strong sense of the futility and absurdity of the human condition"[4] — and it is this sense which we recognize and accept, just as we accept Julian's empty profession of faith, at the end of *Tiny Alice*, as a kind of heroic martyrdom.

Hamlet marks the turning point in the history of dramatic characterization. We see for the first time the integrated or seemingly-integrated character collapse in slow stages before us through an ever more intense oscillation between what is and what appears to be. Acknowledged purpose vies with hidden doubts, action recedes into brooding about action. The dramatic action itself becomes a series of sharp reversals and produces an effect not far removed from Sophoclean irony. Human personality is split into forces — instinct, revelation, confession, guilt, assertion, denial — the full spectrum of psychological motivation. In both *Hamlet* and *Tiny Alice* we seem to be inside the character looking out. Against this internal landscape of the soul, action and dramatic plot become a series of independent episodes, all tending toward the resolution implicit in the opening scenes. It is worth noting that the dramatic resolution of *Tiny Alice* resembles the end of Shakespeare's play in the realization of the death wish buried in the hero. In accepting Miss Alice as his bride, Julian has in fact accepted the verdict of death; just as Hamlet, in avoiding the resolution inspired by the Ghost, is doomed to a limbo of ineffectual action, where single-mindedness and strength of will on the part of others must prove victorious over him. The "accidental" resolution of Shakespeare's play is as much a part of the dramatic intention as is Julian's final martyrdom in Albee's play.

The tragic core of *Hamlet* — like that of *Macbeth*, *Julius Caesar*, and *Othello* — has much in common with the existential premise at the heart of the Absurd. *The Zoo Story*, *Who's Afraid of Virginia Woolf?*, *A Delicate Balance*, and *Tiny Alice* all raise existential questioning to tragic proportions and produce an effect not very different from that produced by the Shakespearean plays mentioned. Albee's plays all end with the total exhaustion of the human will, a condition which does not, however, destroy the integrity of his characters. On the contrary, the depression which sets in at the end of *Who's Afraid of Virginia Woolf?*, the rejection and futility which mark the ending of *A Delicate Balance*, the isolation of the characters in *Quotations from Chairman Mao-Tse-Tung*, the pathetic Christ-like attempt of Jerry at the end of *The Zoo Story* to reach out in death to another human being and thus establish a bond between them (even though it is the bond of victim and killer) illustrate the stoic resignation of characters who even in defeat and death are not overwhelmed. Like the grand tragic figures of the Shakespearean plays, Albee's characters create their own tragic dimension, forcing — as it were — a confrontation with fate; and when that fate finally asserts itself and answers the call, they accept it as their own doing.

The tragic dimension in Albee is also a spiritual unfolding. The religious motifs of the mass for the dead in *Who's Afraid of Virginia Woolf?*, the references to Christ, Hell, faith, Cerberus and the redemption through death in *The Zoo Story*, the religious awakening of Julian to an empty faith in *Tiny Alice*, all remind us that the essence of tragedy is the juxtaposition of human vanity and glory, the simultaneous assertion of human freedom and predestined fate. The tension produced by this paradox — what Spinoza calls "insight into necessity" — is of a kind with the tragic tension of Shakespeare's plays. And, interestingly enough, this tension produces in such plays as *The Zoo Story*, *A Delicate Balance*, and *Who's Afraid of Virginia Woolf?* something very similar to Hamlet's feigned madness. Jerry's intrusion into Peter's privacy has a restrained but unmistakable hysteria about it, which comes to the surface gradually and culminates in the calculated attack which forces Peter to react and results in Jerry's death. Madness opens and closes the story of Agnes and Tobias in *A Delicate Balance*; the entire drama revolves about that point of no dimension. Hysteria bordering on a manic-depressive state (and here I am using the word in its clinical sense) threatens to destroy the protagonists of *Who's Afraid of Virginia Woolf?*; and in *Tiny Alice*, madness is the very heart of the matter, for Julian's loss of faith was, as he tells us, identical with the loss of sanity, and reason enough to have himself committed. But the word madness is no more appropriate here than it is in *Hamlet*. As in Shakespeare's play, madness as introduced by Albee is meant to add to the tension of tragic opposites; it is never a retreat of the conscious will but a means of purging it.

All that has been said so far suggests the paradox of freedom and links up the existential world of the Absurd with the tragic world of Shakespeare. Both Hamlet and Jerry do what is inevitable, what has been programmed for them, what they are shaped to do — but they do it by means of seemingly arbitrary decisions, irrational impulses, license. It is the same kind of insight into necessity which we see in Macbeth and Brutus, who, like Hamlet, accept at the outset a misleading cue, recognize it later for what it is, and in attempting to correct the direction that they have taken succeed only in fulfilling the initial design. This acknowledgement of freedom as insight into necessity is clearest in *Macbeth*, where the hero accepts the prophecies of the witches and then attempts to work against those which threaten to undermine what he has done, bringing about — in his futile efforts — the very things predicted by the witches. The "tomorrow" speech is the realization of the paradox and the acceptance of it. Brutus attempts to justify what he has already consented to do in his soul — namely, the murder of Caesar — rationalizing his deed by the suggestion that Caesar will become the tyrant he fears. But Caesar never gets to prove Brutus right; and in the course of the play, we watch the noble Stoic disintegrating under the doubts that plague him and which rise to haunt him at key moments in the later action.

In the same way, Martha in *Who's Afraid of Virginia Woolf?* forces George's hand and brings about the "death" of the fictional son — who is also the young George, the innocent dream of success, hope of fulfillment, the myth that holds them together. Julian's account of the six years spent in the asylum takes on a horrible fascination as we hear him recall the incidents of that time in language which is at the same time sexual and mystical, and we are made acutely aware of the fact that the past is not dead and buried but very much alive in him. At the end of the play, destiny moves from mystery to light, from objective statement to subjective reality and acceptance, through human volition. What we witness is the translation of an external dictum — an oracular promise, if you will — into an internal purpose. The mysterious bond between the witches and Macbeth, Brutus's stoic determination to do the right thing, Hamlet's acceptance of the Ghost's challenge, Julian's strange identification of sexual abandonment and religious ecstasy, Jerry's obsession with his role as a Christ-like figure, Martha's hysterical efforts to destroy herself through George and the final disintegration of the son-myth all point to the resolution of the existential, tragic question: fate and human will ultimately become one and the same.

The psychological reversals, the paradox of human will and predetermined fate, the contradiction implied by the simul-

taneous acceptance and rejection of the prophecies, are reinforced throughout, in *Macbeth*, by skillful juxtaposition and unintentional irony. Ross hails Macbeth "Thane of Cawdor" just
after the witches have greeted the hero with that title and while
Macbeth is still adjusting himself to the strange greeting; the
messenger comes to Lady Macbeth with news of Duncan's imminent arrival, even as she gives voice to the horrible plan she
has conceived, independently of Macbeth; Banquo's ghost appears immediately following the murder and, as it were, at
Macbeth's invitation; the Porter scene, coming upon Duncan's
murder, intensifies the dramatic tension with its grotesque parody
of reality, particularly with the reference to "hell-gate." Macbeth
broods about how he can get the crown, even as he accepts the
title of Cawdor; having attained the crown, all he can think of is
his rival Banquo; having destroyed Banquo, he discovers a new
threat in Macduff and wreaks his vengeance on the family left
behind; he prepares to go forth into battle, still certain of his
invulnerability, even as he mourns Lady Macbeth's death. In *Tiny
Alice*, the irony implicit in Julian's acceptance of Miss Alice and
his rejection of the experience in the asylum, his instinctive recognition of the strange power of the replica of the mansion and his
acceptance of the invitation to move into the house; his confes-
sions to Miss Alice and his decision to marry her, while rejecting
the sexual implications of his religious mysticism prepare us for
the final paradox, where Julian recognizes his bride as the mysterious darkness of the replica and gives his consent to the marriage with death. In both plays, we witness a Sophoclean unraveling of motives, at first only dimly understood by the protagonists, but gradually drawn into conscious acceptance. As an "extended metaphor of contradiction," *Macbeth* comes very close to
the irony of the Absurd.

Both plays employ imagery of light and dark, sight and
blindness, to remind us of the theme of self-knowledge. I have
always thought of *Macbeth* as the most provocative of Shakespeare's plays in its use of metaphor and symbol to suggest this
transparent allegory. In this respect it deserves a special place of
honor with Sophocles's *Oedipus Rex*.[5] But Albee's *Tiny Alice* deserves to be ranked with them. In that play, Albee proves that
symbol can be used lightly and relevantly to create an allegorical
dimension at once simple and transparent. One example will
suffice — the most impressive one, certainly worthy of the interplay of sight and blindness in *Oedipus Rex* and the poetic
suggestivity of night, visions in sleep, sleepwalking, and blind

prophecies unraveling, in *Macbeth*. Toward the end of Albee's
Tiny Alice, the giant replica of the mansion — which is a kind of
Chinese-box of the microcosm and the macrocosm — is lit up
briefly during the wedding feast of Julian — an ironic suggestion
of what is coming. In this sudden feast of lights, the hidden life
of the replica makes itself seen and lures Julian into accepting
the toast offered to the divinity that resides in it. The replica is,
in fact, a new dimension, expanding in meaning before our very
eyes. Julian accepts it without understanding it — although there
have been enough signals all along to warn him to be cautious:
fire is discovered in the chapel of the replica and everyone rushes
to put it out . . . in the real chapel, upstairs. Lawyer toasts the
newlyweds, wishing them well in their new house, and the lights
go on . . . one by one . . . in the replica. But in the end, when
Julian cries out in his death-agony for some sign of life and certainty, the lights in the replica go out as mysteriously as they had
gone on earlier, and Darkness literally spills out into the larger
dimension of the room as the great chandeliers are dimmed
one by one. The replica is the darkness inside him, and, at his
request, it moves out into the room to engulf him. The giant
doll-house is thus transformed before our eyes into the living
articulate symbol of Julian's spiritual exhaustion. The festival of
light comes to an end, and Darkness becomes a palpable presence as it moves out of its retreat and flows into the room where
Julian lies dying. It is the mystical marriage he had consented to,
the paradox made real. Like a giant mouse-trap, the replica has
been lying in wait for him, for this moment — just as the witches
lure Macbeth with their cryptic utterances, gradually absorbing
his attention, so that he sees and hears nothing else. In the end,
he is transformed into their image, into the self-appointed Mon-
ster of Fate, just as Hamlet becomes finally the ironic means for
the fulfillment of the Ghost's request.

This kind of subtle allegory is as much a feature of the
Absurd as it is of Shakespeare's tragedies, where every image
and reference contributes to the organic structure of poetic expression. Beyond this, the individual images themselves are often as wild and as strange as the language of Ionesco or the early
Albee. The break-up of language — like Dali's bent and dissolving pocket watches — is unforgettably absurd in these dramatists; but the magic hand of chance that makes words say the
seemingly impossible is always at work in Shakespeare. The results are so transparently right, so expressive that we are apt to
miss the absurd conceit of it.

In his moments of highest moral distraction — when he is literally beside himself, torn apart in "restless ecstasy" (III.ii.22) — Macbeth murders his figures of speech even as he murders sleep, to give utterance to the sublimest absurdities of despair. The absurd conceit of the "naked babe" image, for example, reminds us that at moments of greatest tension, Shakespeare's imagery tends to dissolve into a series of kaleidoscopic suggestions, each one sharply defined in itself but, paradoxically, creating a moving image in which the parts — the actual metaphor or simile — give way to the surrealistic movement of the whole. Cleanth Brooks sums up the "naked babe" image as a symbol of "all those enlarging purposes which make life meaningful, and . . . all those emotional and . . . irrational ties which make man more than a machine — which render him human."[6] He reminds us of the cluster of images to which the "naked babe" belongs and the reverberations that are produced as a result of this cumulative linguistic procedure. But it is the moving image which is significant in the context of the Absurd.

> And pity, like a naked newborn babe,
> Striding the blast, or heaven's cherubin horsed
> Upon the sightless couriers of the air,
> Shall blow the horrid deed in every eye,
> That tears shall drown the wind.

Macbeth's imagination — like his vaulting ambition — o'erleaps itself. The babe striding the blast, the angel riding sightless couriers, tears that drown the wind — these images, like such deceptively simple phrases as "ripeness is all," are the very embodiment of paradox. They represent the emptying out of logic and the creation of a new dimension which, taken literally, must appear a patent absurdity. In struggling to articulate what is beyond communicability, Shakespeare approximates the language of the Absurd and pushes dramatic speech to the brink of nonspeech.

Ionesco, of course, immediately comes to mind. But in a slightly different context, think of the absurd paradox of the actor who plays the lead in Pirandello's *Six Characters in Search of an Author*. That actor must insist that no actor can play his part in the production as well as he can, for he is really the character he is playing. He pretends that his acting is somehow beyond the reach of acting. At its worst, this kind of dramatic insight is a stunt; but at its best, it expresses in its tortured diction and its Dali-like dissolving technique the clash of values that sometimes overwhelms us inside, as we try to give expression to our

profoundest feelings. A George Herbert can give the poetic meta-
physic of it in those marvelously suggestive lines —

> O what a thing is man! how far from power,
> From settled peace and rest!
> He is some twenty several men at least
> Each several hour. [7]

Samuel Johnson complained that Shakespeare's style "was
in itself ungrammatical, perplexed and obscure," and while con-
ceding with Dryden and Longinus that the ungrammatical breaks
and figures are indeed "necessary to raise passion,"[8] he favored
generally the effort of 18th-century editors to emend and rectify
the richest imagery into rational, plain language that said very
clearly what Shakespeare would not and did not say. The romantic poets and critics stopped trying to emend the absurdities of Shakespeare's language. Coleridge spoke of its "instructive propriety." Hazlitt and Lamb dwelt with fascination upon it.
Keats saturated his imagination with it so that his own art, which
he called the "magic hand of chance," could always have greatness to play with. Goethe praised its infinite variety. But, as
Wolfgang Clemen observes in *The Development of Shakespeare's
Imagery*, of all the Romantic poets and critics,

> the only one who saw the dramatic relevance of Shakespeare's
> imagery seems to have been the philosopher Hegel. In the first
> part of his "Aesthetic" he analyzes the function of image and com-
> parison in dramatic poetry, illustrating his remarks by examples
> taken from Shakespeare.[9]

In that passage of *The Philosophy of Fine Art*, Hegel answers "the
English critics who have often charged Shakespeare with a su-
perabundant and too varied recourse to the simile [and meta-
phor]." He says that when a great soul is caught in an existential
dilemma — an apparent absurdity that sets his existence on its
head — he must spin out comparisons (like the tales that Albee's
heroes tell of confronting hostile dogs and of killing unresponsive cats) to deliver himself spiritually. "In dramatic art," Hegel
writes, "the dramatis personae appear as themselves the poets
and artists. [When they objectify their feelings in images] this
absorption into something else that is external is the deliverance of the world within . . . it is a victory over the exclusive
obsession of passion and the release from its masterdom." And
then he says: "In following up the course of this liberating process, we will now emphasize several important distinctions to
illustrate which we shall borrow exclusively from Shakespeare,"[10]

How does one accept the unacceptable? How does one

grasp the meaning or, rather, the lack of meaning — the meaningless experience that shatters the soul because it is a tale told
by an idiot signifying nothing? Matthew Arnold expresses it in
these words:

> Ah, love,
>   . . . let us be true
> To one another! for the world, which seems
> To lie before us like a land of dreams,
> So various, so beautiful, so new,
> Hath really neither joy, nor love, nor light.[11]

Leopardi tells us that it is sweet for him to drown in such a sea.
Camus, in his *Myth of Sisyphus,* writes that in a "universe that is
suddenly deprived of illusions and of light," there is a "divorce
between man and his life," and that divorce "truly constitutes
the feeling of Absurdity."[12]

    If that sense of "metaphysical anguish at the absurdity of
the human condition"[13] is indeed the theme of the plays of
Beckett, Ionesco, Genet, and the rest of the modern Absurdist
playwrights, then surely critics of the artistry displayed in developing that theme dramatically might do well to read Hegel's
pages on how Shakespeare handles the theme — in *Macbeth,* of
course; but also in *Henry IV,* where old Northumberland reads
the death of Percy in a messenger's face; and in *Richard II,* where
Henry empties Richard's kingly world, demanding the crown.
Hegel cites these and other comparable passages from *Julius
Caesar* and *Henry VIII* to remind us of the triumph of the absurd,
the vivid poetic telescoping of his suffering by the protagonist
who must, somehow, give vent to it. Hegel writes:

> It is the means whereby the pain of a great downfall is softened. So
> Cleopatra exclaims to Charmian, after she had already put the
> mortal aspic to her breast :
>
> > Peace, peace!
> > Dost thou not see my baby at my breast,
> > That sucks the nurse asleep?
> > As sweet as balm, as soft as air, as gentle —
>
> The bite of the serpent relaxes her members so gently that Death
> is himself deceived and holds himself to be Sleep. And this image
> may well pass as itself a counterfeit of the mild and allaying influ-
> ence of such similitudes.[14]

    Martin Esslin notes that theater has "renounced *arguing
about* the absurdity of the human condition; it merely *presents* it
in being — that is, in terms of concrete stage images of the absurdity of existence."[15] Shakespeare gives us "concrete stage images"
of infinitely more suggestivity. But even in the range of what

most concerns the Absurdists, he remains the master without a peer.

NOTES

An earlier version of this essay appeared in *Comparative Literature,* Vol. VII, Number 3, Fall 1973.

1. See Anne Paolucci, *From Tension to Tonic: The Plays of Edward Albee* (Carbondale: Southern Illinois University Press, 1972), Chapter I. Also, by the same author, *Luigi Pirandello: The Recovery of the Modern Stage for Dramatic Art* (Carbondale: Southern Illinois University Press, 1974), particularly the introductory chapter and the section on the "theater plays."

2. See, Martin Esslin, *The Theatre of the Absurd* (Garden City, N. Y.: Doubleday & Co., 1961), pp. xviii-xx.

3. *Tulane Drama Review*, Vol. 9, no.4 (1965), 144-45.

4. Esslin, p. 234.

5. See Anne Paolucci, *"Macbeth* and *Oedipus Rex:* A Study in Paradox," *Shakespeare Encomium,* ed. Anne Paolucci, The City College Papers I (New York: The City College of CUNY, 1964), pp. 44-70. (See Chapter 8 in this volume.)

6. Cleanth Brooks, "The Naked Babe and the Cloak of Manliness," *The Well Wrought Urn* (1947; rpt. New York: Harcourt Brace, 1959), p. 46.

7. George Herbert, "Giddiness," *The Poems of George Herbert*, with an Introduction by Helen Gardner, 2nd edition (London: Oxford University Press, 1961), p. 117.

8. W. K. Wimsatt, Jr., ed., *Samuel Johnson on Shakespeare* (New York: Hill and Wang, 1960), pp. 52ff.

9. Wolfgang Clemen, *The Development of Shakespeare's Imagery* (New York: Hill and Wang, 1951), p. 14.

10. Anne and Henry Paolucci, *Hegel on Tragedy* (Garden City, N. Y.: Doubleday & Co., 1962), pp. 226-27. (Reissued by Harper and Row, Greenwood Press, and, in 2001, by Griffon House Publications/The Bagehot Council.)

11. Matthew Arnold, *the Poetical Works of Matthew Arnold*, ed. C. B. Tinker and H. F. Lowry (Oxford University Press, 1950), pp. 210-12.

12. Esslin, p. xix.

13. *Ibid.*

14. *Hegel on Tragedy*, p. 231.

15. Esslin, p. xx.

PART FIVE
(247-335)

"THEATER OF THE ABSURD"

"Shakespeare's *Hamlet* and Pirandello's *Enrico IV*," was first published as "The Expressionist Redemption of the Absurd: "Shakespeare's *Hamlet* and Pirandello's *Enrico IV*," in *Hamlet Studies*, New Delhi, India, 1983.

"Comedy and Paradox in Pirandello's Plays" was first published in *Modern Drama*, Toronto, Winter 1977. It was included in 1989 in *Luigi Pirandello*, ed. Harold Bloom, Chelsea House Publications.

"Pirandello and the Waiting Stage of the Absurd (With Some Observations on a New 'Critical Language')" was first published in *Modern Drama*, Toronto, June 1980.

"Albee and the Restructuring of the Modern Stage" was first published in *American Drama, 1945 – Present*, Spring/Summer 1986.

"Albee on the Precipitous Heights (Two Arms Are Not Enough!)" was first published in *Private Tensions and Public Issues*, ed. Matthew C. Roudané. AMS Press, 1993.

CHAPTER 14

SHAKESPEARE'S *HAMLET* AND PIRANDELLO'S *ENRICO IV*

In one of Pirandello's plays, *Right You Are (If You Think You Are)*, the eternal skeptic — Laudisi — alone on stage for a moment, catches sight of himself in a mirror and stops to indulge in a brief conversation with his image:

> There you are! [He points a finger at his reflection in the mirror, which of course points a finger back at him. He smiles.] Come now, which of us is mad, eh? Face to face like this . . . we know who we are, don't we? Trouble is, those others out there don't see you the way I do! And so, my dear fellow, what do *you* turn out to be? In *my* case, here I am, standing opposite you. I can see myself, touch myself. You . . . What are you for the rest of us? An illusion, my friend, an illusion. And yet, look at these madmen — they chase after the illusion in others, full of curiosity, without thinking about the illusion they carry inside them, within themselves! Th:y really believe it's different, somehow.[1]

Others before me have observed that we have in this passage a mirroring of the three-fold psychological perspective within the divergent lines of which Pirandello builds his dramatic universe. I would only add that, if we trouble ourselves to define the constituent vectors of that perspective in the light of what the theater has tended to become since Pirandello's time, we can find some useful distinctions, perhaps the key itself to the essence of modern drama — which starts with Shakespeare, as distinct from ancient drama, the great Greek tragedies and the comedies of Aristophanes.

Pirandello's Laudisi talking to his mirrored self invites us to take dramatic notice of a suggestion (1) of madness, (2) of a dichotomy of consciousness and self-consciousness and its connection with madness (in the passage just quoted, the distance between the speaker and the reflected image in the mirror), and (3) of an obsessive search for the integral mask, for organic personality, for a solution to what Albert Camus described in his *Myth of Sisyphus* as the existential condition of the modern world, "the divorce between man and his environment" — a condition which he labeled "Absurd."[2] These three lines of divergence reflect the Pirandellian dialectic, which — as one critic describes it — is the very act of creation on stage. We see that dialectic fully elaborated in Pirandello's masterpiece *Enrico IV*, a play that is remarkably reminiscent of Shakespeare's. *Hamlet* in the dissolution of character as it moves through a world that must be reinterpreted and reshaped at every moment according to the principles of internal perceptions and personal conviction.

Pirandello himself provides a less equivocal insight into the "absurd" in *Hamlet* when he has one of his characters in the famous early novel *Il Fu Mattia Pascal* (*The Late Mattia Pascal*) explain the difference between ancient and modern tragedy. The speaker is led to say in the course of conversation:

> The tragedy of Orestes in a puppet theater! . . . Now listen to this crazy notion that just popped into my head! Let's suppose that at the very climax of the play, when the puppet who represents Orestes is about to take his revenge on Aegisthus and his mother for his father's death, a great hole were suddenly torn in the paper sky of the theater, what would happen? . . . Orestes would still be bent on revenge, he would still be impatient to bring it about, but his eyes in that instant would be directed up there, to that ripped sky, where all kinds of evil influences would now filter down into the scene, and he would feel his arms grow limp. Orestes, in other words, would become Hamlet. The whole difference, Signor Meis, between ancient and modern tragedy is just that, believe me, a hole in the paper sky.[3]

What sort of evil influences filter down, once we tear open the paper sky of the puppet theater? In the context of Shakespeare criticism, one is tempted to identify them with the humours that poison our resolutions and bring about a dissociation of sensibilities, so that we say one thing and do another. On the surface of things, Shakespeare's *Hamlet* — like Pirandello's *Enrico IV*, as we shall see — seems impotent, withdrawn into a private world of his own; in both plays, the distance between external reality as spelled out for the protagonists by others and their own reflected image of reality creates in us the illusion of their madness; and the fact that in both plays the protagonist assumes the mask of madness to realize internal purpose reinforces the parallels already suggested. The self-consciousness of personality as it realizes its isolation and its peculiar eccentricity with respect to the outer world forces a confrontation with self, and in that confrontation the dichotomy of the "Absurd" emerges.

It is hardly an accident in my opinion, that these two great plays should have provoked, independently, irritatingly negative judgments. We are all familiar with T .S. Eliot's notorious statement that in attempting to express the inexpressible (those "evil influences that filter down through the paper sky of the puppet theater), Shakespeare produced in *Hamlet* an "artistic failure."[4] Ludwig Binswanger reaches a similar conclusion about Pirandello's *Enrico IV* when he tells us that the life of the protagonist in that play is a "form of failed existence" because — he explains — "to exist *as a mask*, that is, not behind but *in* a mask (a role) is the direct opposite of authentic existence and authentic community."[5] The parallel is a striking one and worth probing. In his excellent book, *The Artist's Journey Into the Interior*, Erich Heller throws light on Eliot's notorious statement about *Hamlet*: "There is," he says, "much more to Eliot's essay. . . . [It suffices] in all its strange wrong-headedness, to prove this poet's great critical intelligence."[6] Heller explains:

> Clearly, T.S. Eliot knew what he was saying when he judged *Hamlet* an artistic failure because the hero's emotion exceeded his concrete situation or the "objective correlative." It is the more surprising that Eliot judged as he judged; for what he condemned is the occasion itself of Romantic art, including his own.
>
> Perhaps he did not mean it. Mean what? It is the most persistent and most troublesome question of the Romantic mind. For having lost its world, it can never do what it means; and what it means cannot be done. And when it is done, it says: I did not mean it — just as Hamlet did not mean to kill Polonius.[7]

For Heller, what Eliot calls the "artistic failure" of *Hamlet* is in fact the play's great achievement. "Shakespeare . . . succeeded . . . in creating, paradoxically speaking, the 'objective correlative' for a subjectivity Romantically deprived of any adequate 'objective correlative.'"[8]

Critics of the "Theater of the Absurd" have begun to search for the kind of "subjective correlative" Heller is pointing to here. In his intriguing study of Samuel Beckett, for instance, Vivian Mercier presses the argument that a new critical vocabulary and a totally new approach is needed if we are to penetrate the meaning of the "Absurd." He illustrates his point by setting up his book as a series of dialectical inversions, chapter headings like "Gentleman/Tramp," "Ireland/The World," and the title of his book is quite obviously a paradox: *Beckett/Beckett*.[9] It is the only example I know of in which a critic deliberately moves away from traditional critical definitions and principles and strives to find a new language — a new critical language — that will throw light on the phenomenon of the "Absurd." Anticipating Mercier's attitude, Heller — in the passage quoted — suggests that we view

Hamlet in such terms: Shakespeare's play, he tells us in effect, must be regarded as the "surpassing tragedy" of the Romantic mind searching for subjective correlatives. "Its scene is not so much Denmark as a world whose creator appears to be at cross-purposes with the creator of the human soul."

By Romantic art, let me say quickly, Heller means Modern art generally; in this he is following the Hegelian distinctions — and although I don't mean to dwell on them, we must keep in mind that Heller's explanation is consistent with Hegel's notion of subjective modern art as spiritual inwardness, the penetration of self.[10]

Having said this much about some of the provocative critical suggestions that seem to encourage comparison and contrast between *Hamlet* and *Enrico IV*, I will trace briefly some of the parallels that support what I have put forward thus far, in the light of which the two plays emerge as unique dramatic expressions of the modern condition described by Camus as "the divorce between man and his environment," a new kind of theater in which the first voice of poetry, the *lyric* voice, dominates.

It is, in fact, Hegel who first recognizes in Shakespeare's *Hamlet* that inwardness, that spiritual mirroring of self, the dichotomy of personality which is the characteristic of Romantic art generally and of Romantic or Modern tragedy in particular. (1 will allow myself just this one particularized reference to Hegel because it is central, as we will see). In *Hamlet*, Hegel recognizes the emergence of the *schöne Seele*, the Beautiful Soul of the Modern world, the self-righteous Socratic voice which is both sublime and dangerous. Parenthetically, let me say that a great deal remains to be done in this area of criticism, because for Hegel it was not *Antigone* but *Hamlet* that deserved to be recognized as the greatest tragedy of all time. But that's another story, which I have set down elsewhere and which we cannot explore now.[11] We have in *Hamlet* the same kind of struggle found in *Enrico IV* — the struggle to define an internal landscape that seems somehow to escape definition.

The crucible through which character must pass in order to achieve self-identity in Pirandello's *Enrico IV* takes the form of an intense confrontation with images of the past, identities to be discarded, mirrored images to be examined and shattered. We know how important the image of the mirror is in Pirandello; and we have in *Enrico IV* a pyrotechnic display not of the literal mirror as image (the kind we have in *Right You Are!*) but of reflected images and superimposed masks mirrored back to us by others, a stratification of time through such masks and images, all of which must be destroyed. The culminating scene of the play is in fact a play-within-a-play very much like the dramatic interlude, the Gonzago episode in *Hamlet*. Through it, Henry — like Hamlet — comes to know himself at last. Contradictory masks, intentions, and actions are stripped away; in revealing finally his true identity, the protagonist also reveals the others around him, forces them to unmask. In *Enrico IV* the stratification of roles or masks is the play's most impressive feature: the Marchesa, in her efforts to appear young again, is already a double-mask; in the gown she wore twenty years earlier, the mask is distorted even further in the futile effort to recapture the past — and the contrast is made dramatically visual in the intentional juxtaposition between the Marchesa in her Mardi Gras costume and her daughter Frieda dressed in an identical costume and looking remarkably like her mother twenty years before, at the time that Henry fell from his horse, he too in costume, and suffered a concussion which "embedded" him as it were in his role. As in *Hamlet*, the protagonist provokes a confrontation not in his terms but those of others. Henry, like Hamlet, emerges as the writer producer, director, and leading actor of a script that can no longer be contained in the restricted area of a puppet theater but is now subject to influences from outside. The many roles and masks are finally reduced to the single authoritative voice tempered by the demands of a world that is not that of the protagonist.

In both these plays, the answer to the problem of integral identity emerges in the play-within-the-play. Hamlet writes the script wherein he'll catch the conscience of the usurper, his uncle, who murdered the true King, Hamlet's father. But in the course of the dramatic interlude, Hamlet comes to realize that no one outside himself can ever be expected to understand what has in fact happened. In the dramatic interlude, we see either a brother or a nephew murdering the rightful King, the accepted King. What possible conclusions can the spectators draw other than that? Hamlet, we must remember, has been sworn to secrecy by the Ghost, and he never betrays that oath. The task of explaining will be Horatio's. The drama enacted by the Players serves to reinforce his own certainty (a certainty which never wavers, we must stress, in the course of the play and which was emphatically asserted at the beginning with Hamlet's "O my prophetic soul!") about Claudius' guilt and, paradoxically, alerts him to his own personal dilemma. The interlude drives home the point that he cannot reveal the identity of the murderer and that there is no way in which he can make others arrive at the knowledge or the certainty he carries within himself. The script he has devised or revised as a means to reveal the truth is not self-evident. The play is simply not the crucial experiment he would have it be. It is as apt to catch his own conscience as that of his uncle. (It is the essential dilemma of the relativity of modern experimental science.) Hamlet must kill the King, the Usurper, but on different grounds, grounds that will exonerate him publicly but that do not accord with the private reasons he has accepted from the very beginning in his own soul. The dramatic interlude does succeed, in fact, in a not altogether unexpected way: Claudius realizes his danger and is forced to assume once again the mask of murderer. Through the reiteration of his true intentions, Claudius is finally brought to justice.

The elaborate staging of the traumatic confrontation in *Enrico IV* backfires in much the same way as the dramatic interlude in *Hamlet*. Henry comes to realize the deception practiced on him by his erstwhile friends; but at the same time he also realizes that he cannot ever prove his suspicions. In giving voice to those suspicions, in asserting himself finally through action, he forces another kind of resolution quite different from what he had planned and expected. He stabs Belcredi and in that action commits himself to a new kind of death, a self-imposed mask of madness for avenging a crime which cannot be justified publicly. The public justification for the attack on Belcredi is like Hamlet's killing of Claudius, an "objective correlative" subjectively defined.

In both plays the protagonist appears as a kind of split personality, or more precisely (to avoid clinical terminology) a series of superimposed masks. Hamlet is the "Absurd" in us all, the Socratic voice that cries for truth and listens to its own internal oracle. He is the struggle — through a series of rationalizations — for definition from within. He is the dislocated and alienated voice of the modern conscience seeking expression for its own inexpressible commitment. The nature of the soliloquies in Shakespeare's play suggests an internal life unrelated to external events. In them we detect a kind of floating anxiety hard to pin down, and an attitude which is the very opposite of the Machiavellian ruthlessness reflected in those moments when Hamlet does act publicly. He condemns his friends to death on grounds of mere suspicion — how else are we to assess, objectively, the willingness of Rosencrantz and Guildenstern to help the King discover what is bothering their friend? They certainly don't know what Hamlet knows: for them Claudius is simply the concerned parent complaining about Hamlet's erratic behavior. Hardly the grounds for murder. He deliberately turns against Ophelia in a shocking display of cruel insensitivity, driving her to madness and suicide. He murders Polonius on impulse, not knowing the identity of his victim, and shows no remorse whatever for the deed. He refuses to kill Claudius while the King is praying because he quite literally wants him to go to hell. He makes impossible demands on his mother, newly-married, urging her to give up sex. And so on. With George Herbert we have to cry out:

> He is some twentie sev'rall men at least
> Each sev'rall houre.[12]

In my opinion, these contradictory postures explain a great deal and they put to rest that short-sighted view of the play that tries to force these paradoxical roles into conclusions that rely on objective motivations alone. Hamlet gives all sorts of reasons as to why he cannot kill the king; he gives all sorts of reasons as to why he *does* act in other circumstances that do not involve Claudius' death. In short, he is anything but *impotent* to act when he is convinced in his own mind that he is doing the right thing; what he *does* fail to do is explain the reasons for his actions in clear and convincing terms that accord with objective reality. Except for the murder of Claudius at the end of the play everything he does is triggered by private griefs not altogether clear. His life is given over to death from the very beginning so that, in his actual death, it is spiritually death itself that dies.

In both plays, women precipitate events which lead to tragedy; and in both plays there is an older woman to whom the protagonist is drawn and a younger woman with whom he falls in love. In both plays, the protagonist assumes the mask of madness as a device for stalling others and gaining time, as a temporary escape into a personal world that is at odds with the outer world. The mask of madness in both cases fails; the protagonist is forced to translate his own convictions into terms that are acceptable to the rest of the world. Hamlet dies acknowledging the dilemma which he provoked; Henry retreats into a self-imposed madness in order to escape the demands of retribution. The crucial act, implicit at the beginning of each play, is carried out at the end: both Hamlet and Henry fail to explain their motives completely, but they do succeed in carrying out that crucial act. Hamlet kills Claudius because the King is responsible for a new murder (and indirectly for two other deaths); Henry stabs Belcredi because he is sure that it was Belcredi who occasioned the fall from the horse which resulted in Henry's concussion and loss of memory, but Belcredi has also become Matelda's lover and is not to be trusted. They accomplish what they wanted to accomplish, but for reasons that are not completely clear publicly. In that final confrontation, they come to terms with themselves and assume at last the one true role.

We see in *Enrico IV* the expressionist imperative of the first voice, the *lyric* voice of poetry, struggling for dramatic self-expression in subjective terms; just as we see in *Hamlet* the contradiction occasioned by outward action and internal motivation. In Hamlet's struggle for integral self-definition, as in Henry's impulse to translate his own inner world into an objective reality, we recognize the expressionistic poet attempting to communicate internal certainty in objective terms. From the outside looking in, both protagonists seem to be at moments victims of circumstances and environment, of forces acting upon them, of events beyond their control; but to stop there is to miss the true greatness of the play in each case. In the effort to give expression to their complex inner life — a life of paradoxes and motives never fully revealed — both Hamlet and Henry emerge as creatures of their own contradictions. In them the lyric voice of consciousness struggles for its pitch and timbre, according to its own "subjective correlative."

NOTES

An earlier version of this essay appeared in *Hamlet Studies*, Vol. 2, No. 2, Winter 1980.

1. Luigi Pirandello, "Cosí è (se vi pare)," *Maschere nude I* (Arnoldo Mondadori Editore, 1965), pp. 1065-66. (Translation my own).

2. See Martin Esslin, *The Theatre of the Absurd* (New York: Doubday & Company, 1961), p. xix.

3. See Leonardo Sciascia, *Pirandello e la Sicilia* (Caltanisetta: S. Sciascia, 1961), pp. 17-18. (Translation my own.)

4. T.S. Eliot, "Hamlet," *Selected Essays 1917-1932* (New York: Harcourt, Brace, and Company, 1932), p. 123.

5. Ludwig Binswanger, *Tre forme di esistenza mancata* (Milano, Il saggiatore, 1964). p. 237. See also Gian-Paolo Biasin, *Literary Diseases* (Austin: The University of Texas Press, 1975), p. 114.

6. Erich Heller, *The Artist's Journey into the Interior* (New York, Random House: 1965), p. 130.

7. *Ibid.*, p. 136.

8. *Ibid.*, p, 139.

9. Vivian Mercier, *Beckett/Beckett* (New York, Oxford University Press, 1977).

10. See Anne and Henry Paolucci, eds., *Hegel on Tragedy* (New York, Doubleday & Company, 1965), pp. xvii-xxiv, etc.; Henry Paolucci, trans., *Hegel: On the Arts* (New York: Frederick Ungar Publishing Company, 1979; Smyrna, Delaware: Griffon House Publications/The Bagehot Council, 2001), esp. pp. 36-61, 194-200.

11. See Anne Paolucci, "Bradley and Hegel on Shakespeare," *Comparative Literature*, Vol. XVI, No.3 (Summer 1964.), pp. 211-225; see also Chapters 6 and 7 in this volume. For an earlier discussion of *Hamlet* and *Enrico IV*, see the chapter on "The Creative Madness of *Henry IV*" in Anne Paolucci, *Pirandello's Theater: The Recovery of the Modern Stage for Dramatic Art* (Carbondale, Edwardsville, London, Amsterdam: Southern Illinois University Press, 1974), pp. 89-101.

12. Dudlcy Fitts, ed. "Giddinesse," *George Herbert* (New York: Dell Publishing Co., Inc., 1962), p. 127.

CHAPTER 15

COMEDY AND PARADOX IN PIRANDELLO'S PLAYS

The temptation will always be strong, for those of us analyzing any aspect of Pirandellian comedy, to begin with an examination — or at least, a brief assessment — of the playwright's well-known little book *L'Umorismo* (*On Humor*).[1] I have not wholly resisted that temptation, but I have tried to on two grounds. First, Pirandello's exposition in that book has been carefully examined and evaluated by such experts as Professor Dante della Terza, whose incisive essay "On Pirandello's Humorism"[2] has proved invaluable to most of us interested in the subject, and Professor Antonio Illiano, whose translation of *L'Umorismo* (with Daniel Testa) supplies indispensable notes as well as a fine introduction.

My second reason for resisting the temptation of using *L'Umorismo* as my own critical base in this paper is, I suppose, my own *sentimento del contrario*. That feeling — as Professor Della Terza interprets Pirandello's use of the term — is a sort of categorical imperative. It indicates, Della Terza very acutely observes, "the presence of a subjective 'feeling' that somewhere in the stratified world of our affections there is an emotional explosion that shakes our privileged heritage of sentiments, refusing to accept them as the only ones which really 'are.'"

I experience that sort of explosion when I read *L'Umorismo*, or Croce's criticism of it, or the debate over Tilgher's influence on Pirandello, or Pirandello's responses. Pirandello the literary critic and aesthetician becomes for me, then, simply another character in another Pirandellian play. The experience makes it impossible for me to read Pirandello's discussion of humor as if I thought he were trying simply to be a critical philosopher. What is revealed there is the genius of the comic playwright. The plays have yet to be written; but when they are finally written, it is humor, the *feeling* of the opposite, as distinguished from mere *perception* of the opposite, that will constantly be applied in the best of them. The object of its application is not to form some substantive thing before us that we can then view at leisure, but rather to dissolve what we have before us and show that there is really nothing there — except the imaginative will of the artist functioning as an irresistible dissolvent.

"Pirandello's definition of humorism" (Della Terza writes) "indicates a dilemma at the core of his aesthetic convictions." His "feeling" of the opposite is not a feeling, not a sentiment at all, "since its activity is overwhelmingly critical, analytical, and rational. By trying to give another name to a cognitive activity Pirandello, instead of making his dilemma inconspicuous, as he would have liked, ends up by giving the limelight, unwillingly but revealingly, to an all-encompassing and proliferating imagery suggested by the intrusive concept of reflection."[3]

Read as a revelation of Pirandello's developing dramatic attitude, the essay is surely invaluable. But we simply must not mistake it for an empirically based theory of his own dramaturgical achievement. In that respect I think his essay on the history of the Italian theater is much more illuminating; and I shall have occasion to cite it later. The essay on humor, with its sharp distinction of the comic from the humorous, makes it difficult moreover to relate its meaning to the main content of aesthetic theory which, at least as it relates to drama, does not insist on such a distinction. Comedy, from Aristophanes to Shakespeare and beyond, down to Pirandello himself, of course, has been the chief medium of expression for humor in Pirandello's sense. Neither etymology nor usage justifies insistence on a distinction that assigns the use of "comic" to mere "perception of the opposite." Where I have tried, in what follows, to relate my discussion to the main current of aesthetic theory, I have turned for clarification more often than not to Hegel's usage, which, insofar as it is supported by an organically integrative system of thought, avoids the pitfalls of mere trial and error.

I was struck recently by the closing paragraph of a book on *Humor in Pascal*, that most paradoxical of all modern thinkers. Summarizing the "density of techniques" of what she pointedly calls the "comic humor" of Pascal (to distinguish it from other kinds of humor and other uses of the comic), the author, Professor Olga Russell, supplies us with a long list of distinctions that may be drawn in analyzing the effects of a paradoxical approach to what were for Pascal — as for Pirandello — the "shows of life." The main techniques of comic humor bring into focus, the author writes,

> the unexpected within a sentence, or in a situation, or in a figure of speech; the grotesque, the incongruous; caricature by gesture;

belittling humor, irony in an adjective, or an adverb, or a verb (in the midst of an otherwise straightforward, serious sentence); dynamic and comic antithesis of the small cause and the vast result; the use of derogatory terms or names bringing characters to life in conversation; juxtaposition of the concrete and the abstract, forcing the reader to smile in the obvious attitude of common sense; onomatopoeia as effective as gesture seen on the stage; imagery, concrete and vivid, to point up unreasonableness and foolishness; true comic situations and characters, as in charlatanry in medicine; dramatic situation and crescendo in effect to light up the ridiculous (so close to the sublime); traditional comic themes, *le dupeur dupé*, raised to symbolic meaning; costume as symbol; and the tones of light raillery, teasing, gentle irony, sarcasm, bitter and violent satire.

The author adds that the "humorous effects" of these techniques are "effective for being presented courteously and charitably, in that Pascal shares with all men the burden of human foolishness."[4]

Pirandello makes the same point in *L'Umorismo*, citing De Sanctis's estimate of Machiavelli's "tolerance that understands and absolves,"[5] and stressing how the author of *Don Quixote* makes it difficult for us actually to laugh at his hero by troubling us with feelings not only of pity, but "even, indeed of admiration."[6] Yet I think it is fair to say that Pirandello applies his comic art with an exhaustive thoroughness (at least in his best plays) that is not to be found in a Pascal or a Cervantes. In the closing pages of *L'Umorismo*, it is the destructive or decompositional thoroughness of his *sentimento del contrario* that is emphasized. Where the ordinary artist, the ordinary epic or dramatic poet, will *compose* a character from opposite and contrasting elements, the true humorist will do "just the opposite: he will *decompose* the character into his elements." The true humorist applies a conditional "if," which is but a minute particle of doubt, to begin with — but it is a "minute particle which can be pinned to, and inserted like a wedge into all events." Inserting that wedge, hammering it into the seemingly solid substance of his subject everywhere, the true humorist literally decomposes what ordinary art composes: "hence," in Pirandello's words, "all that is disorganized, unraveled and whimsical, all the digressions which can be seen in the works of humor, as opposed to the ordered construction, the *composition* of the works of art in general."[7]

That surely is the effect of Pirandello's *sentimento del contrario* in his best plays: it penetrates the subject everywhere, cracks its solidity, till decomposition is inevitable. Situations, events, characters, thoughts — all are overwhelmed, pinned with conditionals, hammered till they are shattered, at least in our reflection, into myriad mirrored fragments. If we attempt to piece the fragments together like a jigsaw puzzle, what we get is not a cracked impression of the original thing, but the personality of the comic artist who has made it all his very own precisely in order to dissolve its apparent rigidity.

In my own view, Pirandello's sense of humor could not have had full scope till he turned artistically from narrative expression (which must be objective in what it attempts to tell of human experience) to dramatic expression (which absorbs the objective in the subjective and vice versa). To *feel* the opposite, rather than perceive it merely, is a labor of the dramatic imagination. We all engage in it in some measure day in and day out; but it is the dramatist who brings such labor to full artistic birth in the form of tragedy or comedy, or a mixture of the two. But all the world's a stage! the dramatic imagination cries. And it is when he is convinced that the world is indeed but a place leveled out for players upon which to strut and fret their hour that a dramatic intelligence can begin to people it with such players. The necessity of dramatic art, its reason for being, is to be sought in that perception; it helps us to obey the Delphic Oracle's command to "know thyself." A stage must be cleared so that we can come to see ourselves as we are, in rational reflection. We *are* what reflective reasoning shows us to be. Yet, when that viewing has been done in any society, a time inevitably follows when the reflection hardens so as to become impenetrable, and then, instead of being itself perceived as a rational reflection, rationally real in itself, it becomes for us merely a reflecting surface in which we imagine we see our subjective selves reflected as opposite. The comic spirit, according to Hegel, shatters that hardness, dissolves it, so that comedy is always a reaction to some other form of drama, whether ceremonial in the religious sense, or tragic.

Pirandello, as I said, coming late to the task, does this sort of comic work with a thoroughness that is positively exhaustive. But what exactly is it that he views thus humorously in an exhaustive way? It is absurd to say — bearing in mind that we are talking about a man who invaded the early twentieth-century European stage like a conqueror with his *Six Characters in Search of an Author* — that it is life in general. Pirandello had already applied his *sentimento del contrario* to life in general. What is life in general? As many things as there are minds, and instants of

experience in each mind to perceive its endless flow of multiplicity. *Uno, nessuno, o centomila, Così è (se vi pare)* — we are the
flitting shadows of a dream, with no idea who or what it is that
casts such over-changing shadows.

By the time Pirandello has begun to put his own plays on
stage, he has long since swept away mere life as an object of
artistic, critical, analytical, overwhelming reflection. He has perceived the opposite in life, and perceived the opposite of that
opposite myriadfold. And it is out of the depths of mirrored
opposites that he brings up his *dramatis personae* as creatures of
his *sentimento del contrario*, the feeling of the opposite.

Who is Uncle Simone in *Liolà*? Who is Enrico IV? Who is
signora Ponza? *Liolà* is early, so let us begin with Uncle Simone.
He claims to be a sexually potent old man who could have a
child by his young wife, Mita, if she were fertile; and he has
sought to prove his potency to the world by allowing wicked
Tuzza and her mother, Zia Croce, to claim that he has fathered
the child with whom Tuzza is pregnant. We can see through
Uncle Simone's pretense; we can see easily the opposite. And
the effect is most comical when Uncle Simone attempts to suggest that he might still father a child with his own wife. Zia Croce
heightens the comic effect: it is *no* at seventy; will it be *yes* at
eighty-five? It could be, says Uncle Simone. We must leave time
. . . for time. but we — who read and see the play — know already
at this point what Zia Croce and Tuzza do *not* know: that Uncle
Simone is comical for them at the same moment that he becomes humorous — in Pirandello's sense of the terms — for *us*. It
is true that he cannot father a child with Mita; but he can, in fact,
father one with her in the same way that he allegedly fathered
one with Tuzza. "It's Liolà! I knew it!" Mother and daughter
recognize a real opposite to what they thought they had seen —
laughable to them and to us, at first; but now they can only gnash
their teeth in frustration. *We* smile. It is not perception of the
opposite; it is a *feeling* of the opposite, *sentimento del contrario*.
Uncle Simone is what he is: an impotent old man who wants an
heir. His first wife, who died without bearing him a child, asked
him on her deathbed to get himself a son. God knows he tried.
He seemed to be a fool in trying. In self-defense, his wife cuck-
olds him. A complex sort of fool. In claiming Tuzza's child, he
has announced, in a sense, his willingness to be thus cuckolded.
If only God's grace would fill Mita as it had filled Mary! But
Simone wants a child of his own, not another Christ. If only his
young wife could be filled . . . as Tuzza was filled . . . so that I can

have a child by her as I have been ready to claim I had one from Tuzza![8]

There is something clearly exhaustive in the sense indicated earlier about such humor; certainly it is present in *Six Characters*. The actors who play the characters are not supposed to be actors. They are characters that actors are supposed to play but cannot. They emphasize the difference between what *they* are and what those so-called actors who are trying to play them are. We have paired perceptions of opposites here, as in the case of Uncle Simone. When the curtain comes down, we applaud the actors who have acted the parts of characters that are too real to be played. We recall, perhaps, Hamlet's speech on the subject, marveling that this mere player could act a part so realistically, so passionately, while I — Hamlet — who am *very I*, cannot match the actors expression of passion. Pirandellos six characters must play a whole play in the mood of that Hamlet speech. It is a daring tour de force, but a tour de force still, as compared with *Hamlet* and as compared with Pirandello's own version of *Hamlet*, *Enrico IV*.

There is a powerful suggestion of the opposite generated in *Enrico IV*, and there is also a powerful compounded *feeling* of the opposite. There is much to make one smile in Pirandello's masterpiece — but we could hardly call it humor. Or rather, if there is humor, again let me say, the effect is exhaustive. Pirandello's *feeling of the opposite* presses the humorous to its absolute limits and beyond.

I must admit I have been pressing an Hegelian insight here. Hegel says that it is dramatic comedy and humor in the broadest sense that exhaust all of art. In his lectures on *Aesthetics*, he has a brief subsection called "The Comic Treatment of Contingency"[9] ("Die komische Behandlung der Zufälligkeit")[10] and another titled "Subjective Humor"[11] ("Der subjektive Humor")[12] in which he argues that art's dissolution comes finally not with a tragic bang or a melodramatic whimper but with a comic too-sad-to-laugh smile — or what Pirandello calls humor.

"In humor," Hegel says, "it is the person of the artist which comes on the scene in both its superficial and deeper aspects, so that what is at issue there is essentially the spiritual worth of his personality." Humor, as we noted already, has as its object not to develop and shape a thing before us, but to dissolve what is already ours. In Hegel's words again: "It is the artist himself who enters the material, with the result that his chief activity, by the power of subjective notions, flashes of thought, striking modes of interpretation, consists in destroying and dissolving everything that proposes to make itself objective and win a firm shape for itself in reality, or that seems to have such a shape already in the external world."[13]

According to Hegel, art is most taxed when it is made to sustain a humorous attitude (the *sentimento del contrario* interpreted in a genuine Hegelian sense) toward its subject matter. At the very end of his long lectures on aesthetics, after he has reviewed the entire progression of the arts from architecture through poetry, from the symbolic and classical through the romantic, Hegel speaks finally of dramatic comedy in terms that make me think as much of Pirandello's major figures as of Shakespeare's great Falstaff. A *perception* of the opposite intensified as *feeling* of the opposite is involved in tragedy, as Hegel understands it, as well as in comedy. The "clash of opposites" in tragedy results either in the destruction of the characters who sustain the opposition through one-sided willfulness or in a profound internal conversion that involves acceptance of what had been most seriously resisted. "In comedy," on the other hand, says Hegel, "there comes before our contemplation, in the laughter in which the characters dissolve everything, including themselves, the victory of their own subjective personality which nevertheless persists self-assured."[14] Distinguishing the comical from the laughable, however, Hegel adds: "The comical as such implies an infinite light-heartedness and confidence felt by someone raised altogether above his own inner contradiction and not bitter or miserable in it at all: this is the bliss and ease of a man who, being sure of himself, can bear the frustration of his aims and achievements." And he goes on: ". . . truly *tragic* action necessarily presupposes either a live conception of *individual* freedom and independence or at least an individual's determination and willingness to accept freely and on his own account the responsibility for his own act and its consequences; and for the emergence of *comedy* there must have asserted itself in a still higher degree the free right of the subjective personality and its self-assured dominion."[15]

A. C. Bradley — the great Shakespearean critic — saw, with Hegel's help, the indissoluble link between the comic Falstaff, who drinks and cavorts with Prince Hal, and the final Falstaff, who is rejected by King Henry V. Falstaff's humor is sustained by depth of feeling. "True humor," Hegel writes, "requires great depth and wealth of spirit in order to raise the purely subjective appearance into what is actually expressive, and to make what is substantial emerge out of contingency, out of mere notions." If he is a genuine humorist, the author must proceed with ease, with effortless, unostentatious lightness of expression which, paradoxically, in its very "triviality affords precisely the supreme idea of depth; and since here there are just individual details which gush forth without any order, their inner connection must lie all the deeper and send forth the ray of spirit in their discon-nectedness as such."[16]

In his last plays, Pirandello gives us some very deliberate indications of the depths that sustain the paradoxical multiplic-ity of his art. But the magic of the god-wizard Cotrone (Pirandello's Prospero) in the first play of his great mythic tril-ogy — *The Mountain Giants* (*I giganti della montagna*) — is already present in *Liolà*. Cotrone's house is a place where creatures of the imagination are given, in the mere act of imagining them, a local habitation and a name. The world of *Liolà* is perhaps the greatest proof that Pirandello really had such magic power and did not merely talk about it. Illuminating in this respect is what Hegel has to say of the *level* of humor on which Pirandello, in our view, attempts to operate in *Liolà*. In civilized societies of which we have record, art that draws its materials and especially its characters from the lower classes, Hegel says, tends almost invariably to be comic, for it cannot make the deeds of people externally restricted (as the lower classes are on all sides) seri-ously tragic. The lower-class character can "put on airs" of im-portance, but he cannot *be* important. If he persists in putting on such airs, he becomes comical. Comic characters have the right to spread themselves in whatever way they wish and can do so claiming an independence of action which — because of their restricted potential — is immediately annihilated by themselves, by what they *are*, and by their inner and outer dependence. "But, above all," says Hegel, "this assumed self-reliance founders on external conditions and the distorted attitude of individuals to them. The power of these conditions is on a totally different level for the lower classes from what it is for rulers and princes."[17]

Hegel is not saying that the comic is limited to the lower classes; he is merely pointing out that lower-class characters have a potentially comic effectiveness. A lower-class type with money, for example, who imagines that his money will take him out of the lower class culturally — someone, say, like Nicia in *Mandragola* — is an example of this kind of comic type. Molière's M. Jourdain is another. And so on.

For Hegel, comedy assumes high dramatic importance —

side by side with tragedy — as the vehicle for "pathos," which he defines as the "proper center, the true domain of art."[18] In discussing what he calls the "dissolution of the classical form of art," he observes that comedy cannot rest content with perception of a mere opposition between abiding spiritual values and external contingency. Perception of that kind of opposition, says Hegel in a very Pirandellian mood, is merely prosaic. It takes us, in fact, *out* of the world of art. Comedy must, if not resolve, at least *dis*solve that opposition artistically. True comedy does this by reversing roles, by showing the sham of good intentions and the positive value of a much-condemned social order. "Of this kind of art," he writes, "an example is comedy as Aristophanes among the Greeks has handled it without anger, in pure and serene . . . relation to the most essential spheres in the world of his time."[19]

Hegel extends his observations on the comic and the lower classes into his discussion of painting. I shall not go into his argument except to note what may interest us here in a special way. Using examples from German and Dutch painting, where the subject matter is often taken from the crudest and most vulgar levels of society, Hegel notes that such painting offers us scenes "so completely penetrated by . . . cheerfulness . . . that the real subject matter is not vulgarity, which is just vulgar and vicious, but this cheerfulness . . . roguish and comic . . . the Sunday of life which equalizes everything and removes all evil."[20] The comic aspect, he explains, cancels what is bad and vulgar, and leaves a very *positive* feeling. What better example of *sentimento del contrario*? And what better illustration than Pirandello's *Liolà* — that amoral rogue (the windmill song is the best testimony of this side of his character) — who, in response to Uncle Simone's charge that he, Liolà, is after the old man's money, can sing a love song which is, in Hegel's terms, "the Sunday of life which equalizes everything and removes all evil"? When Eric Bentley writes that we must enter Pirandello's world through *Liolà*, he reminds us of the difference between the genuine Pirandello and modern Pirandellianism, which is pseudo-Pirandellian precisely because it does not have beneath it, around and above it, the Sicilian "Sunday" comedy of *Liolà*. Comedy, in the sense in which Hegel here describes it, is the *redemption* of the vulgar and the bad, just as the substantive drama of Samuel Beckett and Edward Albee, for example, is the *redemption* of the absurd.

Illuminating, with respect to Pirandello's art, is Hegel's

reminder that, in assessing comic power, one needs to be careful to "distinguish whether the *dramatis personae* are comical in themselves or only in the eyes of the audience."[21] Only the former case, he says — agreeing with Aristotle — can be considered comical in the strict sense, as distinguished from the merely laughable. Plautus and Terence preferred the opposite, and their attitude has, of course, dominated modern theatrical entertainment. Pirandello holds with the Aristotelian view, of course, and it lies at the base of his distinction between the merely comical and the humorous in his early essay. Yet surely he is not, any more than Hegel, beneath appreciating the marvelous combination of the two in Falstaff, for instance. We all have at least a vague recollection of Falstaff's famous self-estimate: but most of us, I venture to say, find ourselves enriched (I know I have!) when we turn to Shakespeare's *ipsissima verba* — as I have in this case. Falstaff says: "The brain of this foolish-compounded clay, man, is not able to invent anything that intends to laughter, more than I invent or is invented on me. I am not only witty in myself, but the cause that wit is in other men."[22] On the subject of Shakespeare's treatment of vulgar characters generally, Hegel points out that in the mature comedies they are aggrandized and enhanced above themselves: "Stephano, Trinculo, Pistol, and the absolute hero of them all, Falstaff, remain sunk in their vulgarity, but at the same time they are shown to be men of intelligence with a genius fit for anything, enabling them to have an entirely free existence, and, in short, to be what great men are. . . . In Shakespeare we find no justification, no condemnation, but only an observation of . . . universal fate; . . . and from that standpoint they see everything perish, themselves included, as if they saw it all happening outside themselves."[23]

Pirandello does not touch much on the comic genius of Shakespeare in *L'Umorismo*, where, in fact, he cites with approval Giorgio Arcoleo's view that Hamlet is an instance of the first phase of humor which consists in being able to "*laugh at one's own thought.*"[24] But it is plain that he appreciates the kind of humor that Hegel has in mind in praising Shakespeare's characterization of Falstaff. In his essay on the history of the Italian Theater, Pirandello dwells especially on the side of that history where its vitality is traced back to the "life of the Theatre" itself, which is to say, the experience of the *commedia dell'arte*. We see there, he writes, "actors . . . who begin by writing the comedies they later perform, comedies at once more theatrical because not written in the isolated study," but in the theater itself. "The transitory, impassioned life of the Theater," he goes on to say, "must have taken such full possession of them that the only interest left to them was that of the spectacle itself — a complete absorption in the quality of the performance and communication with the audience. They are no longer authors; but they are no longer even actors, in the true sense of the word." That, according to Pirandello, was the indispensable experience of living theater that permitted Italy, and Italy alone, to dissolve the rigidity of Renaissance forms so that it could "boast of having drained the recovered classical world of all that it had to offer."[25]

What the *commedia dell'arte* did to shatter the rigidity of the Renaissance inheritance, Pirandello understood himself to be doing, dramatically, with the rigidities of a modern theater that had lost contact with its living origins. For an antecedent, he points to Goldoni. Goldoni had learned the lesson of the *commedia dell'arte* even as Molière and Shakespeare had already learned it. But Goldoni had also done something else of even greater importance, from Pirandello's perspective:

> . . . we will never discover the true Goldoni if we fix our attention on the characters that, according to the fashion of the time, he too tried to create — the good natured boor, the grumbler, the miser, etc. They are indeed marvelous; but in the comedies in which they appear as protagonists the truly great author reveals himself, on the contrary, in the subordinate characters, one of whom — the little housemaid, for example — suddenly becomes, like Mirandolina, the center of a comedy of her own; and many others come forward, en masse, to stand there and bicker freely in the streets of Chioggia.[26]

Pirandello's mood here is certainly that of Shakespeare's Prospero even more than of his own Cotrone. What Goldoni gives us in the streets of Chioggia is as marvelous, surely, as the magic storm worked up by Prospero to frighten his prisoners and teach them a lesson. Ariel, you remember, reports back to his master that the charms have indeed worked wonders; the shipwrecked victims of Prospero's tempest are all huddled together, he says, so full of sorrow and fear that,

> . . . if you now beheld them, your affections
> Would become tender.

Prospero, who for the moment has only the *perception* of the opposite, replies simply:

> Dost thou think so, spirit?

But Ariel disarms him, undermining the detached, cold security of the puppet-master, by answering:

> Mine would, sir, were I human.

And Prospero replies:

> And mine shall.
> Hast thou, which art but air, a touch, a feeling
> Of their afflictions, and shall not myself,
> One of their kind, that relish all as sharply
> Passion as they, be kindlier mov'd than thou art?[27]

The art of Pirandello's *sentimento del contrario* is to bring us where Ariel's reply brings Prospero.

I should like, at this point, to extend my discussion to illustrations drawn from Pirandello's plays. First, I must return briefly to *Liolà*, which I consider the key to Pirandello's dramatic world; I shall then touch on the relevance of my earlier remarks in the context of *Cosí è (se vi pare)*, where paradox is embodied in the figure of Signora Ponza; and finally, I shall turn to a consideration of what is certainly Pirandello's most subtle and creative example of the concentric build-up of paradox, *Enrico IV*.

The Sicilian realism of *Liolà*, its easy and traditional structure, the recognizable types — at once characteristic and unique — may mislead us into regarding this early but unusual play of Pirandello's as a struggling toward form, as a preliminary effort of a gifted playwright not yet sure of himself. Nothing could be farther from the truth, in my opinion. *Liolà* — like Shakespeare's early but masterful *Julius Caesar* — is already a perfect expression of what will be the dramatist's peculiar idiom, his unusual and even eccentric style. Pirandello, of course, had Machiavelli's *Mandragola* vividly before him (there can be no doubt about that): *Liolà* is a romanticized aberration of that perverse and bitter redoing of Livy's story of the virtuous Lucrece. Already there is a paradox working itself to the surface in Pirandello's choice of subject. It is the same basic story as that of Livy and Machiavelli; but the perceptions and the feelings of the opposite are inspired by Machiavelli's bitter realism, adapted to a new purpose which redeems the negative, almost unbearable, Machiavellian insights into human nature. Pirandello turns things right side up and upside down again in this early work, producing some of the most complex and paradoxical characters ever to appear on the contemporary stage.

Uncle Simone is drawn undoubtedly as the modern equivalent of Nicia, but how utterly different is his comic posture, if indeed we can speak of a comic posture at all! And how completely ambiguous is his final equivocal decision to accept what

Nicia in *Mandragola* unwittingly consents to accept, thinking that he has outwitted the clever *imbroglioni* who wanted to put something over on him. Nicia is comic in one of the two ways that Hegel talks about: he is comic in the eyes of the audience. Uncle Simone is comic — if at all — in his abstract role as the childless old rich man. But in the play (as we have noted) he takes on many nuances, many complex masks which suggest a secret awareness of the complexities of the situation, an internal confrontation with self which enables him to assert his intention to recognize Mita's child as his for the same reasons that enabled him to accept (for a time, at least) the suggestion that he should allow Tuzza's child to be called his. We sense, in his recognition of that paradox, a sensibility which cannot be attributed to Nicia.

What about Liolà himself? And Mita? Liolà is a seducer, we know, but not the sort of seducer that Callimaco is in *Mandragola*. He is more — let us say — "architectural" than passionate in designing his seduction of Mita. His object unmistakably is to undo the threatened harm that his earlier "seduction" of Tuzza now poses. With her plan to dispossess Mita, in effect, on the strength of Liolà's virility, Tuzza has rather seduced Liolà than been seduced *by* him. Liolà's position is paradoxical to begin with; it parallels, under the circumstances, not so much that of the young lover in Machiavelli's play as that of Fra Timoteo, on whom the responsibility falls to make all things work out for the best, as far as possible, despite the good or bad (mostly bad, in this case) motives of all involved.

In Liolà, Pirandello has created a god-image, a modern Pan who bestows his gifts with charitable abandonment. He makes girls pregnant, but there is no malice in him. He respects the societal order, the lines of demarcation between respectability and personal indulgence. The women who become pregnant are, as a rule, outside the ordinary categories. We are given to understand that there has been no confrontation, no reversal of essential values in those cases. Moreover, Liolà has taken on the children of those seductions and is raising them as his own.

Mita's case confirms those qualities in Liolà which we could only infer from what we learn of his past actions. In her case, self-indulgence is not a factor at all. Liolà adheres to all the rules of respectability in a quirky way, persuading Mita that she must counter Tuzza's selfish move by having a baby of her own by the same means. Why? Because the wicked should *not* triumph in the world; and Tuzza's plan *is* wicked. It is a case, in Pascalian terms, of *le dupeur dupé*, the Bible's deceived deceivers. Mita is surely a victim, to begin with. But in seeking her own, of course, she too takes on paradoxical attitudes. She must be selfish in order to be unselfish. She must submit to Liolà not out of personal desire, but because the essential values below the surface of respectability must be preserved. The threat she faces calls for quick thinking and action. She herself is too naive, too committed to the code of obvious respectability in which she had been raised, to take the kind of initiative Tuzza has already taken. And yet, when her very existence in the social framework is threatened — and not only hers but ultimately Uncle Simone's — she allows herself to be drawn into a new play, not unlike that of Tuzza at first glance, but in the final analysis the very *opposite* of Tuzza's both in the intention which motivated it and the urgency behind it.

Mita and Liolà are, in fact, responding with a *sentimento del contrario* to a nefarious scheme put into motion by others. There is no way out of it, except to reciprocate in kind. The paradox is in the similarity of the two plans which is, of course, a contradiction. Tuzza confesses to Uncle Simone — but to make *her* point and to gain *her* advantage; Mita does *not* confess, and in maintaining the respectable posture she preserves the essential respectability of her role as mother and devoted wife, as well as her husband's advantage. Somehow, Pirandello makes all of this believable and acceptable. How? By building a complex structure of seduction/non-seduction; intrigue/reaction to intrigue; human cupidity/divine, outgoing love worth of the gods; greed and selfishness/self protection; naive sentimentality/naive self-interest; human initiative/miraculous coincidence; and so on. Paradox is the very texture of the play — the first of Pirandello's complex dramatic contradictions which reinforce, rather than negate, the basic positive premise that ultimately it is the human *will* that structures the universe and gives it meaning. We believe; and in the assertion of that belief, the will is made strong.

But what happens when others try to shatter that belief, try to prove the will is weak? In *Così è (se vi pare)*, Pirandello tackles that aspect of the question, demolishing with the persistence of a grand inquisitor the facts as they emerge, as they are weighed and measured, as they are put forward as evidence. To me the ending of the play is predictable; what is exciting is the cumulative effect of the various sets of arguments, the spiraling toward some kind of "proof," the apparently failsafe scaffolding Pirandello builds up to shake our confidence in facts as external forces acting upon us. What an incredible series of facts, of in-

controvertible evidence! And what an incredible combination
of chance occurrences which seem to make that evidence fool-
proof! Who can dare challenge those facts?

Laudisi, the Socratic skeptic without the Socratic assurance of inner truth, has often been called the spokesman for the
playwright. On the contrary: Laudisi is the pseudo-Pirandellian,
the empiricist par excellence who weighs and measures the contradictions as they surface, who delights in the purely negative
role of exposure, who is not really prepared to trace the truth
but insists on the preliminary leveling process of destruction, of
complacent reality, of spurious facts. In that role, he is the balance which keeps the scale from tipping to one side or the other
for most of the play. At a certain moment, however, skepticism
must give way to something else. Pirandello builds the dramatic
confrontations around the two people in the play who are truly
committed, who have *willed* the truth — each according to his
particular self-assertion — creating it for themselves *ex nihilo*.
Two committed characters; two contradictory truths. Where does
the *real* answer lie? There can be *no* answer at all, so long as the
question is phrased in that way, and the answer is sought in
another external *fact*, or another external combination of *circumstances*. Certainly Laudisi offers no answer. He simply dramatizes the contradictions in the play. Certainly Ponza and his
mother-in-law cannot provide a *single* answer of the kind the
others expect. Their positions are diametrically opposed; and
yet they strike sympathetic chords which remind us that they are
not very far apart in the quality of their commitment. But surely
the answer may be found in Signora Ponza — the object of all the
concern and all the detective work. She certainly can tell us who
she is.

Pirandello drives us relentlessly from one set of facts to
another and another, until there are no facts left to consult; and
then, finally, he presents us with the *embodied* fact, the one person who can give us a direct answer. And here, of course,
Pirandello's *sentimento del contrario* becomes dramatically immediate and visual. Signora Ponza turns out to be the ultimate,
absolute paradox, the last in a series of incredible statements
which are ambiguous in the same way that the oracular utterances of the Delphic priestess were both ambiguous and potentially true in an absolute way. Signora Ponza acknowledges the
paradox of her own essential being by reiterating her relationships to Ponza and to Signora Frola. What is she in herself? The
certainty of their conviction: she is Ponza's wife and Signora Frola's

daughter. Reality has been penetrated and exhausted in those two assurances. As for the others who want to reach *out* instead of reaching *inside* themselves for meaning: I can only be for them (she says) and abortive fact. Even Laudisi, who undermines so completely the dichotomy of reality and illusion, nevertheless has accepted the premise of fact and fiction. The veiled woman need not unveil for the man who willfully insists she is his wife or for the woman who as willfully insists she is her daughter; but for those who still look outside themselves for direction and assurance, she can be only a clever trick, an incomplete notion, a mystery.

There is a certain humor in all this, just as there was in certain aspects of *Liolà*. There is also a great deal of irony — and not just the verbal kind we find in Laudisi or in Diego Cenci in *Ciascuno a suo modo*, but also irony of situation, particularly in the contradictory postures which the Aguzzi and their friends assume as each set of seemingly irrefutable facts comes to light. Here, as in *Liolà*, the turning of the tables carries a certain comic satisfaction; but the context is a larger, more complex one, always. The final resolution of Pirandellian laughter — even in a play like *La patente* (*The License*) — is always, also, full of pathos. Human compassion and pathos control laughter and direct its effects. One of the best examples of the weaving together of irony, laughter, and human pathos is *All'uscita* (*At the Exit*), where the drama is a series of splintered infinities, an almost allegorical setting in which half-baked ghosts must attain their one overwhelming earthly wish before they can be swallowed up into merciful oblivion. The old man (a kind of anagogical version of Uncle Simone) disappears (his walking stick falling to the ground) only after he has witnessed his unfaithful wife cry at the sight of a little boy, the child she never had and always wanted. The woman herself, just killed by her lover, runs after the cart on which the child sits — condemned, one suspects, to an eternity similar to that of Tantalus, reaching out but never grasping what she wanted most. The philosopher remains, for he will never know truth. There is a comic frenzy about this marvelous one-act play, a great deal in it that is laughable and rather wild. And yet, the total effect is powerfully pathetic in the best sense of the word. The combination of opposites can best be assessed, I think, if we compare this play with Thornton Wilder's *Our Town*, which many have said was inspired by *All'uscita*. the difference, in my opinion, rests ultimately in the subtle juxtapositions of comedy and pathos which Pirandello weaves together into a complex fabric of humor. Human emotions are stripped of all contingencies and revealed in the one true mask.

It is in *Enrico IV* that paradox, combined with the pathos of the human condition seen as tragic and humorous, is given full play and large dramatic expression. There is comedy of sorts in the masked pageant extended to a lifetime of play-acting; humor in the adjustments which the retainers have to make as they join the company before they become aware of the reality of the script they have been given to play; humor, also, in the stratification of deception, beginning with the cosmetic effort of the Marchesa to look younger and ending with the deception of portraits replaced by real, live figures in the deceptive posture of still life. Humor is present throughout the play — even in the madness of the chief protagonist, a madness which is itself a paradox, of course, since at the time of the action of the play, he is no longer mad.

Beyond the humor which rises from the individual extravagances and offbeat postures already described, there is the nervous humor of a script which cannot be fully understood on the surface of things — just as the situation in *Così è (se vi pare)* could not be fully understood so long as reality remained *outside*, experience felt as something *external* acting upon the individual like the cosmetics applied by the Marchesa to hide her age. Why does the Emperor (so-called) do what he does, live in the way he does, insist on the play-acting made real? Why is he rewriting the history of Canossa? That project in itself need not be humorous; but it is, because he is rewriting, in fact, his entire life-script and those of others around him — and in the discrepancy between the large fact and the small private cause a smile is evoked. The would-be historian becomes almost comic in the impossible task he has assumed. Almost, but not quite. There is pathos too in his effort to escape through madness or the fiction of madness; and that pathos is strengthened in us with the realization that madness has been reversed without effecting any visible change. The Emperor chose to remain embedded in his role. A sane person would not do that, would he (we might ask at this point)? But we realize the insignificance of the question in this particular context where logic and consistency are rigorously applied. And it is that fabric of logic and consistency that must be penetrated if humor is to be perfected here. Like Hamlet, the mad Emperor is not really mad; but in the same way that Hamlet assumes heightened comic effects in the play scene, where his hysterical lucidity can mislead the spectator into thinking he really *has* solved the problem of how to kill Claudius and is on the verge of doing so, in that same way the protagonist of *Enrico IV* may appear comic in his direction and production of an elaborate court play which has no reality for anyone except himself. What a waste of energy! we are tempted to say in both cases. It is funny . . . or would be funny, if it were not so sad. It is, obviously, both at the same time.

Perhaps in Pirandello's masterpiece, as in Shakespeare's, we witness a new and unique kind of humor. In both *Hamlet* and *Enrico IV*, there are two sets of images which are never reconciled. In both, every effort is made to resolve the double image which produces fuzzy effects and makes direct purpose hard to fathom. In the protagonists there is more than the surface can ever reveal; the objective correlative is not exact, correspondences are off just a little, and therefore objects and intentions are never perfectly in focus. Pirandello's hero tells us he was ready to return to the world . . . perhaps . . . if everything had gone well — that is, according to *his* plan, *his* script. But the facts of the situation suggest, on the contrary, an impenetrable determination consistent with the earlier decision to remain isolated. Like Hamlet — who is never farther from the revenge he has promised to carry out than he is during the play scene, when he realizes that he cannot tell anyone *why* he should kill the king without sounding mad and breaking his promise to the ghost, and that if he *does* kill Claudius he will appear to be the very same kind of usurper he has judged his uncle to be — the mad Emperor in Pirandello's play has in him, already deeply embedded, the ending of his own play. That ending is consistent with all the rest. Madness is not the question at all in *Enrico IV* (just as it is never the question, really, in *Hamlet*); it is simply one of many masks behind which the pathos of self-reflection is hidden from the world. To the rest of humanity watching the effort from a safe distance, such pathos may indeed appear comic. One could trace with profit, I think, the hysterical effort of both protagonists — Pirandello's Henry and Shakespeare's Hamlet — to come to terms with the world. The hysteria bothers us, even as we smile, or laugh.

All of us must pass through the crucible of consciousness/ self-consciousness/infinite reflection of self. Pirandello, not surprisingly, talks at length and with great insight of the process of self-awareness in *L'Umorismo*. Toward the end of the little book, he writes:

Let us [consider] the construction that illusion builds for each of us, that is, the construction that each of us makes of himself through the work of illusion. Do we see ourselves in our true and genuine reality, as we really are; or rather as what we should like to be? By means of a spontaneous internal device, a product of secret tendencies and unconscious imitation, do we not in good faith believe ourselves to be different from what we essentially are? And we think, act, and live according to this fictitious, and yet sincere, interpretation of ourselves.

We have in this brief passage the explication of the Pirandellian brand of humor as it appears in and through dramatic character: a necessary and paradoxical awareness of extremes. That movement takes on a variety of overtones, colors, and textures in the Pirandellian repertory, a variety which includes comedy and satire, laughter, symbolic metaphorical effects — in short, the entire spectrum of human emotions and reactions. Pirandello describes the full effects as follows:

> . . . reflection, indeed, can reveal this illusory construction to the comic writer and to the satirist as well as to the humorist. But the comic writer will merely laugh, being content to deflate this metaphor of ourselves created by spontaneous illusion; the satirist will feel disdain towards it; the humorist does neither: through the ridiculousness of the discovery, he will see the serious and painful side; he will disassemble the construction, but not solely to laugh at it; and, instead of feeling disdain, he will rather, in his laughter, feel compassion.[28]

Humor is part of pathos; together they contain the full panoply of human emotions and *sentimenti del contrario*. Neither is complete in itself; in opposition they constitute a paradox; but that paradox, the heartbeat of the Pirandellian world (as also of the Shakespearean world), is ultimately one truth, one vision. In the movement from fact to contradictory fact, from extreme to extreme, from sad to happy, from certainty to doubt, that vision emerges (Pirandello reminds us at the close of his book) as a series of delicate balances:

> The oneness of the soul contradicts the historical concept of the human soul. Its life is a changing equilibrium; it is a continual awakening and obliterating of emotions, tendencies, and ideas; an incessant fluctuating between contradictory terms, and an oscillating between such extremes as hope and fear, truth and falsehood, beauty and ugliness, right and wrong, etc. If in the obscure view of the future a bright plan of action suddenly appears or the flower of pleasure is vaguely seen to shine, soon there also appears our memory of the past, often dim and sad, to avenge the rights of experience; or our sulky and unruly sense of the present will intervene to restrain our spirited imagination. This conflict of memo-

ries, hopes, forebodings, perceptions, and ideals, can be seen as a struggle of various souls which are all fighting among themselves for the exclusive and final power over our personality. . . . Life is a continual flux which we try to stop, to fix in stable and determined forms, both inside and outside ourselves, because we are already fixed forms, forms which move in the midst of other immobile forms and which however can follow the flow of life until the movement, gradually slowing and becoming more and more rigid, eventually ceases. The forms in which we seek to stop, to fix in ourselves this constant flux are the concepts, the ideals with which we would like consistently to comply, all the fictions we create for ourselves, the conditions, the state in wich we tend to stabilize ourselves. But within ourselves, in what we call the soul and is the life in us, the flux continues, indistinct under the barriers and beyond the limits we impose as a means to fashion a consciousness and a personality for ourselves. In certain moments of turmoil all these fictitious forms are hit by the flux and collapse miserably under its thrust; and even what does not flow under the barrier and beyond the limits — that which is distinctly clear to us and which we have carefully channelled into our feelings, into the duties we have imposed upon ourselves, into the habits we have marked out for ourselves — in certain moments of floodtide, overflow and upsets everything.[29]

It is highly relevant, I think, that *L'Umorismo* should end with references to Copernicus, who "disassembled . . . the haughty image we had formed [of the universe]"; Leopardi, who wrote a magnificent satire on the subject; and the telescope, "which dealt us the *coup de grâce*: another infernal little mechanism which could pair up with the one nature chose to bestow upon us." Humoristic reflection, he goes on to say, in this case — as in all cases of such reflection — suggests that we invented the telescope "so as not to be inferior." The feeling of the opposite here takes on this form: "'. . . is man really as small as he looks when we see him through an inverted telescope? If he can understand and conceive of his infinite smallness, it means that he understands and conceives of the infinite greatness of the universe. How, then, can one say that man is small?'"[30]

In Pirandello's dramatic universe, the progression can be measured in many ways. The detached skeptic Laudisi becomes the involved skeptic Diego Cenci and finally the vulnerable skeptic Henry IV, who would understand perfectly Hamlet's struggle with the paradox of the human soul:

What a piece of work is a man! how noble in reason! how infinite in faculties! in form and moving how express and admirable! in action how like an angel! in apprehension how like a god! the beauty of the world, the paragon of animals! And yet to me what is this quintessence of dust?[31]

Or the feeling of the opposite in George Herbert's Pirandellian lines:

O what a thing is man! how far from power,
From settled peace and rest!
He is some twenty several men at least
Each several hour.[32]

It is not Laudisi but Henry IV who comes closest to identification with Pirandello himself, who wore at least as many masks each several hour as Shakespeare himself wore and graciously shared with *his* favorite and most celebrated creation: Hamlet.

NOTES

An earlier version of this essay appeared in *Modern Drama*, Volume XX, Number 4, December 1977.

1. Luigi Pirandello, *On Humor*, intro., transl., and annotated by Antonio Illiano and Daniel P. Testa, Studies in Comparative Literature Number 58 (Chapel Hill, N.C., 1974).

2. Dante Della Terza, "On Pirandello's Humorism," in *Veins of Humor*, ed. Harry Levin, Harvard English Studies 3 (Cambridge, Mass., 1972), pp. 17-33.

3. *Ibid.*, pp. 20-21.

4. Olga Wester Russell, *Humor in Pascal* (North Quincy, Mass., 1977), pp. 160-161.

5. *On Humor*, pp. 95-96.

6. *Ibid.*, p. 115.

7. *Ibid.*, pp. 143-145.

8. For a full discussion of individual plays, see Anne Paolucci, *Pirandello's Theater: The Recovery of the Modern Stage for Dramatic Art* (Carbondale, Il., 1974).

9. See G. W. F. Hegel, *Aesthetics*, transl. T. M. Knox (Oxford, 1975), Vol. I, pp. 590-592.

10. See G. W. F. Hegel, *Aesthetic*, edd. H. G. Hotho and Friedrich Bassenge (Frankfurt am Main, 1965), Vol. I, pp. 565-567.

11. *Aesthetics*, Vol. I, pp. 600-602.

12. *Aesthetik*, Vol. I, pp. 574-576.

13. *Aesthetics*, Vol. I, pp. 600-601.

14. *Ibid.*, Vol. II, p. 1199.

15. *Ibid.*, Vol. II, p. 1205.

16. *Ibid.*, Vol. I, p. 602.

17. *Ibid.*, Vol. I, p. 192.

18. *Ibid.*, Vol. I, p. 232.

19. *Ibid.*, Vol. I, p. 511.

20. *Ibid.*, Vol. II, pp. 886-887.

21. *Ibid.*, Vol. II, p. 1220.

22. William Shakespeare, 2 *Henry IV*, I, ii, 8-12, in *The Complete Works of Shakespeare*, ed. George Lyman Kittredge (New York, etc., 1936).

23. *Aesthetics*, Vol. I, pp. 585-586.

24. *On Humor*, p. 102; italics in text.

25. Luigi Pirandello, "Introduction to the Italian Theater," transl. Anne Paolucci in *Genius of the Italian Theater*, ed. Eric Bentley (New York, 1964), pp. 24-25.

26. *Ibid.*, p. 27.

27. William Shakespeare, *The Tempest*, V, i, 18-24.

28. *On Humor*, p. 132.

29. *Ibid.*, pp. 136-137.

30. *Ibid.*, pp. 141-142.

31. William Shakespeare, *Hamlet*, II, ii, 316-322.

32. George Herbert, "Giddiness," cited by James Thomson, "Sympathy," *Essays and Phantasies* (London, 1881), p. 242.

CHAPTER 16

PIRANDELLO AND THE WAITING STAGE OF THE ABSURD [WITH SOME OBSERVATIONS ON A NEW 'CRITICAL LANGUAGE']

In his *Myth of Sisyphus*, Albert Camus defines the feeling that in our time has replaced the security of a "world that can be explained by reasoning, however, faulty," as the result of "the divorce between man and his life, the actor and his setting." Lifted from his familiar moorings, "man feels a stranger. His is an irremediable exile. . . ." This existential condition is what "truly constitutes the feeling of Absurdity."[1] Almost four decades have gone by since Camus wrote these words; literature has exploded many myths and has found new fertile ground since his time; and it is hardly surprising that French playwrights should have proved the most consistent in exploring what Camus had recognized as the prevailing mood of our century. Theater of the Absurd owes a great deal to Camus; but the man who restructured the modern stage for a corrosive scrutiny of a world in which we are no longer at home and who provided the sustained dramatic energy for the task was Pirandello. It was Pirandello who first shifted the dramatic sights to the fragmented internal world of self, forging a new language for the purpose, a new stage. Without him, Theater of the Absurd might not have come into being; certainly it would have taken a very different direction. His influence on Sartre, Beckett, Ionesco, Pinter, Albee, Wilder Gelber, Anouilh, Giraudoux, O'Neill, and Camus himself makes him without a doubt "the most seminal dramatist of our time."[2]

Whatever the extent of his existential commitment (certainly not as obvious as Beckett's or as strident as Ionesco's), Pirandello effected profound organic changes in the theater, changes that divorced the actor from the conventional stage and prepared him for the dramatic dialectic which was to become the insistent burden of the contemporary theater. Pirandello dramatized the very act of creation, reminding us that it is not an easy birth.

How did he do it?

First: he restored to the stage its central importance as the empty potency of the dramatic experience. He saw the stage as something to be shaped anew with each new play, like a poem that creates its special language, its unique configuration, as it evolves. With this vision of the function of the stage, Pirandello restored to theater the old magic of "two boards and a passion." The commitment was not explicit at the outset: but by 1921, with *Six Characters in Search of an Author*, a new theater in fact had been perfected. And, in retrospect, we can see clear indications of what is to come as early as *Liolà* (1916), in which Pirandello sweeps away with a bold reversal of moral polarities the conventions of a threadbare system of fossilized social responsibility and unexamined religious absolutes. The rigorous definitions of his own Sicilian society are already transformed in that early masterpiece into an implicit question that takes us to the threshold of an existential experience. Against a familiar background we witness a transvaluation of values, a destructive commentary on a society which stifles individual life. The result is not social commentary however, but a stripping of conventional masks down to a vulnerable core. What we have is the beginning of that dissolution of character which is the signet mark of Pirandello's dramatic art. Within five years, Pirandello gives us his fullest statement of the conversion of the stage for that purpose in his "theater plays"; shifting relationships, juxtaposition of roles and masks, the rich dialectic which destroys the unexamined life and prepares us for internal conversion through the will, all come together in a totally new but already perfected dramatic medium.

The "theater plays" are a drastic departure from all that has come before. In them the audience itself becomes a "mask," a *dramatis persona* in the making. All three plays reach down into the darkness beyond the footlights, expanding and contracting and giving back, like a distorted mirror in each case, shifting reflections from unfamiliar angles. In these plays the audience becomes an actor outside his role, just as the theater itself is the symbol of the empty potency of the stage. In this characteristic movement from potency to act, Pirandello destroys the opposition between the "reality" of life and the "illusion" of the stage: each becomes, in turn, the image and the reflection of the other in a continuous spiraling toward *identity*.

Which takes us to a second point: the content of the Pirandellian theater is a *process*, and that process is the *dissolu-*

tion of character on stage. And, as a corollary: both this content
and the restructured stage come into being together, as one organic whole.

Pirandello recognized in the spiraling toward definition
the energizing content for his restructured stage, the core of the
dramatic experience. In insisting on the traumatic dissolution
of character as the central dramatic event, he forces all of us into
an actor-audience role, on and off stage. We are drawn into the
confrontation with self — that moment in all of us (and in all of
us as potential or real audience) when we see our external image and recognize the dichotomy that results in the positing of
that image. Alone, in front of a mirror, Laudisi in *Right You Are!*
dramatizes that moment of separation in the dialectic of personality. And Pirandello keeps recalling that separation to the very
end of the play. Laudisi remains a "split" personality, a constant
term: he is, throughout, the corrosive skeptic who destroys the
illusion of reality (and serves in that sense a very positive function) but never overcomes that skeptical moment (and in that
sense is the middle term of negation in the dramatic assertion of
will). He is not (as some have insisted} Pirandello's own spokesman for an absolute philosophy of moral and epistemological
relativity. For Laudisi, as for most of the others in the play, the
veiled woman is nothing more than an "abortive" fact: only Ponza
and Signora Frola are able to accept her, to will her into a paradoxical but not contradictory identity. We can begin to grasp
Laudisi's true function as a dramatic catalyst and Pirandello's
dramatic idiom as an oscillation between extremes when we look
closely at the "theater plays."

In *Six Characters in Search of an Author*, Pirandello gives us
his first explicit cue as to the function of the "mask" in his theater and the kinds of adjustments we as audience, as potential
"masks," must make to function actively in the dramatic exchange.
From this moment on, the audience will never again be excused
from contributing to the process of disintegrated/reconstituted
self. Through a sequence that is at first simple *awareness or consciousness* (corresponding to the recognition of an external unexamined reality), then *self-awareness* or *self-consciousness* (the setting up of the essential dichotomy, *distance* between subject and
object, between external mask and internal self), and finally the
resolution of that oscillation in the *willful assertion* of the reconstituted personality, Pirandello dramatizes the creation of *identity* on stage. We zigzag to the center of being and move through
paradoxes into what is not organic personality but its fragmented

moments of existence. The Pirandellian dialectic is not a simple opposition leading to statement but a kaleidoscopic suggestion of purpose and consistency. The Pirandellian protagonist is a stratification of attitudes, emotions, states of being, often contradictory intentions, not a consistent whole. Between his appearance on stage and his retreat from it, he himself, his fellow protagonists on stage, and — most important — the activated audience must all *unlearn* what was taken for granted and trace the internal pattern in that external fragmented mosaic.

Characteristically, these plays — like so many others in the Pirandellian repertory — end abruptly; the protagonists rush off into the darkness, into oblivion, into the hostile world from which they have (for a brief moment) sought refuge. Endings do not correspond to recognizable resolutions in Pirandello's plays. In the "theater plays," action comes to a standstill as the stage business is interrupted in each case and spills over into a larger dimension. The characters who invade the Pirandellian stage also invade (by implicit extension if not directly) the theater itself and our own individual consciousness, the stage in us all, where we reject rote-like acceptance and take on our individual Socratic roles.

The Pirandellian audience in general, but particularly the potential or actual audience of the "theater plays," may best be described as the first moment of psychological awareness analogous to the posited external reality which is the point of departure for so many of the Pirandellian plays and protagonists. No one, on or off stage, is spared the trauma of definition. In *Six Characters*, where the setting includes the empty theater waiting for the perfected stage to bring it to life, the actors-in-rehearsal are also the potential audience waiting to be absorbed into the dramatic event. They fail: the dramatic creation is stillborn. The actors outside their parts, like the audience not yet present in the physical theater (but very much present, needless to say, in the dramatization of all this!), strive vainly for definition; the intruders with their "real-life drama" remain splendidly isolated, unable to translate their vital life into artistic terms, into a script, into a "finished" drama. The latter cannot be contained on any stage; just as the actors-in-rehearsal — from the opposite side — are overwhelmed by the stage. *Six Characters* is marvelously instructive in its insistence on the unresolved dramatic equation. Through the actors-in-rehearsal, the potential of the empty theater begins to emerge.

Each in His Own Way — the second of the "theater plays" —

carries the unresolved contradiction of *Six Characters* into a second, more complex phase. The physical stage itself becomes a double image, a superimposition: actors perform before an audience, other actors interrupt the intermissions (part of the script, of course) to enact moments of the "real-life drama" which inspired the "stage play." A third set of actors, the "critics," create a drama of their own with widely divergent opinions about the play (obviously Pirandello's ironic revenge against the real critics who would not accept his new theater or could not explain it). These three distinct actions — the inner play (furthest removed in Pirandello's telescoping technique), the seemingly arbitrary moments of the "real-life drama," and the drama of the critics (a whole new set of contradictions) — stretch the dramatic event into the real theater, into the contemporary audience. As in *Six Characters*, the focus keeps shifting; but here the complications are greater. There is an inner and outer audience, actors imitating life (but never reaching the end of their "play"), actors providing the "real-life" ending (which is never seen on the inner stage), critics commenting on both the inner and outer actions, the insistence on underscoring unfinished dramatic business by having the stage-actors refuse to finish the inner play and having the "real-life" actors finally come together, reverse their decisions, and rush off together into the night. In its intriguing parallels and intersecting lines of action, *Each in His Own Way* is as exciting as Eisenstein's film superimpositions.[3] Once again we have an open-ended play, a difficult dramatic birth. Life and art come together in kaleidoscopic configurations; there are no simple recognizable patterns.

In the third of the "theater plays" — *Tonight We Improvise* — we have the closest approximation to what might be called the "perfect" performance. This play, like the other two which preceded it, is still abortive, open-ended, a series of fragmented impressions; it too proves too large for the formal stage; but something new has been introduced. The "stage" audience and the audience in the actual theater are the same; the "stage" play and the "real-life" drama are superimposed on the one stage; and, for a moment, the inner and outer play come into sharp focus.

As in the other two plays, the stage action keeps dissolving before our eyes. Dramatic formalities are shattered again and again as actors move in and out of their roles, as they force the audience to take sides in their quarrels, as they "block" them into contradictory postures. The spectators are taken in by the dispute in the wings between the actors and the "director"; they accept the delay and wait patiently for the play to begin; they are jolted out of the dramatic illusion when the actors rush to the aid of their leading lady, who has collapsed: they assume a conspiratorial role as the actors appeal to them and explain, at the end, that all they really need is the script, never mind the director!

For a brief moment, Mommina — the leading lady of the stage play — succeeds in doing what the stage-actors in *Six Characters* and *Each in His Own Way* had tried to do: she is transformed into her mask, becomes her role, and overcomes the dichotomy between the "illusion" of acting and the "reality" of life. It is the only moment of its kind in all three "theater plays," the one flawless superimposition, the one sharply focused identity. Mommina's part calls for her to die from frustration and despair; the actress playing the part actually faints; her fellow actors, in consternation, rush to her side. Their amazement and confusion become the amazement and confusion of the theater audience as well. For, by this time, Pirandello has conditioned us to the demands of role-playing; the stage-actors moving into and out of their formal play have forced us to assume a variety of masks ourselves.

The "theater plays" are a *progressive* sequence which contains, already perfected, most of the characteristics we have come to associate with Theater of the Absurd; the telescoping of time, which brings together psychologically related moments and discards the notion of linear or causal relationship; the splintering of character into attitudes, refracted images, contradictory intentions; the dissolution of the traditional mask into voices that are projections of the single lyric voice of the dramatist himself,[4] the transformation of language into an irritant (not yet Ionesco's intentional cacophony of verbal deadwood or Beckett's *reductio ad absurdum* of philosophic discourse): the insistence on an open-ended structure (it will become static in Ionesco, circular in Beckett): the shattering of uncritical assertion and belief: the erosion of all that is external through an inexorable dialectic — all the dramatic pyrotechnics that have proved efficacious in jolting us out of our complacency. Having found his stride and commitment in these three plays, Pirandello will continue to explore the journey into the interior as both artistic definition and the personal dialectic of freedom. We are all masks. The journey into the self is more than theater.

And in acknowledging the expanding and contracting

stage, the unfinished dramatic business in each of these plays (all are, in a sense, "rehearsals"), the audience must finally accept this inescapable conclusion: the imitation of life on stage, in art, is not imperfect but *impossible*.

In his later plays, Pirandello abandons the dichotomy between life and art and sets up new correspondences in which the stage is the moment of conversion in us all and the drama consists of the struggle of the soul to free itself from the formal postures and masks imposed on it from outside. Two exceptions are worth noting: *The Mountain Giants* (the last of Pirandello's three "myth" plays, written at the very end of his life), where the high purpose of art is shattered against the demands of a technological society that will not be distracted from its single purpose; and *Enrico IV*, the first of many plays in which the drama of identity is seen at close range in the immediacy of familiar human situations but also the culminating statement or dramatic paradox of the function of the stage and the mask, as explored in the "theater plays." Any discussion of Pirandello's "theater plays" must include *Enrico IV* — the most "Absurd" of all his plays and (therefore, perhaps) the most suggestive.

The scaffolding of the "theater plays" disappears with *Enrico IV*; the inner stage has become a living historical fiction, the script of which is still being "revised" and "rewritten." At the other end of the time spectrum, we have a play-within-a-play, a contemporary version (also in costume) of the earlier fiction, put forward by the visitors who come on the scene ostensibly to "cure" the mad emperor. Both of these fictions fail (as fictions always do in Pirandello). The emperor is not really mad, he is certainly not an emperor, and the visitors in their eleventh-century costumes are from a recent past. Both these fictions are open-ended and serve to "frame" the total action. Henry's retreat into the past, at the end of the play, is dictated by external events provoked by the visitors; but it is also a conscious and deliberate decision by a man who has put his private fiction to an inexorable test, the demands of life.

Henry recreates the past in his own image. But the visitors who burst into his restructured world (like the intruders in *Six Characters*) have ideas of their own. They have devised their own historical fiction on a stage which is an ingenious visual superimposition of paintings, living statues in period costume, young and old in identical dress, private intentions masked under historical "roles." Their play is meant to shock the "mad emperor" back to sanity after twenty years. It succeeds only in provoking a tragic confrontation and a violent conclusion, Henry quickly takes over again as the pretenders are unmasked. He is not only the writer, director, protagonist, and producer of his own eleventh-century drama; in him the six characters have found their author.

In its paradoxical complexities, this play has much in common with Theater of the Absurd and, also, with Shakespeare's *Hamlet* (in my opinion, the first dramatic expression of the Absurd). In traditional critical terms, both *Hamlet* and *Enrico IV* (to restrict ourselves to these two for a moment) are "artistic failures";[5] and perhaps in this light we can begin to appreciate the vital truth in Eliot's notorious judgment about *Hamlet*. Pirandello's theater of disintegrating personality, of dialectical inversions, of intentionally misleading motives — like Shakespeare's *Hamlet* — takes us to the threshold of non-art. The rest is not exactly silence; and Shakespeare may well have been ahead of himself in attempting to "express the inexpressibly horrible." Hamlet may be the first "hero" of the Absurd, and the play itself the first effort to "communicate the incommunicable."[6] All of this becomes even more intriguing when we consider how recent criticism of the Absurd has gravitated toward the Hegelian dialectic in the effort to explain "art transcending itself." The best modern critics have insisted, in fact, that objective correlatives no longer work for Theater of the Absurd and a new critical terminology and point of view are necessary. Critical statement has been discarded in the effort to grasp that theater as *process* and the mask of the Absurd as a *surrealistic transparency.*

How does one react to Pirandello's "mad emperor," to Hamlet's mask of madness, to the manic-depressive extremes of Beckett's Estragon and Vladimir, to Albee's Agnes who talks of floating off into madness in *A Delicate Balance.* etc. etc.? How must one approach a dramatic action in which nothing happens but everything changes? Can we speak of actors in the usual sense of the word? Well, of course, they *are* actors but they keep bumping into us, forcing us to make decisions with them, for them. And in those circumstances what sort of characters emerge? Are they really identifiable, or are they sounds, masks, roles searching for the ideal critic?

Hamlet, his own insightful critic, anticipates what Martin Esslin will say of Beckett, who "has very nearly made a play out of silence."[7] What are words words words when the Socratic certainty inside us eludes expression? The ghost of the murdered king in *Hamlet* is, like Polonius and Hamlet himself, full of words

— the most vocal ghost in all the Shakespearean repertory — but he is also the least convincing character in Shakespeare's masterpiece: Hamlet refuses to take action on his terms. Here, as in so many plays of Pirandello, Beckett, Albee, Ionesco, and others, words themselves are a mask, a deceiving posture. What is said does not correspond to an emotional correlative.

I have explored elsewhere the parallels between Shakespeare's *Hamlet* and Pirandello.s *Enrico IV* [8] (and those correspondences deserve to be examined in detail); here, by way of conclusion, I would like to consider briefly the kind of critical language that can help in our appreciation of Theater of the Absurd.

Most critics of the contemporary theater recognize the need for a new critical vocabulary, a new approach, but the only example of a consistent application of new principles is Vivian Mercier's *Beckett/Beckett*. In his preface to the book, Mercier recalls the response of the audience at a symposium which followed a performance of *Waiting for Godot*. Someone asked: "Isn't *Waiting for Godot* a sort of Rorschach . . . test?" The speaker, we are told, was "clapped and cheered by most of those present, who clearly felt . . . that most interpretations of that play — indeed of Samuel Beckett's work as a whole — reveal more about the psyche of the people who offer them than about the work itself or the psyche of its author."[9] Well, yes. Every work of art expands as the reader's interests expand. But something else is at work here. Is it just the psyche of the audience or the critic? Pirandello, we have seen, always tries to get his audience to respond in a profoundly personal way — but that response is not meant to be a purely arbitrary reaction. The Rorschach test is the mirror image in us all, the moment of abstract atomistic response. How do we turn that mirror image into an infinite reflection ("one, no one, hundred thousand") and find the heartbeat of the play?

Mercier suggests that Beckett's success can be traced back to his decision to isolate himself in an unfamiliar environment, to break away from his past — as he did in 1945, when he committed himself to "the total immersion in self, the descent into the core of the eddy."[10] — a Pirandellian journey into the interior, of the kind that Erich Heller describes in his Hegelian analysis of modern art and literature.[11] Mercier quotes a passage from Beckett's work on Joyce in which the commitment is clearly set down: "With Joyce the difference is that Joyce was a superb manipulator of material — perhaps the greatest. He was making words do the absolute maximum of work. There isn't a syllable that's superfluous. The kind of work I do is one in which I'm not master of my material. The more Joyce knew the more he could. He's tending toward omniscience and omnipotence as an artist. I'm working with impotence, ignorance. I don't think impotence has been exploited in the past."[12] Or, as Pirandello tells us: we must lay down the very road on which we walk — every stone along the way. The critic as well as the artist. On or off stage, each of us must find definition.

But how does one reach for definition when all our values and our vocabulary have to be put to a test? How does one shape art out of chaos and find the proper terms to explain the experience?

Mercier sees the answer in the *dialectic*. The structure of his book *Beckett/Beckett* reminds us of David H. Hesla's observation that "the shape of Beckett's art is the shape of dialectic" — a synthesis of the positive and negative, the comic and the pathetic," the yes and the no. Optimism and pessimism, hope and despair, comedy and tragedy are counterbalanced by one another: none of them is allowed to become an Absolute. The very chapter headings are set up as paradoxes: "Ireland/The World," "Artist/Philosopher," "Gentleman/Tramp," "Classicism/Absurdism," "Ear/Eye," and so on. Beckett criticism, says Mercier, is "somewhat aware of each dialectic, but it tends to "emphasize one of the poles to the almost total negation of the other."[13] What Mercier succeeds in doing is to revitalize (unconsciously perhaps) the Hegelian notion of the transcendence of art and the fully-sensitized soul (*schöne Seele*) as the most effective critical approach to the Absurd. "Beckett's anti-heroes do not aspire, so they can never fail. Much of the mirthless laughter they elicit from us springs precisely from this lack of aspiration: they expect so little from life and yet their minimal expectations are frustrated."[14] In their impotence they threaten to lapse into silence. And, by extension, the playwright himself (and others writing in the Absurd idiom) seems to be gravitating toward artistic oblivion. But, as Mercier reminds us, so long as this kind of playwright continues to write, he will not "in this life at least . . . reach either silence or nothingness." What we have (and Beckett is an excellent example) is "a dialectic . . . between silence and garrulity."[15] And, like all dialectical reversals, the two things are intimately related: in their relationship they emerge as both distinct and identical. The "garrulity" of Beckett's "anti-heroes," like that of Hamlet and so many of the Pirandellian protagonists, creates a void; it is the other side of silence. One of the best examples of this tendency toward silence is Edward Albee's *Quotations From Chairman Mao*, where the people on stage indulge in private monologues, addressing not so much the audience as their own integral image waiting for illumination. Pirandello's open-ended arguments on stage — like Beckett's "garrulity" — are often a purging of language.

Martin Esslin was among the first to recognize in the Absurd "a gradual devaluation of language . . . a poetry that is to emerge from the concrete and objectified images of the stage itself." Language "still plays an important part . . . but what happens on the stage transcends, and often contradicts the words spoken by the characters."[16] Mercier's study of Beckett's dramatic art is the first consistent effort to probe the dialectic of the Absurd in critical terms. It reminds us, among other things, that to look for "objective correlatives" in a writer whose work is not so much repeated themes (in that sense what he has to offer is very old indeed) as "fundamental sounds" — Beckett's own phrase —[17] is to miss what is characteristically Absurd. And what has been said of Beckett applies to other playwrights of the Absurd, all of whom work within an ironic medium, definition by exclusion, superimpositions that will not be pinned down to explicit statement. The following description of Beckett's dramatic language could just as well be applied to Pirandello, for example:

> . . . that of a man talking to himself, in the first place the author, and in the second place each individual member of the audience; and this "outer" language between the stage and audience extends also to the "inner" language of the stage itself, where the characters too are men or women talking to themselves. Beckett tells himself a story in the form of a play, each member of the audience tells himself the story in the form of Beckett's play, and within the play the characters tell themselves stories. What is on the stage is not only the occasion for the content of the dialogue with the audience, it is also a metaphor, an image of the dialogue between the author and himself as audience, between the member of the audience and himself as author.[18]

The Pirandellian world is precisely such an expanding experience. The concentric, ever-widening areas of correspondences Mercier defines for Beckett are also those of Pirandello's "theater plays" and *Enrico IV*, where for the first time the stage becomes our own consciousness of the Absurd drama in all of us.[19]

NOTES

An earlier version of this essay appeared in *Modern Drama*, 1980.

1. Albert Camus. *Le Mythe de Sisyphe* (Paris, 1942), p. 18: cited by Martin Esslin. *The Theatre of the Absurd* (New York, 1961), p. xix.

2. Robert Brustein, *The Theatre of Revolt* (Boston, 1964), pp.316-317. See also. Anne Pao lucci, *Pirandello's Theater: The Recovery of the Modern Stage for Dramatic Art* (Carbondale, Il., 1974), pp. 5-6.

3. For an excellent discussion of "Dialectical Form" and Eisenstein's fascination with dialectical superimposition, see Anne C. Bolgan, *What the Thunder Really Said* (Montreal, 1973), Chapter 3, (pp. 55-72).

4. Gottfried Benn, the great Expressionist poet-critic of Germany (whose *Probleme der Lyrik* was quite possibly the source for T .S. Eliot's classic essay "The Three Voices of Poetry") observed that the "three voices" in modern literature have all been absorbed into the one voice: the lyric voice. In this light, his influence on Joyce, Pound, Eliot, etc. becomes especially interesting. For the connection between Benn's discussion and Hegel's discussion of Romantic (Modern) art see A. Paolucci "Introduction: Benn, Pound, and Eliot: The Monologue Art of German Expressionism and Anglo-American Modernism," *German Expressionism*, Special Editor. Victor Lange, Volume 9, *Review of National Literatures* (annual volume 1979, New York, 1979), pp. 10-24.

5. T. S. Eliot, "Hamlet," in *Selected Essays 1917-1932* (New York, 1932), p. 123.

6. *Ibid.*, p. 122.

7. Martin Esslin, "Samuel Beckett's Poems," in *Beckett at 60*, (London, 1967), p. 77.

8. See Paolucci, *Pirandello's Theater*, pp. 89-101.

9. Vivian Mercier. *Beckett/Beckett*, (New York, 1977), p. vii.

10. *Ibid.*, p. 5.

11. Erich Heller, *The Artist's Journey into the Interior* (New York, 1965). See especially his ingenious discussion about Eliot's comments about *Hamlet* (e.g., "[It suffices] in all its strange wrong-headedness to prove this poet's great critical intelligence. It reads as if T. S. Eliot had studied Hegel's theory of the difference between Classical and Romantic art . . . and then decided both to profit from it and to ignore it." (p. 130); and, "Clearly, T. S. Eliot knew what he was saying when he judged *Hamlet* an artistic failure because the hero's emotion exceeded his concrete situation or the 'objective correlative.' It is the more surprising that Eliot judged as he judged; for what he condemned is the occasion itself of Romantic art, including his own. . . . Perhaps he did not mean it. Mean what? It is the persistent and most troublesome question of the Romantic mind. For having lost its world, it can never do what it means: and what it means cannot be done." (p. 136); and still later, "Where T. S. Eliot diagnoses the 'artistic failure' of the play, there lies in truth its achievement. Shakespeare, favored by his age . . . succeeded with *Hamlet* where Goethe . . . had to fail with *Torquato Tasso*: in creating, paradoxically speaking, the 'objective correlative' for a subjectivity Roman-

tically deprived of any adequate 'objective correlative'."

12. Mercier, p. 8.

13. Cited by Mercier, p. 11.

14. *Ibid.*, pp. 12-13.

15. *Ibid.*, p. 18.

16. Esslin, p. xxi.

17. Mercier, p. 18.

18. John Fletcher and John Sparling, *Beckett: A Study of His Plays* (London, 1972), pp. 37-38.

19. A slightly different original version of this paper was read to the Pirandello Society at the Convention of the Modern Language Association of America, San Francisco, December 28, 1979.

CHAPTER **17**

ALBEE AND THE RESTRUCTURING OF THE MODERN STAGE

When in the 1970's — at the invitaion of Harry T. Moore — I wrote my book on Edward Albee, *From Tension to Tonic: The Plays of Edward Albee,* critics were struggling with the novelty of the plays, trying to make them accessible to readers and students trained in traditional structures in which action could be traced to a climax and resolution; character interpreted as a series of responses to events and people against a recognizable set of values; intentions and deeds expressed by the protagonists in logically acceptable terms, as cause and effect; and the different "voices" of a play heard in familiar accents to which we, the audience, could relate. What was painfully clear, very early, was that the Aristotelian categories, which had proved effective for almost two thousand years, no longer worked for critics trying to grasp Albee's new kind of drama. Action, in those plays, did not move predictably from conflict to solution; character was neither integral nor organic; themes were not easily decipherable, and language reflected an arbitrary relationship between meaning and words. I had my own difficulties: instinctively I understood the need for a new critical language, but at the time I was not sure how to define it or even recognize it.

What I did do, by way of a beginning, was to indulge in comparisons between Albee's style and other innovative techniques — new and old. I allowed myself to respond instinctively to certain parallels that suggested themselves to me, howsoever outlandish they seemed. I saw much that reminded me of Dante's poetic transparencies and surreal approach to allegory; and I also recognized the manner of Pirandello, who destroyed stage conventions before our eyes in order to force us to restructure a world where assumed values are called into Socratic doubt for a more vital constructive commitment which is both personal and universal. Through such comparisons I found myself gradually moving toward a new critical approach, one that might serve the purpose. Without rejecting Aristotle (we do so at our own peril, still), I found myself moving toward a new set of critical guidelines, In Albee's plays, cause and effect were often disjoined, rational and irrational motivation equally significant, psychological mechanisms not always clear, language itself often reduced to clichés, non sequiturs, obsessive repetitions and refrains, Much later, I was able to relate the phenomenon of this new stage to what the great German Expressionist poet-critic, Gottfried Benn, had said about the transformation of the three voices of poetry in our time: the lyric, the epic, and drama had taken on the characteristics of the "first voice, " the monologue voice of subjectivity. (See Paolucci, "Benn" 17-20; Eliot, "Three" 96.)

Hamlet and the "Artistic Failure" of the Absurd

T. S. Eliot (who read Benn with profit, both as a critic and a poet) seemed to have had that profound observation in mind when he noted that Shakespeare's *Hamlet* was the "Mona Lisa" ("Hamlet" 124; see also Paolucci, *Hegel* xxviii) of literature and at the same time an "artistic failure" ("Hamlet" 123). Most critics who have focused on the arguments which led to these conclusions have missed the intriguing suggestiveness of Eliot's conclusion in each case, especially as they relate to the Absurd. His remarks become especially intriguing in the light of Hegel's analysis of the modern world as the emergence of the self-conscious man who holds within himself the secret of his Socratic certainty — an oracular certainty that is both sublime and diabolical in its self-conscious isolation, a certainty which Hegel recognizes in the *schöne Seele*, the beautiful soul that creates its own world in its contradictory image. *Hamlet*, for Hegel, is the greatest portrayal of that modern consciousness which isolates and withdraws within itself, insisting on its own absolute values to justify its actions. In Hegelian terms, therefore, Shakespeare's *Hamlet* exceeds the limits of the play *as play* in its total insistence on the idiosyncratic and arbitrary character (*Hegel* 90-91, 214, 219-198; "Rejection" 203).

Or, as A. C. Bradley had noted even earlier (acknowledging his great debt to Hegel): Hamlet is larger than life in the tragic setting Shakespeare has provided, just as Falstaff is greater than the comedy that contains him ("Rejection" 259, 269-270, 273). In bringing together Hegel, Eliot, Bradley, Benn, and others who had ventured into this difficult territory, I began to understand that in *Hamlet*, as in the plays of Albee and other playwrights of the Absurd, art indeed reaches a point where, as Hegel points out, it threatens to become non-art, *to transcend* itself (Knox 80, 89), to become absorbed into a qualitatively different (nonliterary or other than literary) experience. Through these critics

I began to understand how Theatre of the Absurd can be described accurately as theatre on the brink of non-theatre.

It was Vivian Mercier who first made clear, in his *Beckett/ Beckett*, the need for a *dialectical* structure in dealing with the Absurd. Themes will elude us in the Aristotelian format, as will character and action and language as we have dealt with them in the past. Focusing on Beckett, Mercier explains that the only way to deal with the plays is by paradox, contradiction, juxtaposition, opposites forced together. Only then can we begin to appreciate the cyclical nature of movement, the obsessive circling around given points in time and experience, the de-fleshed characters whose humanity nonetheless remains strong and moving. Statement becomes allegory (but the key is not easy to come by); experience is solipsistic; the effort to translate subjectivity into objective correlatives seems to echo the open-ended soliloquies of Hamlet. Without any of the Hegelian insights, Mercier had hit on the most crucial critical issue with respect to the Absurd: Aristotelian terminology had to be dismantled and a new set of guidelines set up to deal critically with this kind of play.

What Mercier says of Beckett applies also, of course, to all playwrights of the Absurd. But while following the lead of the early masters (Beckett, Ionesco, etc.), Albee — deliberately or not — retrieves the illusion of realism, even while dismantling accepted stage conventions. I was reminded of Pirandello, whose language is indeed the language of paradox and contradiction, whose characters are disconcerting and cryptic in stating their intentions. I saw in Albee's plays the familiar Pirandellian technique of setting up realistic situations and recognizable characters only to destroy that so-called realism (the true "illusion"), dismantling the stage buttressing and scaffolding of the past in the process of reconstruction. Shifting from realism to subjectivity, dramatizing the process itself, Albee has proved himself one of the true masters of Theatre of the Absurd.

I found myself comparing Albee's characters with those of Pirandello — the Emperor Enrico IV in particular-as well as Shakespeare's Hamlet. In such protagonists, the struggle for self-definition, while moving inexorably toward self-destruction in Socratic isolation, is set against a deceptively familiar canvas of circumstances and events that lure us into logical explanations. Such characters stumble into realities beyond their control. Events trigger responses, not revelations. We all know the critical "problems" that have attracted so many writers to Shakespeare's "Mona Lisa." We know how many hypotheses have been put forward to explain the delay of Hamlet to do what he has promised and sworn to do. We know how short of the mark all such studies have proved to be: Hamlet, the voice of subjectivity, remains inscrutable to the end. To me, the parallels that had surfaced deserved to be studied more closely.

What has always struck me, about Shakespeare's play, is the discontinuity of the action with respect to the character of Hamlet. What I mean is, the protagonist does not really respond to events as expected and does not — as in other plays of Shakespeare's and in most modern plays down to Ibsen, Strindberg, and Arthur Miller — grow or change as a result of what happens around him. He is at the end of the play what he was at the beginning. Shifting directional signals have taken us through a maze of experiences which may be meaningful to most of the characters in the play, all of whom have clear intentions and short- or long-range plans, but seem not to affect in any organic sense Hamlet himself. The impression was strengthened by the nature of the soliloquies, which are all pretty much the same in tone and psychological thrust — curiously interchangeable. They suggest, together, one long continuous monologue, the expression of some deep-rooted difficulty never fully diagnosed. As a result, the soliloquies in *Hamlet* proved to be a deflecting mechanism, redirecting us from the outer play, the sequence of events, to an inner life that waits for definition. To speak of Hamlet's delay and to explain it in terms of expressed intentions and aborted motives is to miss Shakespeare's surrealistic juxtaposition of inner and outer layers of consciousness. Hamlet lives and moves in a world that is his own private territory, where events are translated into terms meant to provoke answers already in place. Under no circumstances will Hamlet kill Claudius to avenge his father's murder. When he does kill his uncle he does so because he has been incited, on the spot, by the knowledge that Claudius has set out poison for his nephew and in so doing has in fact caused the death of the Queen, Laertes, and Hamlet himself: Hamlet responds to one set of circumstances while saying that he is doing something else, really. He stumbles into a series of confrontations which dramatize his inability to spring the trap set for him, until he is forced to react on the spot to the murder of his mother and his friend. Sworn to secrecy, his plotting becomes an ironic arid tragic joke. The masque and the short play he writes do not confirm anything he did not already know, nor do they serve to expose the King in any way:

what the Court witnesses is a play about a nephew who murders the rightful King; what we the audience witness is a frustrated consciousness struggling for expression and recognition. Hamlet's undirected nervous energy comes through in his obsessive need to talk: he is the precursor of Lucky and Pozzo in *Waiting for Godot*, Brother Julian in *Tiny Alice*, Jerry in *The Zoo Story*. In this kind of play a great deal happens but nothing really changes — or, everything changes but nothing really happens.

Like most of the protagonists of the Absurd, Hamlet does not direct action; he responds to it passively. He reacts (as when he changes the letters carried by his friends to England and insures their death instead of his own), but he does not have an effective master plan. He moves from point to point, with a certain amount of energy but without commitment. In these terms Hamlet has little in common with Macbeth, Brutus, or Othello. Not only is the protagonist uncommitted and unconvinced in what he does, he is in a very real sense outside the movement of the play. Hamlet's difficulties are never solved; he moves as a spectator around oases of action, scrutinizing circumstances which have little to do with his subjective inner life. The action of the play is seen as though through the wrong end of the telescope, reduced to insignificance, set at a great distance from the real inner life of the protagonist and the mystery he cannot communicate. He displays the same obsessive circling around an undefined core that we find in the protagonists of the Absurd — the same elusive psychology, the same disruptive and self-destructive forces at work, the same excesses which give us the nagging sensation that we are experiencing certainties gone to rot. We are made conscious of the smell of decay and death. The obscenity of Pozzo explaining Lucky's catatonic presence is no different from the obscenity of Hamlet's musing about Yorick's skull.

Which brings us to the subject of madness. How anyone can read Shakespeare's play and not be struck by the simultaneous lucidity and hysteria in Hamlet's behavior is hard to understand. But to speak of madness in a clinical sense, in his case, is misleading. Hamlet is obviously driven to the edge of the "reasonable" world, that world of realities to which we all adjust as our compromise with the conventions that shape our daily lives and make possible relationships with others. For Hamlet that world is unreal, and yet it forces him to take sides, to do things he would prefer not to do. What engrosses him is his inner life, the sorting out of motives which he himself cannot fully understand. How else can we explain his curious insensitivity to those around him, the distance he places between himself and people like Ophelia, for instance, whom he drives to madness of a real kind, Polonius (whose murder, by "mistake," is glossed over and quickly forgotten), his ruthless plotting against Rosencrantz and Guildenstern, whom he sends to their death simply because they wanted to help the King — in their eyes still the trusted ruler and concerned parent? The critical response to these questions and similar ones suggests not madness but a double image of a Machiavellian realist, ruthless in his immediate dealings with the world, when his "terms" are clear to him, and the "beautiful soul" searching within itself for the absolutes, the oracular certainties that will explain his being, the core of his identity. Hamlet's excesses are quite similar to those of the protagonists of the Absurd, who pushed to the brink of consciousness, fail to communicate in those terms we all accept by force of habit. In such cases, as in Hamlet's, communication is reduced to monologue, language is splintered into a mosaic of impressions, irony takes on a tragic-comic aspect that is funny and pathetic at the same time. In Shakespeare's Hamlet as in the protagonists of the Absurd, the ironic oscillation is the means to self-awareness, self-assessment, and, finally, redemption — at least in the knowledge that one has been true to one's innermost and most persistent instinct for self-definition.

In his role as the undefined personality searching for identity in terms that will satisfy his inner life, Hamlet reveals the distracted "hero" of our existential world. He offers no answers to his frustration, he simply traces experience to basic questions: *Who am I? Where do I belong in this setting? How can I properly explain my actions?* Reduced to its existential core, Hamlet's personality, paradoxically, may be easier to grasp. He has no purpose that will serve to satisfy the demands made on him, no direction to insure meaningful action, no convictions in consistent terms. Friendship, love, family are all undermined in a world where there is no center holding things together. In this perspective, Hamlet reveals a great deal about what he can *not* do, contrary to his stated purpose. His actions fall into a pattern not so much of indecisiveness as of futility. His actions lack organic meaning.

In not conforming to the conventional structures of action, character, themes, and language, Shakespeare's play suggests comparisons with the Absurd. The action in *Hamlet* spirals around a shifting core; the character is fragmented into many moods, outbursts, plots, and counterplots not easily grasped in terms of direct provocation from outside sources. Hamlet himself seems to be traced around two main foci, creating a double image which is never resolved into a single focus. Hamlet tantalizes us with the unexplored and unexplained depths of his soul; we wonder at his obsessive need for self-assertion, for so much talk that resolves nothing and goes nowhere. Hamlet loses nothing and gains nothing in the course of the play; but in trying to grasp the distorted image he projects, we come closer to the confusion in our own lives.

After Shakespeare's *Hamlet*, the first plays to take on the existential question in expressionistic, surreal terms in a large way were Pirandello's "theater plays" and *Enrico IV*: Robert Brustein describes Pirandello's genial innovation as the "dramatization of the very act of creation" (133; see Paolucci, *Pirandello's Theater* 5-6). And if we accept that transformation as the destruction of the conventional habits of play-writing and the introduction of a multi-faceted distorted experience which invades the stage and forces the audience to become active in the reconstitution of the play as play, then Pirandello is indeed the Father of the Absurd and the first great heir of the avant-garde experience Shakespeare depicted for us in his *Hamlet*. The Pirandellian protagonist is undefined and his stage is an everlasting shifting kaleidoscopic pattern. Emperor Enrico IV creates the world in his own image, and — like Hamlet — lashes out when that world is threatened in any way. He is the same oracular voice of truth and doom, the actor in search of his unattainable mask, the beautiful and dangerous Socratic soul working toward definition.

Pirandello's "mad" emperor, like Ionesco's insane Professor and Beckett's hysterical/tyrannical Pozzo, is the unresolved Hamlet in contemporary dress. He has isolated himself from the world, trusts no one, is shrewd and cunning about his own pressing interests, is ready to play games in order to expose his erstwhile enemies, moves precariously among strangers in his mask of insanity, provokes confrontations that are self-destructive, kills at the end. Like Hamlet, Henry hides his intentions — whatever they are — behind the convenient assumption of madness (in Henry's case, amnesia resulting from a concussion). He continues the charade, even after he has regained his memory and his "reason." His habits do not change; until he chooses to confide in his servants that he has been in his right mind for many years, he poses as the Emperor who is writing the true history of Canossa, in his own image, and whose enemies are

masked behind the enemies of the eleventh-century Emperor
who defied the Pope. Pirandello creates layers of consciousness,
as Shakespeare does in *Hamlet*, creating images that suggest the
infinite suggestivity of the movement from sheer consciousness
(we all share in it) to self-consciousness (the dichotomy that leads
to confrontation with the self) to identity (the oscillation between
the images thus created). Pirandello makes this genial superimposition visual on stage by setting up a Chinese-box type of
superimposed layers very like those represented in the replica
of Albee's *Tiny Alice*: paintings showing the "Emperor" and the
Marchesa, twenty years earlier, in the costumes they wore on the
fateful day when the young man fell from his horse and suffered
a concussion; the daughter of the Marchesa and the nephew of
the "Emperor" (in their twenties) in similar costumes; and the
Marchesa and the Emperor in those same costumes but twenty
years removed from the time represented in the paintings. There
is, also, the here and now, the immediate stage, the present setting, where the confrontation takes an unexpected turn and the
"Emperor" recognizes and kills his enemy.

Why has Henry chosen to live in the past he has created?
He tells us that it is too late for him to catch up with the world,
but this kind of talk — like Hamlet's excuses and justifications —
is not wholly convincing. Even if we accept his explanation, why
has he insisted on continuing the charade? He suggests that perhaps he might go back into the world "out there," but then why
does he provoke his old enemy as he does? Like Hamlet, Henry
forces the inevitable to its conclusion. What had been tolerated
as an eccentric "mask" of insanity now becomes a terrible reality: he must forever live out the role of the "insane" Emperor in
order to remain "free."

In his early masterpiece, *Il fu Mattia Pascal*, Pirandello explains — through one of his characters — the difference between
the ancient and modern theatre:

> The tragedy of Orestes in a puppet theatre! . . . Now listen to this
> crazy notion that just came to me! Let's suppose that at the very
> climax, when the puppet who represents Orestes is about to take
> his revenge on Aegisthus and his mother for his father's death, a
> great hole were suddenly torn in the paper sky of the theatre, what
> would happen? . . . Orestes would still be bent on revenge, he
> would still be impatient to bring it about, but his eyes in that in-
> stant would be directed up there, to that rippled sky, where all
> kinds of evil influences would now filter down into the scene, and
> he would feel his arms grow limp. Orestes, in other words, would
> become Hamlet. The whole difference, Signor Meis, between an-

cient and modern tragedy is just that, believe me: a hole in the paper sky (*Pirandello's Theatre* 2, my translation).

How marvelously appropriate the image is! Distracted from purpose and meaningful action, Hamlet is at the mercy of the forces around him. His energies are undiminished but others direct them. It is not remarkable in the light of Pirandello's insight into the crucial change that takes place between ancient and modern tragedy that he should have given us in his Emperor Henry IV the contemporary counterpart of Hamlet, a man without identity, struggling to know himself, an actor embedded in his role, a personality no longer integral or whole. Enrico IV, like Hamlet, is incapable of heroic action, but he displays all the grandeur of self-conscious commitment. In both, disorientation is the key to understanding. In both, also, we witness a Sophoclean reversal of movement: each step forward is a step backward. We spiral toward recognition of the inevitable.

Albee's Kaleidoscopic Technique

I like Albee because he reminds me so much of the total theatrical experience which Pirandello has taught us all to appreciate. Pirandello understood the need for the shifting stage where conventional methods are discarded as we watch and characters move within their own self-defined limits. Other playwrights of the Absurd have dramatized with greater impact than Albee perhaps the cyclical movement of action, the idiosyncratic personality shattered into isolated responses and repetitive experiences, language as the expression of suggestive sounds and empty forms of rhetoric; but what makes Albee stand out, in my opinion, is his insistence on giving us the Pirandellian sense of realism on stage, drawing us into the play and slowly pulling away the scaffolding that separates us from the core of the experience, casting us as participants in the drama. I was struck recently in reading Albee's "Introduction" to Louise Nevelson's work to find this conviction articulated by the playwright himself. Describing the emotional and intellectual involvement he experienced on viewing Nevelson's structures, but particularly "Mrs. N.'s Palace," Albee explains how that piece especially invites one literally to enter Nevelson's world and become engulfed by it. He recalls an earlier similar experience, when he sat in the reconstruction of a room Mondrian had designed: "imagine a Mondrian painting twenty by twenty feet; then imagine it a cube; then imagine yourself placed in the center of the cube. On both occasions — the Mondrian and the Nevelson — I had been transformed from spectator to participant" (*Louise* 29). His conclusion that Nevelson's "worlds" constitute "alternative space . . . a fathomable reality in the midst of the outside chaos" is applicable to Albee's own work: *Tiny Alice* surely is the most startling example of an "endless house" that is itself a sculpture and a symbol of "alternative space" (*Louise* 30). It is not surprising that Nevelson — for Albee — is one of the "few people who saw instinctively to the core of . . . *Tiny Alice*. . . ."

All great art, Albee tells us (echoing Goethe's "all art is arrogance") is "an act of aggression"— aggression against "the familiar and the 'easy'" — which is why, as he puts it, "very few creative artists are hired as critics in the popular and influential media" (*Louise* 16). The "arrogance" of art involves always a new set of guidelines; every artist creates his own language and his own world — and this is nowhere clearer than in the Theatre of the Absurd, where the conventional medium is deliberately destroyed before our eyes. Through chaos we reach some understanding of what is possible.

What Albee does best is precisely what Pirandello had put forth "arrogantly" on his new stage: an evolving experience, a flowing series of contradictions that force the audience to shift from illusion to reality from what appears to be to what is and to reverse the terms taken for granted until reality becomes a large question and illusion (so-called) takes on immediate and vivid meaning. How else can one explain the "theater plays" of Pirandello, or even his late "myth" plays, where social, religious, and artistic values are put to a fierce scrutiny and the world restructured on the basis of an individual commitment? In *Each in His Own Way*, Pirandello shows us the shifting stage itself, carrying action back and forth from the lobby (which may be the very lobby of the theatre in which all this is going on) to the stage and back, forcing us into a double image, two sets of actors, two stories, two dramas, both of which remain open-ended. In *Enrico IV* the double focus is turned into a genial superimposition, a telescoping technique (as we observed earlier) that forces us to reconsider every incident described, every emotion experienced. It is theatre that dramatizes our own paradoxical intentions and forces us to play them out in our own "structuring" of the action in each case.

And that is precisely what Albee does best. In *Tiny Alice* he has created a perfect superimposition not only of characters but of setting. The replica is the larger house and the infinitesimal flash of recognition in us all; the unholy trio who force Brother Julian to confess his despair are also his saviors, for in the knowledge of his limitations he himself recognizes salvation. Death is welcome only because there is no other possible answer; and in the sudden disappearance of the three "guests" we read the end of a chapter, the culmination of an experience which doesn't require any commentary, since we have all gone through moments of conversion, one kind or another. The play ends with the clear echo of past and future moments converging and reinforcing the present one. The musical effects of the language, always strong in Albee, provide the subliminal reinforcement of this large equation.

In the Absurd such effects are vital. They provide the emotional language in the same way that internal rhythms provide the essential clues to meaning in free verse. Refrain, repetition, echoes, forms that are familiar to us in other contexts (the "mass for the dead" in *Who's Afraid of Virginia Woolf?*; the musical "frame" at the beginning and end of *A Delicate Balance*; the spinning around an allegory that is a religious echo and the descent into Hell in *The Zoo Story*; the obvious reversal of primitive and sophisticated attitudes in *Seascape*) are found in all of Albee's plays to help bridge the distance between the absurd reality we take for granted and the illusion which becomes real, once we learn how to recognize it (just as "Absurd" describes the vital theatre of our time and the unchanging realistic theatre is the true absurdity). Beckett makes excellent use of musical effects, as does Ionesco; but Albee employs them best not only in the large varieties of arias for single, double, and triple voices but also in the larger structures of fugues, cantatas, and operatic effects.

Albee reminds us also of Pirandello in his story-telling abilities. This, too, lulls us into thinking along familiar "realistic" lines, but like Pirandello, Albee uses the story technique as an allegory very often, a way to help us grasp what is not stated, what cannot be fully understood through statement. The story of the cat and Tobias's relationship to the animal in *A Delicate Balance*, the story of the dog in *The Zoo Story*, the story of the Boy/Son in all its stratified aspects in *Who's Afraid of Virginia Woolf?*, the constant reaching for memories that surface unexpectedly and seem often unrelated to the larger drama — in making the fullest use of structures we recognize or at least can relate to and accept in those terms, Albee enables us to work out the "script" with him. And it is precisely in this use of the traditional stage and familiar conventions to redefine action, character, themes, and language in the new terminology of the existential experience in us all that Albee shows himself most innovative. Beckett, Pinter, Ionesco, Stoppard, Giraudoux, and Genet have all concentrated on one or more aspects of the stripped stage; but Albee — like Pirandello — has shown us the way to that new stage by dramatizing the excesses that must be cleared away in order to see ourselves in the mirror image of the play through which our own subjectivity is objectified.

Like Pirandello, Albee unobtrusively places us on stage and we find ourselves listening in or overhearing conversations. We must find our own way into the experience. Whatever the "Terror" in *A Delicate Balance*, we feel its horror and give it whatever name is ours to give. Jerry in *The Zoo Story* makes us uneasy; we know the type and prefer to avoid him, even though we are not quite sure what harm he can do. But our instincts are right; and Peter's instincts are those of the audience. And so we find ourselves getting nervous watching and listening to Jerry force Peter to respond to him; and we recognize in Peter's undefined caution some kind of imminent disaster. I'm reminded of what Albee said in answer to an interviewer's comment that "the idea of anyone character's possessing all of the truth seems a bit dogmatic, if not naive": "I think every character should be permitted to have some portion of the misunderstanding," was his reply. The spectator too, I would add. In the same interview Albee speaks of "resonance" in art, the need for directing the attention "to a sense of rhythm, to a sense of order — to a comprehension of what it is to be, to be aware of oneself." The usefulness of art, he explained, "has to do with the fact that it makes us understand consciousness and bring some order into the chaos of existence" (*Louise* 10). For Albee — and he has said this in many different ways and at many different times — theatre is personal discovery and each of us must enter into the experience on our own terms. In the true Pirandellian sense, we all become actors in search of our own mask.

A curious feature of Albee's work is his early experimentation (in *The American Dream* and *The Sandbox*, for instance) along the lines of Beckett and Ionesco — the defleshed abstract stage where language becomes an irritating puzzle and familiar conventions are struck down harshly, without any effort at salvaging some measure of our experience. The early plays are a deliberate exercise in stark existential drama. Later — interestingly enough — Albee returns to that kind of technique (*Quotations from Chairman Mao*), where dramatic dialogue disappears altogether and a new kind of monologue takes its place, one in which the actor addresses himself/herself to the inner consciousness of the spectator. In the early one-act plays mentioned, Albee was no doubt shaping his own talent in the exciting mold of the contemporary German and French playwrights; but in the later play, he seems to have circled back to that stripped stage in his own terms, experimenting with the most avant-garde techniques as though deliberately pushing them to the edge of non-theatre. We are reminded of Pirandello's naked masks.

Briefly, Albee empties the stage and gives us "voices" that are almost disembodied, emotions already in full bloom, forcing communication to its extremest limits. In such a play Albee comes very close to — perhaps goes even further than — playwrights like Beckett and Ionesco; but it is a mark of his sharp critical sensibilities as a dramatist that he should have chosen to continue in a tradition which "saves" realism while demolishing it. I find that kind of theatre much more genial, and more exciting too. Without forcing comparisons with other playwrights, we can say, surely, that an Albee play is shifting ground, a series of superimpositions that we the audience must adjust to if we are to enter the play and experience its expanding orbits. Again, perhaps the best way to appreciate and understand Albee is to come to him through Pirandello's dramatic art. Both use the stage as a distorted mirror in which movements and faces and words and emotions are reconstituted in the effort to recognize what we think we know.

Eventually, of course, it is an understanding not only of Existentialism but also of Expressionism that gives us the best insights into the new art of our twentieth century, particularly Theatre of the Absurd. "Modern art," as Walter Sokel explains in *The Writer in Extremis*, "abandons the illusion of three-dimensional space in favor of a freely constructed space, and deviation from the law of causality does not prevent the artist from pursuing his particular design." Summarizing Kant's aesthetics as the artist's "arbitrary freedom to create according to his intentions" — art as a universe of its own and the artist as "the creator and legislator of a universe" (Sokel 9-10; Clark 157) — Sokel applies that insight into the artistic practices of our time. Whether we agree with his argument or not, his application of that critical discussion to literary phenomena is interesting in our context. One of these phenomena, Literary Cubism (represented by such authors as Pound, Eliot, and Joyce), "is more radically experimental than Surrealism . . . but at the same time much more objective. Its point of departure is an objective situation rather than the personal subconscious. It relies on the latter, too, but . . . emphasizes experiments with language rather than imagery and metaphor." Cubism, surrealism, "and their fusion in Expressionism" insist on the abandonment of "external frameworks" together with all other vestiges of "traditional treatment of character" (Clark 163-164). Victor Lange gives us an excellent literary summary of German Expressionism and its implications. Speaking of Gottfried Benn ("the only successful purveyor of Expressionist prose"), Lange notes that the German writer "renders 'consciousness' with a full awareness of its superiority over a reality that is devoid of an inherent order." The "principle of focusing upon the objective world and thereby transcending its oppressive disjointedness is elaborated by the Expressionist poets in a variety of ways. One, and perhaps the most striking, is the attempt to disturb and mobilize the reader by a succession of syntactically simple statements which, in their taciturn manner, produce an almost mythical effect." We feel in the work of such Expressionist poets as Jakob van Hoddis or Alfred Lichtenstein not "self-preoccupied" minds but minds "intensely object-directed" (31). Lange cites Wassily Kandinsky, who in 1910 defined the tenets of Expressionism in his book *On the Spiritual in Art*, where he underscores — as Martin Buber had before him — the notion of ecstasy as central to all Expressionist art: "the manner by which the artist, in detachment from his immediate experience of the fortuitous, the chaotic world of objects, recognizes in the work of art an opportunity of giving shape to that consciousness beyond self." Like Buber, Kandinsky believed in the capacity of art to "regenerate the world through . . . pure 'inwardness'" (Lange 33).

"Ecstasy," "intensely object-directed," abandonment of "external frameworks," "freely constructed space," the "objective situation" as the point of departure, the superiority of "consciousness," "pure inwardness" — Expressionism had already defined and illustrated the new world of art, that same world which Pirandello shaped for the stage and which we recognize also in Albee. Expressionism together with the Existential mood of isolation and self-conscious brooding has forged Theatre of the Absurd and helps to explain it as a commitment to the monologue of art, which addresses itself to itself, or to nobody.

Albee's "New Realism": A Delicate Balance

A great deal has been written to date about *A Delicate Balance*, but it might be worthwhile reviewing the play in the light of what has already been said about the influence of expressionist and existential currents on the playwrights of the Absurd. It should be clear, at the outset, that I do not propose to trace direct sources or parallels; I wish simply to show that the play contains many of the characteristics discussed in the first half of this paper, that it is very much in the tradition of the Absurd, and yet that it maintains throughout a realism that enhances the surreal and cryptic design which Albee had already mastered early in his career. I should add quickly that almost any play would do as well, as an example in this context; what is said about *A Delicate Balance* may just as easily be applied to *Who's Afraid of Virginia Woolf?*, *Tiny Alice*, or *All Over*.

Mercier's suggestion that critical assessments of the Absurd must be articulated in the same language of paradox and contradiction found in the plays themselves can serve here as a practical guide. I have devised my own set of opposites:

1. *Particular-Universal*. As in his other plays, Albee quickly sets the stage in realistic every-day terms, placing characters in the most ordinary situations, showing them in obvious and often humdrum relationships, and introducing familiar excesses: in this case, alcoholism and sexual indulgence. The house is perfectly recognizable as the kind one expects to find in a fairly affluent suburban community; the people are quite ordinary in that context; and the routines that are depicted are just that — the lull before and after dinner, before breakfast, during breakfast. There is nothing in the setting and the people to suggest anything more than circumstances and individuals we know or have met at sometime or other. What quickly alerts us to other vibrations and resonances is the *language*, especially the far-fetched and outlandish comments of the characters, who seem to swing from the commonplace to the private and mysterious without any warning. In the midst of predictable ironies and outbursts we sense a darkness threatening to take over. There is a superficiality about everything that we see and the people who move in and out of these ordinary settings; but the unexciting is the perfect backdrop for the *bizarre* climax of the play — a climax suggested by Agnes's first speech, the opening speech of the play, in which she speculates, not without humor, on the possibility of her going mad. She returns to the same private theme at the very end of the play — a beautiful frame for the shifting moods and realities, the inconstancies, the unarticulated subjective life of the protagonists.

Fear of madness, hysteria, hyper-restraint, obsessive talk, are expressed as monologues in the midst of dialogue. We are

ready, instinctively, by the time Edna and Harry appear on the
scene, for the Terror they drag in with them: a state of being
that is never defined or explained. In that Terror we surely are
meant to read whatever is unbearable, frightening beyond words.
Each of us must give content to the word and the experience of
Edna and Harry. Against the backdrop of a seemingly normal
setting, friends suddenly turn into enemies; the known becomes
a terrifying unknown; and all familiar relationships and objects
are threatened. In this genial juxtaposition (much more could
be included here by way of illustration, of course), we come to
recognize the universal in the particular and, more important,
the shifting scene (from normal to eccentric) as the solid backdrop of the play, against which the symbolic suggestions of the
undefined Terror become crucial. Like a black hole in the midst
of a star-filled sky, Edna's and Harry's Terror stuns us with its
large implications. We need not know, really, what frightens
them; we can fill in our own exaggerated fears. And, like Agnes
and her family, we too trace a magic circle that will protect us
from the evil lurking beyond it.

  2. *Monologue-Dialogue.* The opening and closing scenes of
the play (mentioned earlier) are the best examples of Albee's
use of conventional dialogue to promote the *single* voice of subjectivity. Here are the opening exchanges:

> AGNES. What I find most astonishing — aside from that belief of
> mine, which never ceases to surprise me by the very fact of its
> surprising lack of unpleasantness, the belief that I might very eas-
> ily — as they say — lose my mind one day, not that I suspect I am
> about to, or am even . . . nearby . . .
> TOBIAS. There is no saner woman on earth, Agnes.
> AGNES. . . . for I'm not that sort; merely that it is not beyond . . .
> happening; some gentle loosening of the moorings sending the
> balloon adrift — and I think that is the only outweighing thing:
> adrift; the . . . becoming a stranger in . . . the world, quite . . .
> uninvolved, for I never see it as violent, only a drifting — what are
> you looking for, Tobias?
> TOBIAS. We will all go mad before you. The anisette. (3)

The end of the play does more than echo the beginning; it measures the distance we have come. The exaggerations, the tensions, the outbursts and tirades have taught us how to see and
read the play. The closing lines set up resonances that are familiar.

> AGNES. What I find most astonishing — aside from my belief that
> I will, one day . . . lose my mind — but when? Never, I begin to
> think, as the years go by, or that I'll not know if it happens, or

maybe even *has* — what I find most astonishing, I think, is the wonder of daylight, of the sun. All the centuries, milleniums — all the history — I wonder if that's why we sleep at night, because the darkenss still . . . frightens us? They say we sleep to let the demons out — to let the mind go raving mad, our dreams and nightmares all our logic gone awry, the dark side of our reason. And when the daylight comes again . . . comes order with it. *(Sad chuckle.)* Poor Edna and Harry. *(Sigh)* Well, they're safely gone . . . and we'll all forget . . . quite soon. *(Pause)* Come now; we can begin the day. (170)

Has it been a dream for all of us, then? Will the day be just another ordinary day? The play ends where it began — in more ways than one. Nothing has really changed. The same difficulties will surface, the same quarrels, the same inexpressible longings, the same unanswerable questions. The day that is beginning is the same day that has just ended.

Dialogue turns into monologue most dramatically in Tobias's answer to his friends' request for asylum. We need not quote that incredible passage: it is central to the play and to our understanding of the paradox of Albee's monologue-dialogue. What should be noted is the internal dialectic that Tobias gives expression to — the absolute willingness to help his friends with the absolute and terrible realization that he must also, in the same way, protect his own. The Terror is like a highly contagious disease: it will spare no one. And so, Tobias — the quiet, understanding, even-tempered husband/father/brother-in-law/ friend — must make a decision in paradoxical terms. I want you. I don't want you. The experience is shattering; but it soon settles deep in the recesses of his soul, where so much else that is inarticulate has found its dark shelter. Tobias regains his composure soon enough. But we know, as we move into what appears to be the solution to a, well, sort of family problem, that we have experienced a trauma and an unanswerable question.

2. *Cliché-Epiphany.* Any passage in the play will do to illustrate the manner in which Albee oscillates from — on one side — the ordinary and trivial, the cliché, the banal to — on the other side — some kind of illumination that leaves us wondering. The familiar is used as a setting into which a mystery is dropped; and because this contradiction is the characteristic *movement* of the play, we are constantly off balance, always wondering what we are *overhearing*, what might be about to happen on a different level of perception. We are on edge, nervous, apprehensive, not knowing what these wide swings mean, when something might explode. The beginning of Scene Two, Act Two is typical.

JULIA. No! You! Sitting there! Like a combination . . . pope, and .
. . "We will not discuss it"; "Claire, be still"; "No, Tobias, the table
is not the proper place"; "Julia!" . . . nanny! Like a nanny!
AGNES. When we are dealing with children . . . .
JULIA. I must discover, sometime, who you think you are.
AGNES. You will learn . . . one day.
JULIA. No, more like a drill sergeant! You will do this, you will not
say that.
AGNES. "To keep in shape." Have you heard the expression? Most
people misunderstand it, assume it means alteration, when it does
not. Maintenance. When we keep something in shape, we maintain its shape — whether we are proud of that shape or not, is
another matter — we keep it from falling apart. We do not attempt
the impossible. We maintain. We hold. (79-80)

The idea of *holding* things together is central to the play. At the
end, Agnes will hold on, after all, and not float away into madness. Tobias in his excruciating self-criticism confesses that he
could not hold on to the cat, the only creature he had ever felt
anything for. Later, in the same Scene:

JULIA. . . . Harry and Edna: what do they want?
CLAIRE. Succor.
JULIA. Pardon?
CLAIRE. Comfort . . . Warmth. A special room with a night light,
or the door ajar so you can look down the hall from the bed and
see that Mommy's door is open.
JULIA. But that's my room.
CLAIRE. It's . . . the room. Happens you were in it. You're a visi-
tor as much as anyone, now.
JULIA. But I know that room.
CLAIRE. Are you home for good now? . . . Are you home forever,
back from the world? To the sadness and reassurance of your par-
ents? Have you come home to take my place?
JULIA. This is my home! (91-92)

The split-level conversation is typical. Throughout the play the
subjective voice keeps coming through, making itself heard in
the midst of the most commonplace observations and quarrels.
What we have is the superimposition found in *images*, the suggestion of a comparison between what is easily apprehended
and what is not at all recognizable. The result is very much like
the effect of imagery in poetry. Occasionally, this kind of superimposition gives way to *metaphor* — as in the story of the cat. The
comparison with the neighbors' impossible request and all the
implications of that request are embedded in Tobias's unexpected
reaction, a reaction that is both angry and compassionate, a paradox that must be related both to his attitude toward the cat and

his contradictory feelings for Edna and Harry. Does the cat, in its inconsistency, resemble its owner? Is the cat true to his nature and is it to be compared with Edna and Harry? The lines are not at all clear, but in the suggestiveness of the various applications of the story to the actual events of the moment, we understand the mystery of escape and return, giving and taking, the paradox of love.

4. *Indirection-Statement.* The most impressive display occurs in Act Two, Scene Two, with Edna and Harry, where — independently — many phrases seem altogether clear and simple but taken in context appear confusing at the very least. Here are some of the statements in that scene:

> You must . . . what is the word? . . . coexist, my dear.
> You have come to live with us, then. . . . let me comb your hair, and rub your back.
> Well, I think it's time for bed.
> Friendship *is* something like marriage, is it not, Tobias? For better and for worse?

But these ordinary phrases are part of an extraordinary scene, in which dialogue keeps shifting from basic statement to exaggerated similes and images, such as:

> *If* we come to the point . . . *if* we are at home one evening, and the . . . terror comes . . . descends . . . if all at once we . . . NEED . . . we come where we are wanted, where we know we are expected, not only where we want; we come where the table has been laid for us in such an event . . . where the bed is turned down . . . and warmed . . . and has been ready should we need it. We are not . . . transients . . . like some. (116-117)

Or:

> Are you going to stay up, Tobias? Sort of a nightwatch, guarding? *I've done* it. The breathing, as you stand in the quiet halls, slow and heavy? And the special . . . warmth, and . . . permeation . . . of a house . . . asleep? When the house is sleeping? When the people are asleep?

Or:

> And the difference? The different breathing and the cold, when every bed is awake . . . all night . . . very still, eyes open, staring into the dark? Do you know that one? (119)

This effort at trying to make one's private world comprehensible to others, by indirection, is a constant motif, part of a fugue-like effect, in which the most simple statements take on some of the mystery.

I would suggest, by way of conclusion, that it is in the integration of language and musical effects — the arias, the large choral voices, the weaving of melodic strains — that Albee ultimately stands alone. The title of my book was meant to direct readers to the harmonies of recurring phrases, the counterpoint of answers turned into questions, questions turned into arguments, arguments taking on the intensity of personal frustration: the resolution of *tension to tonic*.

NOTES

An earlier version of this essay appeared in *Studies in American Drama 1945-Present*, Volume 1, 1986.

Albee, Edward, *A Delicate Balance* (New York: Atheneum, 1966).

_____. Introduction, *Louise Nevelson: Atmosphere and Environments* (New York: C. N. Potter, 1980).

Brustein, Robert, "Luigi Pirandello," *The Theatre of Revolt* (Boston: Little, Brown, 1964).

Clark, Richard C., "Review Article: Sokel, Kafka, and Kant," *German Expressionism*, Special Editor Victor Lange, *Review of National Literatures*, Vol. 9 (1979), 151-170.

Eliot, T. S., "Hamlet," *Selected Essays: 1917-1932* (New York: Harcourt, Brace and Company, 1932), 121-26.

_____. "The Rejection of Falstaff," *Oxford Lectures on Poetry* (Bloomington, Indiana: Indiana University Press, 1961), 245-74.

_____. "The Three Voices of Poetry," *On Poetry and Poets* (New York: Noonday Press, 1961), 96-112.

Knox, T. M., trans., *Hegel's Aesthetics*, 2 vols. (Oxford: At the Clarendon Press, 1975).

Lange, Victor, "Expressionism: A Topological Essay," *German Expressionism*, Special Editor, Victor Lange, *Review of National Literatures*, Vol. 9 (1979), 25-46.

Mercier, Vivian, *Beckett/Beckett* (New York: Oxford, 1977).

Paolucci, Anne, "Benn, Pound, and Eliot: The Monologue Art of German Expressionism and Anglo-American Modernism," *German Expressionism*, Special Editor Victor Lange, *Review of National Literatures*, Vol. 9 (1979), 10-24.

_____. *Pirandello's Theatre: The Recovery of the Modern Stage for Dramatic Art* (Carbondale and Edwardsville: Southern Illinois University Press, 1974).

_____. *From Tension to Tonic: The Plays of Edward Albee*, Preface by Harry T. Moore (Carbondale and Edwardsville: Southern Illinois University Press, 1972, third printing, 1973).

Paolucci, Anne, and Henry Paolucci, eds. *Hegel on Tragedy*, (New York, Doubleday, 1962; Harper and Row, 1974; Greenwood Press, 1975; Griffon House Publications, 2001).

Sciasca, Leonardo, *Pirandello e la Sicilia* (Caltanissetta: S. Sciascia, 1961).

Sokel, Walter, *The Writer in Extremis* (Stanford: Stanford UnIversity Press, 1959).

CHAPTER 18

ALBEE ON THE PRECIPITOUS HEIGHTS (TWO ARMS ARE NOT ENOUGH!)

The dogmatic assertiveness of playwrights like Arthur Miller has made Americans very much aware of the impact, on theater, of current political and racial issues. The Greeks, as we know, were the first to use theater to educate the public in matters of common interest, both in their tragedy and comedy; and theater at its best will always reflect such concerns. But dramatic art must be more than one-dimensional (as Ionesco reminds us), more than a political or social tract; artistic priorities dictate autonomous "voices" on stage. Our mainline American theater, unfortunately, suffers from not only a prolonged commitment to social drama but also from an only lightly veiled realism which even now justifies John Gassner's comment about its being in a state of "protracted adolescence."

Compared to the revolutionary dramatic changes that have come about in the last fifty years with Pirandello, Beckett, Ionesco, Pinter, Giraudoux, Genet, and more current playwrights like Sam Shepard, much of our theater does indeed seem stale and repetitive — especially in its insistence on a political "message" and social reform. The only American dramatist who has succeeded in bringing the innovations of the contemporary theater into a new dramatic balance of public issues and private tensions is Edward Albee. His work, however, has yet to elicit the response it deserves — not the least reason being that the critics simply have not done their homework. They seem more at ease with the familiar themes of our realistic theater, revivals of classics, or the musical superhits to which most audiences have become addicted.

Albee himself has repeated in interviews and lectures that he writes to dramatize what is wrong with society and to shock us into awareness. How he does it varies and continues to change. In his early plays — the one-acts especially — the political and social message was clear and sometimes strikingly partisan. *The American Dream* in its stark realism and semi-caricatures shows us the American middle-class family in its worst light. Grandma is the only person who has insight and compassion — but she is old and not in control of the situation. In *The Death of Bessie Smith*, Albee started out with a strong political message about racism, but, as he explains in the preface to the work, the play changed even as it evolved. What started out as a political statement turned out to be something quite different: the characters who might easily have evolved into prototypes of vicious racism, etc., became autonomous and independent voices. Even Nurse (perhaps originally meant to be the "villain" of the play) turns out to be human in her excesses and doubts. In short, Albee never betrays his characters; which is to say that he allows them every chance to show themselves at their best — even when they are not in our corner. It is the tradition of Shakespeare, whose "villains" — it has been said — "are artists in their own right."

Reading back from his recent *The Man Who Had Three Arms* to *The Lady From Dubuque* and *Who's Afraid of Virginia Woolf?*, one gets a clear sense of Albee's developing place in the best tradition of Pirandello, Beckett, Ionesco, and Pinter. "Public issues" and "private tensions" are always the focus, dramatized in terms that are compelling innovative and beautifully accessible to most serious theater-goers. In satirizing critics, professional lecturers, professors, all who pontificate (*The Man Who Had Three Arms*), Albee scrutinizes with devastating clarity those who profess to "educate" others. Private tensions assume a Pirandellian intensity in *The Lady From Dubuque*, where the theme echoes in some ways the social existential malaise of *Who's Afraid of Virginia Woolf?* while the insistent burden of the wrenching of death, the eternal moment of separation, spells out the large universal "commonplace" in an oratorio in which the different voices blend, clash, come to terms. What might have been a cliché turns out to be an exciting combination of masks, voices, melodies in major and minor keys, as always (in Albee at his very best) — a dramatic moment of crisis translated into musical and allegorical effects that refine the theme as well as the soul (as Aristotle would say). Albee himself has said and written that he didn't discover at some point in his life that he wanted to be a playwright but that he was one and simply did not recognize the fact at once. Some are born to write poetry, some to write plays; Albee, in his own words, at one point realized that he could be nothing but a playwright, that he was "programmed" for just that. And, he might have added, as a playwright he could never allow non-dramatic imperatives to intrude, no matter how compelling in themselves.

Albee's major achievement is the balance he has struck, in

all his plays (including the more virulent tirades of the early years), between public issues and private tensions, between political/social/racial reform and the requirements of genuine art. We shall have an opportunity to examine this balance more closely, later in this article, but a word is in order here about his understanding of the vital need for promoting serious American playwrights as part of the mainstream, and not simply in Off-Broadway and Off-Off-Broadway productions. He challenges the Broadway stage, with its musicals and revivals, as the truly "absurd theater" and has done a great deal on his own to educate the public — students especially — about the best in our American theater tradition. Certainly the time is ripe for reopening the question of national funding for a national theater with long-range plans and budget. The French and Germans have shown clearly that change can become part of a national tradition and that the public can be guided to appreciate new stage conventions that reflect the pressing issues of our time and place. Will our day ever come? Or will we be forever repeating ourselves in an outdated language, persisting in that gross amateurish posture described by John Gassner?

Albee, like so many of the German and French dramatists of the 50s and beyond, realized from the very beginning of his career that part of the playwright's commitment is to renew the tradition, to rework the medium to suit the times. Consciously or instinctively, he followed the counsel of that greatest teacher of the modern craft of writing, Ezra Pound: "make it new." From his first appearance on stage (in Germany, with *The Zoo Story*), Albee showed himself to be such a writer: an individual talent well-schooled in his own tradition but a writer destined to "make it new" with flair and ingenuity rooted in the American temperament but nurtured also by appreciation of the new theater abroad. What he created was an awareness of the great potential for our American theater in the years ahead; he has found a genuinely American dramatic voice for our current "public issues" and "private tensions."

Not surprisingly, it was in Germany and then in France and Italy that Albee's innovative talent was first recognized. The excitement he generated abroad is reminiscent of what Shakespeare, on another level of international fame, experienced, but only centuries after his death. For Shakespeare it happened during a lull in his English popularity, in the late 18th and 19th centuries. Some of the great German critics, poets, and philosophers of the time — Schlegel, Goethe, Hegel — took up the "English Bard" as their very own: *unser Shakespeare!* And they did so with an imaginative excitement that soon became contagious. The leading critics and writers in one after another of the European nations with great literary traditions of their own followed Germany's example; and the excitement finally returned to England and the rest of the English-speaking world, to generate a great Shakespeare "revival."

That Albee had the distinction of being hailed as *unser Albee* in Germany at least a whole season before he began to be hailed by anyone as *our* Albee in his native country, is something that must be borne in mind, at least by those of us who are concerned, academically as well as theatrically, with correctly interpreting and assessing his genius — the "high drama" of his "stagecraft." Europeans and American students of classical and comparative modern literature tend to see at once that Albee's is a distinctly American talent capable of making new the old craft of the theater right before our eyes, enriching a tradition that runs from Aeschylus and Sophocles through Shakespeare and his near contemporaries on the continent, down to the leading modernists of the European dramatic revival of the early 20th century, with Pirandello's extraordinary experiments in the lead. Perhaps it is the accessibility of Albee in a wide comparative context that makes him so much more appreciated outside the United States; but that appreciation, as we said, is focused on the American experience as he dramatizes it for the stage.

It is his *American* vision that gives Albee "strong local colour" (T. S. Eliot) and enables us to relate to his plays more effectively in this sense than to those of other dramatists of the Absurd. From the very beginning, he has taken his subjects from the most obvious and ordinary situations, reflecting the American scene in a way that no other American playwright has succeeded in doing. Some of his situations verge on clichés; in this, he matches Ionesco, who can turn the most obvious event or phrase into something strikingly and startlingly dramatic, as he does in the multi-faceted dramatic elaboration of the worn-out phrase "I could kill that child!" in *The Lesson*. Albee, too, takes his commonplace from the life around him, translating them into unfamiliar, sometimes strange and often allegorical readings. *The Zoo Story* turns the ordinary setting of Central Park into a Dantesque hell. *The American Dream* shows us, in allegorically stripped terms but still quite recognizable ones, the emasculated man, the domineering woman, the powerless old and young relegated into corners of existence. *The Death of Bessie*

Smith dramatizes the all-too-familiar racial tensions that dominated the life of the South in the 60s. *Who's Afraid of Virginia Woolf?* depicts the easy boredom and undercurrents of tension in suburban life in a college town, with the added attraction of witty, pseudo-analytical exchanges that suggest incommunicable undercurrents. *A Delicate Balance* picks up again the excesses of an aimless, superficially unruffled suburban existence. *All Over* introduces the notion of death and the agony of the waiting — a subject which Albee later picks up again in the much more dynamic *The Lady From Dubuque*. In *Quotations from Chairman Mao*, we are treated to the kind of ramblings we all indulge in from time to time, with or without an audience. *Tiny Alice* gives us the distorted Pirandellian mirror image of our own petty doubts and skepticism writ large. *The Man Who Had Three Arms* turns the tables on the critics and academics, giving us a grand Pirandellian illusion of "improvisation" (not unlike the brilliant "monolog" of *Enrico IV*), of which we are embarrassingly, an integral part. In all his plays, Albee focuses on a perfectly ordinary situation, draws us into it, and then strips it imperceptibly to reveal an ambiguous, paradoxical, often tragic core.

His characters are chosen in the same way: they are familiar types, in some cases (as in the early one-act plays) close to caricatures. Jerry is the loner, Peter the middle-class, low-level executive; Nurse is a self-centered, potentially bigoted Southerner; the characters in *The American Dream* are stark prototypes, all personality stripped away from them to reveal their worst absurdities and excesses; George and Martha, Nick and Honey are combinations easily recognizable in suburban college communities; Agnes, Tobias, and their family and friends could be our next-door neighbors . . . or ourselves; and so on. An Albee play is indeed an American experience in which people and places and events are basic elements in the dramatic equation — even as the terms of the dramatic equation shift, as familiar places turn into a trap, as "strong local colour" combines with "unconscious universality" to produce some of the most effective stage plays of our time.

This masterful command of stage dynamics alone would suffice to establish the reputation of a dramatist, but Albee goes much further. His "public issues" and "private tensions" are given another dimension in which meaning is not simply an extended parallel or analogy but becomes an infinite question, a Pirandellian open-ended experience which forces each of us to reexamine our priorities and question our easy solutions. In this,

Albee is far removed from such playwrights as Miller or O'Neill or Tennessee Williams. In steering his audience beyond the "apparent" or "obvious," Albee established the "dialogue" characteristic of the new theater. His particular genius comes through in the way in which he draws the audience into the dramatic action by means of paradoxical deflection. He assimilates the new stage conventions easily yet organically. Beckett's technique emphasizes a recurring cyclical pattern of action, characters reduced almost to caricatures, language in which meaning is diminished and symbols are given the burden of communication, parallel events that echo whatever is to be considered important, and so on. Ionesco's technique focuses on the fragmentation of familiar language and the reassembling of the components in new suggestive, bizarre-sounding phrases and sentences; his characters assume the rigid aspect of masks waiting to be stripped away, to be revealed in their naked inadequacies. Albee's way of demolishing the stale conventions is to lead us first into a familiar setting populated with recognizable people and then to unobtrusively transform that world into something waiting to be discovered — our own often grotesque inner soul. But unlike playwrights like Beckett and Ionesco, Albee gives the appearance of following deceptively traditional lines. In his use of the realistic stage, he resembles most closely, Pirandello, clearing the stage of all accumulated debris to restructure it simply and yet suggestively, creating for the first time in the American theater a truly dynamic dialogue between the audience and the play, the play and the world outside the theater — an expanding equation, the most visual example of which is to be found in *Tiny Alice*.

My conclusion about Albee's stagecraft back in 1972 was that, in his best plays, he had achieved a strikingly original "integration of realism and abstract symbolism," and that he had to be perceived as the "best product of the theater of the absurd, with Pirandello rather than O'Neill as his master." (*From Tension to Tonic: The Plays of Edward Albee*, Cross-Currents Series, Preface by Harry T. Moore, Southern Illinois University Press, 1972, 1974). In later essays, focusing on the absurd in Shakespeare, as well as in Pirandello and Albee, I developed comparisons between Albee's stage techniques, especially in *Tiny Alice*, and Pirandello's "theater plays," and argued that full appreciation of Albee's, as well as Pirandello's, achievement in that regard requires us to reconsider Shakespeare's contribution to the theater of our time — the open- ended approach to large questions about human nature and the world around us. Robert Brustein's *Theater of Revolt* has helped us all to appreciate this aspect of Pirandello's stagecraft and its influence on most subsequent dramatists. In a sense, Pirandello was renewing the mechanisms for assessing "public issues" and "private tensions" through the image of the theater as the evolving stage of life — the mirror as the reflection of our infinite fragmented consciousness. His plays demand a telescoping of inner and outer life, a vigorous acceptance of the process of awareness rather than the end *product*. The *making* of our judgments becomes infinitely more important than the *statement* that may emerge.

This technique (as I have indicated elsewhere) is first found in Shakespeare's *Hamlet*, the earliest example of a play which disappoints us even as we are drawn to its hero in the most private areas of our consciousness. T .S. Eliot calls it the "Mona Lisa" of literature, even as he insists that it is an "artistic failure." The contradiction is only apparent: Eliot is right on both counts. The normal artistic standards by which we judge a play (intention/deeds; motivation/action; integral character; etc.) simply do not apply well here. Dramatically *Hamlet* spills over the definitions on hand. The play is a mess of contradictions, unfinished business, aborted plans, improvised plots, and unfathomable impulses that often contradict one another, a double image in which the hero appears as a tortured soul and a Machiavellian villain. Hamlet does not avenge his father's death at all but kills Claudius at the end of the play for immediate provocations, reasons he can accept in his deepest soul and act upon with vigor he has kept in check all along. There is a curious distorted mirror-image (truly Pirandellian) in the characterization of Hamlet and a sense of the larger world seen at a distance as though in miniature or through the wrong end of a telescope. From the onset, Hamlet works *away from* his avowed intention to kill the murderer of his father. He moves by instinct which he himself never fully understands or explains adequately even to himself: he orders his best friends executed on mere suspicion, he stabs Polonius and never once regrets the mistake, he drives Ophelia to madness with his taunts, he forces the new king's hand by revealing his knowledge of Claudius's guilt — a knowledge which cannot be shared with anyone (that promise he does keep!) and which quickly brings about the final bloody climax of the play. The charade in which Claudius is trapped in his own plot and justifiably killed, also destroys innocent bystanders: Laertes, the Queen, and Hamlet himself. Even the soliloquies in this play are out of focus: they appear interchangeable in a way that we do not find anywhere else in Shakespeare. And yet, *Hamlet*, like the plays of Pirandello and Albee, creates such an illusion of reality, of cause and effect, of rational and reasonable argument, that critics are still struggling to find a way to reconcile the contradictions of the play, to find "meaning" for its progressive internalization of motives. Some critics (perhaps reflecting their own frustrations) have gone so far as to suggest that no one will ever solve the mystery of the play. I disagree. Looking back on *Hamlet* from Pirandello's *Henry IV* and *Six Characters in Search of an Author*; or Albee's *Tiny Alice, A Delicate Balance,* and *The Man Who Had Three Arms*, Shakespeare's *schöne Seele*, the beautiful Socratic soul who answers only to himself according to his own inner convictions and "laws," takes on provocative new features not unlike those of Beckett's Pozzo, Ionesco's Professor, Pirandello's mad emperor, or Albee's Brother Julian and Jerry. Hamlet is indeed the first hero of the Absurd.

Without laboring parallels, it is safe to say that Albee, like Pirandello and Shakespeare before him, deserves major credit for having changed the shape of our dramatic tradition in bold and intriguing ways. But perhaps of even greater importance, he has transformed the illusion of realism into the lyric idiom of the Absurd, giving the whole a distinctly *national* voice, one that expresses not only the fragmented personality struggling toward private definition but also the public aspect of the larger transformation of the *American* setting. In his individual talent he returns to a tradition as old as the Greeks, as enduring as Shakespeare's.

Albee proceeds from a setting that is firmly established and recognizable to an elaboration that is characteristically "Absurd." No other playwright since Pirandello has managed to combine so well the familiar with the unknown, weaving content and structure into an intriguing paradox-an open-ended question. The deceptively simple setting of *The Zoo Story* is Central Park, Peter and Jerry are familiar types (the world of cities is full of lonely and isolated people like Jerry and quietly resigned husbands and fathers like Peter); but in this ordinary setting, these two enter into a dance of death. Strangers at the outset, they become inextricably bound as Victim and Killer. But who is really the victim, who the killer? Is the grotesque parody of a religious sacrifice (beautifully articulated symbolically [and musically] as the high-point of a ritual counterpoint in the *Mass for the Dead*, later, in *Who's Afraid of Virginia Woolf?*) simply a quirky ending to an exercise in the futility of human communication? What is the meaning of this forced brief reltionship which turns into a permanent bond? Here as in other plays by Albee, the key must be sought in the core images woven into the repetitive patterns, suggestive "allegory," and symbolic cues — movement contained within a seemingly static dramatic action.

We find all these characteristic devices already fully elaborated and perfected in *The Zoo Story*, where we are also treated, for the first time, to one of Albee's genial signatures — a narrative within the action of the play. Without fully understanding the implications of such narrative and its connection with the open, established action of the play, we respond automatically, unconsciously, to its vital importance. It is a "core image," similar to the sub-human bestial Satan of Dante (and all other similes that suggest inexpressible horror) or the embodiments of virtue and sin and the allegorical settings of Spenser. Albee's modern transformations of familiar allegorical suggestions enable us to grasp quickly and effortlessly the correspondence between (for example) the dog and Cerberus, the boarding house as an inescapable hell, and the landlady as a sadistic fiend at the gates of a dingy "inferno." We can extend this flash of critical understanding into other areas of the play: Peter is the uncommitted prototype, Jerry is the Christ-figure forcing us into clear commitment, conversion, illumination, and sacrifice. The narrative of Jerry and the dog gives us the first important clue as to how the play should be approached. What at first seems unrelated, arbitrary, and self-indulgent emerges as a language of indirection. The "allegory" of a place of horrors (strongly reminiscent of Dante's *Inferno*) is so transparent, so easily accessible to the understanding, so widely applicable, and the telescopic adjustment extending it to other parts of the play so natural, that we are justified in our critical instinct. We follow the inexorable spiraling toward violence and death without reference to traditional "action" or "plot," to character as intention/motivation/ realization and language as a familiar structure for communication.

Other examples quickly surface: Tobias's story of his cat in *A Delicate Balance*, Brother Julian's account of his stay in the asylum in *Tiny Alice*; the story of the fictional son in *Who's Afraid of Virginia Woolf?* (with all its religious reverberations in the suggestion of a litany for the dead, the telegram received and eaten like the holy wafer, the Latin parody of a Mass, etc.); the reminiscences of the Man in *The Man Who Had Three Arms*, stories that take up in effect the major part of the "action" on stage; the remembered past in *Quotations from Chairman Mao*, where we witness and hear an extended monolog verging on the psychoanalytical.

Albee's narratives also remind us that private tensions — the individual's probing for personal resolution — have a direct impact on the nature of public issues. In the overhauling of stage conventions, Albee clarifies the connection between the private self and the public image. Personal difficulties cannot be resolved in a vacuum — if they can be resolved at all. The individual reaches out for recognition and in that effort is destroyed or paradoxically enlightened through the awareness of others to his predicament.

The attempt to articulate the "Terror" of isolation destroys relationships that had never been threatened before. The narratives in Albee's plays often are the effort to reach out for understanding, for sympathy through the language of indirection and allegorical suggestion. They serve dramatically in the same way that Pirandello's "inner" story serves in his "theater plays" and *Enrico IV*. The core story is an expandable and replaceable example that forces us to translate the "script" into our own emotional terms, educating us in the continuing "catharsis" of acceptance and rejection: the vulnerable exposed self and the compromise we assume in our public image. The myth of the son, the ultimate and indescribable "Terror" that lurks in all of us, the hell which we carefully refuse to acknowledge in our daily lives are Albee's suggestive cues as to the proper reading of the plays. We learn about relationships by trying to understand the *social* effect of Edna's and Harry's "Terror" on the rest of us, or the profound impact on George and Martha of their carefully nurtured *public* myth of a son. And what we learn, finally, is that relationships are themselves a deflecting mechanism that enables us to survive. The bottom line is not to change relationships and to try to improve them, but to recognize the limits of endurance in the private self.

Albee's plays, one may therefore suggest at this point, dramatize accepted public or social conventions, standards, values as the static backdrop against which the individual struggles for private definition. *Who's Afraid of Virginia Woolf?* clearly plays on the excesses of suburban life, the self-destruct impulses in so many modern marriages. Audiences relate easily to what they recognize as some of the social aberrations of our time. But the play has no lasting social commentary, no powerful or explicit "message" in those terms. In a similar vein, *A Delicate Balance* lures us into a familiar set of circumstances: again, suburban couples (but this time not as exciting and vitriolic as Martha and George) settled in a way of life which has no large questions or answers, until Edna and Harry ask for total commitment — complete conversion to their instinctive demands on the part of their best friends. As in *Who's Afraid of Virginia Woolf?* the triggering mechanism for cosmic revelations is a familiar social setting. In *The Man Who Had Three Arms* the audience finds itself in the midst of a public lecture which is a personal confession of inadequacies, a private harangue against the world — a transparent allegory in which all of us must find our own equivalent for a "third arm." In *The Lady from Dubuque*, the fears of others in the face of death is a familiar kind of personal language translated into large resonances about indifferent fate and the uncaring gods. Every Albee play is a new quest doomed to a new failure simply because of the nature of things in the world; but in expressing their irrepressible urge toward recognition, Albee's protagonists strip away all pretenses, all the masks behind which we all hide.

The dialectic of private commitment and public assertion, contradictory inner motivations and aggressive role-playing in public is beautifully compressed in Albee's telescoping of time and distance, myth and reality, fact and fiction. He teaches us to read events as they evolve and take shape: the musical burdens of his dialogue tune the ear and instruct us in correspondences, echoes, refrains; words flow into patterns that are more than the sum total of their meaning. In plays like *Quotations from Chairman Mao*, action itself is turned into a single lyric voice indulging in remembered moments, restructuring them into new patterns, probing them in the search for a single theme, a unified purpose. In his "monolog" plays, Albee trains the audience to recognize the voices of poetry in their distinctive resonances, transposing the third voice (drama) into the lyric voice of the poet "talking" to himself or "nobody" (to use T. S. Eliot's definition, which he adopted from Gottfried Benn's Hegelian analysis of *genres*). Vivian Mercier has illustrated this push of theater to the edge of non-theater, insisting that a new critical language must be found to deal properly with this new set of dramatic conventions (see *Beckett/Beckett*). Both the playwright and the critic force us to ask the question: Is this a play? In the ever-shifting terms of Albee's dramatic *process* the question is predictable.

The answer too, of course, is predictable. What we have is a new kind of stage product that works by correspondences, suggestion, and instinct, all of which find *dramatic* resolution in the consciousness of the protagonist-spectator. In his introduction to the 1969 edition of *Box* and *Quotations from Chairman Mao*, Albee offers his own "statement of principles" as to what a serious playwright is basically challenged to do in pursuing his art. A playwright, he says, "has two obligations: first to make some statement about the condition of man (as it is put) and second, to make some statement about the nature of the art form in which he is working." In his case, I believe Albee has combined the two into one large precept, for his dramatic conventions *are* themselves a statement about the condition of man who, more often than not, will accept what is familiar and established rather than examine Socratically the life around him. Like Pirandello before him, Albee forces each of us to evaluate what we see and hear on stage at every moment, allowing us subtle entry into the self-conscious life waiting to be defined in each of us. Albee's plays instruct us in the *discipline* of perception and the *paradoxes* on which we build understanding.

In the preceding pages I have purposely focused on what might be called Albee's *dramatic methodology*. Rather than approach his plays along familiar critical avenues, applying the usual Aristotelian categories (*action, character, theme, language*), I chose to discuss in some detail Albee's approach to the *particular* and the *general*, especially the manner in which he transforms *private* vision and *public* setting into a spiraling open-ended experience. Having come this far, the reader will surely agree that in Albee's plays (1) private tensions and public issues are part of a dialectical *becoming* and not factors in an irreversible and absolute equation, and (2) "meaning" or "theme" can be clarified only by indirection, by a new set of critical standards — not because Aristotle is no longer worthy (we disagree with him at our own risk!) but because the stage mechanisms in the contemporary theater have qualitatively altered. (Aristotle himself, were he alive today, would be the first to recognize the need for a new critical language and would remind us that his critical norms were "descriptive" and never "normative.") The enlarging of the Aristotelian theory has in fact been accomplished by one of the greatest disciples of the Greek philosopher in the modern world: Hegel. It was Hegel who, long before most of us were ready to accept it, wrote that in our age, when the spirit has probed the innermost recesses of its consciousness, art threatens to "transcend itself," to burst through the established limits (as defined by Aristotle), seeking a new level of critical understanding. The twentieth century has experienced the bursting of the artistic bonds in non-representational painting and sculpture, in architecture that resembles sculpture, in drama that has blended the third voice of autonomous "distanced" stage performance into the first, lyric, voice of the poet talking to himself (at best, meant to be "overheard" — as Eliot reminds us). It is through Hegel that we begin to understand how the theater of the Absurd comes perilously close to the edge of "non-theater."

I have reviewed Hegel's multi-faceted analysis of ancient and modern drama in many ways, in a number of articles and books; I refer to it here only to remind readers that our two greatest English critics — A. C. Bradley and T. S. Eliot — have proved the effectiveness of Hegelian insights and have applied them to their work with striking results. Bradley's analysis of Falstaff still waits for Hegelian clarification on the part of Shakespearean critics; and Eliot's essay on *Hamlet* (among others) will emerge, in due course, as a thoroughly Hegelian illustration of the limits of art — the "beautiful soul" who answers only to his own inner imperatives, the Socratic *daimon* that dictates to the individual conscience.

It is clear that both Bradley and Eliot (the one, directly; the other, indirectly) found in the Hegelian analysis of drama the most effective guidelines for their handling of what was truly "avant garde" in Shakespeare's work, where "character" is larger than life and explicit motivations do not always correspond to action. In our own day, critics like Eric Bentley, John Styan, Vivian Mercier, and Robert Brustein have applied, deliberately or instinctively, similar approaches to their study of Pirandello and the dramatists who followed him. Without necessarily committing themselves to "Hegelian" interpretations, these critics, each in his own way, have recognized the value of "indirection," of "spiraling" open-ended critical approaches in dealing with Theater of the Absurd; their success has proved the efficacy of the method. But we must credit Albee with forcing critics, perhaps without their conscious awareness of it, into new structures of interpretation. In defying traditional approaches to the stage, he made familiar critical categories virtually inapplicable. His concept of the "mask," his metaphorical structuring of language, his circling in refrain-like sequences to an approximation of meaning and his layering and echoing techniques forced the best critics to assume new dramatic guidelines in order to do justice to the quirky structure and unfamiliar language patterns of the plays.

It may be fruitful, at this point, to approach two of Albee's most daring theater products informally from a Hegelian point of view in order to prove the efficacy of such applications to Theater of the Absurd. I chose two plays that are very much alike, even at a distance of almost twenty years: *Box and Quotations From Chairman Mao* (pub. 1969) and *The Man Who Had Three Arms* (pub. 1987). Both plays (one, of course, is a double play!) are virtual monologs, both translate the third voice of poetry (the dramatic voice) into the first voice (the lyric voice), both reduce familiar setting to a kind of metaphor, both depersonalize character without destroying individuality, and both move in a telescopic range creating space as the memory calls forth people, places, and events. Both plays have a lyric intensity, an immediacy that is not found anywhere else in Albee's work.

In these two plays, more than in any other of his mature works, Albee displays an instinctive Pirandellian confidence in using strategies reminiscent of Shakespeare's in *Hamlet*, where action remains static in a vortex of shifting internal revelations. Voices are often depersonalized — although the stories they tell are meticulously detailed and repeated at times from a number of angles. Dramatic interaction of characters is replaced in these plays with a single overriding role, all others deliberately diminished so that the single voice seems to dominate the stage. In his own careful directions at the beginning of the printed text of *Box and Quotations from Chairman Mao*, Albee suggests that ideally the two plays should be interwoven into one stage experience but that, if *Box* is staged separately, it should be repeated twice or three times without any intermission or break. Like Pirandello, Albee is opting for an evolving consciousness on the part of the audience rather than sheer passive acceptance. He insists on it. He points out that the voices must be orchestrated in a particular way in order to reach resolution, in order to move from tension to tonic. Indirection is the key.

Mao, in his public image, addresses the world at large and the future, delivering his views, the tenets of his philosophy, impersonally, without emotion, without distraction. The Long-Winded Lady, on the other hand, seems to be all distraction, all emotion — total involvement in a circumscribed personal tragedy. Mao speaks to eternity, to faceless crowds; she appeals to no one, or — more precisely — to the unresponsive ghosts in her irrevocable past. Interspersed are the verses of The Old Woman, a kind of ballad about her own wretched life. The disembodied Voice from Box suggests a kind of rehearsal, a director in the wings setting up the stage. Any passage will contain elements of this four-part cantata as it rises and falls through repetitions and refrains to . . . some kind of musical tonic. One example will do:

OLD WOMAN.   She was somewhat dressy, an' hadn't a
                    pleasant smile —
                    She was quite conceity, and carried a heap o'
                    style;
                    But if ever I tried to be friends, I did with her,
                    I know
                    But she was hard and proud, an' I couldn't
                    make it go.

LONG-WINDED LADY. *ME!* WHAT ABOUT ME! (*Pause.*) That may
                    give the impression of selfishness, but that is
                    not how I intended it, nor how it is . . . at all. *I* .
                    . . am *left.* (*Helpless shrug.*) He isn't. I'll not touch
                    his dying again. It was long, and coarse, and
                    ugly, and tested the man beyond his . . . beyond
                    anyone's capacities. I dare you! I dare anyone!
                    Don't scream! Don't hate! I dare anyone. (*Softer.*)
                    All that can be done is turn into a beast; the
                    dumb thing's agony. And maybe that's enough
                    comfort: not to know why. (*Pause wistful, sad.*)
                    But I am *left.* (*Mao crosses inside rail to D.R., in-
                    side box.*)

VOICE. (*From* "Box.") And the beauty of art is order.

CHAIRMAN MAO.   We desire peace. Hoever, if imperialism insists
                    on fighting a war, we will have no alternative
                    but to take resolution to fight to the finish be-
                    fore going ahead with our construction. (*Mao
                    steps outside of box.*) If you are afraid of war day in
                    day out, what will you do if war eventually comes?
                    (*Mao crosses D.L.*) I have said that the East Wind
                    is prevailing over the West Wind and war will
                    not break out, and now I have added these explana-
                    tions about the situation in case war should break
                    out. Both possibilities have thus been taken into
                    account. (*Mao bows, crosses U.L. outside rail to in-
                    side box at L. rail opening.*)

OLD WOMAN.   She was somewhat dressy, an' hadn't a
                    pleasant smile —
                    She was quite conceity, and carried a heap o'
                    style;
                    But if ever I tried to be friends, I did with
                    her, I know
                    But she was hard and proud, an' I couldn't
                    make it go.

Even a small "frame" such as the one just quoted is sufficient to impress us with (1) the insistent musical structuring of Albee's dialogue, in which the rise and fall of emotion is not expressed or suggested metaphorically but carried, as it were, within repetitions, refrains, incompleted or truncated efforts at communications, woven into the insistent solid "burden" (Mao) and the shifting fugue-like effects of the melodic (the women), the movement from major to minor, manic to depressive, the *forte* and *pianissimo* alternating in recurring patterns as memories are exorcised; (2) the spiraling around independent but somehow interrelated "foci" of awareness"; (3) a kaleidoscopic design suggesting the various facets of a theme: order, art, political stability, personal hopes, world peace; moral uncertainties, tragedies beyond exorcism, death and dying; (4) the isolation of each "voice" and body, the total lack of human interaction and communication.

In *Box and Quotations*, we are also struck by that same quality one observes in *Hamlet*: a concentric movement of the parts around an unchanging core. I have noted the strange quality of the soliloquies in *Hamlet*: they are virtually interchangeable, surfacing as a result of some event, yes, but coming back again and again to some large unresolved, undefined, incommunicable obsession. The same quality exists in Albee's play. We seem to be circling to some large truth, without ever getting close to target, to the vision of an organic *whole*. The action of the play remains (as in *Hamlet*) static; there is no unambiguous theme. The past is fixed, the future determined. Independent voices resonate and echo in their efforts to find the "tonic" that will give meaning to all the shifting views — that will bring the unending dialectic to a resolution. It is this overriding musical structure, the independent efforts toward a related theme, the shifting *points of view*, the *mosaic* never fully accessible in its entirety, contrasts evoked rather than *expressed*, and the entire mechanism of *deflection* that makes *Quotations* not only a powerful play, as enigmatic as *Hamlet*, but also one of the best expressions of Theater of the Absurd. It proves, also, the clarity of the Hegelian notion of "art transcending itself": for in this play, more than in any other with the exception of *The Man Who Had Three Arms*, Albee stretches the limits of the traditional stage almost to the breaking point. Character is a state of being, a memory bank, a Voice; Action is a telescopic adjustment as vision sweeps across a given prescribed point; Theme is a consciousness of contradictory impulses, an effort to "express the inexpressibly horrible"

(Eliot's phrase, this time to account for the "artistic failure" of *Hamlet*). Language becomes refrains, repetitions of shattered statements, unfinished phrases, shards of consciousness as they reflect some remembered emotion, obsessive phrasing, unwavering dogmatic statements and halting stutterings juxtaposed to create a widening orbit of paradoxes. Even the setting — a deck on an ocean liner, where a "cube" is the source of "Voice" and a carefully defined space limits the movement of Mao — is an illusion of solid ground, the endless shifting sea the reality.

I confess to a certain satisfaction, as a critic, in finding my early insistence (1972) on Albee's musical structuring confirmed in the playwrights own "General Comments" to *Selected Plays of Edward Albee*, Introduction by Edward Albee (Nelson Doubleday, Inc. Garden City, New York, 1987). In the Introduction, Albee insists on instructions to directors and others who might take on the play that they are to adhere closely to the "patterns" he has set, for any alteration "may be interesting but. . . . While the lines must not read metronome-exact, I feel that a certain rhythm will come about, quite of itself" (206). Underlined words, dots and dashes, exclamation points, omission of exclamation points, capitalization for loudness, commas, periods, semi-colons, colons, are all very clearly indicated to suggest speech rhythms, stresses, and emphases. It was with a sense of excitement of discovery that in 1972 I hit on the title *From Tensiom to Tonic: The Plays of Edward Albee* for my first book-length study of his major plays up to that time. I am convinced more than ever that to understand Albee's work critics must recognize the large role musical suggestion plays in all his writings.

Box and Quotations from Chairman Mao was completed in 1968 (published, as I indicated earlier, in 1969); *The Man Who Had Three Arms* first appeared as a manuscript in 1982 and was published, somewhat altered, in 1987. Although almost twenty years elapsed between the writing of the two plays, they have much in common — in the same way that the abstract symbolism and directness of plays like *The American Dream* becomes a symbolic transparency in *Who's Afraid of Virginia Woolf?* In both combinations we see stage experimentation turn into new stage conventions. We are also made very much aware of the consistency of Albee's approach as he evolves new techniques. And as his talent expands, the *organic* quality of his vision becomes even more impressive.

In both sets of paired plays we sense a deepening of emotional sensibilities and a growing feeling of *compassion* both for individuals and for the human condition generally. In both pairs we recognize a dramatic agility in which (to use Pirandello's famous phrase) "il sentimento del contrario" — the sensitivity to the paradoxes of life and the tragic-humorous effects which emerge from such awareness — becomes almost unbearable in the oscillation between exhilarating near-hysteria and depths of depression — a powerful display of counterpoint. There is also, in the combination we are exploring in this article, a wider view of things, easier access for the audience on a literal level. In *The Man Who Had Three Arms*, we are in fact part of a Pirandellian magic show: the theater is the setting, intermissions are worked into the script itself, the audience is addressed by the actor who comes out of his stage role to comment on it, and so on. This play is appealing in my opinion for reasons that are not necessarily *dramatic*. It is a *tour de force*, mesmerizing in its effect. Other plays may appeal more directly in familiar terms (e.g. *Who's Afraid of Virginia Woolf?*, *The Zoo Story*, *A Delicate Balance*, *All Over*) and may even have a more profound effect on audiences. But in *The Man Who Had Three Arms* we sense power at its peak, the playwright in total command of his medium — and in a totally new and unexpected way. This play is to Albee's repertory to date what *King Lear* and *The Tempest* are to Shakespeare's, what the late "myth" plays are to Pirandello's repertory.

Nowhere is the telescoping of time, the paradoxical inversions, the unique fusion of tragic and comic elements, the painful humor characteristic of the Absurd, the linguistic acrobatics, the agonizing private tensions coming into conflict with public postures, and the sense of *no exit* and no reprieve more powerfully rendered than in *The Man Who Had Three Arms*. The 1987 (final) version is very much in keeping with the open-ended quality of such classics of the Absurd as Beckett's *Waiting for Godot*, Ionesco's *The Lesson*, and Pirandello's "theater plays." The *suggestion* of a recurring repetitive action, a single moment of existence writ large, a hypnotic obsessive response to optimistic resolutions both in life and on stage gives this play tremendous impact. It also brings the audience into the action easily and genially, reminding us particularly of Pirandello's *Each in His Own Way* and — an even closer parallel — *Tonight We Improvise*, where the audience in the theater serves on two levels: as the actual theater audience and the audience addressed directly or indirectly by the director and the actors, as they move in and out of their formal roles on stage. In both cases, the audience is an integral part of the play.

The Man Who Had Three Arms makes much greater demands, however. In this play, the audience is *provoked* into reaction, bombarded with direct and indirect insults, and forced into embarrassed laughter which is not quite the usual comic cathartic. The audience soon understands that the speaker's diatribe is meant for them, too. Man and Woman, playing host for the occasion, instruct the audience indirectly as to their part by taking on a variety of "masks" as Himself calls upon past events and the people in his life. Ultimately, however, the play is a one-man show (as in a way *Box and Quotations* was a one-woman show). Himself provides the cues, casts the parts, and establishes the mood; he rewrites the script as he moves from one stark memory to another; he directs the entire proceedings. He is Albee's version of Pirandello's Emperor Enrico IV — the author who has found his characters.

The audience in the theater is the sounding board for the escalating hysterical outbursts of Himself; and as he moves from episode to episode, the audience takes on a variety of different roles. The targets, expressed or suggested, are many: the public at large with its morbid curiosity, greedy agents, unsupportive wives and children; dinner speakers generally; hosts of dinner speakers generally; committees who set up the dinners for public speakers; the unscrupulous press; all who "profess" anything in public, including teachers and drama critics — the pseudo-intellectual, pseudo-educated professional class; promoters of best-sellers; and all who prostitute themselves in the name of *culture*. By having the speaker address the real audience directly, Albee has turned the entire theater into his stage. The audience may not respond directly — Man and Woman are the intermediaries — but they are forced to share with the speaker his most agonizing and pitiful revelations. But let's go back a moment.

Himself — like anyone giving a lecture or professing anything in a public setting — is addressing an audience. He is the 231st lecturer in a series called "Man on Man." He seems confident in a nervous way, overcompensating for being the third and least distinguished choice of the committee. He talks in a kind of feverish mounting momentum, rambling: he tells anecdotes; he fixes with hard intensity on such things as the gluey soup they had at dinner; he gradually targets his ingratiating hosts for his ironic barbs; he attacks in different moods the multilayered audience (hosts, spectators, the present theater crowd watching drama through this kind of telescopic lens, the critics, us) stripping them of all pretense even as he destroys his own dignity. We are aware of ourselves, the audience, as part of the oscillating machinery of the play, part of the clouded reflection of a crazy image that is never quite in focus. In addressing us, the real audience watching all this, Himself assigns us the roles he creates in his evolving monolog script; and we, the implicit term in a large metaphor, trigger everything happening on stage.

Well, almost everything. Himself provides one of the longest of Albee's *narratives* within a play — after all, he is there to tell his story, in the same way that the long Monolog of the Long-Winded Lady in *Quotations* is a fragmented account of *her* story. Himself is there as a last-minute third choice of the committee (as we said earlier). With him on stage are the Man and Woman — the hosts for the evening. These two seem impatient — they want to get on with the program, get through with it. But Himself has a lot to say about . . . himself . . . before he focuses on the events that made him notorious — the extraordinary story of how he grew a third arm and became wealthy, sought-after in the lecture circuit because of that grotesque happening, and, after a while, when the arm *un*grew and withered, how he lost everything. He has not reconciled himself to the rejection by his family and, even more important, his audience. Throughout this fragmented account, Man and Woman assume the roles evoked by the speaker. They also provide the slides called for at a certain moment, moving in and out of dramatic postures and taking on a variety of voices at those moments when the narrative seems on the verge of exceeding its prescribed stage limits.

There is story-telling, pictures, role-playing, and even an unprogrammed intermission announced by Himself so that he can get a drink of gin (which his hosts refused to bring him on stage). This pyrotechnic display comes to an abrupt end when Woman orders someone off stage to lower the curtain and force the speaker to stop his rantings. Himself is not through, however. He is agitated, grows angry. Woman ignores him. As far as she's concerned, he is through. The ordeal is over until next time, another speaker. What has she or the audience understood?

Of course the end is a surprise and yet predictable in the open-ended cyclical structure of Albee's plays. Behold! A new growth has started, somewhere else of course. The past will soon turn into another glorious future.

The end of the play reminds us of the ambiguous quality of Albee's humor. Himself is an expert at caricature — of himself and others. In his ironic thrusts and bizarre tortured account of his third arm and the events that followed, he bares his wounds with a kind of obscene enthusiasm, forcing the audience to look upon them — and literally, to look at the place where his third arm had been. He laughs and no doubt the audience laughs with him and in the same nervous way. It is a bad joke. We are part of it. We encourage it. But in doing so we also become fair targets for the destructive criticism of Himself, who vents his venom on us as the representatives of the world that has destroyed him.

In 1985, Albee said that of all his plays *The Man Who Had Three Arms* "is the one for which I have received the most enthusiastic and favorable response from people in the arts — my peers." And a couple of years later (1987), he said substantially the same thing, adding that the play is "greatly admired by my fellow playwrights and greatly loathed by the tastemakers who were — oddly enough — its subject."

Albee's account of how and when he "discovered" that he himself was a playwright takes on special relevance in this context. He found his "dramatic voice" — he tells us — "while composing *The Zoo Story*." In a passage worthy of Eliot's discussion on the organic nature of the literary genres, Albee explains: "Something very, very interesting happened with the writing of that play. I didn't discover suddenly that I was a playwright; I discovered that I have been a playwright all my life, but didn't know it because I hadn't written plays. . . . And so when I wrote *The Zoo Story*, I was able to start practicing my 'nature' fully."

The potential of that dramatic "nature," already clearly in evidence in *The Zoo Story*, has been actualized in impressive ways in the last thirty years, and continues to surprise us. With *The Man Who Had Three Arms* Albee's high art of stagecraft reaches a true milestone and paves the way for others to follow, both as playwrights and critics. By taking the dramatic event to the very edge of non-theater, in the great tradition of Shakespeare, Pirandello, and others in the Theater of the Absurd, Albee, like Pirandello in his late and greatest plays, has *reconstituted* the stage, reappropriated the genre in a daring dialectic which lesser artists would not take on. Just as Pirandello, after the genial experimentation of the "theater plays," produced the theater play par excellence in *Enrico IV*, the play in which all the novelties of the earlier plays were reabsorbed in a new "traditional" context, so Albee, after the magnificent display of theater about to "transcend itself," produced one of his most memorable plays, it too in a new "traditional" context in which the most outrageous most effective features of contemporary experimentation find their organic newly-reconstituted stage. For this alone, if nothing else, Albee deserves to be honored as the greatest of our American playwrights — the most daring and most successful.

He is, also, our most American playwright in giving stage utterance to our characteristic setting, our cherished values, re-evaluating all that we take for granted and prodding us to new conclusions. In his own effort, he has shown us the way. The strident absolutes of his early years as a playwright have been tempered, although the spirit is still as adamant and unyielding. His attitudes have mellowed; his humor has found even more fertile ground. He is that rare being who, while remaining the same over the years, has never repeated himself, has never diminished his talent in any way.

Albee's mastery of the stage was first recognized abroad, as we know; but the time is ripe for us to claim him as ours, both in the academy and in theater and drama criticism. For those of us who shared the excitement of his "experiments" thirty odd years ago, the mounting interest in Albee's work, especially among younger playwrights and scholars, is gratifying. He has combined our American tradition (Eliot's "strong local colour") with the larger view of man in his environment and time (Eliot's "unconscious universality"). These two opposing themes, the particular and the general, are, Eliot tells us, the characteristic features of any new literary landmark. An author who has both in his sights will inevitably alter the tradition that has preceded him, however subtly. "Tradition" responds to "individual talent" in due course and absorbs it into the continuum.

No doubt Albee will give us much to talk and think about in the years ahead. But the large pattern is clear enough, even at this point: surprises will follow the predictable simplicity of his paradoxical techniques, and public issues and private tensions will always be expressed as an open-ended journey of discovery.

PART SIX
(337-384)

SOPHOCLES, DANTE, ARTHUR MILLER

"The Oracles are Dumb or Cheat: A Study of the Meaning of *Oedipus Rex*" was first published in *Classical Journal*, March 1963.

"*. . . should be of great interest to those of us who teach that beautiful play year after year.*" "*News and Ideas,*" College English (*May 1979*). Translated into Chinese by Aloysius Chang, for *Youth Literary*, No. 271, July 1976.

"Art and Nature in Dante's *Purgatorio*" was first published in *Italica*, Special Anniversary Issue on Dante, 1965.

"Arthur Miller's *Death of a Salesman*: "The 'Tragic Hero' Redefined" was first published in *The World & I*, July 1992.

CHAPTER 19

THE ORACLES ARE DUMB OR CHEAT: A STUDY OF THE MEANING OF *OEDIPUS REX*

Aristotle's praise of the *Oedipus Rex* of Sophocles as one of the best constructed of the Greek tragedies[1] has never been seriously challenged by critics, but the application of his well known definition of the tragic hero to Oedipus[2] has raised and continues to raise some real critical difficulties. These have been summarized most clearly by H. D. F. Kitto:

> Is Sophocles telling us that Man is only the plaything of Fate? Or does he mean, as Dr. Bowra suggested, no more than that the gods have contrived this awful fate for Oedipus in order to display their power to man and to teach him a salutary lesson? Or is Sophocles simply making exciting drama, leaving the philosophical implications unexplored?[3]

Kit to rejects the first two possibilities. Oedipus represents mankind with all its strength and weaknesses; his tragedy is characteristic of the struggles and sufferings of man. For Kitto the play is clearly a tragedy of character:

> What happens is the natural result of the weaknesses and the virtues of his character, in combination with other people's.[4]

And yet, as one critic observes, the punishment suffered by the hero at the end of the play seems out of all proportion to the defects in his character:

> Even when we take into account the passion, the pride, and the curiosity of Oedipus we still feel that the criminal has been in a measure "the victim of a mistake" — that he is a mere puppet in the hands of some superior and relentless power.[5]

This insistence that the play is something more than a tragedy of character, that it must be interpreted in terms of human and divine laws, reappears in a recent study by Peter D. Arnott, who thus summarizes the essence of Greek tragedy:

> How far was man responsible for his own actions, how far compelled by the will of heaven? What happens when sacred commands and human compassions conflict?[6]

There is no doubt that Sophocles represents Oedipus as rushing toward his terrible doom unawares, recoiling with horror from his crimes, and yet assuming full responsibility for his actions. Trained as we all have been by Aristotle, we may well feel that Oedipus must be held guilty if the play is to make sense. But can he really be held responsible for sins which are committed unconsciously? Whitney J. Oates states the alternatives very clearly:

> Oedipus in some sense is presented as master of his own destiny, or else it is meaningless that at the end of the play he does not excuse himself by pleading that he did not know what he was doing, but rather accepts full responsibility as a moral agent for all his acts, whether done in ignorance or not.[7]

Although Oates indicates his preference rather emphatically, he nevertheless leaves the question open, offering no proof for the opinion that Oedipus controls his fate. Bolder critics have chosen the other alternative, some indeed not hesitating to conclude that "there is no meaning in the Oedipus Tyrannus,"[8] that there is merely "the terror of coincidence . . . a frightful groundwork of accident,"[9] that the moral judgments which give rise to the difficulty are entirely those of the reader[10] and that, in fact, the *Oedipus Rex* is exactly what, according to Aristotle, ought to be avoided in tragedy.[11]

Were Aristotle and Sophocles wrong after all? Is Oedipus exaggerating his sense of guilt, or is there something in the characterization of the hero which critics have missed?

The difficulty is a serious one, for it threatens to undermine not only the tragic character of the hero, but the very basis for tragedy, as traditionally accepted and understood. If Oedipus is simply a puppet moved by the unseen strings of fate, if there is no free choice involved in the original action which brings about the tragic consequences we witness, then Oedipus cannot be regarded as a tragic hero, and the situation which unfolds does not assume tragic proportions. If, on the other hand, the artistic instincts of the dramatist are to be trusted, then we must be prepared to show that Oedipus does in some way direct his actions, that somewhere along the line he makes a choice which determines all subsequent action.

This choice must be of a very special kind. It is not the "choice" Oedipus makes in his encounter with King Laius on a lonely mountain road; it is not the "choice" between sending for Tiresias and the shepherd or not sending for them; and, although he consented freely "to marry a woman old enough to be his mother,"[12] all talk of "choice" is meaningless here, since Oedipus had no suspicion whatsoever of his true relationship to the

Queen. All these so-called "choices" are in reality consequences of a decision made long before, one which clearly reflects problems which were, Arnott reminds us, "as momentous for the Greeks as Free Will and Original Sin are for Christianity."[13]

In order to understand properly the nature of the "tragic choice" here involved, it might be well to recall — by way of introduction to our discussion — Hegel's description of the kind of conflict found in the *Oedipus Rex* and best illustrated in the *Antigone*. A. C. Bradley correctly emphasizes Hegel's assertion that the tragic conflict is not a struggle between good and evil (there is no "tragedy" inherent in such a struggle) but a struggle between two equally justified "laws," both of which are good and both of which demand obedience.[14] This is, Bradley reminds us, a fundamental condition of Greek tragedy. The tragic hero is he who finds himself in the peculiar situation of having to choose between two *goods*.[15] Ordinarily, these goods exist side by side and are respected and acknowledged by all, without danger of any conflict. Most people, for example, fulfill their religious obligations and their obligations as citizens without any serious difficulty. Once in a while, however, a man or woman is singled out by fate and forced to insist upon one of these universal "laws" to the exclusion of the other: For the Greeks, a person thus singled out was usually under a family curse and his tragedy was part of the expiation demanded by the gods. Such a curse is inescapable, but tragedy itself begins to unfold only with the choice which the person makes consciously and freely between the two goods. Destiny or the gods prepare the stage — as God prepared the stage for Adam's assertion of freedom — but it is the hero who acts out the tragedy, who springs the trap set for him and seals his own doom.

Where does Oedipus face a dilemma of this kind? Perhaps the best way to answer the question is to follow up those clues to the personality and character of the hero which reveal an inner struggle, a reversal of values. Dramatically, such a struggle is hinted at in the contrast between the rational and the irrational, the constant play on light and darkness, sight and blindness, fact and revelation. These contrasts serve, as has often been noted, to heighten the theme of the play, that man's wisdom consists in acknowledging the superior power of the gods and submitting to it; but, as we shall try to show, they also serve in a quite special way to call attention to the one choice for which Oedipus is directly responsible, for which he assumes responsibility, and for which he is punished. This choice rests ultimately on the conscious and repeated attempts by the hero to reconcile his rational faculty with his irrational fears, fears that he tries to overcome but which in the end he recognizes as manifestations of a power beyond human rationality. From this point of view the play assumes, as Sigmund Freud has observed,[16] tremendous importance as a study of the unconscious, of hidden yet active impulses which lead the hero to the very catastrophe he tries, consciously, to avert. Seen in this light, those moments in which the action moves forward become especially significant. We notice, for example, that in every case it is Oedipus himself who provides the impulse for the movement of the action. We notice, also, that when the action does not move in the direction anticipated, he is all too ready to criticize the very authorities he has called upon. The real clue to his psychological state lies precisely in this wavering, the willingness on his part to call upon divine help in critical moments and the contempt with which he rejects divine manifestations when the crisis is past, when he feels himself in full control of the situation. Let us examine the play with this contrast in mind.

Oedipus has sent to Delphi to seek the help of the Oracle in lifting the plague from the city of Thebes. Hearing that the city is suffering because of the presence of Laius' murderer, he swears — with that fine irony which is the keynote of the play — that he will not rest until he has tracked down and punished the murderer and vows to take the son's part, just as though he were Laius' son.[17] He counts on the aid of the gods again for the next step, calling upon Tiresias, the blind prophet, to help him detect the criminal. But when Tiresias tells him point blank that he, Oedipus, is the murderer; the king turns upon him with contempt, ridiculing prophecies and soothsayers, calling him "sightless," "witless," "senseless," "mad," a "decrepit fortune-teller," a "prophet fraud," scorning his prophetic gift as mere "mystic mummery," and reminding the seer that no one can hurt a man who "sees":

> You child of endless night! You can not hurt me
> Or any other man who sees the sun.[18]

We must remember that, here as elsewhere in the play, the sun suggests something more than the source of physical light. Day and night, light and darkness, sight and blindness — among the most effective literary devices of the play — point up the contrast between truth and error, between the wisdom of man and the wisdom of the gods, the truth hidden in darkness and the lie which lives in the light, a theme which reaches its magnificent climax in the scene where Oedipus, all the "facts" of the case before him, sees the truth of divine "revelation" at last and turns from the world of light into a self-inflicted night of blindness.

Perfectly confident in his knowledge of the truth about himself, Oedipus rejects the revelation of Tiresias in the first scene of the play, reminding everyone that oracles and birds are mockeries of truth, that it was he, not Tiresias, who solved the riddle of the Sphinx through the insight of reason. He is confident of his innocence. He believes that he sees the truth as plainly as he sees the light of the sun. His assurance does not diminish when, after Tiresias' departure, he volunteers to answer Creon's queries: "Put your questions. I am no murderer.[19] Tiresias' accusations disturb him, of course, but in an unexpected way. He does not for a moment doubt his innocence, but interprets the charge as an attempt to wrench the crown from him, a conspiracy led by Creon to seize power. He is scornful of the prophet's words because the wise man does not need oracles. He is led by reason and the light of wisdom, and through these can destroy all human intrigue.

Even Jocasta joins in this repudiation of the oracles:

Set your mind at rest.
If it is a question of soothsayers, I tell you
That you will find no man whose craft gives
    knowledge
Of the unknowable.[20]

The Queen, trying to heal the breach between Creon and Oedipus, recalls the circumstances of Laius' murder as the best proof of the fallibility of oracles, but her account serves, instead, to raise the doubt which makes Oedipus seek out the one man who can tell him something of the circumstances of the murder. When Oedipus confides in the Queen, she too begins to be troubled and does not hesitate to seek out the very gods she had repudiated before, visiting the altars as a suppliant bearing branches and incense. But this submission is short-lived. When the messenger arrives from Corinth with the news of old Polybos' death, she exults:

O riddlers of God's will, where are you now!
This was the man whom Oedipus, long ago,
Feared so, fled so, in dread of destroying him —
But it was another fate by which he died.[21]

And when her husband enters, she greets him with:

Listen to what this man says and then tell me
What has become of the solemn prophecies.[22]

Jocasta's exultation and confidence are echoed by Oedipus himself who, hearing the news of the messenger, regains his former
assurance and bursts out with this tirade against oracles and soothsayers:

> Why should a man respect the Pythian hearth, or
> Give heed to the birds that jangle above his head?
> They prophesied that I should kill Polybos,
> Kill my own father; but he is dead and buried,
> And I am here — I never touched him, never,
> Unless he died of grief for my departure,
> And thus, in a sense, through me. No. Polybos
> Has packed the oracles off with him underground.
> They are empty words.[23]

He can even consider the possibility of having contributed to
Polybos' death by his departure, but that possibility does not
trouble him in the least. The oracle, after all, had been very specific; and he knew with certainty that he had not murdered
Polybos. Even in his moment of triumph, however, he cannot
bring himself to forget or repudiate the second part of the oracle.
He refuses to return to Corinth because the woman he believes
to be his mother is still alive. To dispel these fears, the messenger reveals that Oedipus was a foster child, thus precipitating
the climax of the play and the final revelation of the circumstances of the king's birth and the identity of his true parents.

This series of reversals from certainty and hope to doubt
and despair is part of the basic dramatic texture of the play and
is meant to suggest the interrelationship between the truth of
reason and the truth of divine revelation. The rational man sees
at last the limits of his self-sufficiency. The king's confidence
crumbles only when the investigation he himself has initiated
brings the ultimate fact to light. It is the reasonable explanation
he sought all along, and, ironically, it is precisely the reasonable
explanation to which he finally yields. When Oedipus is faced at
last with the terrible truth, when he has probed into the secrets
of his past and comes to know himself, he sees at last the full
implications of the present and its intimate connection with all
that has gone before:

> Ah God!
> It was true!
>   All the prophecies!
>   — Now,
> O Light, may I look on you for the last time![24]

He sees not only the truth of the prophet's accusation, the unal-
terable course of his destiny as predicted by the Oracle, the use-

lessness of his attempt to deflect the will of the gods; he sees, also, the ordering of coincidences in a meaningful chain of willful acts, what Hegel calls "the completed deed" in all its fullness:

> . . . a hidden power shunning the light of day, waylays the ethical self-consciousness, a power which bursts forth only after the deed is done, and seizes the doer in the act. For the completed deed is the removal of the opposition between the knowing self and the reality over against it. The ethical consciousness cannot disclaim the crime and its guilt. The deed consists in setting in motion what was unmoved, and in bringing out what in the first instance lay shut up as a mere possibility, and thereby linking on the unconscious to the conscious, the nonexistent to the existent. In this truth, therefore, the deed comes to light; — it is something in which a conscious element is bound up with what is unconscious, what is peculiarly one's own with what is alien and external: — it is an essential reality divided in sunder, whose other aspect consciousness experiences and also finds to be its own aspect, but as a power violated by its doing, and roused to hostility against it.[25]

The frailty of human wisdom, the limits of reason, the blind pride of man who disdains the gods are recognized in this moment of revealed truth. Insight into necessity makes Oedipus free at last. But it is not mere recognition of necessity which makes him a tragic hero; having become a truly free agent, he must assume full responsibility for all his actions. Only in this way can the original imbalance be corrected. As Hegel points out, we must take care not to confuse our modern notions of guilt and innocence with the Greek concept of right and wrong. For the Greeks a free man, a man who is not a victim or slave of circumstances and environment, is one who assumes full responsibility for all that he does, whatever the intention behind his actions. Oedipus

> slays his father, marries his mother, begets children in this incestuous alliance, and nevertheless is involved in these most terrible crimes without active participation either in will or knowledge. The point of view of our profounder modern consciousness of right and wrong would be to recognize that crimes of this description, inasmuch as they were neither referable to a personal knowledge or volition, were not deeds for which the true personality of the perpetrator was responsible. The plastic nature of the Greek on the contrary adheres to the bare fact which an individual has achieved, and refuses to face the division implied by the purely ideal attitude of the soul in the self-conscious life on the one hand and the objective significance of the fact accomplished on the other.[26]

Hegel's distinction between the Greek concept of ethical responsibility and the modern concept of personal guilt and innocence must be kept in mind if we are to make sense of the outcome of *Oedipus Rex.* Oedipus recognizes the accomplished fact as his doing and takes the blame for it. As Hegel points out, no judgment is more intolerable in this connection than the insistence that a hero of this type has acted "innocently."

> It is a point of honour with such great characters that they are guilty. They have no desire to excite pity or our sensibilities.[27]

Hegel's brilliant analysis of the tragic hero in Greek drama is particularly relevant in any attempt to explain why Oedipus assumes guilt for actions which, by modern standards of right and wrong, cannot be condemned. But, as a matter of fact, the actions we witness in the play are merely the unfolding or working out of a decision made much earlier and related to the events we actually see in a precise sequence. Oedipus' tragic choice is his fully conscious decision to leave Corinth and thereby escape the prediction of the Delphic Oracle. But in choosing human wisdom and self-sufficiency he was forced to reject the truth of divine inexorable fate. Unable to accept the terrible decree of the Oracle and confident in his own resources and powers, he rejects the prediction of the gods on the level of consciousness but continues to acknowledge it on an unconscious level. His flight becomes, therefore, a race on a treadmill, creating an illusion of real movement away from the starting point. His decision to leave Corinth starts this movement — a movement in the very direction of the catastrophe he so desperately tried to avoid. From a purely human point of view, the decision he makes is, as Hegel insists, noble and good. To have remained with his foster parents — his real parents, as far as he knew — would have meant, in his eyes, inviting disaster without lifting a finger to avert it. He could not sit back and wait for the blow to fall; his sense of honor and goodness would not permit it. He sacrifices happiness with his parents in order to spare them a fate worse than death, to protect them and himself from the curse of the gods. His instincts are unquestionably good; his intentions are beyond reproach. But from a divine point of view, his choice was, in effect, an attempt to outwit the gods, a kind of boast that he could match himself against their almighty power. He is guilty of *hybris* — but of a very special kind. Oedipus is indeed a proud man, the rational self-sufficient man, as we have insisted; but what is tragic about his predicament is that, whatever his decision, it must, by the very nature of the alternatives, be good; or, to put it another way, whatever his decision, he will in the end be forced to reject one of two positive and equally compelling values. We see in the course of the play how he tries to undermine one of these values for the sake of the other, insisting again and again that prophecies and omens are nothing more than superstition. The choice by which he determines the course of the action is a rational, responsible choice, made in full possession of his faculties. But, as Hegel points out, its full implications remain hidden until the moment when the undeniable evidence is produced. In the recognition and acceptance of the "completed deed," Oedipus is restored at last to "health," the conscious choice is seen in its relationship to the consequences which have resulted from it, and the truth of the meaning of that original choice is grasped clearly and unmistakably.

The suffering which he tried to escape appears to him, in the end, as the necessary prerequisite for peace and salvation. He accepts it willingly as the only means by which he can restore the harmony and balance which he destroyed by choosing one good to the exclusion of another. He comes to understand at last the full tragic significance of denying the omnipotence of the gods and relying on purely human powers. The full expiation comes, of course, in the *Oedipus at Colonus*, when the humbled king, all the destructive passions drained from him, submits willingly to the dictates of the gods whom, in the earlier play, he had consciously disobeyed.

The power of the gods is great indeed. Oedipus moves toward his defeat, in *Oedipus Rex*, contributing to it by his own free choice. Might he have saved himself by remaining in Corinth? The gods, Sophocles seems to be warning us, can do anything, regardless of place or time. Where their will is involved, suppositions are meaningless. Destiny is inescapable. Oedipus — exalting the rational mind, the sensitive conscience over and above divine imperatives — cannot avoid his tragic fate. If the gods are truly omnipotent, their will must come to pass. Whatever he does, Oedipus — like Adam and Eve — will in the end be working with fate, exerting his freedom of choice in the fulfillment of a divine, all-powerful design.

NOTES

An earlier version of this essay appeared in *The Classical Journal*, Volume 58, No.6, March, 1963.

1. L. J. Potts, trans., *Aristotle on the Art of Fiction*, (Cambridge 1953): "But of all disclosures the best are those that arise out of the story itself and cause astonishment by probable events; as in the *Oedipus* of Sophocles . . ." (p. 39); "Disclosure produces its finest effect when it is

connected with Irony, as the disclosure in the *Oedipus* is . . ." (p. 31); "As for extravagant incidents, there should be none in the story, or if there are they should be kept outside the tragedy, as is the one in the *Oedipus* of Sophocles . . . (p. 37).

2. *Ibid.*, p. 33: "the kind of man who neither is distinguished for excellence and virtue, nor comes to grief on account of baseness and vice, but on account of some error; a man of great reputation and prosperity, like Oedipus and Thyestes and conspicuous people of such families as theirs."

3. H. D. F. Kitto, *GreekTtragedy, A Literary Study*, 3d ed. (New York 1961), p. 136.

4. *Ibid.*, pp. 136-7.

5. Clifton W. Collins, *Sophocles* (London, 1871), p. 20.

6. Peter D. Arnott, *An Introduction to the Greek Theatre*, (London, 1959), p. 164.

7 Whitney J. Oates and Eugene O'Neill, Jr., eds., *Seven Famous Greek Plays* (New York 1950), p. 120.

8. A. J. A. Waldock, cited in G. M. Kirkwood, *A Study of Sophoclean Drama* (Cornell studies in classical philology, vol. 31). p. 33.

9. *Ibid.*, p. 33.

10. G. M. Kirkwood, pp. 75-76: "To what cause Sophocles wants us to ascribe the fate of Oedipus is a problem that has elicited many and various answers and is often regarded as the key to the play. But what if Sophocles never intended there to be an answer? What if the fate of Oedipus is simply a mythological datum, to be accepted and built into the study of Oedipus without comment or solution? We can enjoy the play most fully, and best avoid misunderstanding it, if we take the simple approach that these questions suggest."

11. Philip W. Harsh, "Implicit and Explicit in the 'Oedipus Tyrannus,'" *AJP* 79 (1958) 255: "According to both Whitman and Knox Oedipus is a man of superior virtue, 'which makes the play correspond fairly closely to Aristotle.s description of what tragedy should avoid: "the spectacle of a virtuous man brought from prosperity to adversity — this moves neither pity nor fear: it merely shocks us.""

12. Kitto, p. 137.

13. Arnott, p. 164.

14. A. C. Bradley, "Hegel's Theory of Tragedy," *Oxford Lectures on Poetry* (London, 1950), pp. 67-95.

15. The Hegelian theory is often recalled — through Bradley and not Hegel, I am convinced — simply to be dismissed, although such dismissal is rarely justified on clear grounds. The following passage from D. W. Lucas' *The Greek Tragic Poets*, reprinted recently in Francis Connolly's *The Types of Literature* (New York 1953), is an example of this kind of "criticism." Speaking of the *Antigone*, Lucas writes: "Though

Hegel, or his interpreters, have clouded the issue by taking the *Antigone* as an example of the fusion of two partial rights in a higher synthesis, there is no doubt that in the eyes of Sophocles Creon is wrong and Antigone is right, and Creon's end points a moral as clear as that of the *Ajax*. It is less easy to know what we are to make of the end of Antigone" (p.675). The Hegelian theory is precisely what enables us to explain the end of Creon and the end of Antigone within a single critical framework.

16. Sigmund Freud, "Dreams of the Death of Beloved Persons," *Great Essays in Science* (New York, 1957), pp. 366-386.

17. Sophocles, "Oedipus Rex," *The Oedipus Cycle*, Engl. versions by Dudley Fitts & Robert Fitzgerald (New York, 1949), p. 14.

18. *Ibid.*, pp. 19-20.

19. *Ibid.*, p. 29.

20. *Ibid.*, p.36.

21. *Ibid.*, p. 47.

22. *Ibid.*, p. 47.

23. *Ibid.*, p. 48.

24. *Ibid.*, p. 62.

25. G. W. F. Hegel, *The Phenomenology of Mind*, tr. J. B. Baillie (London, New York, 1931), p. 490.

26. Hegel, *The Philosophy of Fine Art*, tr. F. P. B. Osmaston, vol. 4 (London, 1920), p. 319.

27. *Ibid.*, p. 321.

CHAPTER 20

ART AND NATURE IN DANTE'S *PURGATORIO*

One of the most interesting, but relatively unexplored features of the *Purgatorio* is the unusual pattern of the descriptions of the "lessons" on the terraces, where the moral of the sinner's experience is compressed into sharp, vivid representations suggesting a progression from the material plastic arts of architecture and sculpture, to music, painting, and poetry. This progression culminates in the grand display of poetic virtuosity at the very top of Purgatory, where art as such seems to reach its extremest limits and reconstituted nature, the condition of the world and man before the fall, takes its place. Nowhere is Dante's inexhaustible imagination more in evidence than in the constantly shifting imagery of sight, touch, hearing, smell, and speech, with which, in the *exempla* on the terraces of Purgatory, he articulates a magnificent tribute to the fine arts, and in his attempt to enlarge — in the Earthly Paradise — familiar techniques and introduce new ones suited to the new problems of super-human experience.

The unique quality of the *Purgatorio* as a whole has been noted by writers like De Sanctis and Momigliano, who suggest that the second canticle is not simply the middle term in a moral progression from Hell to Heaven, but the true antithesis of the *Inferno* and *Paradiso*. In the Christian-Platonic sense, Hell is the semblance of reality, and Heaven, reality itself; Purgatory is the memory of the one and the anticipation of the other, an ephemeral experience totally different from the well-defined error of the first and the clear truth of the third canticle. It is a world of shadows and images,[1] a hazy autumn day,[2] through which the dark violence of the *Inferno* filters through into the *Paradiso* and there is transformed into the violence of an all-consuming love. In the *Purgatorio*, appearance and reality strive one against the other, in the precarious balance which is human life and experience. It is the place of recognition, where familiar everyday images interrupt divine meditation. Dante, the narrator-pilgrim, assumes a dramatic role in the *Purgatorio*, participating in the emotional life of the community and joining in the activities of its members. He is enraptured, for example, by Casella's singing; he is instrumental in the "recognition" of Virgil by Statius; he becomes himself a protagonist in the meeting with Sordello; he accepts the "commissions" for prayers, entrusted to him by the penitents; he is addressed again and again with spiritual intimacy as *frate* — and, at the very top of Purgatory, he becomes the chief protagonist in the reunion scene with Beatrice, the only place in the entire poem where he refers to himself by name.

The *Purgatorio* is the fleeting image of life, the nostalgic, sadly-sweet condition of the soul longing to be made beautiful (to use Dante's words); poetically, it is a masterpiece of paradox. Nowhere is this clearer than in the representation of the *exempla* on the terraces of *Purgatorio*. For, while insisting on the breakdown of sensory perception as the necessary prerequisite for the "reconditioned" or spiritualized body, Dante also is emphasizing the power of human art. In a series of representations which suggest the different categories of fine art, he employs the language of sensory experience to break down the conventional limits of art and prepare the reader for the superhuman experience which transcends artistic expression. The enlargement of sensory perception as a preparation for the *Paradiso* culminates in the Earthly Paradise, where human art — as we said — gives way to reconstituted, flawless, nature. This *tour-de-force* is especially interesting for what may be described as Dante's theory of the progression of the fine arts.

The first terrace depicts the most "solid" of the representations, the only clearly defined material picture, effected in a kind of architectural, ornamental sculpture. The second is in the form of an auditory phenomenon — a kind of echoing, reverberating sound which resembles but is not identical with the human voice and may, perhaps, be compared to a musical effect. The third is an ecstatic vision, a kind of internal, vivid painting, such as one associates very often with dreams. The fourth is the first of the *exempla* to make use of identifiable human mediums — the sinners themselves. Two appear at the beginning of the long column of penitents, chanting in unison — for the benefit of the rest — reminders of those narratives which constitute the virtuous lesson, and two others at the end, providing reminders of narratives illustrating the opposite, negative, lesson. In the fifth of these *exempla*, the medium is a single figure — Hugh Capet — who provides in his own lyric voice the lessons of poverty and liberality, and their opposite, avarice. The sixth representation is a kind of echo of the preceding one — a single voice, heard but not seen, coming from a tree. In the last, the seventh *exemplum*, the virtuous lessons are dramatized so to speak; the unified "chorus" which sings "*Summae Deus clementiae*" (XXV, 121), ends the hymn, always, with an example of chastity, uttered in a loud voice; two other groups cry out, in a kind of counterpoint, reciting examples of unnatural lust, while giving dramatic expression to the spirit of reconstituted love by briefly and chastely embracing one another each time they reach the limits of their restless forward and backward movement.

In this last representation. Dante makes clear that the singing, the weeping, the physical tokens of chaste affection, the loud cries, go on without interruption throughout the scene. Moreover, the visual, auditory, and oral impressions that characterized the earlier *exempla* are here combined in a single setting, a synthesis of visible action and lyric outbursts of musical and pictorial elements. The sculptured bas-reliefs of the first terrace, the musical disembodied reverberations of the second,[3] the painting of the third are rearticulated through the human medium in the next four terraces, where the human voice is heard speaking or singing — first, to an audience, then to itself, and, finally, in dramatic exchanges, where personality is given full expression.

The order of the representations is in itself significant. The first *exemplum* is — as we noted earlier — a combination of architecture and sculpture, the most "classical" and material of the arts, depicting scenes of humility on a marble-like wall which marks the first ledge, where the proud are committed and expiate their sins. The second representation, as Momigliano has observed, suggests a musical effect: Dante hears a loud unembodied "voice" literally fly past, uttering — or, more properly, "singing" — "*Vinum non habent*," over and over again:

La prima voce che passò volando
"*Vinum non habent*," altamente disse,
e retro a noi l'ando reiterando. (XIII, 28-30)

[The first voice which passed by in its flight loudly
said, *Vinum non habent*," and went on repeating behind us.][4]

The third, the ecstatic vision on the terrace of the wrathful, suggests a kind of painting. I was caught up — Dante tells us — in a dream and saw many persons in a temple, and a woman,

ed una donna in su l'entrar con atto
dolce di madre dicer: "Figliuol mio,
perchè hai tu così verso noi fatto?

Ecco, dolenti, lo tuo padre ed io
ti cercavamo".... (XV, 88-92)

[and a woman about to enter, with the tender attitude
of a mother, saying: "My son, why hast thou thus dealt with us?
Behold thy father and I sought thee sorrowing"....]

These last two representations — together with the next four —
suggest the so-called "romantic" arts. With music and painting,
the god (sculpture) in the temple of art (architecture) opens his
eyes and ears to life; but it is in poetry that he reveals his innermost thoughts and feeligs.

In the next four terraces, Dante makes use of identifiable
human mediums for the articulation of the *exempla*. On the terrace of the slothful, Mary's visit to Elizabeth is recalled by the
first two of a column of sinners, in a kind of objective, "epic"
utterance — or, what Eliot has called, "the voice of the poet addressing an audience, whether large or small." On the terrace of
the avaricious and prodigal, it is Hugh Capet who utters the
lesson of Mary's poverty, in the single voice of the lyric poet —
"the voice of the poet talking to himself," as Eliot describes it, "—
or to nobody." Among the gluttonous, a human voice coming
from a tree (a kind of echo of Hugh Capet) extols Mary's tem-
perance. The seventh *exemplum* on the final terrace is a dramatic
synthesis of epic and lyric elements combined to create movement and harmony in a vivid, almost choreographic, action. The
lustful appear as a chorus who recall, in unison, Mary's chastity
— *"Virum non cognosco"* — against the dialogue between the two
groups who sinned against nature, the entire representation suggesting not the directness of the lyric or the objectivity of the
epic but clearly distinguishable "characters" who create, through
a kind of dialogue, an immediate, dramatic action.[5]

Whether or not Dante ordered these *exempla* consciously
or simply followed his poetic intuition, their arrangement is interesting as a progression from material and tangible artistic
expression, to immaterial, intangible expression, articulated by
human agents; architecture and sculpture give way to music,
painting, and poetry. The moments of poetry may be distinguished, in turn, in the traditional sequence of narrative or epic
voice, followed by the subjective or lyrical voice, and culminating finally in the dramatic, which is the synthesis of the other
two.

The "inspiration" which integrates these various expressions of art is, of course, the life of the Virgin Mary. Her virtue is
the focus for the entire series of *exempla*.

But the most interesting thing about these representations is the effort on Dante's part to impress upon the reader the idea that, within the conventional limits of art, communication is already breaking down — or, rather, that the content of art is on the verge of exceeding the possibility of expression. The bas-relief sculpture of the first terrace, Dante tells us a number of times, is more than mere sculpture. It seems to speak out:

> . . . non sembiava imagine che tace. (X, 39)

> [. . . it seemed not an image which is dumb.]

The visual impact awakens the sense of hearing:

> . . . à due miei sensi
> faceva dir l'un "No," l'altro "Si, canta." (59-60)

> [. . . to two of my senses, made the one say. "no," the other, "yes, they do sing."]

The perfumed smoke of the censers is almost a physical reality for both the eyes and the nose:

> . . . al fummo degl'incensi
> che v'era imaginato, gli occhi e il naso
> ed al si ed al no discordi fensi. (61-63)

> [. . . at the smoke of the incense which there was imaged,
> eyes and nose were made discordant with yes and no.]

The banners of Trajan's procession create an illusion of movement:

> . . . e l'aquile nell'oro
> sopr'esso in vista al vento si movieno. (80-81)

> [. . . and the eagles in gold above him moved visibly to the wind.]

The whole representation comes to life through the awakened sensory apparatus; it is, Dante says, a kind of "visibile parlare" (95). So too, the chant he hears go by, in the next terrace, is more than music; just as the "painting" which he sees within the depths of his enraptured imagination can also be *heard*, indicating the threshold of another form of art.

There can be no doubt that in these suggestive representations of virtue and vice Dante was doing much more than establishing religious and moral *exempla*. He was, in effect, paying a last, glorious tribute to the fine arts, to the most beautiful of all human achievements, before entering upon the superhuman experience of the *Paradiso*. His intention is made perfectly clear, I believe, at the end of the series just reviewed, where the entire progression is climaxed by a beautiful exaltation of poetry, the most immaterial, most nearly divine, of all the fine arts. Already in Canto XXIV, Bonagiunta da Lucca had recalled Dante's lovely poem, "Donne ch'avete intelletto d'amore" (51) and had provided the occasion for a review of Dante's *ars poetica*; in Canto XXVI, the last of the terraces of penitents, Guido Guinizelli and Arnaud Daniel, the two great masters of Dante, are immortalized in the poetry of their disciple. And, when human art as such is on the verge of exhausting itself, when "artificial" beauty gives way to the flawless "natural" beauty of the Earthly Paradise, Dante sums up the entire progression with his grandest and final tribute to worldly poetry, echoing the lines of Virgil commemorating Dido's love for Aeneas. Beyond that point lie waters as yet unexplored by human art; poetry alone — the highest of the arts — can dare to venture upon them, but it can do so successfully only by transcending itself.

The paradox is perfectly obvious, of course, and sets up powerful poetic tensions. Religion and theology threaten to absorb poetry, but they never actually do. The poetic tensions thus created are felt from the moment Dante steps into the Earthly Paradise — the threshold to the heavens of light and love. At that moment, he assumes a wholly new poetic attitude, marking the change not only by the description of a mysterious, symbolical pageant, but also by an intensification in the sensory impressions and an almost complete breakdown of descriptive language. The deserted aspect of the place, when Dante first comes upon it, the sudden appearance of the lithe, graceful figure of Matelda, alone in that place, the approach of the colorful procession and the live, allegorical "lesson" enacted before Dante's eyes all contribute to the uniqueness of the moment. Dante has reached the limits of human nature and of human moral correction; the Earthly Paradise is the condition of man before the fall — not only an inconceivable and unachievable state for man in his actual condition, but also an inexpressible one. Dante's wonder at this moment is, therefore, unique; poetically, it is described by means of a magnificent display of color, sound, and movement, which strains his perceptive faculties to their limits and suggests a variety of heightened analogies. With the appearance of Matelda, the difficulty of expression is at once apparent in the intensification of figurative language, particularly the simile.

Matelda's singing reminds Dante of Proserpine,

". . . nel tempo che perdette
la madre lei, ed ella primavera." (XXVIII, 50-51)

[". . . in the time her mother lost her, and she lost
the spring flowers."]

She approaches with the grace of a dancer:

> Come si volge, con le piante strette
> a terra ed intra se, donna che balli,
> e piede innanzi piede a pena mette. . . . (52-54)
>
> [As a lady dancing, turns with feet close to the ground
> and to each other, and hardly puts foot before foot . . . .]

She turns to Dante with modest, downcast eyes:

> . . . non altrimenti
> che vergine che gli occhi onest avvalli . . . (56-57)
>
> [. . . not otherwise than a virgin who drops her modest eyes . . . .]

And when she looks up, the love in her eyes evokes this powerful image:

> Non credo che splendesse tanto lume
>   sotto le ciglia a Venere, trafitta
>   dal figlio, fuor di tutto suo costume. (64-66)
>
> [I don't think so bright a light shone forth under
> the eyelids of Venus,
> pierced by her son, against all his wont.]

So eager is Dante to reach Matelda that the short span of water separating him from the lovely lady seems wider and more frustrating than the Hellespont was to Leander :

> più odio da Leandro non sofferse,
>   per mareggiare intra Sesto ed Abido,
>   che quel da me, perchè allor non s'aperse. (73-75)
>
> [endured not more hatred from Leander for its turbulent waves
> 'twixt Sestos and Abydos, than that did from me, because it
> opened not then.]

The similes in this canto overwhelm the imagination.[6] Dante seems to be making a deliberate effort to impress the reader with the fact that the language of conventional poetry is no longer adequate to express the experience of the Earthly Paradise. With his entrance there, Dante has moved into regions incomprehensible to fallen man, and — therefore — indescribable, except by special poetic dispensation. Significantly, it is at this moment that Beatrice makes her appearance. Her presence here (and throughout the *Paradiso*) provides Dante with the special grace or inspiration needed for the last phase of the poem.

Linguistically, the canto is especially interesting as a review of Dante's highly sophisticated style and for his insistence that conventional art is no longer sufficient for his purposes.

The appearance of Beatrice on the threshold of Heaven, her review of Dante's life and her part in it, and the new insight (and inspiration) she now brings to the poet, are enhanced by the subtle variety of poetic imagery; the importance of the canto

as the new beginning of Dante's spiritual life is beautifully reinforced on the level of language. For instance, Dante deliberately
forces the reader to recall, at this moment, the *stilnovist* conventions of the beginning of the poem and, indirectly, to measure
the distance covered since that time. Virgil says to Dante, just
before the appearance of Matelda and Beatrice:

> Mentre che vegnan lieti gli occhi belli,
>   che lagrimando a te venir mi fenno,
>   seder ti puoi . . . . (XXVII, 136-138)

> [While the glad fair eyes are coming, which weeping
>   made me come to thee, thou canst sit thee down . . . .)

The happy Beatrice about to appear is thus linked to the weeping, sorrowful Beatrice of the opening of the *Inferno*. And yet,
interestingly enough, even the earlier Beatrice, while echoing
the *stilnovist* idiom of the *Vita Nuova*, had already passed into a
larger, more profound tradition.

The familiar vocabulary is all there in *Inferno* II: the lover
is identified with the"cortese" (58, 134)[7] and the "fedele" (98),
the "donna" is"gentil" (94), the *stilnovist* sequence is suggested
in words like"crudele" (100), "duro giudizio" (96), "pietà" (106),
"pietosa" (133), "soccorso" (65), "soccorri" (194), "soccorse"
(133). But the familiar vocabulary in the new setting of the *Inferno* only heightens the change it has undergone since Dante's
earlier poetic phase. In the *Vita Nuova* it was the poet who sought
pity, who wept over the cruelty of his lovely lady and asked for
help;[8] here, instead, in the Limbo of Hell, the petitioner is
Beatrice. The lovely lady comes to plead with Virgil to help Dante,
and Virgil is — in the tradition of the courtly lover — inspired to
immediate obedience:

> "tal che di comandare io la richiesi" (54)

> ["so . . . that I prayed her to command"];

> ". . . tanto m'aggrada il tuo comandamento,
> che l'ubbidir, se già fosse, m'è tardi" (79-80)

> [. . . so grateful to me is thy command, that my obeying, were it
> done already, seems tardy."]

Dante himself is moved to exclaim:

> "Oh pietosa colei che mi soccorse,
> e tu cortcsc ch'ubbidisti tosto
> alle vere parole che ti porse!" (133-135)

> ["O compassionate she, who succoured me! and courteous
> thou, who quickly didst obey the true words she gave thee!"][9]

The *stilnovist* interview between Virgil and Beatrice is, in effect,
the resolution of the conflict described in so many of the son-

nets and *canzoni* of the *Vita Nuova*; in the opening of the *Divine
Comedy*, the lover and his beloved have reached at last a level of
mutual communication. The lady is no longer silent; the love-
dialogue heretofore impossible has now begun.

The *stilnovist* tradition of the spell-bound, obedient lover
is developed still further, at the beginning of the *Purgatorio*. Cato
remembers his liege-service to Marcia :

> "Marzia piacque tanto agli occhi miei,
> mentre ch'io fui di la . . .
> che quante grazie volse da me, fei." (*Purg.* I, 85-87)

> ["Marcia was so pleasing to mine eyes back then . . .
> that every grace she willed of me I did."]

But here again, as in the opening of the *Inferno*, the reader is
conscious of a change. The obedience exacted by Marcia's beauty
has given way to another kind of obedience, exacted by another,
more beautiful lady:

> "Ma se donna del ciel ti move e regge,
> come tu dì', non c'è mestier lusinghe:
> bastiti ben che per lei mi richegge." (91-93)

> ["But if a heavenly lady moves and directs you, as you say,
> no need is there for flattery: enough that you ask me in her
> name."]

It is no accident, therefore, that, coming to the Earthly Paradise,
the entrance to the superhuman experiences of the *Paradiso*,
Dante should have marked the moment, once again, with echoes of the *stilnovist* school,[10] enlarging the traditional implications to include a totally new situation.

The development of the earlier love tradition is emphasized by means of obvious parallels: Beatrice had come to Virgil
in Limbo to rescue Dante from the dark forest in which he had
almost lost himself; now, when she is about to appear to her
lover, he is again in a forest, alone, but this time serene and
happy instead of fearful. The muted light which impressed Virgil,
the lovely eyes dimmed by tears, even the love-sick eyes of Ve-
nus herself, are part of a consciously elaborated progression,
aimed from the beginning toward a reconstitution and enlargement of the *stilnovist* idiom, to include a totally new kind of love
experience.[11]

The appearance of Beatrice — whose face remains veiled
all through the scene — sets in motion a whole psychological and
physiological apparatus which, immediately, recalls the familiar
stilnovist language: "spirito" (*Purg.* XXX, 34), "stupor,"
"tremando," "affranto" (36), "occhi" (37), "occulta virtù" (38),
"amor," "potenza" (39), "percosse" (40), "l'alta virtù," "trafitto"

(41). Dante seems to be saying: this is where I left off in the *Vita Nuova*; let me remind you of what Beatrice meant to me at that time and how far I have come since then.[12]

The language of this canto is memorable in still other ways. The luminous air of the Earthly Paradise had already presented Dante with the first of the many problems of superimposing light on light: with the appearance of the mystic procession, "l'aer luminoso" (*Purg.* XXIX, 23) turns to"foco acceso" (34) and the figures of the pageant appear as moving candelabra and living lights — "vive luci" (62) — whose brightness lights up the waters of the river. Beatrice herself now appears clothed in the color of living flame — "vestita di color di fiamma viva" (XXX, 33). In addition, there is a curious insistence on "child" images. Side by side with the sophisticated language of the *stilnovist* tradition are charmingly naive images:

> Tosto che nella vista mi percosse
>   l'alta virtù, che già m'avea trafitto
>   prima ch'io fuor di puerizia fosse.
>
> volsimi alla sinistra col rispitto
>   col quale il fantolin corre alla mamma,
>   quando ha paura o quando egli e afflitto . . . . (XXX, 40-45)[13]

[The instant that lofty virtue struck my sight, which already had pierced me ere I was out of my boyhood, I turned to

the left with the trust with which the child runs to his mother when he is frightened or when he is afflicted . . . .]

With the image of the naive child — " prima ch'io fuor di puerizia fosse" — the biographical event which marked the culmination of Dante's early life is here brought vividly before us. The image serves, also, to convey the message that this moment at the top of Purgatory is the real beginning of Dante's *vita nuova*.[14] He is once again a child on the threshold of life. Beatrice suggests this in her account of Dante's early life,[15] in which she scolds Dante for having mistaken, in a sense, Francesca for Beatrice. It is not surprising that Dante should have wanted to mark this special moment with language which is beautifully reminiscent of the *Vita Nuova* — while suggesting, simultaneously, the "correction" and "revision" which he has made of that early life, with a new kind of imagery.[16]

This emphasis on a new poetic language comes to a culmination immediately following the two *terzine* quoted earlier. Beatrice's veiled appearance sets into motion the familiar *stilnovist* sequence: the virtue emanating from her moves Dante, as it had long before when, still a child, he had first seen her. Dante recognizes Beatrice, at this moment, not by her eyes and smile[17] but by the powerful spirit which moves out of her and strikes him dumb with love. And here he shows the full scope of his poetic versatility, by combining child images with *stilnovist* echoes and Virgilian language, assimilating to his poetic purpose a moving passage from the Aeneid, which would have told Virgil, had he been there to hear it, the whole story. The lines are a marvelous tribute to the pagan poet, as well as a measure of Dante's own powers of assimilation. "I turned," Dante says, to tell Virgil,

> "Men che dramma
> di sangue m'è rimaso, che non tremi;
> conosco i segni dell'antica fiamma."
>
> Ma Virgilio n'avea lasciati scemi
> di sè, Virgilio dolcissimo patre,
> Virgilio a cui per mia salute diè mi . . . (*Purg.* XXX, 46-51)

["Less than a drop of blood is left in me that trembleth not; I recognize the tokens of the ancient flame."

But Virgil had left us bereft of himself, Virgil sweetest father, Virgil to whom for my weal I gave me up . . .][18]

But the *stilnovist*-Virgilian-child imagery is, after all, only the stammering of the shy lover, nothing more than a prelude or introduction to the vision of the beloved. The woman herself has not yet turned or addressed herself to Dante. When she does, it is not as the *donna gentil* or the woman with *intelletto d'amore*, not as *donzella amorosa* or the modest lady with *sembianza umile* and *occhi bassi*, not as the weeping, sighing lady described by Virgil but — strange as it may seem — as some grand commander of a fleet:

> Quasi ammiraglio che in poppa ed in prora
> viene a veder la gente che ministra
> per gli altri legni, ed a ben far la incuora,
>
> in su la sponda del carro sinistra,
> quando mi volsi al suon del nome mio,
> che di necessità qui si registra,
>
> vidi la donna . . . (XXX, 58-64)

[Even as an admiral, who at stern and at bow, comes to see the folk that man the other ships, and heartens them to brave deeds,

so on the left side of the car, when I turned me at sound of my name, which of necessity here is recorded,

I saw the lady . . . .]

In the scene that follows, jewel metaphors first make their appearance, suggesting perhaps the transition from soft, natural colors to the concentrated, pure light of the *Paradiso*. Beatrice's eyes, in *Purgatorio* XXXI (116), are"smeraldi." Later, in the third canto of *Paradiso*, for example, Costanza and Piccarda will appear as almost indistinguishable reflections in clear glass or in a still, shallow pool of water, as hard to make out as a pearl on a snow-white forehead (*Par.* III, 10-16); and, still later, the Virgin Mary will be described as a lovely sapphire — "il bel zaffiro, / del quale il ciel più chiaro s'inzaffira" (*Par.* XXIII, 101-102).

The paradox of the gentle Beatrice of the sonnets and the authoritative Beatrice of the top of Purgatory is effected through a combination of sophisticated love language (drawn from the *stilnovist* tradition and Virgil) and child images. The new Beatrice has little in common with the earlier heroine of the *Vita Nuova*: she is almost cruel in her blunt exposé of Dante's earlier life, relentless in forcing Dante to humiliate himself publicly and to admit his errors, ironic in her barbed remarks to the grown man who behaved like a beardless youth, firm in insisting on the necessity for tears as an outward manifestation of repentance and purification. The delicate memory of the *stilnovist* lady, and the very conventions of that earlier image, are shattered with the appearance of the. admiral-figure whose language of authority shames Dante. Beatrice's new role is further marked by the symbolical language which she is called upon to explicate. The dark allegory of the pageant is an impressive linguistic reminder that the moment is truly a turning point in the poem; in the *Paradiso*, knowledge will come easily to Dante, through Beatrice's smiling eyes and bright smiles, but here — in territory forever lost to man, and amid natural beauties forever beyond his grasp — insight is impossible. The similes of the earlier scene thus become, in the pageant, an embodied metaphor in which one element has been totally suppressed and must be reconstructed by Beatrice.

The poetic eye, through which the eyes of reason and faith will be opened, is here initiated into the mysteries of the beatified soul by a deliberate confounding of external vision and insight, sensory and extra-sensory perception. One of the most forceful illustrations of the poetic challenge Dante assumes at this moment in the poem is the description of the three dancing nymphs who appear in the symbolical pageant, dressed in red, green, and white, respectively. What is interesting about the passage, linguistically, is the difficulty Dante intentionally puts forward in describing the "dress" of the three figures. What he sees is not really dress or color in the usual sense of the words — not "accidents" but "substances" alive with an incomprehensible power of their own. The first of the three nymphs is in red — or, rather, she is redness itself —

> . . . l'una tanto rossa
> ch'a pena fora dentro al foco nota . . . . (*Purg.* XXIX, 122-123)
> [. . . one so red, she hardly could be seen in the fire . . .]

The second is all in green, or, rather, she is *made* of green; the color seems to emanate from within :

> l'altr'era come se le carni e l'ossa
> fossero state di smeraldo fatte; (124-125)
> [the next seemed flesh and bone of emerald . . . .]

The third is like new-fallen snow:

> . . . la terza parea neve testè mossa . . .(126)
> [. . . the third seemed new-fallen snow . . . .]

The studied effort for precision emphasizes the difficulties Dante wants to put squarely before his readers; it is as if he were trying to say, Don't think of these as simply colors of dress, but as the visible manifestations of natures that are full of love, faith, and hope. These dancing nymphs — or, more precisely, dancing colors — are virtues; but mortal eyes can discern them only as colors, the outward symbols of those virtues. To heighten the sensory experience, to remind the reader that what he sees is a very inadequate expression of the reality before him, Dante thus insists on the paradox of appearance and reality, inverting the terms, so that the reality so often hidden under the appearance of things comes to the surface and destroys the illusory externals.

Throughout the closing cantos of the *Purgatorio*, Dante is consciously at work fashioning a new language for his daringly new voyage of discovery through waters which"giammai non si corse " (*Par.* II, 7). In this prelude to the magnificent vision of the *Paradiso*, the reader witnesses what is perhaps Dante's grandest display of virtuosity -a self-conscious, controlled use of figurative language, color,[19] poetic echoes, allegorical representation, and vivid symbolism, marking the impressive finale to human art and the wondering, child-like beginning of his vision of eternity. The dizzying effect of the sudden changes in style is, in a sense, the reader's first experience with the linguistic pyrotechnics he is about to witness in the journey through heavenly light.[20]

Art, in its traditional balance between intuition and expression, thus comes to an end with the appearance of the divine messenger who is herself the embodiment of divine inspiration and the source of intuitive understanding. The warning in the opening lines of the second canto of *Paradiso* is the warning of a poet conscious of a new task, of a new language to be fashioned for a new subject matter. The poetic challenge is at the root of the beautiful image at the singing skiff which draws the listener with its magic song:

> O voi, che siete in piccioletta barca,
>   desiderosi d'ascoltar, seguiti
>   retro al mio legno che cantando varca,
>
> tornate a riveder li vostri liti:
>   non vi mettete in pelago; che forse,
>   perdendo me, rimarrete smarriti. (*Par.* II, 1-6).

> [O ye, who in your little skiff, longing to hear,
> have followed on my keel that singeth on its way,
>
> turn back to your own shores; don't venture on the open sea;
> for losing me, you may be stranded.]

And, of course, this challenge is the greatest paradox of all; In insisting that the limits of art have been shattered and that the poet is about to venture into hitherto unexplored regions, Dante has left us some of the grandest poetry ever written. The gradual progression from material to immaterial art on the terraces of Purgatory and the studied difficulties of describing the condition of nature before the fall from grace represent a new chapter in the history of poetry. In thus suggesting, in the *Purgatorio*, the limits of art, Dante has left behind the most impressive testimony as to its possibilities, extending and perfecting his artistic talents, in the *Paradiso*, even as he describes the glorious absorption of poetry in religious experience, of the human word in the Word of God. [21]

NOTES

An earlier version of this essay appeared in *Italica*, XLII, 1, 1965.

1. See Francesco De Sanctis, *Antologia Critica sugli Scrittori d' Italia*, ed. Luigi Russo, 2nd edition (Firenze, 1933), p. 249: "L'Inferno ci sta in rimembranza; il paradiso ci sta in desiderio . . . ."

2. See Attilio Momigliano, *La Divina Commedia* (Firenze, 1948), p. 799 n. 94-96: "Il *Purgatorio* è una sfumata, raccolta, nostalgica giornata d'autunno: L '*Inferno* e il *Paradiso* non sono stagioni medie, ma estreme e, ciascuna a suo modo, violente. Soltanto si può dire che nel *Paradiso* si vede la vigoria dell'*Inferno* filtrata attraverso la spiritualità del *Purgatorio*: e perciò la terza cantica non si potrebbe immaginare e spiegare senza la mediazione della seconda. L'epica pienezza interiore di certi passi del *Paradiso* è il potenziamento spirituale dell'agonistica gagliardia dell'*Inferno*.

3. Momigliano, p. 359 n. 36.

4, All excerpts from the *Purgatorio* (both Italian and English) are from the Carlyle-Wicksteed edition, *The Temple Classics*, (London, 1941). I have, in some instances, made minor revisions.

5. T. S. Eliot, "Three Voices of Poetry," *On Poetry and Poets* (New York, 1961), p. 96. See also; Anne and Henry Paolucci, eds. *Hegel on Tragedy* (New York, 1962), pp. xxii-xxiv. (Reprinted 2001, Griffon House Publications.)

6. Cf. Irma Brandeis, *The Ladder of Vision* (New York, 1961), p. 131: "The metaphors of the *Inferno* are indeed few, its similes largely designed 'to make us see more definitely the scene,' but the *Purgatorio* is quite another story. Not only are the *Purgatorio's* metaphors numerous but in the majority of them visual clarity and interpretative insight are there together (with a marked purpose of 'adding to what you see '), while in a few (the most striking), visible likeness drops away in favour of insight."

7. *Inferno*, Carlyle-Wicksteed Edition, *The Temple Classics*, (London, 1920).

8. There are passages in Dante's earlier works where the lady shows some compassion — e.g. the lovely lady at the window (*Vita Nuova, Son.* XIX) — but there is no real "dialogue" on equal terms, such as Dante is introducing here for the first time.

9. Beatrice has, in fact, come to her lover's aid in anticipation of his own request. The actual request that moves her comes from a heavenly source, as she explains to Virgil: "Donna è gentil nel Ciel, chc si compiange" (94); "Lucia, nimica di ciascun crudele" (100); "Al mondo non fur mai persone ratte / a far lor pro, nè a fuggir lor danno, / com'io, dopo cotai parole fatte . . ." (109-111).

10. See Momigliano's notes on Dante's use of *stilnovist* language in the *Inferno* and *Purgatorio*, especially p. 16 n. 62-63: ". . . la Commedia si presenta come la continuazione e la conclusione dell'autobiografia poetica della *Vita Nuova* . . . ." See also his notes to *Purg.* XXX, 34-39, 37-42, 40-42 (p. 493).

11. Victoria Ocampo, *De Francesca a Beatrice* (Madrid, 1928), p. 123, sums up the transition from the earlier *stilnovist* language to the new descriptive language of the *Commedia* as a transition from *eyes* and *mouth* to loving *glances* and *smiles*: "Beatriz responde a la súplica de Dante, no con la boca y los ojos, sino con la sourisa y la mirada: alma de la boca, alma de los ojos, cuya posesión material es imposible."

12. For a discussion of the relationship between the psychological and physiological apparatus of the *stilnovist* poetry, see A. Paolucci, "Ezra Pound and D. G. Rossetti as Translators of Guido Cavalcanti," *The Romanic Review*, December, 1960, pp. 256-267, especially pp. 266-267.

13. For other "child" images, see Dante's description of his fear at having to cross the wall of fire separating him from Beatrice, and Virgil's attempt to get him to cross by minimizing the obstacles — exactly as one would do with a stubborn child: *Purg.* XXVII, 20-42, especially ll. 41-42 ("il nome / che nella mente sempre mi *rampolla*"): also ll. 44-45 ("indi sorrise / come al *fanciul* si fa ch'è vinto al *pome*"). [Italics are my own.] See also, in this connection. E. Sanguineti's references to the "fantolin"

images, "Canto XXX, "*Letture Dantesche. Purgatorio,* ed Giovanni Getto (Firenze, 1958), pp. 616-617.

14. Cf, R. Labusquette, *Les Beatrices* (Paris, 1921), p. 575, n. 1.

15. See especially ll. 115-145.

16. This transition is further markcd by Beatrice's reference to Dante's journey up to that point.

17. Beatrice, as we have pointed out, remains veiled until after the pageant.

18. *Aencid,* IV, 23: "Agnosco veteris vestigia flammae," Just before this utterance, when Beatrice first comes on the scene, she is welcomed with a shower of flowers and another line from Virgil: "Manibus o date lilia plenis!" (*Purg.* XXX, 21).

19. The description of the Earthly Paradise, and particularly the mystic procession, is the only passage in the entire poem where Dante indulges in "word painting." Color is certainly not the dominant feature of the *Divine Comedy*: the *Inferno*, even at its bcst, is a gray twilight region; the *Paradiso* is blinding light; the *Purgatorio* alone has touches of fresh, bright color — and nowhere are they so striking and so numerous as in the Earthly Paradise.

20. Erich Auerbach has thus enumerated Dante's variety of poetic voices: ". . . the Provençal poets and the *stil nuovo*, the language of Virgil and of Christian hymns, the French epic and the Umbrian Lauds, and terminology of the philosophical schools and the incomparable wealth of the popular vernacular which here for the first time found its way into a poem in the lofty style . . .", *Dante, Poet of the Secular World,* tr. Ralph Manheim (Chicago, 1961), p. 97.

21. The poet's difficulties in attempting to describe such an experiencc have been beautifully recorded, in English, by Coleridge in"Kubla Khan." But it is Shelley, of all the English lyric poets, who perhaps comes closest to Dante in the deliberate attempt to suggest, through poetry, an expcrience which cannot be wholly contained by poetry. (See especially his "Hymn to Intellectual Beauty," where the power of life and inspiration is described in Platonic terms which take the mind far from material "reality" and force it to focus on an internal reality of spirit and thought.) One of the best examples of dramatic poetry exceeding the limits of art is Shakespeare's *King Lear*, where — as A. C. Bradley has notcd —"pity and terror. carried perhaps to the extreme limits of art, are so blended with a sense of law and beauty that we feel, at last, not depression and much less despair, but a consciousness of greatness in pain, and of solemnity in the mystery we cannot fathom." *Shakespearean Tragedy* (London 1950), p. 279.

Chapter 21

Arthur Miller's
Death of a Salesman:
The Tragic Hero Redefined

On June 24, 1984, the *New York Times* carried a review by Norton Houghton of Arthur Miller's book-length account of the spring 1983 Beijing production of *Death of a Salesman,* which the playwright had been invited to direct.[1] Miller's record of the enthusiastic mainland Chinese response to *Salesman* never made the best-seller list (Bob Woodward's *Wired* was the No.1 nonfiction entry for that week — a vivid reminder that politics is often more gripping than fiction or drama); but Miller was understandably gratified by what could be interpreted as a resurgence of interest in his work. A less sanguine view might instead interpret the excitement over the Beijing production as a curiously delayed reaction to a play written over four decades ago, when the polarization of economic interests in our country and the world — the legacy of the Great Depression — was the Large Theme. For the Chinese, *Salesman* confirmed their unyielding view about capitalist oppression and the victimized individual struggling for place — a sign not so much of Miller's revitalized reputation as a reflection of Chinese reactionary thinking and their unchanging attitudes toward what the capitalist West represents.

The Chinese success of *Salesman* also reminds us that Miller still sees himself in the role of political and social reformer and still enjoys that role immensely, even though the conditions and realities that made that role impressive in the 1940s no longer exist in the same way. Still at least two generations behind in their political ideology and practice, the Chinese saw in *Salesman* the timely expression of their own dated reactionary opposition to capitalist ideals (recent events in China confirm their hard-line tactics when opposition is voiced in any way). The Beijing *Salesman* worked for the Chinese just fine. And where his "message" does not elicit the same response and enthusiasm of the 1940s, Miller takes on new roles in the public forum.[2]

Critical assessment of Miller's achievement is still ambiguous. At a distance of forty years or more, drama critics (or, more precisely "scholar-critics" as Robert F. Moss calls them)[3] like Eric Bentley, Robert Brustein, John Simon, and Richard Gilman, pretty much agree that Miller's "chief felony appears to be his uncompromising commitment to what he calls 'social drama,' by which he merely means a work that demonstrates the inter-penetration of man and society, with special attention to the welts that the human community can raise on the back of its residents." Such theater or art, for these critics, is "automatically rancid," "left over from the thirties," nothing but "old dramas of social protest by people . . . [who] attributed evil to an oppres-sive economic system instead of to human nature."[4] Brustein sees *Incident at Vichy* as a return to the theater of the thirties, "a period the author seems never to have left." Bentley calls *The Crucible* "a political melodrama, a 'conflict between the wholly guilty and the wholly innocent.'" Moss himself sums up the "com-pulsion" that seems to have alienated a certain class of critics as a "compulsion to bring people to the judgment seat, to require moral responsibility from them."

In spite of the scholar-critics, Miller's plays — and *Salesman* especially — have sold very well, one reason being, no doubt, the use of his texts in most drama courses in colleges throughout the country. The question really must be, finally: *Will Miller's plays survive as dramatic vehicles beyond their obvious value as expli-cators of an important period in history?* The answer seems to be, yes, of course. Miller's work — in spite of often polarized posi-tions on social and political realities — is not what Ionesco calls "one-dimensional." (The possible exception is *Incident at Vichy*.) If it were, we would not still be reading and writing about his plays.

Still, Miller's fall from grace in recent years has been at-tributed by some critics to his insistence on a dated theme. And where Miller departs from that theme, as in *After the Fall*, he seems to be less interesting, less compelling. Allan Wallach sums up his review of the revival of the play in October 1984 in the headline: "Well-Acted Wordiness." *The Creation of the World and Other Business* (1973), in spite of optimistic advance notices and articles, lasted twenty performances; and *The American Clock* (1980) did not fare much better. Even Wallach, who maintains perhaps the best balance between failings that must be noted and a dedicated allegiance to Miller, wrote about *The American Clock*: "It's time to ask whether [Miller] isn't written out on his favorite subject."[5] "I am always looking for America," Miller wrote when (as he put it) "masquerading as a journalist," in August 1972, he attended the Democratic convention. The trouble is that the America he is looking for, his image of it, has long since been appraised and cataloged. The enthusiasm of discovery is no longer there in the same terms — except possibly for the Chinese in Beijing.

Perhaps more lasting, in a larger way, are Miller's *All My Sons* and *A View from the Bridge* — works that in their own ways reinforce a literary tradition rather than a political view. In the first, Miller has provided our age with an impressive modern version of something approximating Greek tragedy (a topic on which he has written and continues to comment with vigor); in the second, he has given us a truly moving drama of human frailties and emotional conflicts that far outweigh whatever social message the play may carry. From this perspective, *Death of a Salesman* is less compelling although perhaps more idiosyncratic in its internalization of a trapped soul struggling in existential terms for some kind of resolution.

Miller's Greek Tragedy/Greek 'Hero': Misdirections?

In the late 1960s, as a Fulbright lecturer in American drama at the University of Naples, I had occasion to speak on Arthur Miller both in the university context and in public lectures that took me on tours of Austria and Italy. Even then, the most important aspect of Miller's work that seemed to merit critical focus was his insistence on promoting the notion of the traditional *tragic hero* in a modern context. For him Willy Loman was a tragic figure, and the forces that were responsible for crushing him were in some way related to those absolute values that the playwright has adopted as his single and major theme throughout: the oppressive and destructive economic system, the absolutes of capitalist big business, and the struggling poor. In my lectures on Miller, I stressed the tragic elements in his plays — especially (as has already been mentioned) the impressive dichotomy portrayed in *All My Sons* and the less apparent but equally compelling opposition in *A View from the Bridge*. It cannot be denied that Miller has deliberately set out to portray the little man, or the modern middle-class bourgeois victim of the system, as a tragic figure, but I also made sure the students recognized the fact that any connection with Greek tragedy had to be regarded as a loosening of definitions, a poetic image rather than a valid critical point.

Without undermining Miller's insistence on the tragic — after all, the playwright's intentions certainly must be accepted as such, and in Miller's case he has repeatedly made the point — we can nevertheless examine the validity of his notion in a context that throws light on its limits as well as on its positive aspects. Miller is not the first to suggest that the old idea of a tragic hero who is in a special category and position, who represents an entire people and nation, who brings down with his fall much else, must be expanded to include modern types like Willy Loman. Still, the transition and the method of expanding the idea must be approached with care if we are to retain the Aristotelian distinctions in a valid context. (Aristotle himself, I'm sure, would have been the first to insist — had he lived later — that his conclusions about Greek tragedy could not be applied to modern drama.)

In my university classes, Miller was received with enthusiasm. His work was familiar to many of the students (quite a number of Italian translations of his plays were already available at that time, both in single-work texts and in collected volumes of more than one work); and, in spite of the limited availability of American drama and theater critics in Italian translation, students were able to discuss Miller's plays well, since those works constituted part of the familiar tradition of realistic drama. As part of that tradition, Miller's plays drew intelligent response both in academic and public lectures — better response than, say, the plays of Edward Albee, whose innovations and paradoxical stage techniques were at the time difficult to assess, unfamiliar, strange, and went counter to an established stage conventions.

By insisting on the "tragic," Miller ensured his common man a status far beyond that of the usual realistic protagonist. He saw his plays as modern confrontations in the Greek style, his emphatic themes as absolutes in a modern context, his protagonists as embodiments of an entire community. The question is: Are such correspondences valid? In the democratization of the modern spirit, where the individual becomes a law unto himself, an idiosyncratic absolute who answers — dangerously, at times — only to himself, where values are no longer divine dicta beyond question and demanding total obedience, where divine edicts give way to laws based on community values (fidelity, honor, family, love, friendship, loyalty, etc.); in such a "translated" world, the hero inevitably takes on the Socratic ambiguity that finds resolution not outside but only and exclusively within himself.

Miller's idea of tragedy, especially as it applies to his own plays, is inexorably bound with his overriding concern with justice. The lines of guilt and innocence must be clearly defined, he has insisted time and again — even though critics like Eric Bentley have taken him to task for what appears to be a simplistic and non-dramatic principle. For Miller, right and wrong are always clear; blame can never be ambiguous.

For the Greeks, on the other hand, personal guilt or innocence was not the point at all, we should recall. Justice was not a simple matter of right or wrong defined in conventional morality or in the accepted legislation of a political community. Miller-type justice, it must be said, was never a consideration in the *Antigone*, for example — not even in *Oedipus Rex* or *Agamemnon*. The chain of events of *Agamemnon*, for example, suggest at first a kind of guilt-punishment equation; but a closer look demolishes that simplistic notion, for Clytemnestra, herself guilty of murder and adultery, is also seen as a victim. And even Orestes cannot be acquitted in human terms as having exacted no more than simple justice. For the Greeks, the dilemma was always awesome in that man and woman were seen trapped in circumstances of their doing and also fated by the gods. The superhuman dimension made all the difference. It will never again surface in later drama — even Shakespearean tragedy shifts to a notion of internal redemption made possible by the Christian dispensation.

The Greeks understood well enough that human beings are individually responsible not only for what they *do* but also for what each suffers to be done *to* him or her. Oedipus — despite the energetic efforts by critics down the centuries to free him of all guilt and responsibility for his actions — openly assumes the blame and passes judgment on himself. That reality must be accepted if Greek tragedy is to be properly understood. The word blame in fact, as applied to the Greek hero, must be carefully distinguished from Miller's use of it. The Greek tragic experience is the medium for greater insight into man's limitations and the all-powerful gods, whose will is not always clear to us. The outcome is profounder insight into *freedom as necessity* — the absolute assertion of the will and full acceptance of the notion of divine omnipotence.

Miller's plays not only ignore the profound paradox of human freedom pitted against all-powerful gods and an inexorable fate but depict, in fact, the values of a community or people as absolute and incontestable. *Human* values, though often in contradiction with man-made laws and traditions, are held up as absolutes; those who transgress such laws are clearly guilty. Punishment and blame, therefore, follow in this view of tragedy; and justice is never ambiguous. The paradoxical question that surfaces at the end of every Greek tragedy is missing from Miller's plays; never does the Miller hero rise above his guilt to assert, at the same time, the righteousness of his "gods" and his responsibility for opposing their will — even when the hero's opposition was in the cause of freedom, as in the case of Oedipus.

Willy Loman is a burned-out salesman who alternately lashes out at the people around him as the agents responsible for his lack of success and commiserates with himself in the isolation of his self-pity. The culprit seems to be the system that produced him and locked him in, the economic realities that trap people like Willy Loman in a grinding process in which the individual is either made inhuman in his dealings with others or is crushed completely. Miller's *Salesman* defies all efforts to compare it to anything resembling Greek tragedy. To speak of the large human tragedy, the existential vacuum of life, in order to justify assigning guilt and blame simply will not work. All good theater evokes large human sympathies, and Miller's plays are no exception. They simply cannot be compared with Greek tragedy in any close reading. *Salesman* is a play about a man who, like so many of us, looks back hopelessly at his life, measures his accomplishments against his dreams, and comes out a loser. That is a human equation but not a tragic one — certainly not in the Greek sense.

In true modern fashion, Miller stresses the psychological facets of that human self-confrontation, the tensions produced within the individual whose instincts want to salvage things, and the difficult efforts at explanation and interpretation when he confronts them. The emotional strains produced by these psychological tremors constitute the power of Miller's plays. Aside from the "messages" and the efforts to "redeem" his priorities in Greek tragic terms, Miller's work is modern in every way — certainly in the penetration of character and the multifaceted aspects of the tortured soul struggling to redeem himself and his humanity.

When the multifaceted character is undermined in modern drama, when a play becomes a vehicle for a given message, for a cause, for a self-indulgent analytical experiment, dramatic balance is lost. Miller's plays have been uneven in this respect, and he has been criticized severely for staging matters that might better have been published as op-ed articles in the *New York Times*. But the playwright has never veered from his commitment to causes large and small that he believes in and wants others to recognize and accept in the same way. In the preface to the Italian edition of his plays, Miller insists on this mission for the playwright, noting that a character takes on dramatic significance only in his assumption of a cause — a challenge to be accepted or rejected. In his eyes, the more concentrated the purpose, the greater impact the play will have. And — echoing in his own way the lesson of Oedipus — he insists that before a person acts he must make every effort to confront the full implications of his actions. Life is meaningful only after such an effort has been made.

Unlike most modern playwrights (with the possible exception of Eugene O'Neill), Miller deliberately stresses the Greek notion of tragedy in his plays, trimming it to suit his dramatic needs. He himself, moreover, often exceeds the limits of his role as playwright, inserting his voice into the action as social and political arbiter, the voice of justice. Here, too, he departs radically from the Greek experience. His inspiration is more the "ruthless criticism of everything existing" that has long inspired social criticism in Western Europe and the United States. It is a legacy of Hegelian-Marxist humanism.[6]

Building on Aristotle: Hegel's Theory of Drama

While always showing the profoundest respect for the Aristotelian analysis of dramatic art, Hegel, in his lectures on the subject, applied Aristotle's insights to the study of a vastly expanded corpus of great dramatic works, including oriental drama as well as the crowning achievements of Shakespeare in comedy and tragedy. In his tirelessly comprehensive treatment of global drama, Hegel not only defines and distinguishes the concepts themselves but also — to his immense credit — provides his readers with examples that are limpid and unforgettable as proof of the applicability of his carefully worked-out arguments.

A. C. Bradley, the noted Shakespearean critic, was (though few have really understood this or are even aware of it) thoroughly Hegelian in his thinking and criticism — a subject certainly deserving of careful study (long overdue!). Bradley opens his provocative essay, "Hegel's Theory of Tragedy," in *Oxford Lectures on Poetry*,[7] with this stunning tribute to the German romantic philosopher and aesthetician, whose theory he proceeds to explain, illustrate, extend and criticize in one vital point, which for years has misled scores of critics:

> Since Aristotle dealt with tragedy, and, as usual, drew the main features of his subject with those sure and simple strokes which no later hand has rivalled, the only philosopher who has treated it in a manner both original and searching is Hegel.[8]

Aristotle was always in Hegel's large view of the subject he dealt with; but it is to his credit that he formulated a new theory for modern tragedy — particularly Shakespearean tragedy — that stands on its own. In addition, his thorough knowledge of every aspect of the Aristotelian discussion enabled him to review it from an exciting and fully consistent point of view, both in its applications to the Greek stage and as a vital base for his own insights into the modern form.

GREEK TRAGEDY. Hegel distinguished not one but several types of confrontations, conflicts, oppositions, modes of tragedy, and reconciliations — the result of much careful reading of the original Greek texts. He singles out for discussion three major types of conflict (reminding us that each has many variations). The first, in which the nature of Greek tragedy comes through in stark fashion, where the protagonists embody a certain absolute right and defend it to the death, is the kind found in Sophocles's *Antigone*: there, unyielding divine laws are in opposition on a collision course. The dilemma that results is awe-inspiring and terrible. In this kind of conflict, the mutually justified claims are reinstated as part of an inviolate whole only when the characters, who embody the conflicting aspects of that dilemma, are both destroyed. Whatever sense of waste we experience in this kind of ending where the best among us must sacrifice their lives is mitigated by the grand spectacle of positive forces once more in position, the balance of divine and human prerogatives once more established.

Hegel notes that, in the Greek confrontation, the spokesperson of one absolute claim recognizes simultaneously the opposite claim and its supporter. Antigone recognizes Creon's right to punish her for insisting on mercy for her brother, who has betrayed Thebes, just as Creon — in the dilemma of his struggle as uncle and ruler — is mortified by Antigone's plight (and his son's sacrifice) while ultimately upholding the claim of the nation to protect its people. For the Greeks, both claims were unanswerable in themselves, both divinely ordained. There is no guilt and innocence in this context — except perhaps in the subtle notion (analogous to Original Sin) that somewhere along the line a whole race, an entire people, has been singled out to suffer, for reasons not always altogether clear or acceptable in clear terms, the awesome dilemma of a conflict in which both sides are destroyed. In Sophocles' play, it is Antigone who assumes the grand and typical Greek tragic posture in her unyielding insistence on maintaining the familial ties and all that they demand. There is never a moment of doubt in her, although she feels throughout the horror of what is to come. (Perhaps some measure of what the Greeks felt in such confrontations can be found in Shakespeare's history sequence — *Richard II* to *Henry V* — where the divine authority to rule is questioned but never undermined and the strength, power, and leadership of the usurper is never justified.)

In the stark and open confrontation here described, the effect of catharsis is felt most powerfully. The horror of a leader tragically destroyed is felt by all those who follow him through *pity* and *fear*: fear of such a tragic fate, but fear felt at a safe distance, for most people are not in a position to make choices that will result in their tragic fall; pity for the fallen hero as a fellow human being, the emotion that brings the fallen hero and the spectator close again. Through the paradoxical oscillation of fear and pity, therefore, the Greeks found the genial mechanism by which tragedy could be felt as a truly universal experience.

A second type of conflict, Hegel tells us, is found in *Oedipus Rex*, where the confrontation is not as clear as in a play like *Antigone*. In this second type of conflict, one of the terms of the tragic equation is obscured, hidden, only gradually revealed in the actual progression from ignorance to illumination. The certainty of Oedipus, who trusts his rationality and lives by it, his grand insistence on measuring phenomena in an intellectual and sensible way, raises him to heroic status in modern eyes (not the least result of which has been the confusion of critics who would like to insist that it is this quality alone that makes Oedipus a tragic figure); but the play is clearly an oscillation between two contradictory poles, and the rationality of Oedipus is at every turn undermined by his moments of fear, when he calls upon the soothsayers and the reading of omens and flights of birds, and so forth. In this juxtaposition of grand arrogance and human failings, the play gradually spirals to revelation. Seen in this manner, *Oedipus Rex* reveals the same awesome opposition as *Antigone*; the absolute assertion of man's superiority through reason is destroyed by the absolute assertion (hidden at first) of the divine imperative that already had spelled out the king's destiny and that he himself *acknowledged* from the very beginning, in his effort to flee that destiny. In terms of modern preferences, *Oedipus Rex* will always rank high, for it reinforces in magnificent terms the intellect of man, exalting him as the divine arbiter of his fate.

A third type of conflict is one in which psychological penetration of character brings the Greek exemplars closer to our modern drama. The best plays in this category include the drama of vacillating consciences embodied in the major heroes and heroines of Euripides. But Hegel's own preference, among the Greek tragedies, is indeed *Antigone*.

Reconciliations and dramatic resolutions in Greek tragedy, Hegel tells us, are just as many and varied as the conflicts themselves. In *Antigone*, the outcome is dictated entirely by the nature of the mutually destructive absolute claims — there is no other possible solution but the death of the protagonists in order to restore the balance necessary to life. In *Oedipus at Colonus*, the illuminated rational man has found his peace and is welcomed among those favored by the gods. Death is not always the best or only resolution, even in Greek tragedy. And, as we shall see, modern drama — because of its special nature — can avoid the self-destructive kind of tragic end we witness in so many Greek tragedies.

MODERN DRAMA. Included in modern drama, for Hegel, is modern tragedy and the various forms of drama in which community values and democratic attitudes prevail. The only form of modern *tragedy* is Shakespearean — nothing after that fits the definition as he spells it out. Modern drama is a totally new kind of theater, in which divine prerogatives have become man-made laws. Of course, for those interested in tragedy, Hegel's discussion of Shakespeare's works is a provocative and convincing basis for discussion of later drama. Shakespeare could still write tragedy because the Renaissance, as the turning point in modern history when man began to assert his human claims over divine absolutes, could still accept the delicate balance of human and divine prerogatives. For Hegel, the evolution of spirit was bound to turn man to self-validation and self-deliberation in the Socratic terms that both threatened and exalted the modern spirit.

In Shakespeare, the claims are dramatized in a rich and colorful form in which the idiosyncrasies of the individual are indulged within the tragic fabric of the play. The tragic confrontation is on the whole less open and focuses more on the characters themselves than on the awesome destructive action in which claims are denied and reasserted. Aristotle was perfectly right in saying that, in Greek tragedy, *plot*, made up of actions, was the single most important element of the play; and Bradley was also correct in stating that in Shakespearean tragedy the focus shifts and action becomes a function of *character*. The logic behind this is discussed at great length and in many different contexts by Hegel; and, in the large canvas of his philosophy, one can well understand the movement from an almost symbolic adherence to the slow unraveling of themes connected with the place of man in the universe and the utterly compelling dedication to portray human character in all its rich details. (See, for instance, the often-cited example of Shakespeare's Mercutio in *Romeo and Juliet* — a character so appealing in wit, actions, and agility of mind that its author had to "kill him off" to save the play.)

The difference is the movement from the perfect balance of sensuous and ideal that characterized all Greek art at its best, including dramatic art, away from the classical balance of *informing principle* and *receptive matter* (which produces the purest beauty and is most completely realized in the plastic arts, especially classical sculpture). The new direction was to all aspects of man's evolving self-awareness, the psychological culmination of which Hegel characterizes as *romantic*.

From that perspective, modern art (starting first in architecture, sculpture, and painting, and then progressing through poetry and music) becomes a process of constant *internalization* of the productive aesthetic experience. Where *words* are the artistic medium, the process is a steady internalization of the voices of poetry. In our own time, looking ahead with Hegel, Gottfried Benn, and T .S. Eliot as our guides, we may say that this *romantic* phase of evolving art finds its purest expression in the drama of the *lyric* voice of poetry. Shakespeare's dialogue becomes absurdist monologue.

Thus, for Hegel, the *classical* beauty of Sophocles' *Antigone* is transcended in the *romantic* beauty of Shakespeare's art, before the lyric internalization of modern drama characteristic of the "beautiful soul" (*schöne Seele*) turns into the playwright's voice, his dramatic monologue. Anyone who reads Hegel with care will soon realize that, for him, the best example of high tragedy ever written was not *Antigone* (as A. C. Bradley misleadingly seems to suggest) but Shakespeare's *Hamlet*. In that play, Hegel sees (as he sees in the protagonists of *Romeo and Juliet, Julius Caesar*, etc.) the articulate voice of our self-determined, Socratic spirit, dangerous and sublime at once, with its perilous attainment of self-conscious identity through ruthless examination and re-examination of all that is rational and irrational, human and divine in us.

Shakespeare is at the turning point in history, still asserting the divine claims and values by which man must live while exalting the human spirit in all its grand complexities. The *schöne Seele*, the Socratic voice that sifts right from wrong, is beautifully present in Shakespearean tragedy, and in his vision of tragedy Shakespeare can still hold the paradox together. But a new powerful element enters into Shakespearean tragedy and gives it a unique character: *Christianity* .With redemption made possible from within, the tragic hero can come to terms with himself and God in him.

For that reason, Hegel explains, modern tragedy (one must always read *Shakespearean* tragedy) need not have a destructive resolution. The protagonist in Shakespeare is always ready within himself to make adjustments to his fate. And, what is all-compelling is not the outcome itself of Shakespearean tragedy but the manner in which the protagonist approaches it. Since character is indeed the focal point in modern tragedy, the action must be seen as a function of the multifaceted personality and not as a rigorous confrontation of values in which actors assume masks and speak as disembodied voices asserting particular claims. In other words: The death of Hamlet (in this context, at any rate) was not altogether necessary — certainly not as predictable or dramatically motivated as the death of Antigone or Oedipus Rex. In later drama, Hegel emphasizes, all such resolutions can be avoided: Hamlet's death (or Romeo's) indeed appears to be a waste in a way that Antigone's is not.

With modern plays since Shakespeare, the closest we come to Greek or Shakespearean tragedy is drama that upholds community values and hopes. The heroic figures of the past who are a law unto themselves give way to the lawmaker and the community leaders who uphold what has been agreed upon. The values cherished are therefore of another kind — friendship, honor, love, and so forth — all of which find their expression and dramatic power in the familiar oppositions of everyday life. The best examples are the plays of Schiller, Goethe, and Racine.

Molière, as compared with Shakespeare, gives us a reduced kind of comedy, a lesser form in that humor takes on a sharp personal edge directed against the master or the husband or the magistrate, whereas the humor of Aristophanic as well as Shakespearean comedy exposes the excesses in attitudes and habits without demeaning the individual (Falstaff, etc.). Humor very often turns into farce in modern drama.

Because in our day (he says, writing in the first decade of the nineteenth century), we seem to have exhausted the possibilities of self-conscious determination (helped to a great extent by the democratization of institutions that have brought the individual into intellectual and political independence), art appears to be on the verge of *transcending itself.*

The phrase "art transcending itself" for many years was taken lightly by critics — certainly it was rarely understood. Today, with the revolution effected by Pirandello and the dramatists of the absurd, we can easily grasp the genial implications of that statement. Having been exposed to the theater of non-communication (Beckett, Albee, Ionesco, Pinter, etc.) and the new stage conventions in which action does not move in predictable intention/result, language does not measure statement, character is fragmented states of being rather than organic personality, theme is not message or reform but something each of us must retranslate in the viewing and reading of a play.

Having come this far into the new age of theater, we can reexamine both the present forms of drama and those of the past with tremendous new insight into the distinctions Hegel and Aristotle have set out for us. In the Hegelian context, the plays of Miller do indeed fit well as excellent examples of modern drama in which a people, a nation, a race reiterates its most fundamental beliefs against threats from within and without the community Large values are translated into laws that can be grasped in all their implications by the community; and the measure of heroic action is the way in which the protagonist responds to the claims of his people, his race, his community, his nation.

Death of a Salesman: *Reclaiming the Dramatic Territory*

Having reviewed very briefly the important Hegelian definitions of tragedy and modern drama, one can more easily assess Miller's work — especially *Death of a Salesman.* As I mentioned earlier, *All My Sons* and *A View from the Bridge* (the first, especially) have some interesting aspects that suggest a modern-type tragedy along the lines just discussed. *All My Sons* not only poses a confrontation that appears to be a dilemma — Joe Keller's manufacture of defective parts in order to keep his factory open, not lose business, and keep his family provided for (although this kind of conflict cannot bear too close a scrutiny in the traditional sense of absolute values in collision) — but also has the kind of spiraling toward terrible truths, a sense of nemesis and doom, a closing in that targets the free agent as victim found in Greek tragedy. The play is, in fact, an effective medium for teaching the fundamentals of Greek or classical tragedy through a modern play. (A typical cluster for teaching the evolution of tragedy into modern drama might be *All My Sons, Antigone,* and *Richard II,* in that order, with the contemporary work — the most accessible — first.) *A View from the Bridge* is especially effective in its sense of impending disasters (again, nemesis at work), terrible truths coming to light and offending the "gods" of social mores, propriety, whatever it is we wish to substitute for the Greek terms. In other words, there are elements in some of Miller's plays that are strongly reminiscent of Greek tragedy, but to insist that the pathos of the protagonist automatically makes him a tragic figure in the Greek sense is a mistake. Certainly it is misleading to promote that notion with regard to *Death of a Salesman.*

In *Salesman* Miller dramatizes for us, in his familiar realistic mode, the final phase of a life that, while remaining the same, has slipped behind. In Willy's self-conscious effort to assess his total worth, in his empty hopes and last-ditch efforts to pick up again and make things go his way, we grasp in an immediate and recognizable tapestry the vanity of life and man's futile effort to escape the consequences of his failures. There is much love around Willy, but for him the undemanding love of his wife, Linda, and the frustrated affection displayed in contradictory highs and lows by his sons, Biff and Happy, are not enough to give him some measure of peace. He must still try to make up for what he has not given them in the past, for what he cannot give them now or later.

To satisfy this obsessive need to remain the same in circumstances that no longer can support him as he was before, he destroys all the good things around him — love, trust, affection, loyalty. He isolates himself in his grief and indulges in it. On the surface, his obsessive need for recognition among his peers, for maintaining his status and equating that with respect and success, is the kind of excess that might be called a tragic flaw. Still, Willy has no compelling purpose or decision to make — not in *tragic* terms, at any rate. His suicide was the final expression of a distorted view of life.

Salesman (like *After the Fall*) tries to bridge the gap between the old realism and something new by applying stage gimmicks reminiscent of O'Neill's. To our American audiences, who (if John Gassner is to be taken seriously) are still in a state of "protracted adolescence," these innovations had great appeal. The split levels and telescoping of time in *Salesman* bring together in sharp juxtaposition what is meaningful in the past and present, allowing Eisensteinian superimpositions to provide windows into the minds and hearts of the protagonists. Interpretations are thus made easier, the parallels lead us to conclusions, and the characters have a chance to wear a number of masks in their several roles. All of this makes for an interesting departure from traditional stage conventions; and in the case of *Salesman* (which first appeared in 1949), it enabled audiences and critics alike to hail Miller with the genuine excitement of discovery.

Of course, as we said, O'Neill had already tried his hand at such gimmicks — shrinking rooms, superimposition of past and present, splintered psychological voices, Pirandellian masks, even the most obvious allegory in *Mourning Becomes Electra*, where the playwright deliberately uses the structures of Greek tragedy as a given and translates his own dramatic action to accord with the ancient model.

Earlier, Pirandello had shown the way — but, in his case, the innovations are woven into the fabric of the play in ways that suggest an *organic* unity of form and matter that almost defies close analysis. Pirandello's stage novelties are never superimposed on a play as an after-thought. The mask-on-mask, image-within-image techniques of his "theater plays," the infinite progression of actors rehearsing in their roles, coming out of their roles, assuming new roles ineffectively, working toward greater realism in the roles; of actors playing not roles but characters training and directing the other set of actors to play the characters, watching and interrupting at every turn because the actors playing the characters are not reading lines to the characters' satisfaction — these innovations cannot be taken out of the play without destroying everything else about it. It was, in fact, Pirandello who first showed the way in this area; among us, the only playwright who has continued to use and develop Pirandellian stage innovations is Edward Albee.[9]

In his use of such innovations, Miller has provided a welcome dimension to what might have been a static and repetitive play. The telescoping of time, juxtaposition of places, the variety of voices and masks all help to make *dramatic* what is a rather uneventful present. Such innovations have indeed given a kind of Pirandellian intensity to the eternal moment, fragmented into its many components. Just as important, I think, they have jolted audiences into greater receptivity in the theater. There is no doubt that such innovations helped to make *Salesman* a success among American and European audiences.

The stage techniques described helped dramatize economically and effectively (as in *After the Fall*) the personal reminiscing in which the characters of *Salesman* rummage in their memories for signs of lingering hope and life. The play is, in fact, about the past. The melodramatic ending seems almost detached from the rest of the play. The lasting impact of the action is provided by the splintered insights into what might have been or was briefly. Although, in one sense, Willy's suicide is a fitting conclusion to a series of events that suggest serious psychological disturbances coming to a head, it is not a compelling dramatic event; it is anticlimactic, a kind of punctuation to bring things to a conclusion. Compared with the endings of Albee's *Tiny Alice* (the suggestion of a recurring infinite pattern about to begin again) or *Who's Afraid of Virginia Woolf?* (the winding down to incommunicable despair about to reactivate the isolated monsters inside us); O'Neill's *Long Day's Journey into Night* (the illumination of past secrets and the reenactment of remembered joy in a context of hopelessness); Pirandello's *Henry IV* (the buried past disinterred in all its ugly suggestion); Beckett's *Waiting for Godot* (non-communication and language found wanting) — the ending of *Salesman* is simply a dead end.

The play's major achievement, in my opinion, is precisely in the penetrating insights of its characters, the evolution from consciousness to self-consciousness. In the process, the debris of the past is sifted and swept aside for easier access to some kind of intuition. In the manner of the "beautiful soul" indulging in his Socratic self-righteousness, Willy gives us a striking display of coming into his own, finding his paradoxical identity through soul searching. His values are clear and unambiguous; he has taken the measure of what is right and good (in the manner Hegel describes) and sees himself as both victim and instigator. The quality that appeals to us in Willy is precisely this paradox and his unwillingness to deny what went wrong in order to insist on what he thought was right. His sons are less interesting as independent voices restructuring the past. They seem trapped in their father's situation, held to base by his inability to snap out of it. Their voices are predictable in a different way: They reminisce about the past knowing — as we do — that the future will be just the same. In a way, they serve to mirror Willy's frustrations and limitations. In the sons we see the failures of the father once more surfacing.

Although Biff and Happy do not emerge as masters of their own destinies (and, of course, their emotional but frustrated relationship with Willy is a major factor in their inability to move on), they echo Willy's moods and enrich the play with the aftershocks of Willy's major emotional tremors. They are inexorably bound to Willy, even as they criticize and belittle him. His fate is theirs. And, although not said in so many words, one can guess that their lives will not be very different from Willy's.

Willy's system has discarded him; he has nowhere to turn. This obvious cliché is always there, as a backdrop to the action; but it is the penetrating assessment of this by Willy and others around him that gives the play its power. The interplay of dramatic voices responding to him produces symphonic reverberations. In this respect, *Salesman* succeeds.

The system that made him and used him now rejects him cruelly when he no longer serves it well. The system is impersonal. It rewards those who can keep it going and discards those who cannot keep up. Willy has undermined himself all along, it is clear; but the system, too, is a major protagonist in the play, for it has set the guidelines and established the parameters that have ruled Willy's life. Perhaps the system needs to be changed; perhaps Willy placed too much faith in what could not save him when his effectiveness diminished. Whatever the nature of the message in these terms, it cannot be called tragic.

Writing on the subject of *tragedy* and the *common man*,[10] Miller draws upon Joseph Wood Krutch's "The Tragic Fallacy"[11] in an attempt to redefine the Aristotelian terminology to fit his and other modern plays. We have alluded to the difficulties created by A. C. Bradley in his effort to redefine the Aristotelian and Hegelian definitions. Miller's efforts to expand the old Aristotelian theories remind us that we would all do well to study what Hegel has actually said in these matters, rather than attack windmills and reinvent the wheel. [12]

For Hegel, the high point of tragedy was not to be found among the Greeks (in spite of his great admiration for them) but among the Elizabethans, who "in their mastery of the exposition of fully developed human characters and personality . . . are exceptionally distinguished; and among them, and soaring above the rest at an almost unapproachable height, stands Shakespeare."[13] What this preference means is that, from Hegel's philosophical vantage point, man evolves spiritually to full self-awareness only in the modern world. Tragedy, in its modern phase, reflects the attainment of that height or depth of self-awareness as fully articulated, genuinely *dramatic* personality (Shakespeare); and the best example of the multifaceted spiritual experience we all share in our modern world is *Hamlet*.

Miller is correct in saying that "in this age few tragedies

are written," and that "we are often held to be below tragedy." We can take such observations to mean that the old tragic demi-gods or heroes above man-made laws no longer exist in our modern world, and that tragedy is therefore no longer possible. But Miller denies that. The common man, he insists, "is as apt a subject for tragedy in its highest sense as kings are." And he adds to the confusion with explanations like the following: "If it is true that tragedy is the consequence of a man's total compulsion to evaluate himself justly, his destruction in the attempt posits a wrong or an evil in his environment."[14] But we know that the self-conscious effort toward identity must include (as Shakespeare makes clear in Hamlet) all the worst and best in us. Hamlet is not simply the "beautiful soul" who answers only to himself; he is also the worst Machiavellian and the most self-righteous provocateur. The *schöne Seele* contains in itself all good and evil; the Socratic process has been fully realized in our modern explorations into the inner workings of soul and mind and heart. Evil and blame cannot be posited *outside* the individual.

And yet, in a sense, the self-redemptive modern spirit, as defined and illustrated by Hegel, is not far removed from Oedipus, who indeed posits wrong and evil in his environment (the unfathomable will of the gods), only to come to the agonized realization that his actions (or reactions) have brought on his tragic undoing and that the responsibility is completely his. However, in positing certain values outside the scope of individual choice, in placing blame for certain actions on the environment or a group or another individual, Miller reduces man's freedom of choice, and responsibility (the intrinsic and central core of all tragedy) and in that sense falls outside the Hegelian analysis in which the truly *tragic* hero must somehow come to terms with his short-comings and recognize them in the larger context involving the conflicting claims of others. Plays like *After the Fall, Incident at Vichy*, and *The American Clock* fail as plays — and also as dramatic *tragic* statements in the organically structured Hegelian argument — precisely because the delicate balance of individual *freedom* in the assumption of *responsibility* is destroyed.

In his best plays, Miller draws unforgettable insights into the redemptive spirit of inquiry and knowledge and gives us some of his most touching portrayals. *Death of a Salesman* does not disappoint us in this respect. New students still respond positively to it. Willy Loman and those who cling to him give us a moving picture of the modern soul struggling toward fulfillment and understanding, toward insight into necessity.

NOTES

An earlier version of this essay appeared in *The World & I*, "Currents in Modern Thought: Drama " LII, 1, 1965.

1. Arthur Miller, *"Salesman" in Beijing* (New York: Viking Press, 1984).

2. Arthur Miller, "Politics as Theater," *Times*, (New York, 4 Nov. 1972), 33.

3. Robert F. Moss, "Arthur Miller Reaches for Former Glory", *Saturday Review*, September 1980, 22.

4. Moss, 23.

5. Allan Wallach, *Newsday*, 14 Dec. 1980.

6. Robert C. Tucker, ed., *The Marx-Engels Reader* (New York: W. W. Norton, 1972), 7.

7. Reprinted in *Hegel on Tragedy*, Anne and Henry Paolucci, (New York: Anchor Books, Doubleday & Co., 1962; Harper & Row, Greenwood Press; Griffon House Publications), 367-88.

8. Paolucci, *Hegel on Tragedy*, 366.

9. For a quick summary on this subject, see Robert Brustein's conclusion about the influence of Pirandello on contemporary playwrights in Anne Paolucci: *Pirandello's Theater: The Recovery of the Modern Stage for Dramatic Art* (Carbondale, Il., Southern Illinois Press, 1964), 5-6.

10. Arthur Miller, *New York Times*, 27 Feb. 1949, II, 1-3.

11. Joseph Wood Krutch, *Modern Temper* (New York: Harcourt,

Brace, 1929), 115-43.

12. My own efforts to correct Bradley's misleading notion that Hegel preferred Greek to Shakespearean tragedy may be found in "Bradley and Hegel on Shakespeare," *ComparativeLiterature*, Summer 1964, 211-25. (See Chapter 6 and 7 in this volume.)

13. Paolucci, *Hegel on Tragedy*, 85; see also 21, 24-25, 95-96, 162, 234-35, etc.

14. Gerald Weales, ed., "Miller on *Death of a Salesman*," *Arthur MIller: Death of a Salesman* (New York: The Viking Press, 1967), 143.

ABOUT THE AUTHORS

HENRY PAOLUCCI was well acquainted with Hegel and other modern, Greek, and Roman philosophers long before he graduated from The City College of New York; his father and older brother had instilled in him the love of books early in his life. At Columbia University, after several years in Italy and North Africa as a navigator in the US Air Force, during World War II— his rich cultural preparation was honed to scholarly perfection. While working on his dissertation at Columbia University, he was chosen Eleanora Duse Traveling Fellow and spent a year in Florence.

His wide range of intellectual interests was reflected in the variety of subjects he subsequently taught: English literature at Iona College, Greek and Roman history at Brooklyn College and The City College; a graduate course in Dante and Medieval Culture at Columbia University; and, from 1967 to 1991, at St. John's University, undergraduate and graduate courses in U.S. foreign policy, history, political theory, St. Augustine, Aristotle, Machiavelli, Hegel, astronomy and modern science.

On his own initiative, he became proficient in Greek, Arab, and Jewish texts and read with tremendous appreciation the works of Karl Adam, Henry Adams, Adolf von Harnack, Benedetto Croce, Karl Jaspers, Giovanni Gentile, Kant and dozens of other important writers in the many areas that interested him. He translated Cesare Beccaria's *On Crimes and Punishments*; Machiavelli's *Mandragola*; and sections of Hegel's *Philosophy of Fine Art*, in a single volume, *Hegel on the Arts*. Among his other works are *The Achievement of Galileo* (a collection of writings, with several translations of his own), Maitland's *Justice and Police,* as well as *The Political Writings of St. Augustine*, and (with Anne Paolucci), *Hegel on Tragedy* (the only anthology of its kind). His keen analyses of US foreign policy were clearly in evidence in his first full-length study, the now classic *War, Peace and the Presidency* (1968).

His early criticism of the policies of Henry Kissinger (*Who Is Kissinger?* and *Kissinger's War: 1957-1975* [1980], reissued together with some new material in 2002) anticipate current revisionist writings on the subject. *Zionism, the Superpowers, and the P.L.O.* (1982), and *Iran, Israel, and the United States* (1991) are especially relevant today.

In 1969 he launched *State of the Nation* — a monthly newsletter on American foreign policy and continued as editor and chief contributor for over a decade. During those years and up to the time of his death, he encouraged younger scholars and colleagues to participate in academic meetings sponsored by The Walter Bagehot Research Council on National Sovereignty, a non-profit educational foundation he established in the mid-sixties. Named after the founder of the British journal, *The Economist,* who was also a literary man and a frequent contributor to journals and magazines of his day, The Walter Bagehot Research Council has became a publishing outlet for books in a variety of fields. Paolucci himself, like Bagehot, also wrote for the leading journals of his day: *National Review, Il Borghese* (Rome), *Il Resto del Carlino* (Rome), and for the Op Ed pages of the *New York Times.*

In 1964, he was chosen to run for the US Senate, as the New York State Conservative Party candidate, against Kenneth Keating and Robert F. Kennedy. His campaign drew much interest (the "Scholarly Candidate": *New York Times*). In 1995, the Party honored him with its prestigious Kieran O'Doherty Award. He continued as Vice-Chairman of the Party until his death.

A lover of Brahms, Schubert, Mozart, Chopin, and Beethoven, as well as Scott Joplin and Cole Porter, Professor Paolucci also found occasion, over the years, to develop his own musical skills. Several of his original compositions were used in Anne Paolucci's videoplay *Cipango!*; others have been incorporated in her recent full-length play, *In the Green Room.*

In 1991, he retired from St. John's University with the title of Professor Emeritus of Government and Politics. He died on January 1, 1999.

ANNE PAOLUCCI was born in Rome, Italy. She attended public schools in Rome and New York City, received her B.A. from Barnard College (English and Creative Writing), her M.A. (Italian literature) and Ph.D. (Comparative Literature) from Columbia University, where she was awarded the first Woodbridge Honorary Fellowship. Both she and her husband spent a year, as Fulbright Scholars from Columbia, at the University of Rome. She later returned to Italy for two years as a Fulbright Lecturer in American Drama at the University of Naples. While there, she saw her first full-length play, *The Short Season*, produced under the auspices of the American Embassy. The play was later staged at the Cubiculo in New York by Nicholas John Stathis and Maurice Edwards. She herself produced and directed Albee's *The Zoo Story* during her stay in Naples.

In 1969, after several years with The City College of CUNY, she went to St. John's University as their first University Research Professor and a member of the presidential staff. Her first project at St. John's was the creation of a new journal, *Review of National Literatures* (1970), which in 1976 became the annual publication of the Council on National Literatures, an independent non-profit educational foundation she launched to promote multicomparative literary studies through representative "overviews" of the emergent and/or neglected literatures of the world. From 1970 to 2000, thirty-six volumes of *RNL* and more than a dozen volumes of the companion series, *CNL/World Report*, were published. In 1986, she created "Columbus: Countdown 1992" in order to promote new critical writings and art works featuring the age of discovery.

She was invited to Queens College as "Distinguished Adjunct Professor," visited Yugoslavia twice as guest of the Ministry of Culture, attended several international symposia in Canada, lectured throughout Italy and in Hong Kong, as well as in the major academic centers of Australia, where she spent seven months at the invitation of the Humanities Research Centre of The National University in Canberra.

In 1981, as Associate Director of "Shakespeare Summerfest" (a five-month multi-media project at The American Museum of Natural History in New York), she organized 12 bilingual dramatic programs using established theater groups and actors for the weekly performances.

She has an honorary degree from Lehman College (CUNY), served on The North America Advisory Board of the London Globe Theatre project, was Vice-President of the Dante Society of America, and is the recipient of the "Golden Lion" Award of Order Sons of Italy as well as the first recipient of their national Elena Cornaro Award (named after the first woman ever to receive a Ph.D. [Padua, 1648]). The Pirandello Society of America (which she headed for 17 years) honored her with its commemorative 25th anniversary medallion; Canada awarded her its gold medal for the Quincentenary (1992), and the Republic of Italy bestowed on her the title of "Cavaliere Order of Merit" in 1989 and later the title of "Commendatore." In 1986, President Reagan appointed her to the National Council on the Humanities, where she continued to serve under Presidents Bush, and Clinton (1986-1993). In 1996, NYS Governor George Pataki appointed her to the Board of Trustees of The City University of New York and, in March 1997, named her Chairperson of the Board — the first woman to hold that office.

Her books include *Luigi Pirandello: The Recovery of the Modern Stage for Dramatic Art* and *From Tension to Tonic: The Plays of Edward Albee* one of the first major critical assessments of Albee's works. She is also the author of four books of poetry, a novella, and three collections of short stories.

As a team, the Paoluccis complemented each other in many ways, but perhaps what will be remembered best is Henry Paolucci's ease in dealing with philosophical and scientific matters and Anne Paolucci's skill in assimilating and bringing into her own intellectual life new works and authors like Hegel. Each recognized in the other's strengths the impetus that made for a productive and exciting exchange, one that lasted almost five decades. •